SUSTAINABLE PEACE

SUSTAINABLE PEACE

Power and Democracy after Civil Wars

EDITED BY

Philip G. Roeder and Donald Rothchild

CORNELL UNIVERSITY PRESS

ITHACA AND LONDON

Cornell University Press gratefully acknowledges receipt of funding from the Carnegie Corporation of New York, through its International Peace and Security Program, which aided in the production of this book.

First published 2005 by Cornell University Press
First printing, Cornell Paperbacks, 2005

Printed in the United States of America

Library of Congress Cataloging-in-Publication Data

Sustainable peace : power and democracy after civil wars / edited by Philip G. Roeder and Donald Rothchild.
p. cm.
Includes bibliographical references and index.
ISBN-13: 978-0-8014-4373-2 (cloth : alk. paper)
ISBN-10: 0-8014-4373-3 (cloth : alk. paper)
ISBN-13: 978-0-8014-8974-7 (pbk. : alk. paper)
ISBN-10: 0-8014-8974-1 (pbk. : alk. paper)
1. Peace-building. 2. Conflict management. 3. Civil war–Political aspects. I. Roeder, Philip G. II. Rothchild, Donald S.
JZ5538.S76 2005
327.1′72–dc22 2005013976

Cornell University Press strives to use environmentally responsible suppliers and materials to the fullest extent possible in the publishing of its books. Such materials include vegetable-based, low-VOC inks and acid-free papers that are recycled, totally chlorine-free, or partly composed of nonwood fibers. For further information, visit our website at www.cornellpress.cornell.edu.

Cloth printing 10 9 8 7 6 5 4 3 2 1

Paperback printing 10 9 8 7 6 5 4 3 2 1

Contents

Figures and Tables

Figures

Tables

Acknowledgments

The inspiration for this research project on the impact of power-sharing institutions on political stability and democracy began in the fall of 1999 at a conference in Washington, D.C., sponsored by the Carnegie Corporation of New York. A generous grant from the Carnegie Corporation and the sustaining encouragement and patience of Stephen J. Del Rosso, Senior Program Officer at the Corporation, were vitally important because these gave us the wherewithal, time, and freedom from other obligations to move from initial, embryonic inspiration to this published volume. In La Jolla the University of California's Institute on Global Conflict and Cooperation provided much needed organizational and logistical support. Ronald Bee of IGCC provided extensive expertise in shaping the project and proposal for successful submission to Carnegie and then execution. Maissa Sanders, Katy Vicknair-Harris, and Rosalee Kitaen shepherded two faculty members who were often clueless about the details of organizing conferences and managing grants. They organized a series of spectacularly pleasant meetings that encouraged us to be more productive. Roger Haydon of Cornell University Press guided us and the manuscript through the shoals of the review process and oversaw the production of this volume. To each of these individuals and the directors of the institutions involved, we are profoundly grateful.

P. G. R. & D. R.

La Jolla and Davis, California

SUSTAINABLE PEACE

1

Dilemmas of State-Building in Divided Societies

Donald Rothchild and Philip G. Roeder

On April 15, 2003, near the city of Nasiriyah about 50 Iraqis assembled on a military base for the first of a series of meetings around the country to discuss broad outlines of a constitution for postwar Iraq. A special adviser to President George W. Bush, Zalmay Khalilizad, presided over the meeting. The discussions took place in difficult circumstances. Despite the security provided by U.S. troops, some invitees stayed away for fear their lives would be endangered. Others boycotted the meeting. On the streets of Nasiriyah some three thousand Iraqis protested against the Americans, who guided the discussion and set bounds on what was permissible in designing a new constitutional order. Despite such obstacles, on July 13 the Americans convened a 25-member interim Governing Council for Iraq and within eight months (March 8, 2004) the Council had ratified an interim constitution for their country. But then the process of constitutional development hit a stone wall: 12 of the 13 Shiite members of the Governing Council announced grave reservations about the interim constitution they had just approved. Grand Ayatollah Ali al-Sistani, the supreme cleric in the Shiite community of Muslims, objected to the interim document, declaring that it "places obstacles in the path of reaching a permanent constitution."[1] A wave of protests swept the Shiite areas of central and southern Iraq. Shiite Imams denounced the interim constitution as "illegal" and declared the authorities who had adopted it to be "illegitimate." The interim constitution was dead soon after arrival.

Many of the problems faced in Iraq have been confronted by leaders in other ethnically divided societies after severe conflicts.[2] Leaders of different

1. Dexter Filkins "Iraqi Constitution is Signed Despite Shiite Reservations," *New York Times* 9 March 2004, 1.

2. For example, see Carlotta Gall, "Afghans Clash at a Conference to Work Out a New Constitution," *New York Times* 30 December 2003, A11; Carlotta Gall, "Ethnic Morass Bogs

ethnic communities, usually with foreign powers looking over their shoulders and frequently with foreign powers guiding the negotiations, must reach agreement on political institutions that will permit them to live together peacefully and democratically. Typically the first task before these leaders or the foreign powers is to devise transitional arrangements for the short term. These must provide the modicum of political stability necessary to conduct elections to a constitutional assembly and the security for delegates to assemble, conduct constitutional debates, and craft political institutions to maintain stability and foster democracy for the longer term. To get leaders of different ethnic groups to come to the bargaining table, particularly after a period of intense hostility among them, it may be necessary to make concessions simply to initiate the transition to sustainable peace. To gain Kurdish support at the bargaining table, for example, the Americans and the Governing Council had to offer the Kurds significant political autonomy in the new Iraqi political order.

In attempting to design governing institutions that will foster democracy in a country where politics has often been autocratic and has recently been in turmoil, leaders of ethnic groups may demand protections against the tyranny of the soon-to-be-empowered majority. Leaders of minorities fear that simple majority rule may leave them permanently on the losing end of most policy decisions. Yet guarantees to minorities such as the Sunni, Kurdish, Christian, and secular Iraqis can outrage leaders of the majority, like the Shiite Grand Ayatollah Sistani, and bring complaints that these guarantees infringe the very basis of democracy—rule by the people. Leaders of minorities may urge the adoption of special protections, such as the right to maintain traditional religious courts, provide separate education, or establish armed formations for self-defense. Yet some of these protections may increase the risk that severe conflict will resume—and at an even more intense level. Some leaders of minorities may demand protections that the majority fears will threaten the survival of the country over the longer term. For example, many Arabs feared for the continued unity of Iraq if the Kurds were granted their demand for a united, autonomous homeland.[3]

Since 1990 leaders of ethnic groups, of governments in ethnically divided societies, of governments providing foreign intervention forces, and of international organizations such as the United Nations have confronted these sorts of issues in over 50 conflicts in more than 36 countries. In at least 19 conflicts the leaders of ethnic groups agreed to formal institutional arrange-

---

Down Afghan Talks on Charter," *New York Times* 1 January 2004, A6; Carlotta Gall, "Afghan Council Gives Approval to Constitution," *New York Times* 5 January 2004, A1.

3. Steven R. Weisman, "U.S. Presses Iraqi Kurds to Compromise on Issue of Autonomy," *New York Times* 8 January 2004, A5; Edward Wong, "Making Compromises to Keep a Country Whole," *New York Times* 4 January 2004, 8.

ments—and in some conflicts they reached an agreement on multiple occasions (Table 1.1). In some of these agreements the parties accepted secession of part of the country and establishment of new sovereign states such as Azerbaijan, Croatia, and Slovenia. Elsewhere the parties agreed to continue to live together in the same state, such as Bosnia, Macedonia, and Sudan, but with expanded rights for minorities to participate in governing the state they shared with other ethnic groups and to govern themselves through autonomous institutions. Yet there were also over 40 ethnic civil wars in the 1990s that had not yet ended by early 2004 (Table 1.2). Some of these cases, such as the ongoing Basque conflict in Spain and the Assamese conflict in India, had earlier resulted in institutional arrangements to expand the autonomy of the ethnic groups, but these failed to end the conflicts. Many of the cases, such as the Abkhazian and South Ossetian wars in Georgia, resulted in ceasefires, but a decade of on-again-off-again negotiations failed to yield agreement on the institutions that would govern these peoples and territories.

How can leaders craft political institutions that will sustain the peace and foster democracy in ethnically divided societies after conflicts such as civil wars? Under turbulent conditions the leaders of ethnic groups, govern-

Table 1.1. Major settlements in ethnically divided societies, 1990–2003

Country	Year(s) of settlement
Azerbaijan	1991
Croatia	1991
Slovenia	1991
Eritrea	1993
South Africa	1993
Rwanda	1993
Burundi	1994
Bosnia	1995
Sierra Leone	1996
Northern Ireland	1998
Kosovo	1999
Afghanistan	2001
Burundi	2001
Macedonia	2001–2002
Burundi	2002
Congo	2002
Democratic Republic of the Congo (Zaire)	2002
East Timor	2002
Democratic Republic of the Congo (Zaire)	2003
Côte d'Ivoire	2003
Iraq	2003
Sudan	2004

Sources: Based on data from Owen 2002, 388–389; Gleditsch et al. 2004.

Table 1.2. Ongoing ethnic civil wars, 1990–2003

Country	Crisis area/group
More than 1,000 battle-related deaths in at least one year	
Azerbaijan	Nagorno-Karabakh
Congo (Democratic Republic)	East
Georgia	Abkhazia
India	Assam
India	Kashmir
India	Punjab/Khalistan
Indonesia	Aceh
Myanmar	Karen
Myanmar	Shan
Philippines	Mindanao
Russia	Chechnya
Sri Lanka	Eelam
Sudan	Darfur
Sudan	Southern Sudan
Yemen	South Yemen
More than 1,000 battle-related deaths, but not in one year	
Bangladesh	Chittagong Hill Tribes
Côte d'Ivoire	North
Croatia	Serb
Myanmar	Kachin
Senegal	Casamance
More than 25 battle-related deaths in one year, but fewer than 1,000 total	
Angola	Cabinda
Comoros	Anjouan
Ethiopia	Afar
Ethiopia	Ogaden
Ethiopia	Oromiya
Ethiopia	Somalis
Georgia	South Ossetia
India	Jarkhand
India	Manipur
India	Nagaland
India	Tripura
Israel	Palestine
Moldova	Dniestr
Myanmar	Arakan
Myanmar	Kaya
Myanmar	Mon
Niger	Air and Azawad
Niger	Toubou
Papua New Guinea	Bougainville
Russia	Dagestan
Spain	Basques
Turkey	Kurdistan

Source: Based on data from Gleditsch et al. 2004.

ments, and international organizations are challenged to design political arrangements that can simultaneously meet the tests of representativeness, democratic accountability, effective governance, and political stability. The task is daunting because these societies are divided by deep communal distrust and uncertainty about the future. In a context of limited strategic choices, state leaders and diplomats must craft institutions that can both initiate the transition to peace and democracy in the short term and facilitate the consolidation of these over the longer run. The charge is critically important but awesome.

Viewing majoritarian democracy as a potential source of heightened interethnic conflict, practitioners and academics have responded to this task by championing various institutional arrangements that they label "power sharing." Indeed, as recent experiments in ethnically divided Bosnia, Burundi, and Afghanistan illustrate, power sharing has become the international community's preferred remedy for building peace and democracy after civil wars.[4] Peacemakers introduce these institutional arrangements in an attempt to guarantee ethnic groups a role in governmental decision-making or to ensure policy outcomes with a fair allocation of scarce governmental resources. At critical junctures in the transition from intense (sometimes violent) conflict, these power-sharing arrangements may offer a compromise acceptable to most ethnic elites. They attempt to limit the uncertainties of democratic politics and to increase the security of all groups by including group representatives in the state decisionmaking process. This in turn supports expectations of reduced conflict in the future (Holsti 1996, 8).

The interest of the international community in power sharing increased significantly in the 1990s, as governments in the United States and Europe searched for options that would maintain the peace after brutal civil wars as well as facilitate the consolidation of democracy after less violent conflicts such as that in Macedonia. With little experience in promoting power-sharing arrangements in post–civil war situations and surprisingly little empirical evidence that power sharing facilitates the consolidation of peace and democracy in ethnically divided societies in the developing world, the international community nonetheless plunged ahead with a series of experiments with power-sharing institutions. Diplomats and politicians initially felt vindicated by their choice because power sharing seemed to offer an inclu-

4. For example, soon after the American intervention in Afghanistan, major newspapers featured op-ed articles that called for power sharing or consociationalism in Afghanistan and, in order to avoid future "Afghanistans," power sharing in such diverse countries as Russia, China, India, and Indonesia; see, for example, Richard Hrair Dekmejian, "One Nation, Loosely United," *New York Times* 18 December 2001; Stanley A. Weiss, "Tasks for Russia, China, India and Indonesia: Avert the Next Afghanistan," *International Herald Tribune* 11 July 2002; Ottaway and Lieven (2002).

sive compromise that initiated a transition from intense conflict in such diverse settings as Bosnia, Afghanistan, and Côte d'Ivoire. Yet it soon became evident that these short-term accommodations to initiate a transition to peace and democracy have come with high longer-term costs: *The very same institutions that provide an attractive basis to end a conflict in an ethnically divided country are likely to hinder the consolidation of peace and democracy over the longer term.*

This volume presents ten research projects by social scientists who examine many of the premises of these recent power-sharing experiments. Not facing the immediate and pressing demands for action that diplomats and politicians encounter, the authors have had the luxury to look back in time and to other parts of the world for comparative empirical evidence to test the policy assumptions of the practitioners. On the basis of the evidence, we will advance two major claims. First, there is an inconsistency between short-term benefits and longer-term costs associated with the specific institutional arrangements and the broader strategy that come under the heading "power sharing." We call this the dilemma of power sharing. Second, contrary to the claims of advocates for a power-sharing approach, there are other institutional alternatives that are likely to lead to a more enduring peace and a more democratic polity. Indeed, using the evidence presented in this volume, we will advance an alternative strategy of institution building for sustainable regime change after conflicts in ethnically divided societies. We label this institutional arrangement "power dividing" and advance it as part of a broader strategy of nation-state stewardship.

The Classic Options

In academic circles the choice of institutions suitable to ethnically divided societies has been painted in stark terms—a choice between power sharing, on one hand, and instability, dictatorship, or ethnic domination, on the other. When scholars found that power sharing was not a sufficient guarantee of peace, they prescribed either some form of oversight by external powers or partition of the disputed state into separate sovereign states. Thus, the traditional menu of options has tended to highlight three choices: (1) the choice between majoritarian democracy and power sharing (Lijphart 1977, 1995), (2) the decision whether to establish a foreign protectorate (Walter 1999a), and (3) the decision whether to partition the state (Kaufmann 1996, 1999; Sambanis 2000). A central conclusion that emerges from this volume is that there is an overlooked alternative to majoritarian democracy and power sharing—what we call "power dividing." This alternative is more likely to lead to the consolidation of peace and democracy in conditions that typically prevail after civil wars and is less likely to require

Table 1.3. Power sharing and its alternatives

Non-democracy	Constrained democracy	Full democracy
Colonial domination	Power sharing	Majoritarianism
Autocracy	Protectorate under foreign power(s)	Partition into independent states
Hegemonic exchange		Power division

the extraordinary steps of either protectorate or partition to sustain over the long term (Table 1.3).

Majoritarian Democracy

The case against majoritarian democracy in ethnically divided societies begins with the Westminster model of British democracy—a notably straightforward model of majority rule. In the United Kingdom Parliament is controlled by the majority party—and the government normally does not include minority parties. The majority itself emerges from elections in which Members of Parliament are selected in single-member districts by getting as few as one vote more than the nearest competitor. The losers get nothing. The majority in Parliament is supreme over all other branches and all subordinate levels of government. The Parliamentary majority, it used to be said, could do anything but turn a man into a woman, and now, with the miracles of modern medicine, even that is possible. There is no separation of powers to permit parallel branches to stand against Parliament, no federalism that reserves decision rights to constituent jurisdictions, and no bill of rights that places the rights of private citizens beyond the reach of Parliament.

The case against using this Westminster model in highly pluralistic societies emerged from decades of scholarship on state building in developing countries that seemed to confirm John Stuart Mill's thesis in *Considerations on Representative Government* (1962 [1861], 82–91) that ethnically pluralistic societies are inherently unstable and require "a constitutionally unlimited, or at least a practically preponderant, authority in the chief ruler." J. S. Furnivall (1944) extended this with the argument that plural societies cannot be held together by the rule of law and need some external force—a colonial power in the case he was considering—to maintain unity (also see Smith 1969). Alvin Rabushka and Kenneth Shepsle (1972, 217) supported this conclusion using formal analysis. They pointedly rejected the contention that "the resolution of intense but conflicting preferences in the plural society [is] manageable in a democratic framework."

The brief against the Westminster model warned that majoritarian democracy does not protect minorities sufficiently. Indeed, given the power of central state institutions and their command over economic resources, the result after civil war could be increasing central dominance in public affairs as a new government sought to consolidate its control and to mobilize the society for reconstruction and development. When civil wars left behind great antagonisms, a dominant ethnic political party might be tempted to use its majority position in government to discriminate against, even tyrannize over, minority groups. In a majoritarian democracy with a dominant ethnic political party, alternation from one government to another is less frequent and inclusion of minorities in governing coalitions is unlikely. When majoritarian democracy becomes ethnically exclusive, the political system is less likely to be stable over the long term—threatening the survival of both peace and democracy. We contend that this brief exaggerates the dangers of democracy and overlooks the alternatives available to make democracy work in ethnically divided societies.

Power Sharing

The alternative to majoritarian democracy has most often been a form of power sharing among ethnic elites. The power-sharing strategy embraces three main objectives: inclusive government, group self-government, and proportionality (Lijphart 1977, 1985, 1995; Nordlinger 1972; Sisk 1996). The designers of postconflict settlements attempt to promote these outcomes through power-sharing institutions. Thus, in order to ensure that the decisionmaking process includes representatives of all major ethnic groups, the authors of postconflict constitutions have often introduced constitutional provisions that mandate that the incumbents in key posts, such as the president, vice presidents, prime minister, cabinet ministers, and speaker of the legislature, must mirror the ethnic configurations of society. The attempt to grant ethnic groups the power to govern themselves has often led to the creation of autonomous homeland administrations within the common state. In the pursuit of proportionality in allocation of the most valuable state resources—which includes appointment to prized governmental, military, and civil service positions—constitutions or fundamental laws often provide a formula for allocation of positions and budgetary funds.

Power-sharing regimes depend on cooperation among ethnic elites. They range across a spectrum from partial democracy to soft authoritarianism (such as hegemonic exchange regimes; Rothchild 1997, 13–15). In order to promote political stability in ethnically or religiously divided societies, power-sharing regimes provide for less participation by the public at large and less contestation among ethnic elites than commonly found in majoritarian democracies. Fearful that in an openly democratic polity hard-liners from each ethnic group will stir popular demands for a larger share of economic resources, more political and civil service positions, and still greater political autonomy, moderate leaders from different communal interests act in concert to limit democracy and maintain the power-sharing arrangement.

Yet, the success of power sharing depends on the continuing commitment of the leaders of ethnic groups to moderate their own demands and their ability to contain hard-line elements within their own communities. Such moderation and control are likely to be in short supply after a civil war. Moreover, we will argue that the incentives created by power-sharing institutions themselves encourage ethnic elites to escalate their claims. And they empower these elites with the means to back their demands with political brinkmanship. For these reasons, power sharing may get ethnic leaders to leave the battlefield, but then after a short lull transforms the bargaining room into a new battlefield.

Protectorate under Foreign Power(s) or International Organization(s)

Where power sharing alone is inadequate to maintain the peace, academics have advised governments of foreign powers to further constrain democracy by establishing protectorates that restrain the majority and protect minorities. Foreign interveners have been particularly valuable during the negotiation and early implementation phases of power-sharing arrangements (Carnegie Commission on Preventing Deadly Conflict 1997b). In addition, as Barbara Walter (1999a) notes, agreement on this third-party involvement sends a credible signal to the negotiating partners that all signatories are serious about peace. On various occasions the role of external guarantors has been institutionalized. At the Paris Peace Conference following World War I the Allies sought to ensure the rights of minorities through a regime of minority treaties that the League of Nations would guarantee (Musgrave 1997, 32–61; Krasner and Froats 1998). Daniel J. Elazar (1982, 1994) has argued that we should expect international organizations to play an increasingly important role as external guarantors in the future. The decade-long presence of the High Representative in Bosnia and Herzegovina is perhaps a manifestation of this new role in maintaining the peace.

One noteworthy example of a long-term institutionalized third-party guarantee has been the continuing role of the British Crown in some Commonwealth countries—through the agency of the governors general. Agreement by ethnic elites to retain this institution can make their commitment to accommodation more credible. Jenna Bednar, William Eskridge, and John Ferejohn (2001) attribute the stability of Canada's federal system for nearly a century after the British North America Act in 1867 to the unique role of the Judicial Committee of the British Privy Council in London as a court of appeal for the Canadian provinces and the equally unique role of the British Parliament that had to approve amendments to the Act. These provided a credible commitment that the rights of the provinces—notably Quebec—

would not be usurped by the central Canadian government. Conversely, where these links have been broken, as in Zimbabwe, there has been little to restrain national leaders intent on altering their relations with minorities.

Yet in recent decades countries such as the United States have been reluctant to assume the long-term burdens implied by a commitment to protect a power-sharing agreement in a country like Rwanda. And states like Iraq have been unwilling to submit to this type of abridgement of their sovereignty for an extended period. Even many Commonwealth members have limited the powers of the governors general. Moreover, many of the parties to a civil war may object to one or the other protector. Prior to an agreement it may be difficult for all parties to find an external guarantor that all consider neutral. Once an agreement is implemented some ethnic elites may come to see the involvement of the external powers as highly partisan. For example, in maintaining an existing pattern of relations the interveners often appear to favor ethnic groups who fare better under the status quo. In Northern Ireland, Brendan O'Leary (1989) notes, direct rule from London after 1972 sought to introduce "a supposedly neutral authority above the rival subcultures" of Northern Ireland. London's agents were at first seen by both Ulstermen and Irish as honest brokers, but within a decade the latter came to see London as upholding social, economic, and political arrangements that discriminated against the Irish. British sanctions against violations of the peace—particularly, the policy of "criminalization"—"backfired most spectacularly" because it was seen as directed at only one of the parties to the conflict. In Sri Lanka the Indian government, which mediated the India–Sri Lanka Agreement in 1987 and dispatched the Indian Peace-Keeping Force to implement the accord, found that soon neither side supported its role. The Indians encountered stiff resistance from the Tamil guerrillas—the Liberation Tigers of Tamil Eelam—and finally withdrew from the country upon the request of the Sri Lankan government (Wriggins 1995; Bose 2002).

In short, in the contemporary period the option of external guarantors is unlikely to become a common means to make democracy work in ethnically divided societies after civil wars over the longer term. This still leaves all parties with the problem of getting the institutions right for the longer term.

Partition into Independent States

Where significant communities do not wish to remain within a common state, partition may be the only way to make a successful transition from intense conflict to stable peace and democracy. Even where the communities do not reject a common state, but the leaders of the communities do not trust the commitments of other ethnic leaders, partition may be the only way to peace and democracy. The secessions of Norway and Ireland in the last century did not threaten existing democracy, and the secession of Finland and the partition of Israel, India, Czechoslovakia, and even Yugoslavia permitted stable democracies to develop in some successor states where it might have been stunted had outside powers attempted to maintain a unified state. Indeed, in a large-scale comparative study Nicholas Sambanis (2000, 459–464) finds that in the newly independent states created by partition after civil wars, democracy was stronger than in states that remained whole after civil wars. A close look at Sambanis's data also shows that *partition*—as we use the term here to mean division into separate independent states—can lead to more durable peace. The likelihood of residual violence in the first two years after the end of a civil war was 53.8 percent in the 104 cases that did not involve territorial separation of the parties. It was slightly higher (63.6 percent) in the 11 cases of territorial power sharing that did not result in independent states recognized by the international community. Alternatively, it was substantially lower (30 percent) in the 10 cases where partition resulted in new sovereign states recognized by the international community. In short, according to this data set, the likelihood of residual violence was highest under territorial power sharing and lowest under partition into independent states.[5]

Partition creates borders between the contending communities in an effort to reduce the risks and costs of potentially destructive ethnic encounters. By removing one of the most contentious issues from the bargaining table—that is, the issue of control over the government that governs them all—partition typically lowers the stakes in the conflict between these communities. The process can be peaceful (Czechoslovakia) or bitterly contentious (India, Palestine, or Ireland). Its proponents argue that where ethnic communities are intermixed, when violence escalates, and when the state is unprepared or unwilling to guarantee the peace, the "separation of people into defensible enclaves" becomes essential to restoring peace and stability (Kaufmann 1999, 223). Nevertheless, plans for a "civilized divorce" (Tullberg and Tullberg 1997, 247) may encounter at least three difficulties: There may be no agreement on the boundaries between ethnic groups, and this may lead to even more deadly international conflicts among the successor states. The economic costs of divided and shrunken markets may be steep. The division of the state can create new minorities, cause increased refugee flows across borders, and lead to ethnic cleansing in the successor states.

5. We use Sambanis's (2000, 447–49) data shown in his Table 1. The eleven cases of territorial separation without independence include Azerbaijan 1996, Cyprus 1964 and 1974, Georgia 1993 and 1994, India 1965 and 1994, Moldova 1994, Russia-Chechnya 1996, Somalia 1991, and Tajikistan 1994. The ten cases of partition into separate independent states include China-Taiwan 1947, Ethiopia-Eritrea 1991, India 1948, Israel-Palestine 1949, Korea 1953, Pakistan 1971, Vietnam 1975, Yugoslavia-Bosnia 1995, and Yugoslavia-Croatia 1991 and 1995.

These complications underscore that partition should not become a preferred solution to civil wars in ethnically divided societies. It may be the best option when ethnic groups are so distrustful of one another that they are unable to live together in a stable democracy and demand institutionalized power sharing as a condition for their agreement to coexist with their adversaries in a single state. In these circumstances, partition into separate states may be a less costly way to initiate a transition to peace and democracy and to consolidate both. Nevertheless, even in these instances the partition option does not eliminate the need to get the institutions right for ethnically divided societies.

The Dilemma of Power Sharing: Ending the War, Losing the Peace

This volume engages this debate over options with new, more systematic evidence from researchers within the academic community. This evidence points to a dilemma: Power-sharing institutions frequently facilitate a transition from civil war, but they thwart the consolidation of peace and democracy (also see Adekanye 1998, 32). In order to analyze the role of power sharing in transitions from civil war it is useful to divide the transition into two interrelated phases—the *initiation phase* and the *consolidation phase* (compare Rothchild 2001). The timelines and tasks of the transition to peace and the transition to democracy will not be identical. Thus, the initiation phase of the *transition to peace* begins with a cessation of hostilities, includes such tasks as separating troops, establishing monitoring mechanisms, demobilizing, disarming, and decommissioning troops. The consolidation phase of the transition to peace consists of establishing a preponderance of the means of coercion in the hands of the new government and fostering at least broad acquiescence in, and hopefully widespread belief in the legitimacy of, this preponderance so as to end armed challenges to the central government. The initiation phase of the *transition to democracy* begins with the task of establishing a common administration accepted by the parties previously locked in conflict and culminates with the holding of the first, founding elections in which their members participate as citizens of a common state. The consolidation phase of the transition to democracy seeks to institutionalize procedures that increase expectations of continuing accountability of the governmental bureaucracy to elected officials and of these elected officials to the public at large through regular fair and free elections (Linz and Stepan 1996; Shin 1994, 143–146). Both transitions involve convincing members of the majority and the minority that into the future they will more effectively achieve their ends by working within the existing institutional structure than working against it. These transitions both require efficient and accountable government as well as procedures acceptable to all parties to the original agreement whereby the original institutions can evolve to meet changing contingencies.

The dilemma of power sharing emerges from the gap between the promises needed to initiate the transition and the performance necessary to consolidate peace and democracy. At the end of a civil war, the parties' agreement to accept the constraints associated with power-sharing institutions is a powerful signal of their commitment to resolve future disputes peacefully and not to abuse the other side once it has laid down its arms. In particular, the willingness of the majority to tie its hands or at least to submit to rule by a power-sharing government is a costly signal that may convince minorities of the majority's commitment to treat them fairly. Yet, once the leaders turn to the task of consolidating the institutions and rules of governance, these same power-sharing institutions are likely to prove unstable, to create incentives to escalate future ethnic conflicts to more destructive levels, including violence, and to place obstacles in the path of consolidating full democracy. For example, parties may demand executive power-sharing arrangements, electoral rules that provide for proportional representation, and territorial autonomy as conditions for signing a peace settlement. Oversized coalition governments with mutual vetoes, however, may erode the efficiency of government over the longer term and increase the likelihood of decisionmaking deadlock. Electoral systems like list proportional representation in large, multimember constituencies may hinder the development of links between citizens and their legislative representatives (Barkan 1995). Autonomous regions may become states within the state that can sabotage the central government. It is a cruel irony that power-sharing arrangements may be necessary incentives to facilitate agreement to a peace accord in the initiation phase but threaten the long-term prospects for stable peace and democracy in ethnically divided societies in the consolidation phase.

The dilemma of power sharing is particularly difficult because power-sharing arrangements for the short term are inextricably linked to the institutional arrangements that are likely to prevail in the longer term. If this were not so, it would be a relatively easy matter to separate the institutions of the two periods and resolve the power-sharing dilemma. The parties could initiate the transition from civil war with interim power-sharing institutions and a sunset provision that stipulates a termination date for power sharing. In this interim period the parties would negotiate entirely new institutions that would be better able to consolidate the peace and democracy. This was the apparent hope of the designers of the peace process in Afghanistan. In that country, the process began with a temporary government under Hamid Karzai facilitated by the occupying power. Six months later a Loya Jirga (assembly of notables from around the country) convened to elect a new interim government and legislature. The plan also envisioned that 18 to 24 months later national elections would select yet another, more permanent legislature.

Yet, there are at least two reasons why the institutions of the initiation phase are linked to those of the consolidation phase. First, initiation-phase arrangements typically empower the political actors who design the institutions under which consolidation of peace and democracy is expected to take place. As observers of the Afghan transition have noted, the decisions made at each stage constrained the choices made at the next. At each step the interim institutions empowered a specific cast of political actors—most notably and regrettably, the regional warlords—who then became the dominant parties in the negotiations over the design of the next set of political institutions.[6] In Iraq, early decisions willy nilly led to the privileged place of Kurdish and Shiite leaders in the negotiation of a new constitution as the most important secular Iraqi alternatives were eliminated. Only later did the occupying authorities try to bring in tribal leaders as a political force that might cross-cut the now overarching religious and ethnic divide.[7]

Second, parties that demand power sharing as a condition for agreeing to initiate the transition to peace and democracy typically demand guarantees that these arrangements will continue for the long term. In the search for an agreement to end a conflict, parties that fear being submerged in a post-conflict democracy will look for ways to give power-sharing arrangements greater permanence. They may therefore be unwilling to sign an interim agreement to initiate a transition that contains a sunset provision unless they are given strong assurances that they will have a say in the design of the institutions for the consolidation phase. And in doing so, they are likely to seek to perpetuate those very relationships that weaken governance and democracy.

Introduction of third-party enforcers does not resolve this dilemma. Outside parties—such as the United Nations or North Atlantic Treaty Organization (NATO)—might try to get the weaker groups to agree to institutions that are better suited to the task of the consolidation phase by adding commitments to serve as an external third-party enforcer (as occurred in Bosnia). Yet, the commitment made by third-party enforcers to take appropriate action is not necessarily credible in the eyes of minorities. In particular, if minorities believe the enforcers will withdraw after a relatively brief period of time, they are likely to demand power-sharing institutions that jeopardize the long-term survival of the peace and democracy by giving the minorities the means to defend themselves once the third-party enforcer withdraws. The presence of third-party enforcers during the initial phase typ-

6. See, for example, Tom Zeller, "Of the People, By the Warlords," *New York Times* 24 November 2002, 14; Amy Waldman and Carlotta Gall, "A Young Afghan Dares to Mention the Unmentionable," *New York Times* 18 December 2003, A3.

7. Edward Wong, "Iraq Secular Leaders Seek to Thwart Islamist Power," *New York Times* 22 February 2004, A10.

ically does not diminish the underlying need for reliable institutional protections for vulnerable groups.

The Strategy of Nation-State Stewardship

The strategy of nation-state stewardship includes a description of the institutional arrangement that we regard as best suited to consolidating peace and democracy after intense conflict has occurred, and guidelines concerning both the form and timing of interventions by the international community and the occasions when partition may be the best option. This strategy is guided by the objective of constructing political institutions that express a people's shared sentiments on constituting an independent state. This shared sense of nationhood both defines the boundaries of the state and limits the realm of governmental responsibilities within those borders.

Curiously, in the debates over power sharing and majoritarian democracy, we believe a much earlier institutional response to the dangers of simple majority rule has been largely neglected—the power-dividing arrangements that we associate with the U.S. Constitution. In the logic of James Madison one limits majorities not by empowering minority groups with parts of the government's powers, but by expanding individual liberties and rights at the expense of government and by empowering different majorities in independent organs of government. There are three elements to this power-dividing strategy—civil liberties, multiple majorities, and checks and balances. In short, divided-powers democracies allocate state powers between government and civil society with strong, enforceable civil liberties that take many responsibilities out of the hands of government. They distribute those responsibilities left to government among separate, independent organs that represent alternative, crosscutting majorities. For the most important issues that divide the ethnic groups, but must be decided by a government common to all ethnic groups, power-dividing institutions balance one decisionmaking center against another so as to check each majority.

First, in the constitutional allocation of decision rights the power-dividing strategy takes many decisions out of the hands of government and places these in the hands of individuals—that is, leaves key decisions to the private sphere and to civil society. In sponsoring the U.S. Bill of Rights, Madison recognized that limits on the decisionmaking rights of government were just as important as limits on any single majority within the government. For example, Madison sought to take one of the most divisive cultural issues of his day—religion—out of the hands of government. With a constitutional provision that prohibited any laws infringing the free exercise of religion or the separation of church and state, the Madisonian solution sought to lower the stakes in politics. These limits on government also had a salutary effect on civil society and created the most favorable institutional conditions for interests to become fluid and "self-determining" rather than fixed and "predetermined" by government. Because a liberal regime of extensive rights also tends to make it easier for fissures and competition to emerge within a dominant ethnic group, wide-ranging individual liberties for unfettered expression and association also increase the likelihood that the majority will divide into separate interests.[8] As a consequence, ethnic identities in a republic with power-dividing institutions are more likely to be limited to specific policy issues, and ethnic majorities find it much more difficult to sustain political hegemony of their ethnic group over a broad range of policy. Competition within the dominant ethnic group leads some subgroups—typically those disadvantaged by the status quo—to look outside the ethnic group for allies. This does not represent crosscutting cleavages at work (Lipset 1960), but a variant of the oligarch's dilemma (Roeder 1993; Ramseyer and Rosenbluth 1996).; that is, it does not depend on competing loyalties that bind individuals across ethnic lines, but on competition within the majority ethnic group and the self-interested pursuit of advantage among factions.

Second, in the design of governmental institutions, the power-dividing strategy contrasts sharply with both the Westminster and the power-sharing models, for these fuse legislative and executive powers, and they grant supremacy to the combined Parliament-Government. Power dividing favors separation of powers at all levels of government among independent branches of government and even separate specialized agencies that represent different majorities within the public at large. For example, in many localities the elected city council, school board, and water-basin authority represent the public differently and each empowers a different majority within the public at large. The multiple-majorities approach empowers each of the majorities to make decisions within a limited range of policy issues. Three advantages follow from this separation of power: greater efficiency, greater democracy, and multiple majorities. Stephen Holmes (1995, 165) notes that separation of power is "a form of division of labor, permitting—in some cases—a more efficient distribution and organization of governmental functions." Thus, he notes, "an independent judiciary was originally established not to limit power but, on the contrary, to increase the capacity of the government to do its job." Bernard Manin, Adam Przeworski, and Susan C. Stokes (1999, 50–51) suggest that this may be more democratic than the parliamentary model because fused powers give citizens only a single vote—for their legislator. They observe that "governments make thou-

8. William Easterly (2001, 690) argues that "formal institutions that protect minorities and establish clear legal rules for business may be more important in ethnically divided societies than in homogeneous ones" because the former typically lack "the web of informal social networks that span the entire society" and "spawn informal institutions (social capital and trust) that provide assurance against expropriation or broken contracts."

sands of decisions that affect individual welfare, [but] citizens have only one instrument to control these decisions: the vote. One cannot control a thousand targets with one instrument." They propose a power-dividing solution: "Thus, for example, separating monetary from other political decisions and voting separately, and at staggered intervals, for the directors of the central bank would give voters an additional instrument of control." Yet this is also a prudent response to a central problem of an ethnically divided society: Divided-power institutions that empower multiple majorities increase the likelihood that members of ethnic minorities will be parts of political majorities on some issues and many members of any ethnic majority will be members of political minorities on some issues. Moreover, to the extent that some identities are constructed through politics, power-dividing institutions may even lead to identities that are multidimensional, situation- or issue-specific, and crosscutting rather than unidimensional, recurring, and cumulative.

Third, in order to keep each of these decisionmaking centers that represents a specific majority from overreaching its authority, checks and balances pit one against the other (Wood 1969, 446–453). In the *Federalist Papers* Madison (1961 [1788], 324) frames the problem as one of designing institutions so that "the rights of individuals, or of the minority, will be in little danger from interested combinations of the majority." He built on a logic sketched by the Baron de Montesquieu (1977 [1748], 200) that "to prevent the abuse of power, 'tis necessary that by the very disposition of things power should be a check to power." The separation of powers among institutions based on alternative majorities (described in the previous paragraph) makes it more difficult to form a majority consensus to encroach on the rights of minorities and harder to sustain such majorities on many issues over an extended time period. In a well-designed system of checks and balances, attempts to expand one organ's (and one majority's) power at the expense of ethnic minorities cause other organs to resist. Thus, given this logic, presidentialism with a real balance of powers between executive and legislature is typically preferable to parliamentarism in protecting democracy and human rights; bicameral legislatures with competing bases of representation are similarly preferable to unicameral bodies; and independent judiciaries empowered with judicial review over the acts of legislatures and executives are also preferable to weak judiciaries. For decisions, such as decisions about interest rates, that must be made expeditiously, the rules of a power-dividing democracy permit individual organs to reach decisions independently from other organs—as long as the same organ does not make all such decisions. The more such decisions can threaten the stability of the constitutional order, such as amendments to a peace settlement, the rules of power-dividing democracy require concurrent approval by multiple organs empowering different majorities.

In short, the oldest and longest-lasting experiments to make majoritarian democracy work in divided societies—experiments such as the United States and, we would add, Switzerland—have not sought to empower elite cartels. Instead, they have sought to trust civil society and have limited the powers of government by extending civil liberties that can be enforced against the government. In terms of institutional design, they have allocated governmental powers among separate, independent organs constituted on the bases of multiple, crosscutting majorities.

The strategy of nation-state stewardship sees these institution-building tasks as defining key objectives of any foreign intervention and setting conditions to determine when intervention to secure democracy is prudent. In this strategy direct intervention is only occasionally prudent and only when the interveners are willing to commit to a multiyear process of building power-dividing institutions. In the institution-building strategy foreign powers and international organizations seek to avoid creating any concentrations of power at either the national or local levels. This, of course, means resisting the natural temptation to create a single unified authority on the other side with which the occupying authority can conduct negotiations and arrange a transfer of power so as to exit quickly. The power-dividing strategy rejects the usual pattern of appointing an interim council of indigenous leaders and then building democratic institutions from this core—outward with the appointment of ministers and interim legislators favored by the interim council and downward with the creation of subordinate provincial and local administrations under the interim council. Instead, the power-dividing strategy leads statesmen and -women to begin at the bottom with elections to such diverse organs as hospital administrations, school districts, and village or borough governments and build upward from multiple, crosscutting constituencies to construct city governments, various crosscutting regional administrations, and diverse national governing organs.[9] The strategy of nation-state stewardship is not based on the claim that these institutions are normatively superior to other forms of democracy, but on the claim that they are prudent when the objective of interveners is the long-term consolidation of democracy in ethnically divided societies.

Before there can be common political institutions, however, there must be a consensus among most of the leaders of the main ethnic groups that together their diverse populations constitute a nation. (In this sense, a *nation* is simply a population that believes it should be united in an independent state of its own; see Breuilly 1994.) This sets limits on the powers of the government that rules them all. They must be willing to submit to some poli-

9. On the importance of creating a rule of law and civil society before empowering central governing institutions, see Paddy Ashdown, "What I Learned in Bosnia," *New York Times* 28 October 2002, A31.

cies that are binding on all ethnic groups. They must be willing to agree to some policy by a majority vote of the nation as a whole. Where there are no or few decisions that they are willing to submit to a majority vote, the leaders do not consider their different people to be parts of a single nation. In particular, when there are no significant issues where members of minority ethnic groups are members of the political majority and members of an ethnic majority are members of the political minority, this may be evidence that there is no nation that unites the ethnic groups. Here political cleavages are unidimensional, recurring, and cumulative. These are conditions in which partition is most likely to be a better solution than power-dividing democracy.

The Organization of This Volume

This book concerns the elements of a successful transition to peace and democracy in an ethnically divided society after a period of intense conflict such as a civil war. A first dependent variable is the stability of different institutional arrangements themselves—did the institutions created as part of the postconflict settlement endure? A second dependent variable is the stability (or duration) of peace—that is, did the institutions created in the peace process increase the length of time that the peace survived, the length of time before there was a resumption of the intense ethnic conflict? A third dependent variable is the successful transition to democracy—did the institutions created in the peace process facilitate the holding of the first fair and free elections in a timely manner and the consolidation of democracy thereafter? Each of our authors focuses on at least one of these distinct aspects of the complex transition from ethnic conflict.

The primary independent variables are various institutional arrangements that affect the likelihood of a successful transition to domestic peace and democracy—where transition includes both the initiation phase and the consolidation phase. For the purposes of this volume, the primary power-sharing institutions include federalism, collective executives, communal legislative chambers, reserved seats in legislatures, the list system of proportional representation with a low threshold, and formal rules mandating proportional resource allocation. Less common types of power sharing include rotational presidencies (proposed for Nigeria under the Abacha regime) and schemes of nonterritorial federalism (such as communal councils proposed for the Austro-Hungarian Empire).

Our definition of what constitutes power sharing reflects a conception of political institutions commonly found among students of comparative politics. Yet in the course of this project we became aware that a separate convention has emerged among students of international relations who use the term "power sharing" more broadly to include many practices that comparativists would not recognize as institutional arrangements—such as ceasefires that leave armies in control of territory. We also became attuned to the differences among comparativists themselves concerning the extension of the term "power sharing" to include policies that are not formally mandated, such as an informal compromise on the proportional allocation of budgets. Although they reflect a legitimate difference, the alternative usages of the same term can be confusing. In the interest of precision, we use the term *power-sharing institutions* when we seek to invoke the narrower list of more formal arrangements such as those discussed in the previous paragraph. We use *power-sharing policies* to refer to policies that can be formal or informal. We use the terms *power sharing*, *power-sharing arrangements*, and *power-sharing provisions* to bracket agreements that can be informal as well as formal. By preserving the distinction we are able to investigate such questions as whether informal arrangements constrain the development and performance of formal institutions.

The chapters in this volume ask five questions about the impact of various institutions on transitions from intense conflict to democratic stability in ethnically divided societies. We began with questions that led us to conclude that there is a dilemma of power sharing. The first concerns a comparison among power-sharing arrangements:

1. Which of the primary power-sharing institutions, power-sharing policies, and informal power-sharing provisions in peace settlements are more likely to lead to stable peace and democracy after deadly conflicts such as civil wars in ethnically divided societies?

The second question concerns a comparison between the initiation and consolidation phases of a transition and the relative effectiveness of power-sharing arrangements in each:

2. In which phase—the initiation phase or the consolidation phase—of a transition are power-sharing arrangements more successful at promoting peace and democracy?

In addition, we ask how contextual constraints—including different demographic, economic, social, or international constraints—affect the ways in which power-sharing arrangements affect the transition from intense conflict. Thus, our third question concerns this second-order constraint on the relationship between power sharing and our dependent variables:

3. Under what circumstances—such as different proportions of majorities and minorities in the population, territorial intermixing of ethnic communities, a previous violent conflict, or third-party protection—is power sharing most successful at maintaining peace and democracy in ethnically divided societies?

We concluded that a combination of favorable conditions is seldom present after intense conflicts. Thus, we turned to the comparison between power-sharing institutions and alternatives to power sharing during a transition from severe conflict in ethnically divided societies. Hence our fourth question is:

> 4. Are alternative democratic arrangements—such as majoritarian democracy, power dividing, a protectorate, or partition into independent democracies—more stable and less conflict producing than ethnic power-sharing arrangements within deeply divided societies?

This and the second question inevitably raise additional ones about the appropriateness of these arrangements at different points in the initiation and consolidation phases of a transition. Moreover, since institutions adopted at one point of a transition constrain subsequent choices, this also begs the question whether institutions that are better for the initiation phase will permit—even facilitate—the emergence of institutions more suitable for the consolidation phase. Therefore, our fifth question concerns the development of a sophisticated, phased strategy:

> 5. Can the introduction of institutions—each of which is designed for a specific part of the transition—be phased in a comprehensive strategy that is more likely to result in the consolidation of peace and democracy?

In selecting cases, we are constrained in reaching generalizable findings by the relatively few examples of successful consolidation of peace and democracy after domestic conflicts, particularly after civil wars, through power sharing or power dividing. The histories of recent experiments in power sharing—such as Bosnia and Afghanistan—are too short to allow us to draw many conclusions. In addition, the continuing role of external actors makes it difficult to assess the viability of these arrangements as self-sustaining institutions for independent countries. Thus, the authors have often had to examine most nearly comparable cases—such as ethnically divided societies that have not recently experienced intense conflict, let alone civil war—in order to find evidence that might permit us to assess the usefulness of various institutional arrangements in the maintenance of domestic peace and the transition to democracy.

The chapters in this volume take three different approaches to the question of appropriate institutions. The chapters in Part I present the dilemma of power sharing and the alternative of power dividing in greater depth. This part addresses the first, second, fourth, and fifth questions concerning the ability of formal power-sharing institutions and informal power-sharing arrangements to sustain peaceful relations and democracy, the phase at which these are most likely to promote such outcomes in a transition from civil war, and the power-dividing alternative to power sharing. In Chapter 2 we review the main problems that arise from power sharing in ethnically divided societies. In Chapter 3, Philip G. Roeder makes a case for the alternative of power division as a more stable foundation for consolidating peace and democracy in ethnically divided societies. He argues that power sharing is more likely to lead to escalating demands from the leaders of ethnic groups, who back their demands with more extreme means, including violence. Alternatively, the power-dividing, or multiple-majorities, strategy of institution building lowers the ethnic stakes in conflicts, achieves efficient decisionmaking without institutionalizing a tyranny of the majority, disperses institutional weapons, and protects the rights of ethnic minorities by linking these to the rights of other types of minorities within the ethnic majority. What are typically cited as successful cases of power sharing in ethnically divided societies, he contends, are actually the result of power dividing.

Do promises in peace settlements of power sharing, as international relations scholars use this term, initiate a successful transition to peace and democracy? Matthew Hoddie and Caroline Hartzell examine in Chapter 4 the terms of peace settlements that ended civil wars between 1945 and 1998 and ask whether provisions that promise executive power sharing (in the central government), territorial autonomy, proportionality in military staffing and control, and proportional allocation of economic resources affected the duration of peace in the initiation phase and the length of time before holding general elections. They find no relationship between executive power sharing and the successful maintenance of peace or timely transition to democracy. Alternatively, they find that provisions for territorial and military power sharing in the initial agreement—such as ceasefires that left each party in control of its own territory and promises of integrating the parties' armed forces into a common army—have been positively associated with the duration of the peace. They also find that provisions for territorial and economic power sharing are positively associated with the timely holding of elections. This sets in stark terms the dilemma of power sharing: A good beginning can, as the other authors in Part I underscore, prove to be the undoing of a transition, if the promise of power sharing is actually implemented.

In Part II the authors address the impact of actual power-sharing institutions and policies after the peace settlement or ceasefire on the different phases of the transition to peace and democracy. They take up the first two questions listed previously. Taken together these four chapters underscore the dilemma of power sharing that we identified earlier in this chapter. In Chapter 5, David A. Lake and Donald Rothchild examine the short- and longer-term stability of territorial decentralization—a primary element of power sharing and recent civil-war settlements in ethnically divided societies such as Bosnia, the Philippines, and Ethiopia. They argue that the *offer of decentralization* can be a valuable incentive in the initiation of a transition to peace because it can serve as a signal of moderation by the majority. In the longer term, however, territorial decentralization has not been a viable arrangement that is likely to lead to the consolidation of peace and democracy in ethnically divided societies in newly emergent countries. Specifically, in large-*n* comparisons they find that "since 1945, warring factions have never realized full political decentralization along territorial lines as part of a civil war settlement" and that even where no civil war has taken place "territorial decentralization is an extremely fragile political institution."

Does the institutional design of a state—specifically, whether it is ethnofederal or unitary—affect the success of democratic transitions and the maintenance of peace in ethnically divided societies? In Chapter 6 Valerie Bunce and Stephen Watts compare states undertaking a transition from socialism and argue that "the ethnofederal successor states, in direct contrast to their unitary counterparts, were weak; their constituent nations unusually conflictual; and their democratic orders compromised from the very start and fragile over time." While existing ethnofederal states probably should not attempt to become unitary, creating new ethnofederal states in deeply divided societies may weaken democracy and the peace. This evidence suggests that in many circumstances ethnofederalism is an imprudent institutional choice for consolidating peace and democracy after civil wars.

In Chapter 7, Benjamin Reilly examines the role of electoral systems in the consolidation of democracy in ethnically divided societies—a tool that has been much favored by policy and academic specialists in recent years. He asks whether proportional rather than plurality electoral systems are the surest way to achieve inclusive governments and stable democracy in these societies—a central claim made by the proponents of a power-sharing strategy. In looking closely at the experience of those ethnically divided societies that have also consolidated democracy, he finds that they have tended to maintain inclusive governments. Yet these democracies have sustained inclusive governments with plurality rather than proportional electoral systems. This favored tool of power sharing may be no better than the alternative of majoritarian (or plurality) elections in the consolidation of peace and democracy after civil wars.

Eduardo Alemán and Daniel Treisman in Chapter 8 explore the impact of fiscal power sharing on the level of secessionist violence. Specifically, they compare the impact of the power-sharing policies of fiscal decentralization and fiscal proportionality with the impact of the alternative strategy of fiscal appeasement. In a comparison of India, Pakistan, Nigeria, and the former Yugoslavia, they find little evidence that fiscal decentralization reduced secessionist violence. In allocating central funds, fiscal proportionality does not appear to have been enough to satisfy potential secessionists; fiscal appeasement that "buys off" the potential secessionists may be the most effective policy. Yet, the weakness of these relationships warns that the impact of any fiscal policy on secession may be very limited.

Part III focuses on constraints such as demographic structure or level of economic development that affect the success of power-sharing institutions in ethnically divided societies. Taken together these four chapters underscore how rare it is to find conditions favoring success in societies recently torn by civil wars. In Chapter 9, Marie-Joëlle Zahar explores the role of third-party enforcers in Lebanon's 140-year experiment with power sharing. She finds that the shifting role of external enforcers has brought both peace and violence. Lengthy periods of stability in the power-sharing arrangements have all been associated with protectorates—first by the Ottoman Empire, then by France, and recently by Syria. Instability has been associated with transitions when outside powers intervened seeking to establish a new protectorate or when an existing protector began to withdraw. Zahar finds that over the longer term, rather than contributing to the consolidation of peace and democracy, Lebanese power sharing has blocked the consolidation of a self-sustaining peace that could survive withdrawal of the protectorate and thwarted the evolution to full democracy, even though these are the stated objectives of parties to recent power-sharing arrangements.

Amit Ahuja and Ashutosh Varshney in Chapter 10 ask under what conditions ethnofederalism might be more stable. For insights they turn to the experience of India—a rare example of a durable ethnofederal democracy. They note that ethnofederalism since the 1950s has not generated divisive political disputes that threaten India's unity and that central institutions (such as the presidency, army, electoral commission, Supreme Court) have continued to serve as honest brokers between center and states and among the states. They identify three factors that account for India's success with ethnofederalism. First, the Indian people are so united by a shared sense of "nation-ness" that aggrieved ethnic groups or states have seldom raised the issue of secession. Second, the Indian population is not bifurcated but fragmented along linguistic or ethnic lines, so that any majority must be inclusive. And third, Indian society is characterized by crosscutting rather than cumulative cleavages. By contrast, these factors are typically missing among states that have recently been torn by intense conflicts such as civil wars. Indeed, at the end of civil wars there is at best only a limited sense of common nationhood among ethnic groups and relatively few significant crosscutting ties. The Indian case highlights how difficult it may be to make ethnofederalism work among parties following intense conflicts.

In Chapter 11, Edmond J. Keller and Lahra Smith examine the implementation of territorial decentralization in Ethiopia since 1991. They find that constraints that one would normally expect to find in ethnically divided societies after civil wars have proved to be major obstacles in the way of effective decentralization in such areas as fiscal policy and education policy. Thus, despite the formal plans of Ethiopia's central government, the regional governments have not come to exercise the autonomous decisionmaking powers allotted them. Many regions lack independent tax bases and sources of funds and so remain dependent on the central government; their administrative resources (personnel and facilities) are insufficient to meet the expanded demands of decentralization; and the implementation effort in many regions has become waylaid by limited accountability among newly autonomous officials, local corruption, and local conflicts among new ethnic majorities and their new minorities.

Timothy Sisk and Christoph Stefes in Chapter 12 examine a rare instance in which the parties to a transition successfully navigated through the dilemma of power sharing—South Africa's phased transition through interim power sharing to majoritarian democracy. They ask whether we can mine any lessons from this experience and find that the successful transition was facilitated by the confidence-building process that developed during the initiation phase. Intergroup confidence in the commitments of all major parties to abide by democratic rules grew in South Africa, as Sisk (1995, 15) explains elsewhere, because, despite deep racial and ethnic conflicts of interest, the communities shared a "sense of common destiny and the realization that hegemonic aims are, in the final analysis, self-defeating." Reassured by gestures of goodwill, the parties developed a new constitutional order with protections for all and cultivated informal power sharing in multiple bargaining arenas at the local, regional, and national levels in politics, society, and the economy. Sisk and Stefes argue that, unlike the experience with power sharing in Northern Ireland and Bosnia, this strategy permitted South Africa to avoid replicating a single ethnic divide in every corner of politics and society.

In the conclusion (Chapter 13) the editors mine these rich chapters for insights that might help us devise more successful policies for transitions from intense conflicts in ethnically divided societies. We put forward nine policy recommendations that seek to avoid the dilemma of power sharing. In brief, we contend that the evidence presented in these chapters, when applied to the recent experience of internationally imposed power sharing, not only underscores the dilemmas of power sharing but also points to additional dilemmas created by international interventions and protectorates. We argue that this evidence suggests the need for an alternative strategy of institution building and international involvement—a strategy of nation-state stewardship that leads to power-dividing democracy.

PART I

Power-Sharing Dilemmas and the Power-Dividing Alternative

2

Power Sharing as an Impediment to Peace and Democracy

Donald Rothchild and Philip G. Roeder

Power-sharing institutions, like all fundamental political institutions, allocate decision rights between the state and society and, within the state, among governmental organs. These institutions in turn constrain subsequent political processes by empowering some political actors rather than others, creating incentives to press some demands rather than others, and making it less costly to press these demands in some ways rather than others. Power-sharing institutions are no different than others in this respect, but in ethnically divided societies after intense conflicts they typically have a set of unintended but perverse consequences. They empower ethnic elites from previously warring groups, create incentives for these elites to press radical demands once the peace is in place, and lower the costs for these elites to escalate conflict in ways that threaten democracy and peace. These dangers can be avoided when power-sharing institutions operate under very special conditions such as a political culture of accommodation, economic prosperity and equality, demographic stability, strong governmental institutions, stable hierarchical relations within ethnic communities, and a supportive international environment. Yet those conditions are unlikely to be present or difficult to sustain after severe conflicts such as civil wars.

In this chapter we review the long-term problems that arise under power-sharing institutions in ethnically divided societies after intense conflicts. It is important to keep in mind that the prescription for power-sharing institutions originated from close study of societies that were ethnically homogeneous—notably Austria and the Netherlands—and had not experienced ethnic civil war in recent history. Our critique does not challenge the account of these earlier successes, only the claim that this model has been successful when transplanted to ethnically divided societies and particularly after periods of intense domestic conflict. This chapter is divided into three parts.

The first identifies the distinguishing characteristics of power-sharing institutions. The second presents the case that when extended to ethnically divided countries these institutions frequently shape political processes so that there are greater incentives to act in ways that threaten democracy and the peace. The third advances the argument that the conditions necessary for successful power-sharing institutions—conditions present in the original cases that inspired this approach—are unlikely to exist or difficult to sustain after severe conflicts in ethnically divided societies.

What Is Power Sharing?

According to the *Oxford English Dictionary* the term power sharing entered the language in 1972 in conjunction with the short-lived settlement in Northern Ireland. In academic circles many of the institutions that have since been subsumed under this rubric were advanced in earlier decades. Particularly noteworthy is W. Arthur Lewis's (1965) discussion of the need for consensus democracy in the developing countries and Arend Lijphart's model of consociational democracy in the Netherlands that he puts forward in *The Politics of Accommodation* (1968). The case for power sharing in ethnically divided societies was made in the 1970s by Eric Nordlinger, who anticipated many others with his monograph *Conflict Regulation in Divided Societies* (1972), and by Lijphart, whose best statement concerning consociationalism in ethnically divided societies remains *Democracy in Plural Societies* (1977). In the following decade Donald Horowitz offered important new insights on this regime type in his *Ethnic Groups in Conflict* (1985).

In invoking the term "power sharing," or its related formulations such as "consociationalism," advocates have used the term variously to refer to institutions, an elite culture (Venter 1983), informal decisionmaking practices (Lembruch 1975), or policies. More recently it has also been used by students of international relations to include informal provisions found in peace settlements and ceasefires that we noted in the previous chapter. In this volume we will limit the term *power-sharing institutions* to formal institutions that distribute decisionmaking rights within the state and define decisionmaking procedures (e.g., Lijphart 1985, 6). Specifically, power-sharing institutions in ethnically pluralistic societies consist of rules that seek to guarantee what we will label inclusive decisionmaking, partitioned decisionmaking, predetermined decisions, or some combination of these. These rules provide what we will call *mandates*, or relatively hard guarantees, and *opportunities*, or relatively soft guarantees (Table 2.1).[1]

1. This distinction parallels some points in Lijphart's (1990b) distinction between consociationalism on the basis of "predetermined" groups versus consociationalism on the basis of "self-determining" groups.

Table 2.1. Illustrative institutional arrangements under power-sharing agreements

	Mandates (relatively hard guarantees)	Opportunities (relatively soft guarantees)
Inclusive decisionmaking	Ethnic allocation of executive posts Reserved seats in legislature Concurrent majorities	Parliamentary government List proportional representation with low threshold Supermajorities
Partitioned decisionmaking	Ethnofederalism Exclusive jurisdiction	Federalism Concurrent jurisdiction
Predetermined decisions	Prohibited decisions Extraordinary amendment procedure	Amendment by simple legislative majority

Inclusive Decisionmaking

In realms where decisions are binding on all members of a society, regardless of their ethnic identity, power-sharing institutions seek to reassure minorities that their interests will be taken into account by guaranteeing participation of representatives of all the main ethnic groups in the making of governmental decisions. In practice power-sharing arrangements are seldom fully inclusive because the dominant political elite typically leaves the leaders of small groups—who lack bargaining leverage—out of the decisionmaking process. Nevertheless, the objective is to include all groups that can threaten political stability if kept outside the arrangements. The ideal of inclusive decisionmaking sets twin objectives: First is the representation of all major ethnic groups in the "central" decisionmaking organs of the state—that is, the organs that have jurisdiction over members of all ethnic groups. Second is decisionmaking procedures within these organs that give a voice in policy outcomes to representatives of ethnic minorities as well as majorities. Inclusion of minority groups in a grand coalition is not a sufficient condition; tokenism is not enough. It is critical that power sharing assigns group representatives in the elite cartel to positions of power such as influential ministries, that these are authentic representatives of their communities, and that they have a real voice in public policy (Rothchild 1997, 65).

In practice, mandates or relatively hard guarantees of representation in decisionmaking stipulate that specific ethnic groups must occupy designated posts of the central government. For example, in Cyprus (1960–1968) the constitution assigned the presidency to the Greek community and the vice presidency to the Turkish community; each community held a separate election to fill its assigned post. The president and vice president in turn each appointed the seven Greek ministers and three Turkish ministers from their respective communities in order to constitute the Council of Ministers. Similarly, under the Global Ceasefire Accord and the Pretoria Protocol on Political, Defence, and Security Power Sharing in Burundi signed in 2003, seats in the national assembly and transitional cabinet must be allocated according to a formula of 60 percent to Hutus and 40 percent to Tutsis; positions in the senate and the regular troops of the security forces must be divided evenly between Hutus and Tutsis (ICG 2004c, 3–4).

More commonly inclusive decisionmaking is guaranteed by setting aside seats within the national legislature—or within a separate upper chamber—for representatives of designated ethnic groups. Cyprus's constitution, for example, guaranteed that 70 percent of the seats in the House of Representatives would be elected by the Greek community and 30 percent by the Turkish community. Under the 2004 Naivasha Protocol on Power Sharing in the Sudan (Sect. 2.2.5), the northern-based National Congress Party is allocated 52 percent of all seats in the transitional National Assembly, while the remaining seats are distributed as follows: 28 percent to the southern-based Sudan People's Liberation Movement, 14 percent to other northern political forces, and 6 percent to other southern political forces.[2] Mauritius expands minority representation in its National Assembly by allocating 8 of its 70 seats (two seats apiece) among the Hindu, Muslim, Chinese, and general populations to ensure representation of the major communities. These are but a few illustrations. Federal states with regions drawn to correspond to ethnic homelands—such as India—often maintain an upper legislative chamber that guarantees equal representation to each homeland.

Alternatively, opportunities for representation in central decisionmaking—that is, relatively soft guarantees—do not assign government posts to specific ethnic groups but provide selection procedures that increase the probability that all major ethnic groups will in fact be represented. Lijphart (1995, 856) has argued for a parliamentary rather than presidential form of government because it lowers the barriers to entry into the government (cabinet) and for elections based on proportional representation rather than single-member districts because they lower the barriers to entry into the legislature. Thus, constitutional designers can increase the likelihood of coalition governments that over time include most of the major ethnic groups by adopting a combination of parliamentary government with elections by list proportional representation in large-magnitude districts with low electoral thresholds. Horowitz (1985, 628–651) advocates voting schemes in presidential elections that require a victor to win support in more than one region of the country. He also calls for legislative elections that permit voters to register their first, second, and lower preferences among candidates and require a victor to command an absolute majority made up of first and lower-ranked votes. In both of these types of elections candidates must broaden their appeals beyond the demands of a single ethnic group in order

2. *Protocol Between the Government Of Sudan (GOS) and the Sudan People's Liberation Movement (SPLM) on Power Sharing* (Naivasha, Kenya, May 26, 2004).

to win; as a consequence, victors are likely to represent coalitions of ethnic groups.

Whatever type of guarantee is used to expand ethnic representation in government, inclusive decisionmaking also depends on decision rules within the government and legislature to ensure that the voices of minority representatives are, in fact, registered in policymaking. Relatively hard guarantees of inclusion in decisions typically require concurrent support from the representatives of different ethnic groups—that is, ethnic representatives exercise a veto over sensitive issues. For example, Cyprus's president and vice president each had an independent "final veto" over decisions of the Council of Ministers and over laws or decisions of the House of Representatives concerning foreign affairs, defense, and security. Relatively soft guarantees may require supermajorities in a common legislature so that, depending on the actual proportions of seats held by the different ethnic groups, sensitive legislation must garner at least some support from the minority communities in order to pass.

Partitioned Decisionmaking

Some issues divide ethnic groups deeply from one another, but policy to address these issues need not be standardized for the country as a whole. Such issues as traditional or religious practices are especially important to ethnic-group members. For these policy realms power sharing typically prescribes partitioning decisionmaking so that separate agencies of the ethnic groups such as communal legislative chambers or homeland administrations make policies for their own members. Rather than bringing ethnic representatives into the political center to reach a common policy, partitioned decisionmaking divides the government's decisionmaking powers in these policy realms and allocates these powers among independent governmental decisionmaking agencies in which specific ethnic groups have greater voice—sometimes what amounts to an exclusive voice.

The most important institutional distinction in granting this type of autonomy to ethnic groups concerns whether power sharing assigns jurisdiction on the basis of the principle of "territoriality" or "personality" (McRae 1975; Coakley 1994). The former creates ethnofederalism; the latter, ethnocorporatism. *Ethnofederalism* is adopted more frequently because of the ease of creating and administering autonomous regions within the territorially based state, but territory is only a proxy for ethnicity. Thus, the Soviet Union's ethnofederalism assigned most responsibility to territorial units that acted in the name of the ethnic group, but many administrations included substantial minorities and sometimes even majorities composed of other nationalities. *Ethnocorporatism* creates jurisdictions that extend only to members of the community and not to all residents within the territory. This includes such institutions as communal legislative chambers, which adopt separate policies for their respective ethnic communities, and communal bureaucratic administrations, such as separate school systems for different ethnic communities residing side by side in the same region.

Forms of ethnocorporatism were practiced in the millet system of the Ottoman Empire that granted autonomy to non-Muslim confessional communities and under the Estonian Cultural Autonomy Law of 1925; it was also associated with the proposals for the Austro-Hungarian Empire offered by Karl Renner, Otto Bauer, and the Austrian Social Democrats after 1899 (Hanf 1991). Cyprus's 1960 constitution created two Communal Chambers—elected separately from the Greek and Turkish communities—that had exclusive legislative jurisdiction in matters of religion, education, culture, and personal status for members of their respective communities. The Communal Chambers were also empowered to create courts to adjudicate civil disputes concerning religious matters and personal status and to impose taxes on members of the separate communities to finance these policies. It is important to note that in power sharing, these agencies of ethnic groups are typically not voluntary associations, but governmental or state institutions. Individuals under their jurisdiction do not freely choose to join—except by escaping to another jurisdiction; rather, compliance is mandatory for everyone within their jurisdiction, and enforcement is backed by the coercive powers of the state exercised by these agencies.

Mandated autonomy—that is, relatively hard guarantees of ethnic autonomy—assign agencies to specific ethnic groups. Opportunities for autonomy—that is, softer guarantees of ethnic autonomy—create agencies that increase the likelihood of ethnic capture (Lijphart 1995, 856; Horowitz 1985, 613–622), but do not guarantee this. Thus, federalism or cantonal autonomy with boundaries drawn without regard to ethnic composition may be a relatively soft guarantee of ethnic autonomy, but they afford geographically concentrated ethnic minorities greater voice in local administration and therefore expanded opportunities for self-governance. Harder guarantees of ethnic autonomy give these agencies exclusive jurisdiction in specific policy realms. Relatively soft guarantees of ethnic autonomy give the central government and ethnic agencies concurrent jurisdiction. The latter is "softer" because it carries significant risk of poaching on the prerogatives of the ethnic agencies by a fiscally and politically dominant central government or even outright preemption by the central government.

Predetermined Decisions

Formal power-sharing rules often set some issues such as the allocation of valuable governmental resources outside the decisionmaking powers of all levels of government. In power sharing these predetermined decisions typically include formulas for proportional allocation of such government resources as educational funds or positions within the bureaucracy and the military. These are issues that the drafters of power-sharing institutions do not feel they can entrust to subsequent generations of politicians and the uncertainties of democracy. Thus, various Nigerian constitutions since 1979 have made balanced recruitment and balanced allocation fundamental principles in federal decisionmaking. The 1999 constitution (Chapter II, Section 14 (3)) specifies, for example, that not only "the composition of the Government of the Federation" but also the composition of "any of its [appointed] agencies and the conduct of its affairs shall be carried out in such a manner as to reflect the federal character of Nigeria." Cyprus's 1960 constitution mandated that the republic's army would consist of 2,000 men; 60 percent were to be Greeks and 40 percent Turks. The police and gendarmerie were to consist of another 2,000 men; of these 70 percent were to be Greeks and 30 percent Turks. Harder guarantees that these decisions will remain outside the jurisdiction of all levels of government prohibit amendments to the formulas or at least mandate extraordinary procedures such as a constituent assembly to enact a change of rules (Attanasio 1991, 1210). Softer guarantees can be amended by some simpler procedure such as a legislative majority.

Of course, there are subtle differences among the proposals for power-sharing institutions. Perhaps the best known is the difference between what is sometimes called the consociational approach of Arend Lijphart (1977, 25) and the integrative approach of Donald Horowitz (1985, 598). *Consociationalism* is characterized by such protections for segmental interests as the grand coalition, mutual veto, proportional allocations, and autonomy. The *integrative approach* seeks to manage conflict through the use of incentives to promote interethnic cooperation in parties and electoral campaigns.

Despite such differences, the power-sharing approach is defined by at least three common characteristics. These approaches share a commitment to what Timothy Sisk (1996, 34) calls "coalescent democracy" as opposed to competitive democracy (Lijphart 1977, 25); thus governments and legislatures represent inclusive coalitions of ethnic groups. They privilege one dimension of social cleavage—ethnicity—in designing institutions and defining policy equity, rather than seeking to identify dimensions of social cleavage in which ethnicity is not the primary dimension that separates majority from minority (Sisk 1996, 44–45). And they tend to concentrate powers—particularly through federalism or autonomy—in a few critical decisionmaking arenas in which ethnic interests must be reconciled either at the electoral stage or in the decisionmaking stage.

The case for power sharing is not simply a scholarly discourse; it is intended as practical policy advice as well. Indeed, many authors have advised constitutional commissions in a number of new democracies in ethnically plural societies on the design of their constitutions (Lijphart 1985; Horowitz 1991). The themes of these authors have been adopted as an agenda for action by a number of governmental, international, and nongovernmental organizations advising new states on institutional design. For example, scholars associated with the United States Institute of Peace have issued studies that examine a variety of alternative power-sharing arrangements to solve ethnic conflicts (Sisk 1996). The International Institute for Democracy and Electoral Assistance has issued a handbook that outlines "options for negotiators" in developing democracy in societies with deeply rooted conflicts (Harris and Reilly 1998). The East Europe Constitutional Design Forum in London has published a handbook on electoral and constitutional models for ethnically divided countries (Chapman 1991). All advocate some form of power-sharing institutions.

The Perils of Power Sharing

The sad irony of power-sharing institutions is that when extended to ethnically divided societies they have created both motives and means for the ethnic elites empowered by power sharing to escalate ethnic conflicts. No matter whether the ethnic elites intended it or not, this escalation has tended to threaten the consolidation of peace and democracy. Specifically, in ethnically divided societies, power-sharing institutions have given rise to at least seven key problems that have thwarted the consolidation of peace and democracy. These are problems that emerge in ethnically divided societies even when there has not been a recent conflict.

1. Limits on Democracy

Power sharing limits democracy. Power-sharing institutions typically seek to create a stable cartel among the elites of ethnic groups (and often other interest groups). As Nils Butenschøn (1985) notes, these "elites in plural societies must deviate from competitive practices of political decision-making on the national level (as is the accepted norm of Western democracies)" and avoid public appeals to their respective constituencies over the issues that are most divisive among groups (Daalder 1974, 607–608). These elites can compromise with one another because they enjoy the "discretionary freedom," as Hans Daalder (1974, 608) calls it, that comes from their "predominance over a politically deferential and organizationally encapsulated following," as Adriano Pappalardo (1981, 365) phrases it. Nordlinger (1972, 73) contends that "a necessary condition for conflict regulation is a form of structured relations between leaders and non-elites in which the leaders are clearly predominant and their demands regularly fulfilled." Yet, carried too far, power-sharing institutions limit precisely those essential elements that define democracy. Democracy requires competition among elites over the important policy concerns of the public and accountability of the elites to the citizenry on these most important policy issues through regular elections. Such elections permit the citizens to select among competing party elites (Schumpeter 1975 [1947]; Dahl 1971).

2. Institutional Weapons

Power-sharing institutions frequently empower the leaders of ethnic groups with the means to challenge the power-sharing agreement. Many institutions of inclusive decisionmaking, such as mutual vetoes, can be used to begin a game of brinkmanship in which each side threatens to force a deadlock in governmental decisionmaking until the other side grants further concessions. Many institutions of partitioned decisionmaking, such as the powers of autonomous homelands in ethnofederal states, can be abused by regional leaders, including ethnomilitary warlords, to press the central government for further devolution and to extract income that can be invested in future fighting capacity (Reno 1998).

This predation in turn can feed the fears and suspicions that give ethnic elites the motive to challenge the power-sharing agreement in anticipation of defection by the other side. Power sharing in the highly charged environment at the end of a conflict is complicated by fear and suspicion among ethnic communities—and frequently by the reality—that each power of government allocated to an ethnic group is an opportunity for it to exploit. Ethnic elites may fear—frequently with justification—that the vetoes or autonomy granted other groups can be used as weapons to extort concessions. Thus, in Cyprus President Makarios complained bitterly of the vice president's use of the veto to wring further concessions for the Turkish minority. Meanwhile, Greeks' complaints fueled fears in the Turkish community that the decision rights of the minority were being threatened.

3. Focus on Interethnic Allocation

Power-sharing institutions shape the agenda of politics and privilege issues of interethnic allocation of power and resources (Daalder 1974, 607; Lijphart 1968, 122–138). Consequently, the issues that divide ethnic groups from one another come to occupy a central place in politics under power sharing, sustain interethnic conflict at high levels, and keep alive fundamental issues of renegotiating the rules of power sharing. For example, ethnic elites under power sharing often debate whether the rules of proportionality disadvantage one or the other group unfairly. This challenge to the predetermined decision is particularly common among elites who believe that the members of their own communities exhibit special skills and achievements (Gboyega 1989, 183) and that proportionality discriminates against their more qualified candidates for positions and in favor of less qualified members of other ethnic groups. Proportionality may leave ethnic groups residing in wealthier regions particularly aggrieved. In Olusegun Obasanjo's Nigeria, for example, minority peoples such as those of the oil-producing areas in the Niger Delta felt marginalized because the greater part of the benefits were allocated to other states on the basis of need (Suberu 2001, 66; Ibelema 2000, 212). Similarly, as the Soviet Union began to democratize, the wealthier Baltic regions were the first to complain that the redistributive policies imposed by Moscow were unfair (Roeder 1991). In each of these cases, issues of allocation were not only points of interethnic distribution but also fundamental questions concerning revision of the power-sharing institutions themselves.

4. The Second-Generation Problem

Even where ethnic elites are initially sincere in their commitments to power sharing, elite incentives—particularly, but not exclusively, in the majority group—change once a power-sharing arrangement is in place—a moral hazard or time-inconsistency problem that might be called "the second-generation problem" in power-sharing institutions (Rabushka and Shepsle 1972; Roeder 1999). Although a majority group may perceive that it has an incentive to make concessions on power sharing at the time a peace accord is negotiated, these incentives tend to shift as the contract becomes a reality. As the need to reassure weaker parties becomes less immediate, the majority party is inclined to focus on the problems of governance and maintaining political power. Its need to act in a conciliatory manner toward ethnic minorities diminishes and the requirements of decisive governance increase, raising questions as to the majority group's continuing commitment to the principle of proportionality in civil service recruitment, regional allocations, or representation in the decision process.

Compromises among elites who negotiated the original power-sharing agreement may become particularly difficult to maintain, and, as a consequence, the power-sharing institutions may be threatened when ambitious, up-and-coming politicians engage in outbidding behavior to outflank the moderate elites within their own community. Under pressure from their constituents to pursue the community's narrow self-interest, the political leaders of the majority community in particular will find it harder to compromise in order to realize the common interest of all ethnic groups and to uphold a long-term commitment to what at times seems to their constituents to be a disadvantageous arrangement. When ambitious, up-and-coming leaders with more radical demands actually succeed in replacing moderates, the upshot is to complicate still further the maintenance of the ruling elite cartel and therefore the ethnic balance of power. For example, Serbian leaders who succeeded Josip Broz Tito as part of the collective leadership of Yugoslavia found they were outflanked within Serbia by more nationalistic leaders such as Slobodan Milošević. The ascent of these more radical leaders made holding the federation together more difficult. Subsequently, the outflanking of Milošević by still more radical nationalists such as Vojislav Šešelj and the addition of these radicals to form a parliamentary majority in Serbia led to a further radicalization of politics in the last year of the Yugoslav Federation (Hislope 1997).

5. Governmental Inefficiency

Power-sharing institutions are designed to expand the representativeness of the state, but this representativeness often comes at the cost of greater governmental inefficiency. Inclusive decisionmaking—particularly by guaranteeing ethnic representation and granting vetoes to ethnic spokesmen and -women—makes policymaking slower and more likely to end in deadlock (Shugart and Carey 1992, 104–105). Partitioned decisionmaking increases administrative costs through the duplication of decisionmaking agencies and bureaucracies (Lijphart 1985, 99). For example, parallel educational systems and parallel courts in the same regions multiply administrative costs. For countries emerging from civil conflict these costs may overtax a very weak revenue base. With additional costs, the government may simply have to deliver less in the way of education and other services. For example, Edmond Keller and Lahra Smith document that Ethiopia has found that it is an enormous financial burden to develop course texts and train teachers to conduct classes simultaneously in the various languages of its regions (see Chapter 11). Ethnic leaders and their constituents may quickly grow disillusioned with a government that cannot help them reconstruct their lives after civil war nor provide them with hope for significant improvement in the future.

6. Governmental Rigidity

Power-sharing institutions tend to be inflexible and unable to adapt to rapidly changing social conditions during a transition from intense conflict. In reassuring all major groups about their autonomy or representation at the political center, power-sharing institutions freeze a status quo that makes political change difficult. Yet, a postconflict environment may demand dynamic arrangements that can shift over time, as socioeconomic interests change and new actors enter the political process. In general, however, institutions—particularly strong institutions that represent credible commitments to power sharing among ethnic groups in divided societies—are likely to be sticky. Lebanon's inability to adapt its institutions to a changing social environment except in the face of political crisis and finally civil war attests to this stickiness. Balancing the competing needs for strong institutions and flexible institutions through power sharing may be well beyond the abilities of constitutional designers.

This is particularly problematic for completing the transition to democracy. In exceptional cases such as South Africa during its transition from apartheid to nonracial democracy, power-sharing institutions have facilitated the evolution of stable intergroup relations leading to full democracy. What begins as a pact among ethnic elites must be transformed into dense webs of interdependent relations among an expanding set of political participants. Once in place, power-sharing institutions must evolve with the steady adoption of more democratic rules. Yet, power-sharing institutions typically create the conditions for the dominant political class to resist change. This resistance may lead to escalating political conflict and repression. Excluded politicians may be too impatient to remain deferential as behind-the-scenes negotiations and compromises slow or even block the transition to democracy. In the face of opposition from the elite cartel, often the only way for new politicians to break into politics is through the transformation of the power-sharing arrangement itself (Rose 2000). In reaction the dominant elites may respond—indeed, they are expected to respond in order to maintain their structured predominance—with repression of the leaders questioning the system in the name of democratization. For example, Lebanese power sharing broke down as newcomers challenged the preeminence of traditional elites, these elites attempted to reassert their authority with repression, and the elites found it imprudent to continue honoring many of their commitments to one another under the old power-sharing rules. Since power sharing is often an elitist approach, it tends to resist not only political adaptation to social change but social change as well (Rothchild 1986).

7. Inadequate Enforcement

It may be difficult to enforce the rules of a power-sharing arrangement against opportunistic behavior by the leaders of ethnic groups that are the major parties to the agreement. It is sometimes difficult to distinguish sanctions from predation. Attempts by group leaders—and even attempts by a central government that is supposed to be above all ethnic groups—to sanction violations of the rules frequently escalate conflict among ethnic groups and threaten the agreement. Without an external guarantor to ensure stability, especially in the early phases of implementation, aggrieved interests can always find reasons to renege on their commitments. Domestic enforcement agencies can be captured by ethnic interests, and even when they are not captured, the leaders of some ethnic groups may believe these agencies are partisans of one side. Thus, in the last years of the Soviet Union, when Mikhail Gorbachev attempted to enforce rules against Estonia and Georgia that prohibited union republics from discriminating against their own minorities, this action was taken as escalation of a conflict between the union-republic governments and Moscow, and it provoked counterescalation by union-republic leaders. Gorbachev was seen as a partisan of an empire that kept Russians in a dominant position over Estonians and Georgians. Domestic enforcement agencies run jointly can become paralyzed by the same opportunistic behavior that they are supposed to monitor and sanction. Designers may try to decentralize monitoring and enforcement among the parties to the agreement by permitting ethnic elites to sanction one another for failure to fulfill commitments, but this leads to a proliferation of institutional weapons that makes power sharing even more fragile.

Perhaps the best indication of all these intrinsic difficulties in implementing power sharing is the high mortality rates for power-sharing arrangements. Many of the cases cited by power-sharing advocates as successes have, in fact, ended in failure. Such failures result in the collapse of democracy, renewed ethnic conflict and violence, and the abandonment of the power-sharing arrangement. For example, among the 16 experiments with power-sharing institutions cited by Horowitz (1985) in *Ethnic Groups in Conflict*, 12—Burma, Chad, Cyprus, Ethiopia, Guyana, Iraq, Lebanon, Nigeria (1960–1966 and 1976–1983), the Philippines, Sri Lanka, and Sudan—were subsequently discarded (although some later reappeared in another form).

The Unlikely Conditions Necessary for Success

Under proper conditions, the experience with power sharing may be more positive. According to proponents of the power-sharing strategy, seven conditions can favor the success of power-sharing institutions—even in ethnically divided societies. Yet, in ethnically divided societies few if any of these conditions are typically present at the end of conflicts—particularly after conflicts as intense as civil wars (also see Giersch 2000, 10–14; McGarry and Noel 1989).

1. Elite Dominance

In a power-sharing agreement, the parties must be able to fulfill their commitments in the contract. This means the ethnic elites must continue to assure one another that they can enforce this agreement within their respective ethnic groups and enforce subsequent decisions reached through its inclusive decisionmaking procedures. These commitments may be more credible, as Nordlinger (1972) suggests, when elites have demonstrated predominance within their group. Yet, even in normal times, this type of ethnic solidarity is uncommon. Internal diversity of ethnic groups because of divisions among regions, clans, classes, or personalities complicates the processes of negotiating and maintaining durable power-sharing arrangements. Ethnic leaders must actively develop a common position within the ethnic community before entering into political exchanges with other spokespersons at the political center (Putnam 1988). This two-step process complicates the operation of a power-sharing arrangement and increases the likelihood of governmental *immobilisme*.

In the rapidly changing conditions that prevail at the end of a conflict, it is unlikely that elite dominance will remain secure. Even if the conflict itself strengthened the unity of the ethnic group, the rapid transition from conflict to peace is likely to encourage both splits among elites within individual ethnic groups and the rise of challengers from the stratum of young up-and-coming leaders. For example, in Northern Ireland a roadblock in the path to implementing the Good Friday Agreements arose quickly when it became apparent in the November 2003 elections to the Northern Ireland Assembly that the moderate leaders of both Protestant Ulstermen (the Ulster Unionists) and Catholic Irish (Social Democratic and Labour Party) did not command unified support within their respective communities and could not deliver votes. The two parties that emerged as the largest in the Assembly—the Democratic Unionists and Sinn Fein—could not work together to sustain the power-sharing agreement. Alternatively, where only some ethnic groups are cohesive, and particularly where some possess hierarchical organization, this disparity may pose a threat to other groups that are not organized and may feed fears among the weak about the long-term commitment of the strong to power sharing.

Weakness or erosion of elite dominance within the respective communities can also increase the incentive of members of the power-sharing elite to resist compromises or break commitments among themselves. Problems of credible commitments among the elites of different ethnic groups may become particularly acute when the balance of factional power shifts within their respective groups (Lake and Rothchild 1998, 15). As extremists within a group gain a substantial following and effectively challenge their representatives in the elite cartel, the existing elites may find it very difficult to continue support for power sharing. It is true, as John McGarry and Brendan O'Leary (1993, 27) assert, that "the leaders of the rival ethnic communities must fear the consequences of ethnic war and desire to preserve the economic and political stability of their regions." Yet, in many circumstances they fear the relatively remote probability of ethnic war less than they fear the immediate threat to their political position from radicals within their respective communities.

2. A Culture of Accommodation

Where a trans-societal bargaining culture is present, as in Belgium, Switzerland, and India, it facilitates the negotiation of intergroup issues. Where this culture exists only as an elite culture, limited to the power-sharing leaders, there may still be a basis for sustained compromises—although a much more fragile basis. Major group actors come to anticipate that their rivals will reciprocate their positive moves, and, when this occurs, they are able to interact according to the rules of the political game. Such a bargaining culture involves a willingness to resolve conflict through an iterative process of political exchange and reciprocity. Where they share a bargaining culture, parties to an agreement are more likely to accept costs in the short term or in individual decisions because they expect greater gains in the longer term or in subsequent decisions. Yet even in the best of conditions, these cultures develop slowly: Eric Nordlinger estimates this must be present in a society for at least two generations to prompt meaningful conflict-regulating behavior (Nordlinger 1972, 59).

Sadly, in societies emerging from intense conflict, ethnic groups may have less reason to trust one another and less experience with negotiation and compromise. After a civil war a culture of accommodation may take longer than two generations to emerge. A weak bargaining culture may strengthen through the experience of negotiating a power-sharing arrangement and its implementation, but the absence of a bargaining culture in the short-term may preclude the initial compromises. Where the leaders of ethnic groups do not accept the same basic norms on managing conflict or where the constituencies of leaders are not prepared to act in accordance with these agreed-on rules, a power-sharing arrangement is unlikely to prove an effective tension-management institution. As in Cambodia, Angola, Rwanda, or Côte d'Ivoire, the ability and incentive to invest in a complex power-sharing arrangement simply may not be present (Laitin 1987, 275). In short, after an intense conflict, typically there is no culture of accommodation and there is too little time for a culture of accommodation to emerge to sustain power sharing and facilitate consolidation of peace and democracy.

3. Sincere Commitments

It can be difficult to consolidate peace and democracy under power-sharing institutions after intense conflicts because the agreement to establish power-sharing institutions often invites insincere commitments in the initiation phase. Power-sharing institutions can be particularly unstable because they are a compromise among parties to a conflict in which there is no clear victor. This is likely to be the case when power-sharing institutions represent a compromise between a central government fighting to keep the country united and secessionists seeking separation and independence. The basic compromise permits the various parties to believe they can achieve objectives that are fundamentally incompatible with the objectives of other parties. Power sharing can be especially attractive to parties that have reached a hurting stalemate on the battlefield because it can be an opportunity to achieve their objectives by less costly means. For example, secessionists may believe that the autonomy in a power-sharing arrangement will give them the opportunity to develop the capacity that they need to make a successful bid for independence at a later date. Even where leaders do not believe they can improve their chances of achieving their objectives by peaceful means, they may see the power-sharing arrangements as an opportunity to build the resources they need to prevail in a future round of fighting. Thus, power-sharing institutions create incentives for insincere commitments in the initiation phase that in turn threaten success in the consolidation phase.

Even where leaders are sincere, the suspicion that the other side is insincere in its commitment to power-sharing institutions keeps these arrangements unstable. Thus, groups that control the central government often seek to limit the autonomy of homeland administrations because they fear these measures may become the tools for ultimate secession. Alternatively, the leaders of homelands may demand greater autonomy because they fear the central government is not committed to respecting the rights of weaker parties. In Macedonia, for example, the Macedonian majority objected to granting autonomy to the country's Albanian minority because they feared this was a first step to secession. The Albanian leaders—some of whom did hope to follow the example of Kosovo in neighboring Serbia—saw the objections of the Macedonians as evidence that the Albanian minority needed still greater autonomy to protect its interests. This has led to an ongoing struggle over power-sharing institutions as each side attempts to strengthen its position.

4. State Strength

By the term *state strength* we refer to an effective and legitimate government and administrative bureaucracy. This describes the central government's relationship to society, which parallels—and sometimes competes with—the relationship of each ethnic leadership to its particular part of society: The central government and administrative bureaucracy must be able to implement the decisions reached by the elite cartel and ethnic agencies. A state is strong when it is responsible and responsive—and citizens perceive it as such. State strength grows when the state's agencies mediate among the competing groups rather than becoming a party to one side of these disputes (Rothchild 1997, 246).

Yet after particularly destructive civil wars, the state is typically weak and frequently partisan. As Kenneth Menkhaus and Louis Ortmayer (2000, 236) note regarding Somalia, the "emphasis on power-sharing formulas may not be relevant where there is no state within which power can be shared." Even where the state has survived, but is "soft" and unable to regulate or penetrate society effectively, it cannot implement decisions made through inclusive decisionmaking. This inability to implement policy can erode the legitimacy of the agreement. Where many citizens view the central government as illegitimate and where they see its administrative bureaucracy as partisan and biased in its implementation, this further erodes the success of power-sharing institutions.

Initial state capacity may be particularly important because imposition of power-sharing arrangements can weaken the state. For example, a commitment to proportionality may ensure that authentic group representatives will be selected for high positions of state, given important ministries, and allocated sufficient positions and resources to meet their and their constituents' minimal expectations. Yet these may not be the most effective decisionmakers and implementers in demanding times. In addition, power sharing is inherently at odds with the development of a nonpartisan state, because assigning parts of the state—such as regional administrations, specialized courts, or high-level posts—to specific ethnic groups with the expectation that these institutions will protect the interests of the respective ethnic groups makes those parts of the state intrinsically partisan. In Bosnia and Herzegovina each member of the collective presidency and collective judiciary is a representative of a constituent ethnic group with little interest in making the common government work or developing a common, nonpartisan state. They have repeatedly deadlocked on big issues as well as trivial issues, such as the design of an all-Bosnia license plate (Farkas 2001, 12; Talentino 2002, 34).

5. Economic Prosperity and Equality

Economic prosperity and equality among ethnic groups allow the elite cartel to limit conflicts over redistributive issues that might otherwise exacerbate divisions among ethnic groups. An expanding economic pie can allow ethnic elites to elevate the living standards of economically disadvantaged groups even as the other groups continue to see a rise in their own living standards. Under these circumstances, no group need feel imperiled by policies of corrective equity (Lijphart 1985, 124–125). Relatively equal economic opportunities for all groups simplify strategic interactions and allow power-sharing elites to focus on more manageable issues. In this way economic equality facilitates moderation among ethnic elites.

Alternatively, economic hard times can make any attempt to help the most disadvantaged ethnic groups more contentious. In the late Soviet Union, for example, as economic growth rates declined, divisions over developmental policies to help the least developed republics such as Turkmenistan became sharper as the leaders of the more prosperous republics and ethnic groups felt the costs of interrepublic transfers more acutely (Roeder 1991). Structural economic inequalities among ethnic segments increase the likelihood that conflicts will escalate over distribution and may even lead to violence. Very unequal distributions of benefits have had a destabilizing effect on interethnic relations in Fiji and Zimbabwe, requiring the dominant state elite to exert extensive political and military control and making power-sharing arrangements less stable. In cases where the dominant political elite is unprepared to correct the glaring inequalities in society, it may contribute to a significant backlash on the part of some ethnic groups, emboldening them to rebel and undermine stable political relations.

Of course, structural inequalities do not inevitably lead to deeper conflict under power sharing (Collier 2000, 7). Where the advantaged community accepts the need to institute redistributive policies—as Chinese political leaders have in Malaysia—this concession can be seen by other ethnic elites as a costly signal of a commitment to corrective equity and reduce the threat to power-sharing institutions (Horowitz 1991, 470).[3]

Clearly, intense conflicts such as civil wars typically do not leave behind prosperous economies. They tend to exacerbate demands for equity—even when the conflict did not make inequality worse. And they are unlikely to foster the interethnic generosity that might facilitate addressing equity problems that keep alive interethnic resentment.

6. Stable Demographics

When the rates of population growth among the various communities are relatively even, established formulas of balanced representation in the legislature are more likely to remain relatively acceptable over time. Few groups

3. Domestic economic inequalities can be further exacerbated where ethnic groups are differentially integrated into the global economy. Where the state is weak and some ethnoregional interests engage in trade relations with neighboring countries outside of central government control, it can increase domestic socioeconomic inequalities and heighten intergroup tensions. In Africa, for example, the diamond trade has incorporated some regions into the world economy, but in such a way as to exacerbate the power inequalities among local elites. Reportedly $300 million in "conflict diamonds" were smuggled in the 1999–2000 period from Sierra Leone through Liberia to international markets, greatly advantaging the rebel Revolutionary Unity Front (RUF). (Although the RUF was not an ethnic group but a criminal group that controlled the diamond mining area, it was invited into the power-sharing executive for a time.) The effect of this trade was to privilege one local element against the others, undermining state and international efforts to build power-sharing institutions in that country (*Africa Confidential* 2000, 2).

will be in a position to demand readjustment in the power-sharing institutions to reflect the changing demographics in society, and well-represented ethnic groups will be better positioned to insist on maintaining the initial bargain. Alternatively, uneven rates of population increase can destabilize power-sharing institutions.

In the Lebanese conflict, for example, Mary-Jane and Marius Deeb (1995, 125) write that what was at issue was "the amount of power that each group would hold in government (notably in Parliament) and the amount of territory it would control." Under the National Pact of 1943, an elite power-sharing arrangement established a rigid formula for the representation of confessional interests in the political process. This formula, based on the 1932 census, soon proved out of date, and the rapidly growing Muslim community (and particularly its Shiite component) became restive under what it saw as a discriminatory formula. This dissatisfaction contributed to the breakdown of the National Pact and the brutal civil war of the late 1970s. After resisting institutional changes that might have averted civil war and after several failed attempts to reform these institutions and end the war earlier, at the Ta'if Conference in 1989, the Muslim and Christian deputies finally agreed to reform the basis of confessional representation, moving from a 6:5 ratio to one representing Christians and Muslims equally (Zahar 2002).

Demographic stability is uncommon in ethnically divided societies, especially after severe conflicts. This instability is explained by various factors. Civil wars often change patterns of migration into and out of regions (particularly after ethnic cleansing). Distributions of populations between urban centers and the countryside shift as one ethnic group or another flees for safety. Rates of childbearing may rise in some ethnic groups and fall in others. Thus, civil wars can lead to short-term or enduring changes in patterns of population growth among ethnic groups and in their geographic distribution.

7. A Constructive Relationship with the International Community

The relationship of internal actors with outside powers (foreign states, international organizations, or transnational actors) can be critical to the maintenance of power-sharing institutions in ethnically divided societies. Yet the precise pattern of intervention that will help power-sharing institutions to consolidate peace and democracy is no simple matter. External actors are often quite limited in their ability to impose power sharing on the internal conflicts of other societies, as indicated by the experiences in Côte d'Ivoire, Burundi 1994, Sri Lanka, and Cyprus. "The attempt to create power-sharing by fiat [in the face of unfavorable conditions]," Brian Barry (1975, 410–411) remarks, "is attractive but, I suggest, ultimately misguided." For over a decade the concerted efforts of the international community have been unable to persuade the parties to agree to power sharing in Azerbaijan's war with the Karabakh Armenians, Georgia's wars with the South Ossetians and Abkhazians, or Moldova's conflict with the Transnistrians (King 2001b). Efforts by mediators to use diplomatic pressure to secure the adoption of a power-sharing agreement in Burundi in 1994 faced considerable local resistance (Ould-Abdallah 2000, 72; Denyer 2000). Any attempt to simply paper over local resistance with a power-sharing agreement is unlikely to prevent a recurrence of conflict. Effective power sharing requires extensive local participation in the negotiation process to provide the new contract with political legitimacy. Risks increase significantly with external manipulation when local commitment to the agreement tends to be half-hearted and often a matter of tactical advantage. Later, once the external powers withdraw, the willingness to maintain the agreement may decline. This is the continuing danger in Bosnia and Herzegovina.

Nevertheless, at critical junctures as a peace agreement takes hold, a third-party actor (or coalition of actors) can intervene in an ethnic confrontation and attempt to create or restore the balance between contending groups. It can apply pressure and offer incentives to push majority and minority interests to accept difficult confidence-building mechanisms on the ceasefire, disarmament, demobilization, reintegration of armies, run-up to the founding election, and negotiation of the principles of governance (including power-sharing arrangements). An outside power is able to play a pivotal role because it is in a position to reassure the various internal rivals about their security during the precarious transition period (Walter 1999a, 61). In Zimbabwe, Namibia, Sudan (1972), Liberia (2003), Burundi (2003), and El Salvador, among others, third-party actors played a significant role in developing a consensus on the institutions of power sharing for the future. And in Northern Ireland, the 1998 Belfast Agreement creatively linked power sharing with an institutionalized role for the governments in Dublin and London.[4]

4. Transnational actors such as nongovernmental organizations (NGOs) can supplement these constructive engagements, yet not all private international involvements have been positive. Foreign private interests have at times worked closely with local warlords to destabilize local relations, as in the Democratic Republic of the Congo, Sierra Leone, and Liberia, and at times private international agencies have been charged with interference, even weapons transfers. In Sri Lanka the ties between separatist-inclined Tamils of Sri Lanka and those living across the Palk Strait in the Indian State of Tamil Nadu have raised deep suspicions among the majority Sinhalese, who charge the foreign Tamils with training and supplying weapons to the insurgents. And in the Southern Sudan, where a civil war raged, Sudanese President Omar Hassan al-Bashir accused international relief organizations of supplying the rebels with much-needed war materials (Reuters, July 23, 2000). International terrorist networks like al-Qaeda may supply arms and expertise to ethnic groups, such as the Chechens, so as to strengthen their ability and resolve to carry on a war against a central government. Yet it should be stressed that these are unusual cases; private international organizations have been supportive for the most part of a host country's development and therefore contribute in critical ways to many experiments with power sharing.

Yet as the experience in Zimbabwe, Côte d'Ivoire, and Northern Ireland shows, the third parties have seldom been able to sustain power-sharing institutions beyond the initiation period and the time of direct intervention. In the end the only reliable "guarantee" of stable strategic interactions among groups is the presence of legitimate and effective domestic governance. The task of building strong, responsive governments and effective civil societies is a long-lasting one, requiring considerable nurturing on the part of political and community leaders. Professionalism must be encouraged in the military and civil service, the media must be assisted, secondary schools and universities modernized, the rule of law extended, and the linkages between the formal and informal economies made more effective. The pace of development quickens when supportive interactions with foreign governments, international organizations, nongovernmental organizations, and other private transnational interests buttress these efforts (Prendergast and Plumb 2002), but local political actors play the critical roles in achieving these objectives.

Conclusion

In short, power sharing in ethnically divided societies emerging from conflict unites former opponents in an unsteady coalition of convenience. These arrangements often represent the most pragmatic of accommodations in order to initiate a transition from conflict; they are compromises to which all parties can agree. Particularly where the parties to the power-sharing arrangement have recently been involved in an intense conflict, such as a civil war, power sharing may emerge as a necessary compromise that reflects the military capabilities of the adversaries on the battlefield and the need to secure a quick commitment to a peace agreement. They can reassure weaker parties about their security and well-being following a civil war and reduce tensions in societies undergoing the transition from authoritarian rule to democracy. Such arrangements may prove mutually beneficial, enabling the major interests to build the trust necessary to sustain stable relations through an iterative bargaining process.

Yet inherent difficulties exist in the transition from short-term necessity to long-term democratic consolidation. The achievement of a self-enforcing, democratic equilibrium, one where "all the relevant political forces find it best to continue to submit their interests and values to the uncertain interplay of the institutions," involves a complicated shift from adversarial to coordinated and trusting behavior (Przeworski 1991, 26). Power sharing can make this shift to democracy more difficult. It may also make the consolidation of the peace more difficult. Power-sharing institutions tend to be short-lived. The usual inducements to cooperation may be weak in societies emerging from intense ethnic conflict. Ethnic elites will have had little opportunity to establish their own reputations or to verify the reputation of others for fulfilling commitments. Ethnic elites are likely to be skeptical about the continuation of the political "game" into the future and so less inclined to expect that fulfilling commitments now will be reciprocated by other elites in the future.

Where there are no democratic alternatives on the table, power sharing is indisputably preferable to continued conflict or authoritarianism. In rare circumstances the agreement on power sharing has become the basis for a transition to democracy, as in South Africa. In these circumstances, it may be judged to be a progressive compromise. More commonly, however, power sharing becomes a fixed institutional basis for future strategic interactions. In these circumstances, a durable peace typically proves beyond reach. The failure of power-sharing arrangements is not an inconsequential matter, for failure results in hostile political memories that can devastate intergroup relations for years to come. In worst cases, it may contribute to a relapse into a new round of civil war.

3

Power Dividing as an Alternative to Ethnic Power Sharing

Philip G. Roeder

In stable democracies institutional guarantees of minority rights against a predatory majority have tended to result in either power-sharing or power-dividing constitutions. The former is associated with continental European democracies such as the Netherlands and Austria; the latter, with the United States. Both were designed as alternatives to unalloyed majoritarianism and over the longer term have shown themselves to be stable institutional arrangements. Yet few of these "model" constitutions in stable democracies have had to cope with the problem of intense ethnic divisions that threaten the survival of the state itself. This poses the question that inspires the empirical investigation in this chapter: Which constitutional arrangement is more likely to lead to long-term stability when implemented in ethnically divided societies that have experienced or are likely to experience civil war? To answer this question, which involves predicting future consequences (always a risky enterprise), social science must look to the recent past. And so this chapter asks: Based on the empirical record so far, which type of constitutional arrangement has been more successful at deterring the escalation of normal ethnopolitical conflict into ethnonational crises that threaten the constitutional order with violence and breakdown?

The evidence indicates that divided-power arrangements are more likely to deter the escalation of ethnic conflict to ethnonational crises. This insti-

I owe thanks to many individuals—to Matt Baum, Neal Beck, Liz Gerber, and Simon Hug for their answers to an endless series of methodological questions, to Dan Lake and Chad Rector for their assistance in collecting data for this project, and to Gary Shiffman for patiently listening to more iterations of my theory than any human should be asked to bear. In addition, I heartily thank Val Bunce, Eben Friedman, Matt Hoddie, Simon Hug, Arend Lijphart, Stephanie McWhorter, Matt Murphy, Akos Rona-Tas, Don Rothchild, and Tim Sisk for careful reading, tough criticism, and constructive suggestions concerning earlier drafts of this manuscript.

tutional arrangement is associated with such early liberal philosophers as the Baron de Montesquieu and James Madison, but has been elaborated over two centuries in practice in various countries; for example, in the United States during its Progressive Era. As defined in Chapter 1, *power-dividing institutions* stress the importance of civil liberties that limit government, separation of powers that create multiple majorities, and checks and balances that limit each majority. Power-dividing institutions ensure the rights of ethnic and other groups through universalistic, individual liberties against governmental intrusion in private and associational lives; these are guaranteed to all citizens whether members of a majority or minority and to all types of groups whether ethnic or not. In this way civil liberties take many decisions, such as the preservation of different cultures and lifestyles, out of the hands of government and entrust these to civil society. Power-dividing institutions do not abandon majoritarianism in governmental decisionmaking—the fundamental principle of democracy that popular majorities should decide the course of government. Yet rather than empowering a single majority in a supreme organ such as the Westminster Parliament, power-dividing institutions empower multiple majorities, each construing the public interest somewhat differently, in separate, independent organs of government. Power-dividing institutions provide more credible commitments to the rights of all minorities—whether based on ethnicity or other identities—by balancing and checking a majority in one governmental organ against several majorities in other organs. In ethnically divided societies these institutions promote a more robust domestic arrangement by lowering the stakes of ethnic conflict within government and checking both predatory governmental leaders and predatory ethnopoliticians. The evidence in this chapter underscores that societies emerging from civil conflicts and new democracies in ethnically divided societies are not limited to a hard choice between so-called Westminster majoritarianism and power sharing. From the beginning of modern representative government and democracy, philosophers have prescribed and practitioners have implemented a third option—power-dividing or multiple-majorities institutional arrangements—and this has been more successful than power sharing at preserving the rights of minorities and deterring escalation of ethnopolitical conflict.

This chapter is divided in four parts. The first presents a theoretical explanation for the greater stability of power-dividing institutions in ethnically divided societies. It begins with a model of escalation of ethnopolitical conflicts. This model sets down an analytic foundation for assessing the impact of power-sharing and power-dividing institutions on the likelihood that normal ethnic conflict will escalate to threaten violence and the breakdown of the institutional order. The second part presents statistical tests of the alternative expectations of the power-sharing and power-dividing approaches against recent experience. As the other chapters in this volume note, there are few instances of successful power sharing after civil wars. Thus, in this chapter I expand the number of cases to include all independent countries in the last half of the twentieth century, whether they have experienced civil wars or not. The results support the claim that the power-dividing model of democracy creates a more robust deterrent to escalation than power sharing. In the third and fourth parts I discuss these results and draw out their implications for policy.

Controlling the Escalation of Ethnopolitical Conflict

The dependent variable in this chapter is escalation of ethnopolitical conflict into ethnonational crises. In this context *ethnonationalism* refers to claims and counterclaims concerning the right of an ethnic group to self-governance within a state of its own (Breuilly 1994, 1, 9).[1] Ethnonational claims belong to the category of constitutional claims—demands for some of the existing state's powers. Unlike other such claims, which may come from democratic reformers, civil libertarians, or corporatist groups, ethnonationalism is a claim that a specified people should be self-governing within a separate, territorially defined state—either as an autonomous entity within a larger state or as a sovereign state (Armstrong 1982, 4–11; Gellner 1983, 1; Haas 1986, 727–728).[2] Ethnonational *crises* challenge the existing distribution of decision rights between ethnic groups and the government of an existing state. The escalation of ethnopolitical conflict to ethnonational crises represents one of the most threatening domestic challenges to an existing state in that it ultimately involves questions about changes not only in the government or the regime but also in the boundaries of the state itself.

The principal independent variables in this chapter are political institutions. This chapter explores whether political institutions can lower the likelihood that ethnic conflicts will escalate to ethnonational crises. This discussion does not assume that any institutional design can long hold together different nations that have already resolved that they do not want to live together in a common-state (Roeder 1999). (The term *common-state*

1. Nationalism as a constitutional claim pressed by politicians against states differs from nationalism as a sentiment that binds individuals within a nation (Connor 1994; Haas 1986), a doctrine developed by intellectuals (Kedourie 1960), an ideology of state power that supports assertive policies, or an agenda of cultural renewal (Hutchinson 1987). By defining nationalism as a type of constitutional claim, I do not intend to deny the reality or importance of these other phenomena, only to assert that they constitute distinguishable variables.

2. There has been some dispute whether the term ethnonationalism should be reserved to claims for sovereignty (Kohn 1945, 18–20), but in practice it is difficult to distinguish these from claims for autonomy. Moreover, ethnopoliticians often vacillate between these two types of claims as though they represent differences of degree rather than differences in kind.

refers to a political jurisdiction that is common to all ethnic groups within a country. In contrast, jurisdictions such as autonomous homeland administrations are unique to only one or some of the ethnic groups.) Yet in instances where most of the population is ambivalent, undecided, agnostic, or indifferent on the secession issue or even supports the continued existence of the common-state, it is plausible that institutions might either deter or facilitate opportunism by politicians.

Ethnopolitical Bargaining

To begin thinking about the ways in which these institutional variables might affect the likelihood of ethnonational crises, we start with a simple model of bargaining between leaders of the government of the common-state and ethnopoliticians of a specific ethnic group—a bilateral relationship that I will call an *ethnopolitical dyad.* In normal politics each side in the ethnopolitical dyad conducts bargaining according to the constitutive rules of the state. These rules allocate decisionmaking rights among a national government, regional or local governments, specially empowered social groups, and individuals. These rules also provide procedures for resolving conflicts among these rights and for adjustments in this allocation.

Conflict is endemic in politics, including ethnic politics. The objective in seeking institutional stability is not to eliminate conflict, but to contain conflict within the constitutive rules and to avoid escalation that calls the allocation of decision rights into question. That is, the stability of any institutional arrangement, including post–civil war arrangements, depends on escalation control—preventing the escalation of claims and actions into crises that threaten to bring down the existing institutions or constitutive rules. The most important forms of escalation that may lead to such crises are escalation in either the stakes or the means of conflict (Smoke 1977, 14; Leatherman et al. 1999, 111–145). In ethnopolitical conflict, escalation in the *stakes* of conflict may begin with claims by the government of the common-state to decision rights previously granted members of ethnic groups or attempts by ethnic groups to exercise decisionmaking rights previously granted the government of the common-state. The stakes may escalate from conflicts over decisionmaking rights within a narrow realm of policy to conflicts over ever more decision rights in more realms and, finally, the right of the ethnic group to decision rights in all realms (sovereignty). So, for example, in the last years of the Soviet Union the conflict between the all-union government in Moscow and the governments of the Soviet union republics such as Armenia became more intense once the latter raised the stakes by broaching the issue of their possible secession and independence. The *means* of conflict escalate when either side initiates actions that increase the losses of the other side. In ethnopolitical conflict the means may escalate from verbal declarations to the mobilization of public boycotts of the other side or from peaceful to violent protests. So, for example, in the late Soviet Union the crisis between Moscow and its union republics grew more intense as one side or the other escalated the conflict from the so-called war of laws, in which each sought to nullify the acts of the other, to embargoes of exports to other regions, and finally to demonstrative acts of violence against the other side. Each level of escalation in stakes or means represents an increasingly intense crisis with rising likelihood of more extensive constitutional change (Kahn 1965).

Calculating common-state leaders and ethnopoliticians decide to escalate conflict in this bargaining relationship when they expect to gain from escalation. Alternatively, they are likely to be deterred from escalation when they believe that escalation will not pay. Deterrence is likely when (1) they do not expect the other side to concede even after escalation and/or (2) they expect that their gains will be less than the losses suffered as a result of the other side's retaliation.[3] Each side's expectations about the likelihood that the other side will concede and/or inflict retaliation depend on their own ability to inflict losses on the other side for failing to concede to their claims and on their own ability to retaliate against the other side's retaliation.

Taking one step back from these calculations of losses and gains from escalation, each side estimates the outcome of escalation by measuring the leverage each has to induce the other to act in desired ways. For ethnopoliticians this leverage over the government of the common-state is measured by their ability to back their ethnonational demands with action that is costly to the government leaders, such as delivering votes to the opposition, organizing protests and demonstrations, embargoing national taxes collected from ethnic-group members, initiating campaigns of terrorist violence, or conducting warfare. For government leaders this leverage is measured by their ability to take actions that are costly to the ethnopoliticians such as depriving ethnopoliticians of public venues for assembly and expression, withholding funds, removing ethnopoliticians from political office, or punishing, intimidating, and suppressing the ethnopolitician's supporters with physical coercion. Mutual deterrence and stability at any level of conflict and, thus, the limitation of ethnopolitical conflicts so that they do not become ethnonational crises, depend on the balance of leverage that each side has over the other.

This balance of leverage, in turn, depends to a significant extent on political institutions, such as power-sharing and power-dividing institutions. That is, the causal chain in this bargaining model (what makes one ethnopolitical dyad different from another) is quite simple: Political institutions affect

3. Whether the first condition is sufficient to deter depends on whether escalation is an inherently costly action.

the balance of leverage. This balance affects expectations about the outcome of escalation. These expectations in turn affect whether common-state leaders and ethnopoliticians choose to escalate the stakes and means of ethnopolitical conflict.

Power Sharing Creates Incentives to Escalate

The power-sharing approach to constitution making begins by identifying the chief troublemakers among ethnopolitical groups and empowering them with a piece of government—usually guaranteed positions within the government of the common-state and within the governments of autonomous regions (Lijphart 2002). Ironically, in the context of the bilateral bargaining relationship between common-state leaders and ethnopoliticians, the institutions of power sharing actually increase the likelihood of subsequent escalation to ethnonational crises. Power-sharing arrangements create incentives for ethnic leaders to escalate both the stakes and the means of conflict. Under power sharing ethnic leaders are more likely to make more extreme demands on behalf of their ethnic groups and to inflict (or threaten to inflict) greater losses on the leaders of the common-state. Simultaneously, these institutions create incentives for common-state leaders to preempt these demands and actions by attempting to centralize decision rights. Specifically, in ethnically divided societies power sharing has three closely related consequences that raise the ethnic stakes in domestic politics and increase the likelihood that either ethnopoliticians or common-state leaders will escalate conflict: (1) the ethnification of all policy disputes and elimination of crosscutting cleavages, (2) the institutionalization of a cross-group contagion of escalating demands, and (3) the concentration of institutional weapons in the hands of ethnopoliticians, providing them the means to back up their escalating demands.

First, under power-sharing institutions in ethnically divided societies politicians have greater incentive to make all issues ethnic issues, and so ethnicity is seldom irrelevant to any policy question that reaches the government. In power-sharing systems, empowered leaders are likely to resist framing policy issues in terms that divide the members of their respective ethnic groups and unite some of them with members of other ethnic groups. Empowered ethnic leaders look for divisive issues that reinforce the unity of their own ethnic groups and their own privileged positions within them. Politicians with other agendas such as labor rights or stimulation of industry must frame their claims as ethnic claims in order to gain access to the most important decisionmaking centers. This ethnification of issues, in turn, leads to the elimination of crosscutting cleavages; only policy divisions that are cumulative rather than crosscutting are likely to reach government. For example, in the final days of the Soviet Union policy disputes over both big issues such as the reform of the socialist economy and little issues such as the allocation of highway taxes were increasingly framed as issues of the sovereign prerogatives of the union republics and their distinct peoples (Roeder 1991).[4]

Second, power sharing increases the incentives to escalate demands and institutionalizes a contagion of escalation among ethnic leaders. That is, the leaders of ethnic groups who defect from the current allocation of decision rights can gain a greater share of the resources of the common-state and a greater share in subsequent common-state decisionmaking. This makes it tempting for all ethnopoliticians to defect from the agreement and demand greater rights. This also raises the probability that other ethnopoliticians who make no such demands will end up being suckers who receive a diminished share of common-state resources and decisionmaking and must contribute a larger share to the maintenance of the common-state government. Thus, any claim by one ethnic-group leader to additional rights must be matched by the leaders of other ethnic groups and preemptive constitutional claims become a dominant strategy for all ethnic groups as soon as they fear that others might defect. Power sharing may unravel through a domino effect of cascading defections. Each demand of an ethnic group for greater rights at the expense of the common-state government inspires others to make similar or greater demands because being left behind will leave them worse off. For example, in late 1991, as Russia's reformist leaders demanded a larger voice in the governing of the Soviet Union and actually began making decisions for the whole union unilaterally, leaders of other republics such as Belarus and Ukraine followed suit to demand an expanded voice and then decided to leave the union altogether. Similarly, in the former Yugoslavia, Serbia's attempt to expand its power within the federal government led Slovenia and Croatia to secede (Gagnon 1994/95). Once Slovenia and Croatia indicated they would pull out, Macedonia and Bosnia felt they could not remain behind as junior partners in a Yugoslavia soon to be thoroughly dominated by Serbia.

Third, the incentive for ethnopoliticians to escalate demands on the common-state government also increases under power sharing because they have the means to back up these demands by inflicting losses on the common-state leaders. Power sharing leads to the concentration of institutional weapons in the hands of ethnopoliticians, who can use them against the national government. Philip Selznick (1960, 2) notes that decision rights can be weapons "used by a power-seeking elite in a manner unrestrained by

4. This escalation of demands so as to extract more concessions from the central government is even prevalent in power-sharing regimes that are cited as the most stable. See, for example, Dale Fuchs, "Basque Parliament to Debate Independence Plan," *New York Times* (November 7, 2003), A10.

the constitutional order" and that these decision rights can be used to change that constitutional order. For example, a veto in decisions of the common-state gives ethnic leaders the power to paralyze the national decisionmaking process. These ethnic leaders can use this veto to threaten mutual disaster until the leaders of other ethnic groups in the common-state government give in. Control over critical revenue sources gives ethnopoliticians leading autonomous homelands the power to starve leaders of the common-state government into submission. Federalization of the armed forces expands the ability of ethnic homeland administrations to employ violence against the common-state government, secede, and bring down the state.[5]

Institutional Instability *or* Destructive Violence

Designers of power sharing attempt to check escalation through a delicate balance of leverage, but this seldom solves the problem of institutional instability and often makes instability more destructive. In seeking the perfect balance of leverage, the designers of power-sharing arrangements are caught between competing demands—making the power-sharing institutions more durable and avoiding violence. To avoid encroachments by common-state leaders and minorities on the rights of the others, the designers of power-sharing institutions typically try to balance the powers of ethnic groups against those of the common-state. To avoid a resumption of violence they try to make the security agencies of the common-state government preponderant. Yet, designers of power-sharing institutions cannot have it both ways: Having privileged a single zero-sum distribution of decision rights, avoiding the Scylla of recentralization raises the risk of the Charybdis of destructive conflict. That is, these designers confront a trade-off between (1) stabilizing institutions and (2) limiting escalation in the means of conflict.

First, finding an allocation of decision rights and institutional weapons that will be durable is difficult when power sharing privileges a single dimension of conflict. Typically, in a state not subject to power sharing the balance of leverage favors the common-state leaders. Yet in power sharing this simply makes ethnic rights particularly vulnerable to encroachment from central leaders—a common reason for the short life of many power-sharing arrangements. Without any means to resist, ethnic minorities must submit to their loss of decision rights. The designers of power-sharing arrangements attempt to make credible commitments to ethnic minorities that common-state leaders will not encroach by providing the minorities with some means to

5. For example, see Bebler's (1993) discussion of Yugoslav federalism. An instructive comparison is the opposite extreme in which ethnopoliticians have no institutionally based leverage over the national government; see, for example, Barany (1998).

defend themselves. Yet this leverage in the hands of ethnic minorities against the central government must not be so great that the ethnic minorities have the upper hand and are able to coerce the common-state government into handing over more and more powers. Thus, the designers of power-sharing institutions often attempt a delicate balancing act that will guard against the twin dangers of recentralization and disintegration. The designers of power-sharing institutions may carefully balance the powers of the common-state against the powers of the ethnic minorities and even create mutual hostage relationships (Walter 1999b). William W. Kaufmann (1956) provides the key enduring insight about stability in these bargaining situations that also applies to stability in power-sharing institutions. In these circumstances stability requires that at any level of escalation, if one side has the option of escalation, the other side must be able and willing to match this. Each side is deterred from escalation by knowledge that, even though "we" might escalate conflict, the other side can match this, and so our chances of gaining our objectives would not improve, but our costs would rise significantly. The search for a perfect balance of powers between national government and ethnic communities may lead to such a knife-edge equilibrium, but this is fragile and easily upset when the advantage shifts—even temporarily—to one side or the other.

Second, nearer the perfect balance of institutional weapons the danger of destructive escalation in means rises. In particular two risks increase: First, it is more likely that both sides will simultaneously calculate that by escalating conflict they will be able to induce the other side to concede (Wittman 2001).[6] (Of course, at most only one side can be right.) Second, the level of destruction and even violence that results when mutual deterrence breaks down is likely to be higher when both sides have extensive capabilities. A significant body of theory and evidence in international relations supports the contention that power parity increases the likelihood of violence while preponderance decreases this (Organski 1958; Bueno de Mesquita and Lalman 1992; Kugler and Lemke 1996). Michelle Benson and Jacek Kugler (1998) argue and provide evidence that this same relationship holds within polities as well—power parity between government and opposition is associated with higher levels of violence.

Because the simple bilateral balance in individual ethnopolitical dyads is so fragile, many in the policy community have borrowed a classic solution to rigidities in international balances of power—a "balancer" or third party that holds the balance. As Edward Vose Gulick (1967, 65) explains, "When one side threatens the security and survival of the other, the third party steps in on the side of the weaker and sees that a balance between independent

6. Consistent with this logic, Hartzell and Rothchild (1997, 153) find that *de*-escalation of conflicts—settlements of civil wars—is more likely when the balance of power is asymmetrical.

powers is restored." In the logic of ethnopolitical conflict balancers are likely to jump to the defense of ethnic groups should the central government's leaders become predatory but are unlikely to join predatory ethnic leaders who seek to renegotiate the terms of the constitution in ways that will bring down the state. In power-sharing arrangements at the end of a civil war this is likely to be the armed forces of a foreign power or multilateral coalition of foreign powers. Finding a domestic balancer is more difficult. In much of the literature on credible commitments the role of domestic balancer is assigned to independent courts, yet, as Lake and Rothchild underscore in Chapter 5, these are seldom adequate to the task in ethnically plural societies. Because the government of the common-state usually appoints judges, defines their jurisdiction, and prescribes their procedures, courts are unlikely to restrain the central government as it encroaches on the decision rights of ethnopoliticians (Bednar, Eskridge, and Ferejohn 2001).

Power-sharing arrangements have not had much success in ethnically divided societies. For example, Arend Lijphart (2002) lists sixteen consociational regimes in the twentieth century. Three of these cases (Suriname 1958–1973, Netherlands Antilles 1950–1985, and Northern Ireland 1999–1999) were not independent states, and four more (Austria 1945–1966, Netherlands 1917–1967, Luxembourg 1917–1967, and Colombia 1958–1974) were not ethnically divided societies.[7] This leaves us with a universe of nine consociational regimes in independent, ethnically divided societies. Six of these failed. Czechoslovakia's four-year experiment with power sharing (1989–1993) ended in partition of the country. Cyprus's (1960–1963) and Lebanon's (1945–1975) experiments ended in civil wars. Malaysia's (1955–1969) experiment with power sharing was particularly rocky: The Malaysia federation saw secession (or expulsion) of one ethnically distinct region (Singapore) and only strong-arm tactics prevented secession of the ethnically distinct Sabah state. Malaysia's consociational government ended in widespread ethnic violence. Fiji's one-year experiment (1999–2000) ended in a military coup. And South Africa's (1994–1996) ended in a peaceful slide into majoritarianism. The median age at death for these six failed experiments was a mere three and a half years. Only three consociational regimes in ethnically divided societies have reportedly survived—Switzerland (1943–), Belgium (1970–), and India (1947–). And, as I argue in this chapter, these cases have been successful to the extent they have

7. The most stable consociational arrangements have been instances in which there is no ethnic divide in society. In Austria and the Netherlands power sharing was an arrangement between political parties representing different ideologies. These two countries were two of the most homogeneous in the world—the dominant ethnic group constituted well over 90 percent of the population in each country at the time of consociationalism.

submerged any ethnic power-sharing arrangements within a larger array of power-dividing institutions.

Power Dividing Deters Escalation to Ethnonational Crises

The power-dividing or multiple-majorities strategy begins from the premise that a fundamental flaw in power sharing is its statist approach that privileges a specific configuration of majority and minorities in the design of the government. Instead, the divided-power strategy empowers individual citizens at the expense of the state, empowers multiple majorities within a common-state government to address diverse policy issues, and makes it more difficult for any one majority to take rights away from minorities by balancing the powers of one governmental organ (and its majority) against other organs (and their majorities) within a common-state. In the context of ethnically divided societies, the divided-power or multiple-majorities strategy takes seriously the constructivists' evidence that for individuals identities, including ethnic identities, tend to be multiple, situation-specific, and fluid over time (Nagel 1994; Waters 1990). Rather than privileging one configuration of majority and minorities through predetermined governmental formulas, the multiple-majorities strategy seeks to create conditions under which citizens can sort themselves into various, alternative configurations of majorities and minorities in civil society and in separate, independent governmental organs.

The power-dividing solution begins with extensive civil rights that empower all citizens and all groups equally, but leaves to civil society rather than the state the decision concerning which groups will form to contest politics at any moment. It divides decisionmaking rights between society and the government and constructs a high wall—in the United States it is the Bill of Rights enforceable in courts—to protect the decision rights that are set outside the reach of government such as decisions whether to support religion and which religions to support. In ethnically divided societies the power-dividing strategy creates only a common-state. It avoids assigning vetoes to identified ethnic minorities within the common-state or alienating some of the state's decisionmaking rights to separate ethnic homelands.

Power dividing permits the majority to rule through organs that make decisions for all ethnic groups. However, it institutionalizes a separation of powers among the governmental organs of the common-state so that no single majority is likely to make all decisions. For example, in the United States the majority that is represented in the election of the president differs from the majority that emerges in the legislative chamber elected from single-member districts apportioned by population and from the majority in the second legislative chamber elected with equal representation of each state regardless of population. Specific decisions such as setting interest rates, regulating aviation among regions, or regulating securities markets are made by bodies with still different configurations of majorities and minorities that represent the public interest. That is, for the sake of efficient decisionmaking the Congress and President have delegated decisions to such administrative agencies as the Board of Governors of the Federal Reserve System; nevertheless, simple majority rule in each agency does not produce domination by the same majority across agencies of the common-state. In decisions where efficiency should be sacrificed to representativeness, decisions of the common-state must win endorsement from multiple majorities, such as both chambers of Congress and the President.[8] To give greater permanence to the allocation of decision rights in the initial agreement and to make these commitments to minorities more credible, changes in the allocation principle require endorsement by these multiple majorities.

Simple borrowing of power-dividing institutions that result in multiple majorities in one country does not guarantee that they will produce multiple majorities in another. Power dividing is a strategy that seeks to avoid either privileging a single dimension along which majority and minorities are defined or replicating the same cleavage in different guises within all institutions. In ethnically divided countries, the logic of power dividing requires identifying alternative, crosscutting divisions in society that do not replicate the ethnic divide and will not be trumped by ethnic differences—such as religion or religiosity, rural versus urban residence, upstream versus downstream river-basin dwellers, producers oriented to foreign markets versus producers oriented to domestic markets, and so forth. In this sense, this strategy begins from the constructivist view that politicized ethnic identities are often endogenous to the political process (Brass 1991). It recognizes the resource mobilization school's insight that it is often the relative availability of resources for political action that determines which political identities—whether ethnic or not—get mobilized into political conflicts (McCarthy and Zald 1987; Leites and Wolf 1970). In ethnically divided societies, by dividing any ethnic majority among multiple crosscutting majorities and minorities, the power-dividing strategy seeks to foster through politics the development of dispersed rather than cumulative cleavages (compare Lipset 1981).

In the context of ethnopolitical bargaining, the combination of power divided among common-state governmental organs that empower multiple majorities and power divided between government and individuals that

8. This concept of *multiple majorities* across organs that make decisions for the country as a whole is different from that of *compound majorities* (as Daniel Elazar 1985 labels it) between central and regional states in a federal state. As an illustration of multiple majorities, see Faust's (1996) discussion of the special formula in the Federal Reserve that Congress used to represent shared and diverging interests concerning inflation; this constituted a different majority than that found in Congress.

empower civil society has four important consequences. First, it reduces the stakes in ethnopolitical bargaining in two ways that reduce the incentive to escalate ethnic demands on government. It takes many decisions out of the hands of government and trusts to civil society and private initiative to fulfill many of the aspirations of individuals for such things as religious expression. In addition, power dividing lowers the ethnic stakes on issues that do fall within the jurisdiction of the government by making it less likely that winners and losers will correlate with ethnicity and less likely that wins and losses across issues will be cumulative. A loss as a minority on one issue—such as the allocation of water in river basins—does not jeopardize one's gains as a member of a majority on other issues—such as interest rates. In short, as an analyst of political opportunity structures (Tarrow 1989) notes, political institutions constitute an important constraint on whether mobilizing ethnic groups is a prudent strategy for ambitious politicians. The divided-powers strategy limits the realms in which it is prudent to make and to escalate ethnic demands.

Second, by creating independent organs with specialized decision authority, power dividing balances efficient decisionmaking in specific areas against the dangers of tyranny by a single majority across issue areas. In addition to the main general-purpose decisionmaking bodies of the central government such as presidents and assemblies, power-dividing arrangements include independent special-purpose administrations with countrywide jurisdiction, such as the Federal Reserve Board. At the regional level, alongside independent multipurpose administrations such as state governments, power-dividing arrangements establish independent special-purpose administrations with crosscutting jurisdictions like the Tennessee Valley Authority. At the local level, city and county governments exist alongside independent administrations for school boards, water districts, and so forth. In power sharing, particularly where consensual decisionmaking places vetoes in the hands of ethnic leaders, deadlock represents a constant threat to the legitimacy and stability of these arrangements. Simple majoritarianism of the Westminster type permits efficient decisionmaking but may be perceived as threatening because it empowers a single majority across all issues. The power-dividing or multiple-majorities strategy achieves decisiveness on each issue but with representativeness across issues and without dominance of a single majority across issues. This further reduces the incentive to frame issues as ethnic demands and to escalate these, because on many issues ethnicity will not be the most effective appeal to win a vote.

Third, power dividing avoids the concentration of institutional weapons in the hands of ethnopoliticians or other politicians. Power dividing does create institutional weapons, but each weapon gives its holder only limited leverage over other common-state leaders. These weapons are less likely than in power-sharing arrangements to accumulate in the hands of ethnic groups and even less likely to accumulate in the hands of a single set of ethnic-group leaders. This also explains why federalism can be so destabilizing in ethnically divided societies. In these arrangements decision rights tend to accumulate in two foci—the central government and the ethnoregional governments. Not only does this tend to define all policy disputes as majority-center versus minority-periphery, but it tends to lead to the accumulation of the means to back up demands in the hands of the leaders of these two decisionmaking foci. Alternatively, by dispersing rather than concentrating institutional weapons among many national and regional majorities, the power-dividing strategy reduces the incentives to escalate stakes and means in ethnopolitical bargaining.

Fourth, power dividing creates conditions for greater stability in the constitutional arrangement itself. Power dividing requires that changes in the regime structure be supported simultaneously by multiple majorities. The simple and obvious institutional obstacle to majority encroachment on minority rights in power dividing is the requirement that any change in the allocation of decision rights must be ratified by the different majorities in separate governmental organs. Power dividing provides credible commitments to minorities that the majority is unlikely to rewrite this guarantee in the future. Yet this may not be enough.

More important, power dividing creates conditions in which many members of the ethnic majority and minorities are likely to recognize shared interests in defending the institutional order. Attempts by an organ of government to infringe on the rights of ethnic minorities are likely to bring defensive alliances with elements within the ethnic majority itself. The liberal regime grants the same civil rights of association and expression to all groups—not just ethnic or cultural groups, but industrial, commercial, labor, and public service groups as well. Many of these groups share an interest with ethnic minorities in preserving these civil rights. However, they do not share an interest in granting ethnic groups the type of rights that would threaten the survival of the state. These other groups are likely to join ethnic groups in defense of their rights, but they are likely to defend the common-state government against any challenges that could undo the basic agreement. For example, in the United States when some members of the ethnic majority have attacked the religious rights of ethnic minorities, such as the right of Native Americans to use peyote in religious rituals, other members of the ethnic majority, such as members of mainstream Protestant denominations that share civil liberties with the ethnic minority, have been among the minority's strongest allies (Pevar 1983).

In stark contrast, the special status granted ethnic groups in power sharing often isolates ethnic elites from other elites and makes their rights more vulnerable to the majority. The allocation of decisionmaking powers in power sharing privileges ethnic elites over other elites and some ethnic elites over others; as a consequence, the empowered elites become isolated from these "disfranchised" elites and their memberships. Both "non-ethnic" elites, such as labor and business leaders, and ethnic elites excluded from the power-sharing arrangement have no interest in defending the rules of a game that discriminate against them and, in fact, have an active interest in changing those rules that privilege ethnic leaders at their expense. If the central government seeks to undo the basic agreement and begins to prey on the special rights of ethnic groups, these other elites are unlikely to jump to the defense of the privileged ethnic groups and may even press the national government to encroach on these privileges. For example, in the Russian Federation leaders of the Russian provinces (oblasts) have been among the strongest defenders of Moscow's attempts to encroach on the prerogatives of the non-Russian republics.

Power Dividing Explains Power Sharing Success

Ironically, evidence for the importance of power dividing as a deterrent to ethnonational challenges in ethnically plural societies is found in the three cases that are often cited as successful ethnic power-sharing systems. In Switzerland, Belgium, and India ethnicity has been only one of several empowered dimensions of conflict and cohesion in society. These polities did not privilege ethnicity, but embedded the rights of ethnic groups within a larger scheme of rights that also empowered groups that cut across any ethnic majority and minorities. In short, power sharing has worked best when it has been a smaller part of a larger multiple-majorities institutional arrangement.

Switzerland. In Switzerland ethnolinguistic identity has been only a latent basis for political action and seldom has represented an important political divide (Bogdanor 1988, 73; Steiner 1969, 296). In part the low salience of ethnicity is attributable to the good fortune of demographic patterns because differences in language, religion, and urban-rural residence cut across one another (Steiner 1974, 255; Switzerland 1993, tables 2.002–2.004). Even so, good power-dividing institutions are an equally important factor. The low salience of ethnicity owes much to the fact that Switzerland embeds the rights of ethnic groups in a set of rights shared by many other, often more salient, groups. Today linguistic groups share similar rights with religious and class groups. All of these groups must express many of their claims through a common set of cantonal decision rights that divide and sometimes trump all three types of social cleavage. Moreover, for the development of individual cultural communities, the Swiss rely heavily on civil society and private action. Indeed, Switzerland, like the United States, comes closer to the ideal of limited government than most established democracies. (For example, government spending, as a share of gross domestic product [GDP], is 47 percent higher in Switzerland's four neighbors than in Switzerland [United Nations 2001a].) The Swiss government is about a third smaller than its neighbors (even after taking into account the different size of the countries) and leaves many more decisions to the private sector or civil society.

In governmental decisionmaking processes no one configuration of interests is privileged (Schoch 2000, iv). Switzerland's bicameral legislature represents the Swiss people by two different formulas—neither of which privileges ethnicity. The collective presidency balances ideological (left-right), cantonal, religious, and ethnolinguistic representation. Decisions may be made by direct democracy in referenda and initiatives, by consensus in the federal institutions, or in cantonal or communal institutions. At every level of government many decisions are made by agencies of self-administration (*Milizverwaltung*), such as the water-supply system in the high valleys of Valais (Linder 1994, 52–54). As Jürg Steiner and Robert H. Dorff (1985, 53) conclude, "it becomes less clear as to how much Swiss decision processes are federal or unitary. . . . The main impression is the great amount of variation from one decision process to another" (also see Steiner 1987). In sum, the Swiss have not created a simple ethnic power-sharing constitutional order; they have empowered civil society and multiple majorities in government, so that winners and losers do not accumulate along ethnolinguistic lines (compare Steiner 1998, 19).

Belgium. Belgian power sharing was most stable as long as ethnicity was not elevated above other group rights and institutional weapons did not concentrate in ethnic foci. It is also, however, an example of the dangers that can result once ethnic power sharing becomes privileged. The original Belgian power-sharing agreement addressed a confessional (religiosity) conflict. It was then expanded to include class differences. Only later were the rights of linguistic groups embedded within this complex, inclusive system of group rights (Lorwin 1966). After World War II government coalitions simultaneously balanced linguistic, confessional, and ideological (left-right) differences (McRae 1986, 186), without privileging one or the other. In the initial response to pressure for greater recognition of Flemish, Walloon, and German communities, complex institutions that divided the linguistic communities among multiple councils led to what one political scientist characterized as a "curiously Byzantine" compromise and another characterized as "an exotic hybrid" between a federal and unitary state (McRae 1986, 168). The multiple majorities maintained stability. Conversely, instability and threats to Belgium's unity have grown as the rights of ethnic groups have come to trump the rights of other groups and, particularly since the adoption of the 1994 Constitution, as the Regional Councils have come to concentrate more institutional weapons in their hands.

The transformation of Belgium's multiple-majority democracy of the 1970s into an ethnic power-sharing arrangement has made Belgium less stable. By the late 1990s Belgians increasingly talked of a "crisis" in Belgian politics, in which politicians seek "to liberate the Belgian polity from its rigidity, caused by its pillarized character and by the colonization of the state by corporate institutions" (van den Bossche 2004, 66). Flemish nationalists demand further consolidation of their separate nation and statehood. Democrats who lament the limited role of the public in the current system have forwarded a myriad of proposals that would make the government more efficient and less political, change the electoral system, and introduce such majoritarian practices as direct election of the prime minister and referenda.

India. In this light, India's ethnolinguistic power-sharing arrangement has remained stable because it is embedded in a more complex set of cleavages and because it concentrates few institutional weapons in the hands of the ethnolinguistic states. India has avoided creating power sharing for what has been its most explosive cultural divide—that between Hindus and Muslims. Indeed, in creating linguistic states in the 1950s the Indian government created a counterweight to what had been the two types of identities that posed the greatest threat of secession from India—Islam and the princely states governed by traditional rulers. Jawaharlal Nehru rejected religion as the basis for new states and blocked plans for a Sikh state based on religion precisely because he feared this would lead to "Pakistan-style" fragmentation (Roy 1962, 188–206; Sharma 1969, 40–48). Division of the princely states such as Junagadh and Hyderabad put an end to jurisdictions that posed an immediate threat of secession after independence. In short, power sharing based on linguistic difference worked in part due to the good fortune that it was not the most important divide in Indian politics and, in fact, worked at cross-purposes to these other divides. Moreover, the autonomy of linguistic states and the institutional weapons in the hands of their leaders have been limited by the ability of India's parliament to dissolve (and create) states by simple legislative act, the national emergency powers that enable the central government to suspend state constitutions and governments, and centrally appointed governors that give the central prime minister the power to dismiss chief ministers and cabinets in states controlled by opposition parties (Santhanam 1960, 7, 10–11; "India: A Country Study" in U.S. Library of Congress). In routine politics, centralization of policymaking results from economic planning, the fiscal dependence of state governments on budgetary grants from the center, and the supremacy of parliamentary legislation except in a few areas reserved to the states. In short, India's ethnic stability also appears to be a result of avoiding the concentration of institutional weapons in the hands of ethnic leaders.

A Statistical Test

To test the claims about the impact of institutions on ethnopolitical conflict, I turn to statistical evidence about the world's major independent states and ethnic groups. As a "first cut" these tests focus on major institutions for which data are readily available for all states and ethnic groups. An advantage to this approach is that this permits a test that gives us some assurance of the generalizability of these findings. A disadvantage is that this does not permit closer examination of less common institutional variations. The statistical tests use logit analysis to estimate the probability of escalation in ethnopolitical conflicts under alternative institutional arrangements. This section is somewhat technical; the discussion of these results in the third section of this paper is more humane.

Cases—Ethnopolitical Dyads

The evidence consists of time-series–cross-section observations on ethnopolitical dyads over time. The time-series unit of analysis consists of nine successive five-year periods beginning with January 1, 1955, and ending with December 31, 1999. The cross-section unit of analysis is an ethnopolitical dyad that pairs leaders of the government of the common-state with ethnopoliticians from an ethnic group within that state—such as Spain's leaders and its Basque ethnopoliticians. This corresponds to the bargaining relationship described in the theoretical discussion.

The observations include all countries with a population that topped (or, in the case of failed states like the Soviet Union, would have topped) one million by December 31, 1999 (United States 2001). The data set omits observations for individual time-periods when at the beginning of the five-year period (1) the state was not independent or (2) the ethnic group either did not constitute at least 1 percent of the country's total population or did not comprise at least two hundred thousand members. The total number of observations is 8,074 dyad-quinquennia—such as Spain-Basques in 1960–1964—that include 153 different states and 658 different ethnic groups.[9]

This data set comprises a different population of cases than is frequently analyzed in large-*n* projects on ethnic conflict—most notably, Ted Robert Gurr's (1999) seminal work. The groups in the data set used here do not include all *minorities* at risk; excluded are non-ethnic regional groupings such

9. If the 8 rump successor states (e.g., the Russian Federation) and newly unified states (e.g., Yemen) are counted as distinct from the states they replaced, then the total number of states is 161. The number of ethnic groups includes 632 individual groups and 26 combined groups such as the Pygmies of Congo (Brazzaville) or the indigenous peoples of the United States. In addition there are 21 external amalgamated groups, such as East Indians living in the United Kingdom.

as the inhabitants of Cabinda or religious subgroups within ethnic groups such as Shiite Iraqis.[10] Moreover, not all the groups in this data set are *at risk*; the list is close to a complete listing of ethnic groups that cross the size threshold—whether they were at risk or not. Where available I use census data to construct the list and populations of ethnic groups; where census data are unavailable I rely on anthropologists' estimates of ethnic groups and their populations. The list of ethnic groups, their populations, and their cultural characteristics were derived from eight sources: Bromlei (1988), Bruk (1986), Bruk and Apenchenko (1964), Levinson (1991), Minority Rights Group (1997), Moseley and Asher (1994), United Nations (1980, 1985, 1986, 1990, 1995), and individual country studies in the area handbook series commissioned by the Library of Congress' Federal Research Division (U.S. Library of Congress).

Dependent Variables—Escalation to Ethnonational Crises

The dependent variables indicate escalation in ethnopolitical conflict to more intense ethnonational crises. In this context, a *crisis* is a public dispute that raises the issue of the ethnic group's right to self-governance and that engages both ethnopoliticians and common-state leaders. A challenge that either side can ignore is not counted as a crisis; a challenge must bring a formal, public response—often a verbal denunciation, sometimes a concession, and other times collective protest or violence. The issues on the bargaining table may include autonomy, unification with a neighboring state, or independence, but all involve the right of the ethnic group to self-governance and attempts to expand or reduce this. The coding makes no assumption that one side or the other initiated a crisis; for example, ethnopoliticians' claims are often reactions to predatory policies of governmental leaders. The data are compiled from *Facts on File* (1955–1999), Gurr (1999), *Keesing's Record of World Events* (1955–1999), Minahan (1996), SIPRI (1987–1998), and Wallensteen and Sollenberg (1998).

The dependent variables indicate escalation of ethnopolitical conflicts along the dimensions discussed previously. Escalation of *stakes* in ethnopolitical conflict to the level of an ethnonational crisis means that constitutional issues concerning the distribution of decision rights are on the bargaining table in that ethnopolitical dyad during the five-year period. Escalation of *means* within ethnonational crises means that at least one side has gone beyond harsh words and begun to engage in collective protest or violence to back its claims. Specifically, the statistical tests employ four different indicators of escalating ethnopolitical conflict.

10. When members of regional coalitions make nationalist demands on behalf of their constituent ethnic groups, these claims are coded separately for each ethnic group.

1. *Ethnonationalist crisis* indicates a dyad-quinquennium in which there was an ethnonational crisis. This includes any public conflict, including declaratory or symbolic acts, protests, demonstrations, and armed conflict, in which the rights of the ethnic group to self-governance are at issue.
2. *Armed conflict* indicates a dyad-quinquennium in which one of these ethnonational crises involved armed conflict between the members of the ethnic group and government. This includes localized contests of violence such as insurgency and counterinsurgency, sporadic acts of violence such as terrorism and counterterrorism, as well as sustained, widespread conflicts involving collective violence such as civil wars.
3. *Intensity of armed conflict* is a three-level (zero to two) index of the intensity of this armed conflict in a dyad-quinquennium. This distinguishes civil war (level = 2) from more sporadic or localized forms of conflict (level = 1) and from no violence (level = 0).[11]
4. *Increase in intensity of armed conflict* is a dichotomous indicator of an increase in the level of the three-step index of armed conflict since the previous five-year period.

Independent Variables

As defined in Chapter 1, power-sharing strategies most commonly prescribe institutional arrangements that provide for both inclusive decisionmaking within the government of the common-state and partitioned decisionmaking among governments of segment-states. A number of countries have developed unique institutional designs for the government of the common-state, such as Lebanon's elaborate parceling of posts in the common-state. The most common institutional arrangements for inclusive decisionmaking, however, are (1) parliamentary government that permits coalition governments rather than winner-take-all within the executive and (2) allocation of seats in the legislature on the basis of group affiliation or nonmajoritarian (nonplurality) voting. Although some unique experiments with nonterritorial ethnocorporatism have been undertaken in countries such as interwar Estonia, the most common institutional arrangement for partitioning decisionmaking is territorial autonomy. These territorial arrangements include what are called "hard guarantees" of autonomy in Chapter 2, such as special autonomous regions that give the homeland administrations of ethnic minorities special rights beyond those enjoyed by

11. In initial statistical tests using ordered logit this was a four-step variable that distinguished civil war (level = 3) from conflicts among small or localized units such as a local (counter-)insurgency or (counter-)guerrilla conflict (level = 2), and from sporadic acts of violence such as sporadic terrorist attacks (level = 1). In ordered logit analysis the second (level = 1) and third (level = 2) steps were not significantly different from one another.

the first-order subdivisions or ethnofederalism that makes homeland administrations the first-order subdivisions of the state. These territorial arrangements also include "soft guarantees" such as federalism that is not strictly based on homelands but creates opportunities for ethnic capture.

Alternatively, power-dividing strategies reject parliamentarism as tending toward the unity of legislative and executive branches and reject the strategy of privileging the ethnic division within the common-state or in autonomous segment-states. Power-dividing strategies advocate separation of powers or branches within the government of the common-state and creation of local governments that divide the homelands of major ethnic groups (compare Hale 2004). Thus, in this view presidentialism with a nationally elected president and locally elected representatives to the legislature is preferable because these multiple avenues of representation create opportunities for alternative majorities to emerge in the legislative and executive branches of the common-state. Similarly, a bicameral legislature that apportions each chamber differently but apportions neither on the basis of minority representation, in effect, empowers alternative majorities within the legislative branch. The power-dividing strategy also counsels against the ethnofederal arrangements that empower ethnic groups within autonomous administrations and the federal arrangements that create opportunities for ethnic capture.

The four different equations for escalation of ethnopolitical conflicts to more intense ethnonational crises use seven independent variables that indicate the presence of either power-dividing or power-sharing institutions. All measure the relationship between the ethnic group and the government of the common-state at the beginning of the quinquennium. Some are specific to the relationship between the ethnic group and the government; others are common to all ethnopolitical dyads in that state. The first three variables describe common-state institutions; the last four describe territorial-autonomy arrangements.

1. *Separation of powers* indicates a presidential or semi-presidential regime in which the populace elected the chief executive of the common-state, such as the American or French president, who exercised more than ceremonial powers (source: *Statesman's Yearbook* 1955–1999; *Europa World Yearbook* 1987–1998).
2. *Bicameral legislature* indicates that the populace elected representatives to two chambers of the legislature of the common-state, such as the House of Representatives and Senate of the U.S. Congress, neither of which allocated seats according to an ethnic power-sharing scheme (source: *Statesman's Yearbook* 1955–1999; *Europa World Yearbook* 1987–1998).
3. *Parliamentarism* indicates that the legislative branch elected the chief executive, such as the prime minister, and that any popularly elected president,

such as the Irish president, exercised largely ceremonial powers (source: *Statesman's Yearbook* 1955–1999; *Europa World Yearbook* 1987–1998).

4. *Territorial autonomy* indicates that the homeland of the ethnic group enjoyed autonomy either in the form of a special autonomous region that placed it above other first-order administrations, such as the autonomous regions of Italy, or in the form of a first-order administration, such as the union republics of the Soviet Union. (Most of these also had power-sharing cooptation of ethnic groups into the legislature by allocating upper chamber seats according to ethnic group or ethnic homeland.) (Source: *Statesman's Yearbook* 1955–1999; *Europa World Yearbook* 1987–1998.)
5. *Second-order autonomy* indicates that the homeland of the ethnic group, such as the national *okrugs* in the Soviet Union or the Indian reservations in the United States, enjoyed autonomy but was subordinate to the authority of first-order autonomies such as the Soviet *krais* or U.S. states.
6. *Disfranchised ethnic group* indicates that within a state that granted some homelands autonomy, the ethnic group in this dyad did not enjoy autonomy.
7. *Non-ethnic federalism* indicates a federal system in which first-order jurisdictions are not based on ethnic homelands, but provide the opportunity for ethnic capture. This includes only those federal systems in which there is significant decentralization of decision rights. (Source: Jaggers and Gurr 1996; Lemco 1991.)

In addition to these institutional variables, the equations include nine other variables to control for constraints other than power-sharing and power-dividing institutions. Each measures some dimension of the context within which the members of each dyad acted.

8. *Duration of democracy* measures the number of years that a democratic regime has been in power. This is derived from the Polity IV data set (Marshall and Jaggers 2000) by multiplying a dichotomous indicator of democracy on the eve of the quinquennium (a composite polity index of 6 or higher) by the duration of the regime (the number of years since a major change in regime-type).
9. *Duration of autocracy* measures the number of years that an authoritarian regime has been in power. This is derived form the Polity IV dataset (Marshall and Jaggers 2000) by multiplying a dichotomous indicator of autocracy on the eve of the quinquennium (a composite polity index of –6 or lower) by the duration of the regime (the number of years since a major change in regime).
10. *Regime in turmoil* indicates that at the beginning of the quinquennium the regime was undergoing significant change due to a constitutional crisis or transition between regime-types. This indicates any state undergoing what

the Polity IV data set describes as an interregnum or a transition (Marshall and Jaggers 2000).

11. *Governor general* indicates states in which the British Crown appointed the Chief of State (governor general) (source: *Statesman's Yearbook* 1955–1999).
12. *Proportion of population* measures the ethnic group's proportion of the country's total population. This is multiplied by 1 if the ethnic group is not the largest in the country and by 0 if it is the largest.
13. *Cultural difference* indicates a major cultural difference within a dyad: The ethnic group either speaks a language that belongs to a different linguistic phylum and group than that spoken by the majority of the country or the ethnic group belongs to a different religion (either civilizational or sectarian differences) than the majority of the country. Consistent with my findings elsewhere (Roeder 2003), early runs show that separate variables for linguistic, civilizational, and sectarian difference do not yield coefficient estimates that are significantly different from one another, so for the sake of parsimony in control variables these are combined in a single dichotomous variable that indicates the presence of any one of these cultural divides within a dyad.
14. *Immigrant minority* indicates an ethnic group that had a nation-state—either an independent state or an autonomous state within a state—that is not adjacent to the country in question.
15. *Gross domestic product per capita* is the natural logarithm of per capita GDP in the year prior to the five-year period. This is denominated in constant 1993 dollars. (Source: World Bank 1999b.)
16. *Relative urbanization* measures the extent to which social mobilization exceeds economic development (Huntington 1968, 53–55). This is the extent to which urbanization exceeded (or fell short of) levels predicted for a country with its per capita GDP in that quinquennium. Specifically, relative urbanization is the standardized residual from a regression of urbanization on the per capita GDP; these are derived from separate cross-national equations for each quinquennium. (Sources: World Bank 1999b; United Nations 2001b.)

Specification of Equations

Estimation of these equations presents two potential specification problems. First, binary time-series-cross-section observations can violate the independence assumption in the ordinary logit statistical models. To test for the robustness of the coefficient estimates, I use the diagnostic for the temporal dependence of the observations recommended by Beck, Katz, and Tucker (1998)—a series of dichotomous independent variables for each of the time periods. None of the signs of coefficients for the institutional variables changed, nor did the statistical significance of any fall below .05 in this diagnostic procedure.

Second, an estimate of the effect of institutions on subsequent conflict must control for the possible endogeneity of those institutions. In particular, a defender of either power-sharing or power-dividing strategies might object that a finding of a positive statistical relationship between their preferred arrangement and subsequent conflict results because constitutional designers are more likely to employ that particular arrangement in instances more likely to experience subsequent escalation—in hope of preventing it. Yet, this is equally true of power-dividing and power-sharing arrangements and since the tests below concern differences between these two strategies, the endogeneity problem should not affect this comparison.

Nevertheless, there are three elements of the specification of the statistical models that address these endogeneity concerns. First, the tests use alternative specifications of the dependent variable. The first two dependent variables measure incidence of conflict that crosses a particular threshold of intensity; the third variable measures the intensity of conflict; and the fourth variable indicates increases in this intensity. In the fourth equation the increase in the level of conflict unambiguously follows the introduction of specific institutions; it does not reflect a continuously high intensity of conflict that began prior to the introduction of institutions. Second, in order to control for the endogeneity of territorial autonomy, all equations include a variable for ethnic groups within a power-sharing arrangement that are not enfranchised by the arrangement. If designers empower groups that are more likely to find themselves in conflict with the government, then power sharing should not be associated with increased conflict for the disfranchised. Alternatively, the power-dividing argument contends that the heightened stakes and contagion effects associated with power sharing should lead even ethnopoliticians from the disfranchised groups to escalate their conflicts. Third, the equations "control for" the most important objective factors, such as cultural difference, that lead to expectations of future conflict and might lead constitutional designers to single out groups for special treatment.

Estimation Results

The results are consistent with the expectations of the power-dividing approach. Examining the first seven variables in Tables 3.1 and 3.2, the signs of 23 of 28 coefficient estimates are as expected by the power-dividing approach—separation of powers between branches (negative), separation of powers in a bicameral legislature (negative), parliamentarism (positive), territorial autonomy (positive), disfranchisement (positive), and non-ethnic federalism (positive). Of these coefficients 20 are statistically significant at the .05 level or better. Only 5 of the 28 coefficient estimates are consistent

Table 3.1. Escalation of conflict to ethnonational crises, 1955–1999, logit estimates

	Ethnonational crisis		Armed conflict	
Variable	Coefficient	(*z*)	Coefficient	(*z*)
Separation of powers	–0.123	(–1.26)	–0.186	(–1.54)
Bicameral legislature	–0.382**	(–2.69)	–0.677***	(–3.27)
Parliamentarism	0.329**	(2.84)	0.523***	(3.89)
Territorial autonomy	1.901***	(17.61)	1.401***	(10.96)
Second-order autonomy	–0.137	(–0.74)	–0.649*	(–2.43)
Disfranchised	0.767***	(5.83)	0.724***	(4.45)
Non-ethnic federalism	0.924***	(7.56)	0.705***	(4.40)
Duration of democracy	–0.006*	(–2.49)	0.001	(0.44)
Duration of autocracy	–0.134***	(–4.21)	–0.017***	(–4.17)
Regime in turmoil	0.454**	(2.85)	0.604***	(3.43)
Governor general	–0.946***	(–4.07)	–2.891***	(–5.51)
Proportion of population	4.539***	(9.05)	3.460***	(5.70)
Cultural difference	1.229***	(14.33)	1.294***	(11.96)
Immigrant minority	–3.255***	(–10.68)	–2.783***	(–7.06)
GDP per capita (logarithm)	1.981***	(6.25)	–0.274	(–0.68)
Relative urbanization	0.008*	(2.46)	–0.009*	(–2.18)
Constant	–4.364***	(–19.25)	–3.414***	(–12.28)
	$n = 8{,}074$		$n = 8{,}074$	
	$\chi^2 = 1{,}072.92$		$\chi^2 = 719.45$	

Significance: *** at .001 level; ** at .01 level; * at .05 level.

Table 3.2. Escalation of intensity of armed ethnic conflict, 1955–1999, logit estimates

	Intensity of armed conflict (ordered logit)		Increase in intensity of armed conflict (logit)	
Variable	Coefficient	(*z*)/{sd}	Coefficient	(*z*)
Separation of powers	–0.182	(–1.52)	0.172	(0.87)
Bicameral legislature	–0.657***	(–3.19)	–0.233	(–0.74)
Parliamentarism	0.481***	(3.58)	0.667**	(2.85)
Territorial autonomy	1.416***	(11.12)	1.229***	(5.68)
Second-order autonomy	–0.643*	(2.42)	–0.389	(–0.84)
Disfranchised	0.715***	(4.37)	0.425	(1.43)
Non-ethnic federalism	0.635***	(3.98)	0.571*	(2.08)
Duration of democracy	0.000	(0.13)	–0.016*	(–2.51)
Duration of autocracy	–0.018***	(–4.31)	–0.003	(–0.48)
Regime in turmoil	0.661***	(3.78)	0.973***	(3.57)
Governor general	–2.826***	(–5.39)	–1.708*	(–2.28)
Proportion of population	3.520***	(5.93)	3.254***	(3.31)
Cultural difference	1.273***	(11.84)	0.911***	(5.13)
Immigrant minority	–2.737***	(–6.96)	–2.055***	(–3.43)
GDP per capita (logarithm)	–0.211	(–0.53)	0.039	(0.06)
Relative urbanization	–0.010*	(–2.47)	–0.013	(–1.79)
Constant/ Cut 1	3.427	{0.276}	–4.762***	(–10.07)
Cut 2	5.318	{0.290}		
	$n = 8{,}074$		$n = 7{,}966$[a]	
	$\chi^2 = 708.84$		$\chi^2 = 145.92$	

[a] Cases dropped if dependent variable was at maximum value in previous time period.
Significance: *** at .001 level; ** at .01 level; * at .05 level.

with expectations of the power-sharing approach. Second-order autonomy is the only one that consistently yields coefficients in line with the power-sharing predictions; however, only two of these coefficients are statistically significant at the .05 level.

The control variables confirm that these institutional arrangements operate under demographic, cultural, and developmental constraints that are very powerful. First, the probability of escalation in ethnopolitical conflict rises as the ratio between the population of the ethnic minority and the rest of the country approaches parity. Second, where ethnic groups are separated by deep cultural divides, such as linguistic, civilizational, and sectarian differences, the likelihood of escalation is significantly higher. Third, dyads involving immigrant minorities show significantly lower probability of escalation. Fourth, protests and demonstrations are phenomena of more developed, urbanized societies, but violence is a disease of less developed, rural societies. Fifth, stable regimes, particularly mature autocracies, are less likely to experience escalation of ethnopolitical conflict.

Discussion of Results

The statistical results are consistent with the claims of the power-dividing approach that recommends separation of powers in the political institutions of the common-state and rejects partitioning of the decisionmaking powers of the state among autonomous ethnic homelands. Power dividing is less likely than power sharing to see the stakes in normal ethnopolitical conflict escalate to ethnonational crises, and it is less likely to see escalation to more extreme means. We can begin estimating how much more instability results from power-sharing institutions by examining the equations shown in Table 3.1 and estimating the probabilities of conflict shown in Table 3.3. I have

Table 3.3. Probability of ethnonationalist conflict in stable democracies under alternative institutional constraints (per quinquennium)

	Ethnonational crisis (%)	Armed conflict (%)
Power-dividing	8.4	3.6
Power-sharing (hard guarantee of autonomy)	58.4	37.0
Power-sharing (soft guarantee of autonomy)	34.7	22.7
Presidential	11.8	6.7
Parliamentary	17.4	12.7
No autonomy	13.4	8.2
Ethnic group with autonomous homeland	50.7	26.6
Disfranchised ethnic group	25.1	15.8
Non-ethnic federalism	28.0	15.3

Note: Calculated from equations in Table 3.1 for an "otherwise average" dyad in which an indigenous ethnic group constitutes 10 percent of the country's population.

selected as the point of comparison otherwise average ethnopolitical dyads that involve indigenous ethnic groups that constitute 10 percent of the countries' population in democracies of average age (10.1 years). In such dyads power sharing with hard guarantees of autonomy was almost six times as likely to see ethnopolitical conflict become an ethnonational crisis and ten times as likely to see this crisis end in armed struggle over the issue of self-determination.[12]

Figure 3.1 plots the rising likelihood of ethnonational crises and of crises in which at least one side resorts to violence as the minority's proportion of the population rises. (These functions are based on the equations shown in Table 3.1. Again the calculations of probabilities are based on an otherwise average indigenous ethnic group in a stable democracy of average age.) Under power sharing with hard guarantees of autonomy the probability of an ethnonational crisis within a dyad starts at less than even odds for the smallest ethnic groups and rises to nearly 90 percent for the largest ethnic minorities. The likelihood of armed conflict in these crises increases more than twofold from 30 percent to 70 percent. Alternatively, under power dividing, the likelihood for each level of violence is lower. Indeed, even dyads involving the largest minorities under power dividing are less likely to see either an ethnonational crisis or a crisis with a resort to violence than dyads involving the smallest minorities under power sharing.

A closer look at the specific institutions associated with each strategy sheds further light on their individual contributions to stability. First, the results show that parliamentary government is consistently associated with higher likelihood of escalation than is separation of powers (presidentialism or semi-presidentialism). In all four equations in Tables 3.1 and 3.2 the coefficient estimate for parliamentarism is positive and statistically significant at the .01 level or better. Consider again the case of the stable democracy of average age and the dyad in which an indigenous ethnic group constitutes a tenth of the country's population: The probability that a dyad would see ethnopolitical conflict escalate to armed conflict was almost twice as high in parliamentary regimes as in regimes with separation of powers between

12. In each function in Table 3.3 all variables are set at their respective means except that Proportion of population = 0.1, Duration of democracy = 10.1; Duration of autocracy = 0; Regime in turmoil = 0; and Immigrant minority = 0. For the power-dividing function Separation of powers = 1 and Bicameral legislature = 1, while Parliamentarism, Territorial autonomy, Second-order autonomy, Non-ethnic federalism, and Disfranchised are set to zero. For the power-sharing (hard guarantees) function Parliamentarism = 1 and Territorial autonomy = 1, while Separation of powers, Bicameral legislature, Second-order autonomy, Disfranchised, and Non-ethnic federalism are set to zero. In tests of the difference between the means of the two probability distributions (King, Tomz, and Wittenberg 2000), we can reject the null hypothesis at the .05 level for all equations except the fourth—increase in intensity from the previous time period.

Figure 3.1 Estimated probability of ethnic conflict, per quinquennium

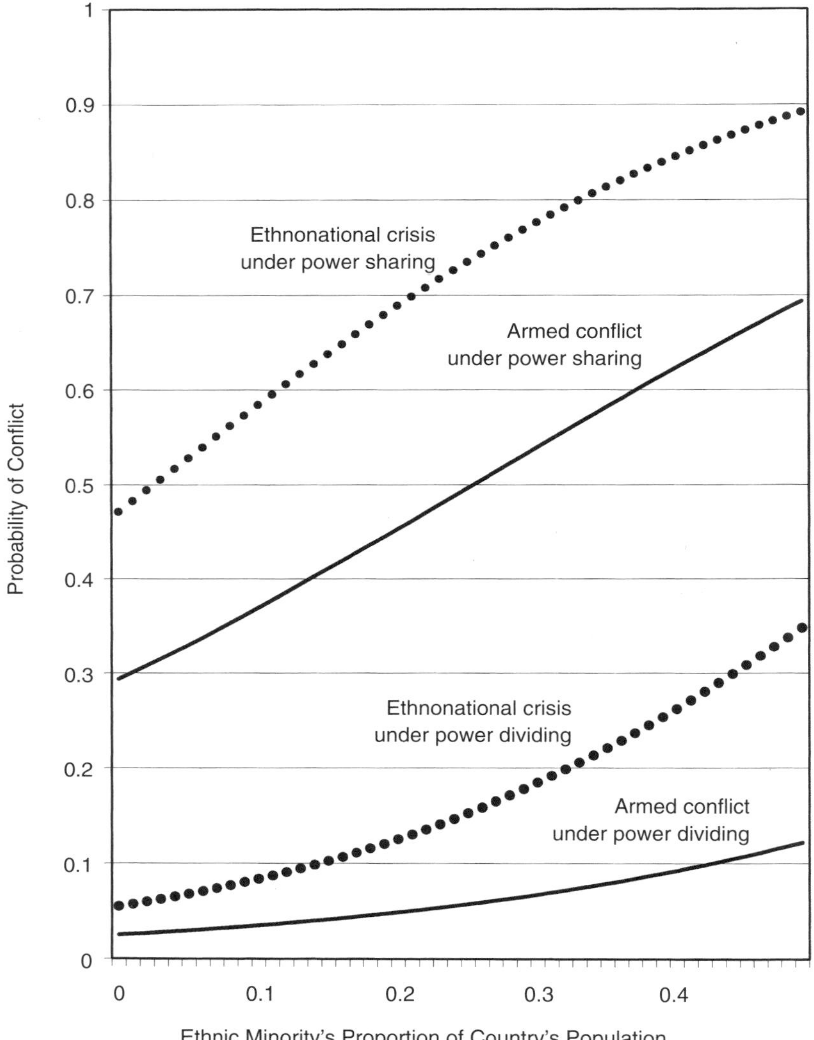

branches (see Table 3.3). Yet this is not the most dangerous power-sharing institution. Second, the probability of escalation was lower in countries with bicameral legislatures with divided majorities and ethnically blind formulas for representation. All coefficient estimates are negative, and three are significant at the .01 level or better.

Third, partitioned decisionmaking associated with separate autoı homelands had the most profound effect of any of the institutions. Ag… the comparison group is dyads in stable democracies of average age that involved an otherwise average indigenous ethnic group that constituted a tenth of the country's population. The likelihood of escalation to an ethnonational crisis that involved armed conflict was three times higher (26.6 percent versus 8.2 percent) when the ethnic group's homeland enjoyed regional autonomy (see Table 3.3). Even soft guarantees of autonomy in ethnically divided societies nearly doubled (15.3 percent versus 8.2 percent) the likelihood of ethnonational crises involving armed conflict.

Closer examination of the patterns associated with territorial autonomy reveal two additional insights: First, power sharing is also associated with more intense ethnopolitical conflict involving ethnic groups left disfranchised by the autonomy arrangement.[13] This is due to the effects of the heightened stakes of conflict and institutionalized contagion where no group wants to be the sucker as others increase their power. Second, the role of institutional weapons is revealed by comparing the likelihood of crisis and armed conflict among disfranchised minorities with the likelihood among empowered minorities in power-sharing polities. The likelihood of crisis with the common-state government was twice as high for dyads involving ethnic groups with institutional weapons (50.7 percent versus 25.1 percent) and the likelihood of armed conflict with the common-state government was two-thirds higher.

The evidence is, of course, only about probabilities. None of this suggests that any institutional arrangement is likely to hold together for long peoples who do not want to live in the same state. The strength of the demographic and cultural "givens" in the statistical models attests to this. In the time span examined in these equations (four and a half decades) political institutions could build on this demographic or cultural base only to deter or facilitate the escalation of ethnopolitical conflict. The institutional arrangements described here stress restraining opportunistic behavior by elites who would exploit these "givens."

Because there are so few examples of successful power sharing or consociationalism after civil wars, these models do not permit us to ascertain whether a special, atypical pattern would emerge if power sharing were applied more generally to post–civil war settlements. Nonetheless, the significance of the institutional constraints in the previous equations, even with the introduction in the equations of a variable for prior regime turmoil, supports the suspicion that these institutions do have an independent effect

13. Cohen (1997, 624) finds that federal states have experienced less intense ethnic conflict. This differs from the finding here that conflicts involving ethnic groups with ethnofederal status are more likely to escalate to more extreme forms.

above and beyond the effect of prior civil war. And that effect is to erode deterrence of escalation after civil war.

Findings from studies of civil war settlements by Caroline Hartzell (2000), Roy Licklider (1995), Edward Luttwak (1999), and Harrison Wagner (1993) give further evidence to support this conclusion. Wagner criticizes power-sharing settlements and argues, "negotiated settlements of civil wars are likely to break down because segments of power-sharing government retain the capacity for resorting to civil war while victory destroys the losers' organization, making it very difficult to resume the war" (Licklider 1995, 681). Licklider's (1995, 685) study of 91 civil wars from 1945 to 1993 confirms this. This relationship is particularly strong in what he labels "identity" rather than "political-economic" civil wars. Following a victory by one side, only a fifth of the identity wars had resumed before 1994. Alternatively, following a negotiated compromise among the previously warring parties, two-thirds of the identity wars had resumed before 1994. Hartzell (2000, 20) finds that even when controlling for intensity of the civil war, level of economic development, and third-party guarantees, civil war settlements imposed by a victorious side were likely to last 170 percent longer than negotiated compromises among the previously warring parties. The compromises keep alive the myth that one has not been (and cannot be) defeated in a contest of arms and leave in place many institutional weapons for a resumption of conflict. As Luttwak (1999, 36) explains, at the end of a civil war "hope of military success must fade for accommodation to become more attractive than further combat." Power sharing is more likely to keep this deadly and destructive hope alive.

Normative and Policy Implications

The argument in this chapter is purely prudential, stressing empirical consequences. Yet this inevitably touches on important normative issues. The argument is that liberalism is also realism. This is an instance in which reality may not be perverse and liberal ideals and prudence reinforce one another. For example, starting with a moral claim derived from Kantian principles that support the autonomy of the individual, the political philosopher Thomas Pogge (1997, 188) proposes "a generalized Golden Rule" for judging claims to rights by ethnic groups: "Base any claims you make for some group(s) on principles by which you would be prepared to judge the claims of any other groups as well. Here is one neat way to 'enforce' this rule: Whenever someone claims group rights for some groups, or for groups of some type, we take her to hold that these rights should be granted to any other claimant group as well." This is very close to the instrumental or prudential rule I have advocated for the design of institutions allocating decision rights. For constitutional designers crafting institutions in ethnically divided societies, Pogge's "generalized Golden Rule" would lead to more robust institutions.

Of course, this begs the question—is it possible to realize this Kantian ideal in deeply divided societies and particularly at the moment of deepest division when ethnic conflicts have escalated to high stakes and extreme means? Certainly there is little hope for power dividing when the sides at the bargaining table will consider only rigid power-sharing institutions with little flexibility for subsequent evolution to power-dividing democracy. Indeed, at the end of a civil war the leaders of ethnic groups intent on checking the leaders of other ethnic groups may be particularly unwilling to open the political process to involve politicians representing non-ethnic agendas. These non-ethnic agendas might take away some members of ethnic groups on some policy issues. In such a situation, power sharing may be the only arrangement with which to initiate the transition. Yet, this short-term expedient increases the likelihood of a recurrence of conflict in the longer term. In these circumstances it might be best to partition the common-state among new independent states.

A second difficulty in implementing the power-dividing strategy of constitution making is its emphasis on extensive civil liberties—the allocation of many decisions to the private sector rather than government. Yet, as Jack Snyder and Karen Ballantine (1996, 61–62) have argued, in the initial stages of a transition, civil liberties may be unsettling: "promoting unconditional freedom of public debate in newly democratizing societies is, in many circumstances, likely to make the problem [of instability] worse." In part these dangers are mitigated by the power-dividing strategy because it lowers the stakes involved in the contest for control of government. Much of the intensity of the conflict described by Snyder and Ballantine arises from the statism that makes capture of the government so valuable. In any event, the power-dividing strategy issues a warning: Failure to empower civil society with extensive civil rights as soon as possible increases the risk of subsequent escalation of ethnopolitical conflict to crises in government. Indeed, a significant body of evidence suggests that democracies experience less political instability and particularly less violence than semi-democratized regimes (Dudley and Miller 1998; Muller 1985; Muller and Weede 1994; Scarritt and McMillan 1995). Not long after the initiation of the transition from civil war, a little liberty becomes more dangerous than a lot.

Despite these problems, many instances in which analysts have advocated power-sharing arrangements fall far short of these extreme circumstances where only power sharing will do. In these instances where some choice is left to constitution makers, the power-dividing strategy recommends three tactics to implement power dividing when the initiation phase throws up obstacles. The first is bringing more players to the bargaining table of constitutional design—not only all ethnic groups and other types of cultural and identity groups but also labor, management, the professions, and various interest groups. Although this runs counter to the usual rules of bargaining, which predict that agreement is easier when fewer parties sit at the bargaining table, it increases the likelihood of a robust outcome from the agreement.

Second, if parties demand some majoritarian or power-sharing institution, constitutional designers can accommodate this, but must check this institution with others that represent society differently. The attempt to find the perfect institution, such as the perfect electoral formula, for ethnically divided societies misses the important point made by the power-dividing strategy: We should not rely on a single formula, but on multiple formulas in the same polity so as to create multiple, crosscutting majorities. For example, if ethnic leaders reject cantonization that divides the homelands of each ethnic group and demand homeland autonomy, then constitutional designers should also seek to create special administrative districts that cut across these homelands. Examples include water basin districts, local education districts, public health districts, and road-development districts, each with special governing boards, elected by majorities in the crosscutting jurisdictions. For foreign donors this means that the massive funds poured into various projects such as irrigation, education, public health, or transportation should not all funnel through the same hands at the central or regional level.

Third, the power-dividing strategy emphasizes rediscovering the virtues of limited government—at least for its practical benefits in conflicts that divide societies deeply. Power sharing has a statist orientation that assumes government is the solution. Where decisions can be made efficiently only if given to institutions with compulsory jurisdiction then the power-dividing approach argues that these decision rights should not accumulate in a single set of jurisdictions, such as homelands, but should be dispersed among separate crosscutting jurisdictions. Yet, early liberals also realized that in areas that are most divisive—such as religion in their day—government should leave those decisions to individuals and to civil society. Mechanisms to take choices out of the hands of government—such as school vouchers—may be appropriate to an ethnically plural society in which education is a flashpoint for ethnonational crises. The commitment to remove decision rights from the state and leave these to citizens has always been liberalism's most radical challenge to a statist world.

4

Power Sharing in Peace Settlements: Initiating the Transition from Civil War

Matthew Hoddie and Caroline Hartzell

This chapter answers two questions about the effects that power-sharing provisions in peace settlements can have on the initiation of a transition to peace and democratic practices following civil war. First, do power-sharing provisions in civil war settlements reduce the likelihood of a resumption of conflict in the early stages of a transition from a civil war? Second, do these same power-sharing provisions create conditions that facilitate the holding of timely elections following the end of hostilities? The dilemma of power sharing identified in Chapter 1 notes a positive role for power sharing in the initiation phase. The offer of power sharing is a costly signal of an intention to respect the rights of other ethnic groups. In this chapter we document that offers of power sharing in peace settlements can, indeed, have the positive effects of fostering stability and democratic practices.

This chapter is part of a scholarly tradition in international relations on ending civil wars and thus follows some conventions that differ from those of debates within comparative politics concerning the value of power sharing. First, our definition of *power sharing* is not limited to the formal institutions and policies identified in Chapter 2. We use a more inclusive definition so that the term *power-sharing provisions* refers to informal arrangements and practices as well as formal institutions and policies. Second, our primary independent variables are the provisions of peace settlements that promise power sharing. These promises are not always implemented, so our independent variable is not a direct measure of institutions and policies actually enacted. Third, we focus only on civil wars that came to an end through a negotiated settlement. This excludes civil wars that ended through victory of one side or the other.

Employing a statistical analysis of the 38 civil wars settled by the process of negotiation between 1945 and 1998, we conclude that inclusion of provisions for certain power-sharing institutions, policies, and informal arrangements in the initial peace settlement is useful in encouraging both stability and elections during what Donald Rothchild and Philip Roeder in Chapter 1 label the initiation phase. Specifically, we find that negotiated civil war settlement provisions that promise territorial or military power sharing are positively associated with the likelihood that peace will endure. Our findings also indicate that the prospects for the holding of timely elections are enhanced by this early mutual commitment among former combatants to institutions associated with territorial power sharing.

We interpret these results as indicating that these power-sharing provisions facilitating a post–civil war settlement tend to send reassuring signals to parties to the conflict that their vital concerns will not be ignored or attacked following the establishment of peace and a new government. Aware that power can be exercised in a variety of ways, societies at the ends of conflicts have looked to different forms of power-sharing institutions and policies to prevent any single set of actors from monopolizing, and potentially abusing, power. While these institutions and policies may be modified at a later date, the reassurances embodied in promises to create power-sharing institutions and policies with the end of hostilities have the favorable effect of enhancing the prospects for reconciliation among the once-warring parties. The offer of power sharing in a peace settlement—whether power-sharing institutions and policies are actually implemented or not—is a costly signal of the parties' commitment to accept a common rule, to resolve conflicts by peaceful means, and to forgo attempts to impose outcomes by extralegal, particularly violent means.

Power-Sharing Mechanisms for Conflict Management

David Lake and Donald Rothchild (1996) attribute the emergence of many instances of civil violence to the security concerns of groups that have been heightened by the problems of communication failures and a sense of trepidation about the capabilities and intentions of their adversaries. These security concerns are likely to be particularly acute immediately following a civil war because all parties have recent, concrete evidence of the hostile intentions of their adversaries.

Given this environment in which security concerns are paramount, groups must craft rules as part of a postwar settlement that are perceived to be: (1) transparent, (2) predictable in their outcomes, and (3) capable of preventing a single collectivity from monopolizing state power. Paradoxically, it is the very capacity of power-sharing institutions to avoid the uncertainty and unpredictability of democracy that make them so attractive as means to initiate a transition from civil war to peace and to elections. Former civil war adversaries do regularly rely on the promise of power sharing as a means to accomplish these goals and manage domestic conflict. Among the 38 negotiated settlements we consider, only one (a failed 1989 agreement to end Angola's civil war) did not include any provisions for the sharing of power.

In terms of creating transparent rules, power-sharing institutions and policies establish a code of conduct for groups in an often chaotic and confusing environment. These rules specify what defines appropriate group behaviors such as how to integrate the military, allocate seats in the legislature, or distribute the budget. Beyond establishing a clear code of conduct, these same institutions and policies provide each collectivity with a means by which to assess and verify the level of commitment and adherence to the agreement by their former adversaries.[1] Defections are immediately apparent if the principles of power sharing are violated.

Power-sharing institutions and policies also provide procedures to manage conflict with outcomes that are predictable. Post–civil war societies are rife with suspicion and concerns about what the actions of some collectivities will mean for the interests of others. In this environment, groups worried about the implications of open-ended competitions for power in which outcomes are uncertain may be tempted to return to war to avoid what they fear may be a worse result.[2] Under these circumstances, uncertainty is the enemy of peace. Stability is more likely to prevail if the new rules for managing conflict can ensure that particular outcomes—such as group representation in the government or a specific allocation of budgetary funds—will, in fact, result.

Finally, and most important, power-sharing institutions and policies contribute to peaceful conflict management by appearing to reduce the risk that any single group will control all the levers of state power. Power-sharing rules can help to minimize this problem from emerging by balancing, dividing, or sharing power among competing groups. Former combatants are more likely to feel secure about the future if they know that rules exist that avoid concentrating power, particularly power that can be used to coerce others, in the hands of a single party (Hartzell 1999).

For these reasons power sharing can be very appealing and reassuring to parties negotiating an end to a civil war. They are likely to hold concerns analogous to states in the anarchic international system. Emerging from an unsettled domestic environment, these collectivities will have an interest in ensuring that they have the means to protect themselves against the predatory actions of others. This may be accomplished by guaranteeing a degree of access to resources that are central to self-defense.

1. For a discussion of power-sharing practices that may serve as security-building measures among former civil war adversaries, see Stedman and Rothchild 1996.

2. Jonas Savimbi's return to war following an initial round of elections in Angola serves as an example of unknown payoffs leading to a reinitiation of hostilities.

Comparing Power-Sharing Provisions

To consider the role that the promised creation of power sharing has on the prospects for durable peace and timely elections, we focus on the 38 civil conflicts that ended between 1945 and 1998 through the process of negotiations. Consistent with the criteria outlined in the Correlates of War project, we define a civil war as those instances in which the conflict produced a minimum of 1,000 battle deaths per year.[3] We consider a *negotiated settlement* to have taken place if representatives of the opposing sides engaged in direct talks that resulted in an agreement.[4] In these negotiated settlements we identify four types of provisions associated with power sharing. Chapter 2 of this volume characterizes *power sharing* as involving critical choices on inclusive, partitioned, or predetermined decision-making rules or combinations of these rules. This definition focuses on power sharing as it takes place within a state's political institutions. Many peace settlements include provisions that promise arrangements or practices that are less formal than the power-sharing institutions and policies identified in Chapter 2. Some of these provisions require initial compromises, such as integration of armed forces, rather than enduring or recurrent practices. Our more inclusive definition of power sharing, derived from the international relations literature, includes all these formal and informal provisions.

Central Power Sharing

Provisions for central power sharing in peace settlements promise to distribute political power in the core governing institutions of the state among groups in the divided society. In peace settlements reached since 1945, provisions stipulate that political power in the central government should be shared or divided among groups in at least three different ways. First, parties may agree to employ a system of electoral proportional representation (PR) for the legislature of the central government. Although the mechanics by which votes are translated into seats under different PR systems vary, these rules share in common the aim to minimize the disparity between a party's share of national votes and the number of parliamentary seats it occupies (Reilly and Reynolds 1998). A case in point is Mozambique's 1992 *General Peace Agreement*, which mandated that election to the Assembly be based on

3. More precisely, we classified domestic conflicts that broke out between 1945 and 1998 as civil wars if they met four criteria specified in the Correlates of War project: (1) The conflict produced a minimum of 1,000 battle deaths per year; (2) the central government was a party to the dispute; (3) there was genuine resistance on the part of both the national government and its adversaries during the course of the conflict; and (4) the war occurred within a defined political unit (Small and Singer 1982).

4. Third-party actors might participate in the negotiating process, but the antagonists themselves had to meet to discuss their demands for ending the war.

the principle of proportional representation. Second, groups may agree to a principle of proportionality in the bureaucracies of the central government. Rules of this nature seek to allocate decision- and policy-making power to groups by appointing a predetermined number of their representatives to positions on courts, commissions, the civil and foreign services, and other corresponding offices. The Salvadoran peace accords, for example, called for the creation of a National Commission for the Consolidation of Peace (COPAZ), which would be responsible for overseeing the implementation of the political agreements reached by the parties. The accords required that COPAZ be composed of two representatives of the Government of El Salvador, including a member of the armed forces, two representatives of the Farabundo Marti Liberation Front (FMLN), and one representative of each of the parties or coalitions represented in the Legislative Assembly. Finally, central power-sharing provisions may be constructed on the basis of proportionality in the executive of the national government. In this instance, groups are guaranteed a voice in the innermost circles of political power via the appointment of representatives to ministerial, subministerial, and cabinet positions. Tajikistan's 1997 peace agreement, for example, called for "co-option of the members of the United Tajik Opposition into the structures of the executive branch," with 30 percent of senior government posts filled by United Tajik Opposition candidates.[5]

In negotiated civil war settlements, provisions for central power-sharing institutions have been more common than provisions for the other types of power sharing. This stands out in Table 4.1, in which we compare power-sharing institutions and policies included in negotiated agreements: 30 of the 38 peace agreements we examine, or 79 percent of the total, include provisions for central power sharing.

Territorial Power Sharing

Provisions for territorial power sharing include both formal autonomy such as federalism and informal arrangements such as ceasefires that leave the armed forces of each side in control of their respective territories. Territorially based power-sharing institutions aim to decentralize power by "placing institutional limitations on unbridled central authority" (Lake and Rothchild 1996, 62). Recognizing that the government is typically the most powerful organization within a country, territorial power-sharing institutions call for the devolution of powers to regionally concentrated groups in the hopes that this will enhance their sense of security. In this form of power sharing, political influence is divided between levels of government through

5. For the full text of the Bishkek Memorandum see www.eurasianet.org/resource/tajikistan/links/bishmemo.html. Retrieved February 2, 2005.

Table 4.1. Power-sharing institutions and policies in 38 civil war settlements

Settlement	Central power-sharing institutions	Territorial power-sharing institutions	Military power-sharing policies	Economic power-sharing policies
Angola, 1975–89	0	0	0	0
Angola, 1989–91	1	0	1	0
Angola, 1992–94	1	1	1	0
Azerbaijan, 1989–94	0	1	1	0
Bosnia, 1992–95	1	1	1	0
Cambodia, 1970–91	1	0	1	0
Chad, 1979–79	1	0	0	0
Chad, 1989–96	1	0	1	0
Chechnya, 1994–96	1	1	1	1
Colombia, 1948–57	1	0	0	1
Croatia, 1991–92	1	0	0	0
Croatia, 1995–95	1	0	0	0
Dominican Republic, 1965–65	0	0	1	0
El Salvador, 1979–92	1	0	1	1
Georgia (S. Ossetia), 1989–92	0	1	1	0
Georgia (Abkhazia), 1992–94	1	1	0	0
Guatemala, 1963–96	0	1	0	1
Guinea Bissau, 1998–98	1	0	1	0
India, 1946–49	1	1	0	0
Iraq, 1961–70	1	1	0	1
Laos, 1959–73	1	0	0	0
Lebanon, 1958–58	1	0	0	1
Lebanon, 1975–89	1	0	1	0
Liberia, 1989–93	1	0	0	0
Liberia, 1994–96	1	0	0	0
Malaysia, 1948–56	0	1	0	1
Moldova, 1992–92	1	1	0	1
Mozambique, 1982–92	1	1	1	0
Nicaragua, 1981–89	1	1	1	1
Papua New Guinea, 1989–98	0	1	0	0
Philippines, 1972–96	1	1	1	1
Rwanda, 1990–93	1	0	1	1
Sierra Leone, 1992–96	1	0	1	1
South Africa, 1983–91	1	1	1	1
Sudan, 1963–72	0	1	1	1
Tajikistan, 1992–97	1	0	1	0
Yemen Arab Republic, 1962–70	1	1	1	1
Zimbabwe, 1972–79	1	0	1	1

Note: Years indicate the beginning and end of each conflict.

the creation of one of various forms of decentralized government including, most commonly, federalism and regional autonomy. *Federalism*, in which "power is devolved equally to all regions and each region has an identical relationship to the central government" is perhaps the best-known arrangement of this type (Ghai 1998, 156). Examples of negotiated settlements that have included federal features are Malaysia and South Africa. In the case of *regional autonomy*, only one or a few of a country's regions are likely to have special powers devolved to them.[6] The 1996 peace settlement in the Philippines, for example, called for the creation of a Special Zone of Peace and Development (SZOPAD) in Southern Mindanao to consist of fourteen provinces and nine cities. Three years after the creation of the SZOPAD, a plebiscite was to be held to "determine the establishment of a new autonomous government and the specific area of autonomy" of this government.[7]

Although there is some debate regarding the utility of territorial power-sharing institutions for stabilizing the peace (see, for example, Chapter 5), 18 peace agreements, or 47 percent of the total, contain provisions for some form of territorial power sharing. Clearly many former combatants find this type of power sharing attractive at the end of a civil war.

Military Power Sharing

In peace arrangements at the end of civil wars, provisions for military power sharing specify details of staffing and control of the coercive agencies of the state. The means most often employed for sharing military power has been to integrate the former antagonists' armed forces in a new common security force. The new army may include equal numbers of each group's troops or a balance formed on the basis of a formula that reflects the relative size of each of the armed groups at the end of the civil war. For example, the 1996 Philippine peace agreement called for the integration of some 7,500 members of the Mindanao National Liberation Force's military wing into the national army and security forces.

To reassure former combatants, particularly those that are members of a minority group, about the manner in which the state's new security forces will be used, peace arrangements may mandate appointment of members of the subordinate group to key leadership positions—such as general, commander, director, or defense minister—in the state's security forces. This ensures they are in a position to monitor the movements of troops and warn of policy decisions that might alter the future composition or use of the state's forces to their detriment. Notable examples of this type of power-sharing policy include the commissioning of Southern Sudan Liberation

6. Some scholars who focus on territorially based institutions use the terms "symmetrical" and "asymmetrical" federalism in place of the terms "federalism" and "regional autonomy." In both cases, the critical difference that exists between the two categories of territorially based institutions is not the degree of autonomy enjoyed by the subunits, but whether the whole state is divided among such subunits.

7. For the full text of the peace agreement between the government of the Philippines and the Moro National Liberation Front see www.usip.org/library/pa/philippines/pagree_07181996_toc.html. Retrieved February 2, 2005.

Movement leader and Anya-Nya Commander-in-Chief Major-General Joseph Lagu as Major-General in the unified Sudanese army and Violeta Barrios de Chamorro's retention of Sandinista General Humberto Ortega as head of Nicaragua's armed forces.

Finally, although it occurs only in rare cases, a peace arrangement may seek to check the ability of the state to use its security forces against the other party by allowing antagonists to retain their own armed forces without complete decommissioning or disarming. The Dayton Agreement crafted to resolve the civil war in Bosnia and Herzegovina, for example, allowed the Bosnian-Croat Federation and Republika Srpska entities that make up Bosnia and Herzegovina to maintain their own separate armies. Provisions for military power sharing of one type or another appear in over half of the negotiated civil war settlements we examine (see Table 4.1). Twenty-two of the peace agreements, or 58 percent of the total, include rules for sharing military power.[8]

Economic Power Sharing

The economic dimension of power sharing is a complex one, involving not only issues of distributive justice but also questions regarding control of economic resources. Faced with these concerns, settlement architects seek to construct policies for the distribution of wealth and income that achieve a balance among groups or at least prevent any single group from monopolizing economic resources. Peace settlements may mandate a specific pattern of resource allocation among groups (usually minorities) or policies targeted at the needs of specific groups or regions. The 1996 peace accord signed in the Philippines, for example, called for the state to provide a Special Zone of Peace and Development in the Southern Philippines with resources to foster development within the region, including basic services such as water and socialized housing and entrepreneurial development support in the form of livelihood assistance and credit facilities. El Salvador's peace accords specified a number of measures for the transfer of lands to former combatants and to those who had occupied lands in war zones.

Provisions mandating the sharing of wealth appear less frequently in civil war peace settlements than the other power-sharing provisions described above. Only 16 of the 38 peace agreements we examine, or 42 percent of the total, mandate the establishment of economic power sharing. The reason

8. Given the frequency with which military power-sharing policies have been constructed, the existing literature on power sharing has been remiss in its lack of attention to this issue. This relative neglect may be starting to change, however, as security sector reform following civil wars has emerged as an issue on regional, national, and international agendas. See, for example, the articles in the first issue of the *Journal of Conflict, Security, and Development* (2001).

why provisions for economic power sharing are infrequently included in settlements may have to do with the perceived costs associated with these arrangements. Governments faced with the costs of rebuilding following a civil war will likely be reluctant, or even unable, to engage in significant investment or resource reallocation.[9]

As the foregoing demonstrates, actors concerned with how best to secure post–civil war reconciliation have devised a number of different power-sharing provisions that constrain the ways in which power is to be exercised in the postwar state. Because the parties to a settlement fear what former combatants may do, should the adversaries come to monopolize state power, considerable effort is spent crafting means by which to share, balance, and divide power among former combatants. Recognizing that there are various dimensions to state power—political, territorial, military, and economic—the architects of negotiated settlements have envisioned power-sharing institutions and policies meant to help balance the exercise of power along each of these dimensions. The promised creation of these institutions and policies serves the valuable function of signaling the shared commitment of all parties to living together in peace in the context of the postwar state.

Hypotheses

In this section we formulate specific propositions about the effects that these promises of power sharing have on longer-term developments—specifically, the duration of peace and introduction of electoral competition. We examine the effects of power-sharing provisions on two dependent variables meant to indicate the degree to which former enemies subsequently reconcile their interests and begin the process of establishing new norms of reciprocity. The two dependent variables focus on the first five years after a civil war.[10] The first dependent variable is the duration of the peace—the time in months until a resumption of civil war—following the signing of a negotiated agreement. The second dependent variable is the number of months that transpire between arriving at a civil war settlement and the holding of

9. According to the Department of Foreign Affairs of the Philippines, for example, national government spending on the socioeconomic development programs called for in the 1996 peace agreement was six times higher during the first four years of the agreement's implementation than the average annual amount spent on those programs in the four years preceding the agreement (*Business World* [Philippines] October 18, 2000). In the case of the Salvadoran peace settlement, the money the Salvadoran government used to purchase occupied lands that it then sold, at rates lower than market interest rates, to those occupying the land, was financed by the United States and the European Union (Spence et al. 1997).

10. Our emphasis on the initial five years following the end of hostilities is a common practice in the study of post–civil war transitions (see, for example, Licklider 1995 and Walter 1997).

the first democratic national elections (what Rothchild and Roeder use to mark the culmination of the initiation phase). Because elections have come to be seen as "the critical turning point at which a society moves from open, antagonistic violence to a new era based on bargaining and reciprocity," it is important to understand the conditions that facilitate or impede the timely holding of postconflict elections (Reynolds and Sisk 1998, 17).[11]

Power-Sharing Provisions

What effect does the inclusion of different power-sharing provisions in a settlement have on the subsequent stability of the peace during the initiation phase? Our expectation is that war is less likely to break out during the initiation phase if negotiated settlements promise to establish power-sharing institutions, policies, or practices that make it difficult for any one group to use state resources to the detriment of other groups.

What effect does the promise of different power sharing institutions and policies have on the likelihood that elections will be held in a timely manner? Postconflict elections are a critical turning point in the transition from armed conflict to stable governance. In the words of Krishna Kumar (1998, 7), elections will ideally "contribute to the institutionalization of a conflict resolution mechanism in the body politic." Yet, because the outcomes of elections are inherently uncertain, as Timothy Sisk has observed, electoral competition may be seen as "a matter of not simply losing office but of losing the means for protecting the survival of the group" (Sisk 1996, 31). Groups that fear for their security may seek to postpone or even prevent the first postconflict elections. Postconflict elections are more likely to become "reconciliation elections" and be held in a timely manner following the signing of a civil war settlement if the agreement includes power-sharing provisions that address the security concerns of former opponents.[12] South Africa, which held its first general elections a little over two years after the signing of a negotiated agreement, is a case in point. The effect of including power-sharing provisions in the initial agreement was to reassure minority groups about the manner in which power would be exercised and the uses to which power would be put, thus lessening parties' fear of electoral outcomes. As a

11. By including a dependent variable reflecting the time in months to the first election we do not mean to suggest that early elections are always in the best interest of states emerging from civil war. If held under conditions of pervasive insecurity and uncertainty, these elections run the significant risk of reinvigorating rivalries and even instigating a new round of hostilities (Paris 2001, 327). Our intention is instead to demonstrate that the promise of power sharing has the potential to mitigate this sense of insecurity and thus increase the odds that timely and peaceful elections will be held and that the outcome will be respected by all parties to the conflict.

12. The phrase "reconciliation elections" was coined by Rafael López-Pintor (1997).

result, not only were elections held, but "[b]y the time the elections were held, widespread consensus had been achieved on the rules of the political game" (Kumar and Ottaway 1998, 236).

Hypothesis 1a. Including power-sharing provisions in a negotiated civil war settlement decreases the likelihood that civil war will resume in the initiation phase.
Hypothesis 1b. Including power-sharing provisions in a negotiated civil war settlement increases the likelihood of holding the transition elections in a timely manner.

Other Influences

Power-sharing provisions are clearly not the only factors with an effect on the duration of peace and the time to transition elections. In what follows we discuss the hypothesized impact of a number of control variables on our two dependent variables. These control variables are also included to address concerns about the potential for endogeneity in our model. It is possible that the inclusion of power-sharing arrangements as part of a settlement and higher levels of conciliatory behavior among former combatants are both determined by other factors. Our control variables address this issue by taking into account those influences that might serve simultaneously to encourage domestic adversaries to agree to power-sharing arrangements and maintain peaceful interactions.[13]

Third-party enforcer. In light of the security concerns adversaries face following a civil war, Saadia Touval (1982), Barbara Walter (1999a), and Walter and Jack Snyder (1999) have suggested that civil war settlements are unlikely to succeed unless the terms of the agreement are enforced by a third party. Walter (1997, 340) explains that third parties are called on to "guarantee that groups will be protected, terms will be fulfilled, and promises will be kept." Third-party promises to intervene to provide for the

13. In her study of negotiated civil war settlements, Barbara Walter sought to address the endogeneity issue by exploring whether power-sharing "pacts," as she called them, were offered only in those cases that were likely to succeed anyway. She found that "most of the factors associated with the peaceful resolution of civil wars did not significantly predict the presence of power-sharing guarantees" (Walter 2002, 100). The only two variables that did appear to be positively related to power-sharing pacts were lengthy wars (not surprising, since long wars tend to be costly wars, thus prompting adversaries to offer one another incentives to bring the war to an end) and the presence of third-party guarantors. As Walter notes, the relationship between power-sharing "pacts" and third-party guarantors is likely to be spurious because power-sharing pacts are usually agreed to before third-party actors offer themselves as enforcers of the agreement. Although our data set and control variables differ somewhat from Walter's, the logic regarding the low likelihood of endogeneity in a model of this nature should still hold.

safety of former combatants are meant to reassure these actors that their commitment to a negotiated settlement will not cost them their lives. If third-party promises to intervene are credible, the peace that follows settlements that provide for third-party intervention should prove more stable in the initiation phase.

Negotiated settlements that call for third-party enforcers should also be more likely to result in transition elections being held in a timely manner than settlements that are not enforced by third parties. Third-party enforcers can help to ensure that electoral conflict does not turn to violence: The presence of the third-party enforcer assures former combatants that no matter how disenchanted some actors may become with the election outcomes, the third party will either deter or quickly contain any violence.

> *Hypothesis 2a.* Provisions for third-party enforcement in a negotiated civil war settlement decrease the likelihood of a resumption of civil war in the initiation phase.
> *Hypothesis 2b.* Provisions for third-party enforcement in a negotiated settlement increase the likelihood that transition elections will take place in a timely manner.

Conflict duration. The duration of the previous civil war is likely to have an impact on the parties' decision to maintain peace and hold transition elections. The civil wars we examine in this chapter range from a relatively brief three-month conflict in Croatia in 1995 to a war that lasted nearly 34 years in Guatemala. The average length of the civil wars in our study is just short of seven years. Although lengthy civil wars tend to have higher costs, longer conflicts have the perverse yet positive consequence of providing parties to a dispute and third-party enforcers with information about the other parties (Mason, Weingarten, Jr., and Fett 1999). During the course of a war of extended duration, adversaries and third-party actors can monitor the extent to which parties cooperate with mediators, uphold or violate ceasefire agreements, and show signs of restraint. Short conflicts provide fewer opportunities for collecting information of this nature and for forming conclusions about one's opponents. Most important, lengthy conflicts may heighten expectations that a resumption of conflict will be fruitless. That is, as the war drags on and opponents fail to do better than fight each other to a stalemate, they are increasingly likely to conclude that they cannot prevail in any resumption of war (Werner 1999). Based on this logic, we anticipate that lengthy conflicts will have two effects. One is that wars of long duration should increase the likelihood that parties will commit to a stable peace. The other is that parties anxious to end a long civil war should be willing to take measures to bring closure to the war, including agreeing to hold the transition elections in a timely manner.

> *Hypothesis 3a.* The longer the duration of the previous civil war, the lower the likelihood that war will resume in the initiation phase.
> *Hypothesis 3b.* The longer the duration of the previous civil war, the higher the likelihood that transition elections will be held in a timely manner.

Conflict intensity. Alternatively, civil wars associated with high numbers of casualties should have the effect of increasing the sense of insecurity within the state, thus making it more challenging to sustain a postconflict peace. The casualty rate has varied from 84 deaths per month in Chad's 1989–1996 civil war to a high of 25,217 deaths per month in India's 1946–1949 civil conflict. Civil wars in which the parties inflicted death on one another at relatively higher rates are likely to increase the overall sense of insecurity—both among the victims who fear a resumption of hostilities and the perpetrators who fear revenge. As a result, parties will be less willing to cooperate with one another to manage future conflict. Under these conditions, former adversaries may have a propensity to be "trigger happy" and interpret even innocuous moves by their opponents as violations of the settlement. Through their own reactions, actors may undermine an agreement (Hartzell, Hoddie, and Rothchild 2001) as well as plans for postconflict elections. For these reasons, higher intensity of conflict should undermine the peace and delay the transition elections.

> *Hypothesis 4a.* The higher the monthly casualty rate in a civil war prior to a negotiated settlement, the higher the likelihood of a resumption of civil war in the initiation phase.
> *Hypothesis 4b.* The higher the monthly casualty rate in a civil war prior to a negotiated settlement the lower the likelihood of holding transition elections in a timely manner.

Stakes of the conflict. A number of scholars have suggested that certain types of civil wars may be more amenable to stable settlements and regularized patterns of competition than others. In particular, identity wars (i.e., conflicts based on ethnic, subethnic, religious, or racial interests) are said to differ from wars of an ideological nature in the sense that the stakes, defined in terms of physical safety and survival, are believed to be greater in the former than the latter (Lake and Rothchild 1996). In addition, the stakes have often been identified as being less divisible in identity conflicts than in ideological wars (Gurr 1990; Licklider 1995). As a result, we expect that mutual accommodation, and by extension a stable peace, is more difficult to reach and sustain in the case of identity-based civil wars in comparison to ideological conflicts. This lack of cooperation seems likely to carry over into the electoral arena as well. Parties organized along identity lines may be more likely than other parties to see the electoral competition as a mirror of the recent conflict. To the extent that this is true and groups clash in the run-up to the transition elections, violence may ensue and elections be postponed or canceled altogether.

> *Hypothesis 5a.* Civil wars centered on identity issues are more likely to see the resumption of conflict in the initiation phase than are other types of civil wars.
> *Hypothesis 5b.* Civil wars centered on identity issues decrease the likelihood that transition elections will be held in a timely manner.

Previous regime type. Actors in countries that are familiar with democratic institutions as a means of managing conflict may prove more amenable to trusting these institutions and the outcomes they produce as compared to those without similar experience. Opponents who have competed for power within the framework of a democratic regime should also have had more experience with the accommodation of competing interests than actors who are the product of authoritarian regimes (Hartzell, Mozaffar, and Rothchild 1999). For these reasons we expect actors in states with previous experiences with democracy to be the most willing to allow the newly created peace to endure and to submit to postconflict elections.

> *Hypothesis 6a.* Previous experience with democracy decreases the likelihood that civil war will resume in the initiation phase.
> *Hypothesis 6b.* Previous experience with democracy increases the likelihood that transition elections will be held in a timely manner.

International system structure. Fen Hampson (1990), and Peter Wallensteen and Margareta Sollenberg (1997) have each sought to determine what effects the end of the Cold War had on civil war outcomes. In general, they have concluded that the end of the East-West struggle is likely to bode well for the stability of settlements because it has meant an end to the superpowers' many wars by proxy and to the competitive arming of warring parties. In the absence of this outside support, antagonists are more likely to commit themselves to a stable peace. The end of the Cold War also appears to have influenced the likelihood of holding transition elections. The international community has been more willing since 1990 to sponsor, organize, and monitor international elections at the end of civil wars than it was previously (López-Pintor 1997). It is unclear whether this is because the demise of the Soviet Union has made these elections less subject to politicization and conflict at the international level or because the "third wave" of democracy underway before the end of the Cold War has a continuing influence (Huntington 1991). These international pressures have made it increasingly difficult for negotiating parties to balk at the idea of holding postconflict elections or to block the elections. The effect of the end of superpower conflict thus has been to enhance the prospects for the holding of timely postconflict elections.

> *Hypothesis 7a.* The likelihood of resumption of civil war in the initiation phase has decreased since the end of the Cold War.
> *Hypothesis 7b.* The likelihood that transition elections will be held in a timely manner has increased since the end of the Cold War.

Data and Method

The formal tests of our hypotheses employ two separate dependent variables—the duration of peace and the time to the first postconflict national election. Our first dependent variable is designed to consider the effect that the promise of power-sharing institutions and policies may have on maintaining the domestic peace during the initiation phase. This indicator is operationalized as the number of months that peace endured following the signing of a negotiated settlement—that is, the number of months until any resumption of civil war. In keeping with our focus on the effect of power-sharing arrangements on the initiation phase, we limit the period of examination to the initial five years following the establishing of an agreement. Our data for this indicator extends through December 1999. With this operationalization of the dependent variable, the 38 settlements are at risk of failure for a total of 1,621 months.

The second dependent variable is the number of months that intervenes between the signing of a civil war settlement and the holding of the first postconflict election for offices in either the national legislature or executive branch. Because our concern is with elections that follow in a timely manner upon the peace settlement, we consider only those elections held within five years of the signing of an agreement. We exclude elections that were held following a postsettlement return to civil war based on the logic that the armed conflict invalidates the provisions of the agreement and restricts the opportunity for participation in the democratic contest.[14] In addition, the elections must be fair and free contests. We exclude those electoral contests that were held in years in which the Polity IV data set indicates that selection of the country's executive was deemed uncompetitive or the situation too anarchic to assess.[15] The latest election included in our data set was held

14. For those instances in which conflict reemerged prior to an election, the case is censored (considered to have left the data set without the event occurring) at the month war broke out.

15. Polity IV's measure of executive recruitment has three codings: selection, dual/transitional, and election. We included all instances of elections in which states are described as determining their chief executive either through a dual/transitional process or election.

in August 2000. There are a total of 1,077 months in which the 38 cases had an opportunity to hold elections.

These negotiated peace agreements appear to be relatively robust. In terms of the maintenance of stability following the agreement, only 12 of the 38 cases (32 percent) experienced a return to domestic warfare, and we estimate the mean survival time of an arrangement within our five-year time frame to be 43 months.[16] Among those countries that remained stable following the signing of a settlement, 18 (47 percent) successfully conducted a free and fair transition election within five years. For the cases in which an election was finally held, the average time from settlement to election was approximately 19 months.

Given our emphasis on comparing the effects of different power-sharing provisions in the initial peace settlement, the model we test includes four dichotomous indicators for each of the different power-sharing provisions in the initial peace settlement: central power sharing, territorial power sharing, military power sharing, and economic power sharing. If the peace settlement includes a provision for one of the four forms of power sharing, the corresponding indicator is scored as one; the absence of such a provision is recorded as zero. The codings for these variables are based on the texts of the settlements. If the text was unavailable, we largely relied on *Keesing's Contemporary Archives* and the annual *Yearbook* of the Stockholm International Peace Research Institute (SIPRI).

Table 4.2 indicates the number of settlements that contain one or more of the power-sharing provisions. Overall, our data show that combatants negotiating an end to civil war often include power-sharing provisions as part of a settlement. Of the 38 negotiated peace agreements constructed between 1945 and 1998, only one, the 1989 Gbadolite Accord to resolve the Angolan civil war, contained no power-sharing provisions. Eight of the agreements (21 percent) included one type of power-sharing provisions; fourteen of the agreements (37 percent) contained two types; ten of the agreements (26 percent) included three types; and five (13 percent) included all four types of the power-sharing provisions.

Elections (dates indicated in parentheses) excluded from the data set based on Polity IV's coding were those in the states of Azerbaijan (1995), Chad (1996), Croatia (1993), Croatia (2000), the Dominican Republic (1966), Guinea-Bissau (1999), Sudan (1972), Tajikistan (1999), and Yemen (1971).

16. Findings employing this data set were first reported in Hartzell, Hoddie, and Rothchild 2001. Since the publication of those results we have refined some estimates regarding the duration of settlements, and this accounts for the greater number of months under consideration in this chapter. In addition, the earlier reported results contained minor coding errors concerning whether some cases were designated as either failures or continuing successes at the censor date. It is for this reason that we identify two fewer failures in this chapter as compared to the earlier study. These corrections in coding were found to have no effect on the substantive findings reported in the original study.

Table 4.2. Frequency of power-sharing arrangements in 38 civil-war settlements

Power-sharing dimensions	Central executive	Territorial	Military	Economic	Settlements
Four	Central	Territorial	Military	Economic	5
Three	Central	Territorial	Military	—	3
	Central	Territorial	—	Economic	2
	—	Territorial	Military	Economic	1
	Central	—	Military	Economic	4
Two	Central	Territorial	—	—	2
	Central	—	Military	—	6
	Central	—	—	Economic	2
	—	Territorial	Military	—	2
	—	Territorial	—	Economic	2
	—	—	Military	Economic	0
One	Central	—	—	—	6
	—	Territorial	—	—	1
	—	—	Military	—	1
	—	—	—	Economic	0
None	—	—	—	—	1

In contrast to the indicators of power-sharing provisions, the other independent variables we employ in this study prove much more straightforward in terms of their coding and do not require detailed explanation. We present the coding rules for all variables in the chapter's appendix.

Methodology

To consider the effect of power-sharing institutions and policies on (a) the duration of peace following a settlement and (b) the time to transition election following a settlement we employ a Cox proportional hazards model.[17] There are a number of advantages to adopting this approach. First, the Cox proportional hazards model was designed to consider factors that might increase or decrease the length of time before a particular event occurs. In these tests both of our dependent variables are events—the failure of an agreement or the holding of elections. For this reason, the Cox model is ideally suited to our purposes.

Second, employing the Cox proportional hazards model is a significant improvement over earlier studies considering civil war settlement stability. Previous research on this topic has tended to define the dependent variable

17. We adopted the Cox proportional hazards model, rather than the alternatives of the parametric exponential and Weibull models, because we make no assumptions regarding whether newer settlements are more susceptible to failure than those that have been established for a longer time period. The Cox model allows for estimating the effects of independent variables on duration time "without having to assume a specific parametric form for the distribution of time until an event occurs" (Box-Steffensmeier and Jones 1997, 1432).

dichotomously—peace settlements that lasted more than five years were categorized as a success; those that proved less durable were classified a failure.[18] The Cox model allows us to consider a much more precise degree of variation in the dependent variable than would have been possible in the earlier approach.

Finally, the hazard rate statistic generated by these tests provides an easily interpretable measure of the influence of a variable on the event of interest. The *hazard rate* is defined as the exponent of the coefficient. Its deviation from the value of one indicates the percent increase or decrease in the likelihood of the incident occurring (Bueno de Mesquita and Siverson 1995, 851). Variables with hazard rates below one decrease the potential of the event happening; variables with hazard rates above one increase the risk of the event occurring.

Given the tests reported, it should be emphasized that the values associated with the hazard rate must be interpreted differently depending on the dependent variable under examination. One of our dependent variables is an event to be avoided—the failure of a peace settlement. In this sense, our main concern is with identifying independent variables with a hazard rate value *less than one* because they contribute to settlement durability. Indicators with hazard rate values *greater than one* are those that are likely to contribute to the undermining of a peace settlement. In contrast, our second dependent variable is typically thought to be a desired goal—the holding of a transition election. Thus, we are primarily concerned with identifying independent variables with a hazard rate value *greater than one* because those are the factors that encourage a quick turnaround to elections. Variables with hazard rate values *less than one* are associated with delaying elections.

Empirical Analysis

We present the findings for our tests in Table 4.3.[19] Although a number of control variables prove to have statistically significant effects, consistent with the substantive concerns of both this volume and chapter we will focus our discussion on the effects of different power-sharing provisions on the two dependent variables.[20]

18. See, for example, Licklider 1995 and Walter 1997.

19. We tested both models for the presence of nonproportional variable effects in the data. Employing residual-based diagnostics, the global tests we ran provided no evidence of nonproportionality in the models.

20. For a more detailed discussion of the effects of the statistically significant control variables on short-term post–civil war stability, see Hartzell, Hoddie, and Rothchild 2001. This chapter considers a wide range of power sharing while the earlier article limited its emphasis to territorial power sharing.

Table 4.3. Cox proportional hazards model estimates

Variable	Duration of the peace		Time to transition election	
	Hazard ratio	Coefficient	Hazard ratio	Coefficient
Central power-sharing institutions	0.68	−0.39	2.67	0.98
	(0.55)	(0.82)	(2.72)	(1.01)
Territorial power-sharing institutions	0.006***	−5.09	2.39*	0.87
	(.008)	(1.29)	(1.24)	(0.52)
Military power-sharing policies	0.05***	−3.05	0.42	−0.87
	(0.03)	(0.58)	(0.31)	(0.74)
Economic power-sharing policies	1.58	0.46	2.06	0.72
	(2.14)	(1.36)	(0.98)	(0.48)
Third-party enforcer	0.02**	−3.71	19.25**	2.96
	(0.04)	(1.53)	(19.64)	(1.02)
Conflict duration[a]	0.19***	−1.66	3.76**	1.32
	(0.09)	(0.49)	(1.87)	(0.50)
Conflict intensity[b]	3.26**	1.18	0.55	−0.60
	(1.69)	(0.52)	(0.27)	(0.50)
Stakes of the conflict	18.58***	2.92	0.92	−0.08
	(12.72)	(0.69)	(0.58)	(0.63)
Previous regime type	0.001***	−6.84	1.46	0.38
	(0.001)	(1.20)	(1.96)	(1.35)
International system structure	3.51	1.26	0.88	−0.13
	(2.06)	(0.59)	(0.38)	(0.43)
Subjects (failures)	38 (12)		38 (18)	
Months at risk	1,621		1,077	
Wald χ^2	100.54		32.52	
Probability > χ^2	0.0000		0.0003	
Log-likelihood	−23.37		−45.63	

Note: All tests are two-tailed. Values in parentheses are robust standard errors.

[a] Ratio of hazard rate to base hazard rate for Duration of Peace is 86.30 (when value set to minimum) and 0.25 (when value set to maximum). For Time to Transition Election these ratios are, respectively, 0.03 and 18.90.

[b] Ratio of hazard rate to base hazard rate for Duration of Peace is 0.02 (when value set to minimum) and 52.66 (when value set to maximum). For Time to Transition Election these values are, respectively, 7.35 and 0.14.

Significance: *** $p < .01$, ** $p < .05$, * $p < .10$.

When employing the dependent variable of settlement stability, the Cox proportional hazards model identifies two power-sharing provisions that increase the likelihood that domestic peace will endure through the initiation phase. We find that agreements that include provisions for establishing territorial or military power sharing tend to increase the length of time that the parties remain at peace. As indicated by the hazard rate statistics listed in the second column of Table 4.3, provisions for establishing territorial power-sharing institutions decrease the likelihood of settlement failure by 99 percent and specifying policies for military power sharing in an agreement decreases the risk of a return to civil war by 95 percent.[21]

When employing the dependent variable of the time between peace settlement and national elections, we find that only establishing institutions for territorial power sharing has the effect of increasing the likelihood of holding timely elections. As indicated by the hazard rate listed in the fourth column of Table 4.3, settlements establishing some form of territorial autonomy increase the likelihood of elections within five years by 139 percent. Over the course of the five-year period we examine, transition elections tend to be held more quickly in those instances in which institutions providing for territorial autonomy have been included as part of a settlement.

Interpretation of Results

Taken as a whole, our results suggest that some power-sharing provisions have a role to play in the initial stages of the process of post–civil war reconciliation. Provisions for territorial and military power sharing assist in creating conditions to strengthen the peace; provisions for territorial autonomy encourage the holding of timely transition elections.

One can understand why groups concerned with stability in the initiation phase after a civil war would find military and territorial power sharing more reassuring than other forms of power sharing. The ability of actors who control the government to inflict physical harm on others in the event of a return to war is most likely to be limited if the peace settlement checks or limits the central government's coercive force and provides collectivities with a territory over which they exercise some form of control. Settlements that provide for territorial and military power sharing promise to leave groups in control of defensible territory and provide them with a check on the use of the central government's coercive forces. The agreement of all parties to provisions that promise these protections sends a costly signal that they recognize the need of the other side to be secure from coercion at the hands of the government during the initiation phase. Whether this commitment is

21. The probability for the indicator reflecting territorial power sharing is based on the estimated hazard rate. This value deviates .994 from the baseline of one indicating that the presence of such a provision decreases the risk of settlement failure by 99.4 percent. We employ a different means to calculate the substantive impact of the two continuous variables, *conflict duration* and *conflict intensity*, that we use in the model. The footnote of Table 4.3 reports the ratio between the hazard rates with the variable in question increased or decreased from its mean value (as indicated in column four) and the "base" hazard rate for which the continuous variables are held at their mean. Following Werner (1999, 924), "[i]f the variable has no substantive effect, the ratio will equal 1.0 because the 'revised' hazard rate and the 'base' hazard rate are the same. The deviation of the ratio from 1.0 thus indicates the variable's substantive effect."

implemented through the institutions, policies, and practices promised in the peace settlement or through some other, subsequently devised arrangement, the commitment sets the transition process in the right direction.

A further striking aspect of these results is the absence of statistically significant findings related to provisions for the sharing of central political power among former adversaries. Conventional understandings of power sharing often emphasize or focus solely on the distribution of offices and influence within the political center. Our results suggest that this particular power-sharing mechanism, at least in isolation, does not have demonstrated ability to assist in the transition from anarchic civil war to a peaceful and functioning democratic polity.[22] It is only when expanding the definition of power sharing to include mechanisms beyond provisions emphasizing the distribution of influence at the political center that such accommodations prove important.

It is also notable that the economic power-sharing provision does not demonstrate an ability to assist in maintaining peace or holding elections following civil war. This finding is particularly surprising in light of recent research suggesting that civil wars are often initiated over the issue of gaining control of a state's natural resources. Such a perspective emphasizes that domestic wars are more frequently fought over issues of "greed" rather than "grievance."[23] Our results suggest that, even if economic interests serve as an initial motivation for the conflict, former combatants tend to view economic concerns as secondary in importance to establishing institutions and policies that they perceive to have a more immediate impact on providing for the security of their group.

Conclusion

Power-sharing provisions in peace settlements have a demonstrated ability to provide a sense of security to former combatants facing the immediate prospect of working together peacefully after a severe conflict such as a civil war. In particular, our research indicates that both military and territorial power sharing have a positive role to play in fostering a postwar peace. These provisions have the demonstrated capacity to set the stage for the period of transition by enhancing a sense of confidence among former enemies that their interests will not be jeopardized in the context of the postwar state. This in turn increases the likelihood that peace will endure and democratic practices will be embraced.

22. For a discussion of the potential for multiple power-sharing mechanisms to be mutually reinforcing, see Hartzell and Hoddie 2003.

23. See, for example, Mats R. Berdal and David Malone 2000 and Paul Collier and Anke Hoeffler 2002.

Appendix: Coding Rules

Central power sharing. Score as "1" if the civil war settlement includes any of the following provisions: (a) electoral proportional representation (settlement or discussion of settlement must specify its use, it is not a reversion to previous use of proportional representation); (b) administrative proportional representation (i.e., appointment of representatives of warring groups to courts, civil service, foreign service, and commissions); (c) executive proportional representation (i.e., appointment of representatives of warring groups to ministerial, subministerial, and cabinet positions).

Territorial power sharing. Score as "1" if the civil war settlement calls for either of the following: (a) allowing one (or more) subunits of the country to exercise control over local issues, without extending those powers to other subunits of the country; (b) providing that all substate units have similar internal governance structures and wield powers separate from those possessed by the central government.

Military power sharing. Score as "1" if the civil war settlement includes any of the following provisions: (a) creation of state's security forces (i.e., army, navy, air force, state militia) through the integration of former antagonists' armed forces on the basis of a formula representative of the size of the armed groups; (b) creation of state's security forces (i.e., army, navy, air force, state militia) on the basis of equal numbers of troops drawn from the antagonists' armed forces, (c) appointment of members of armed faction(s) who do not dominate the state, or of weaker armed factions, to key leadership positions (i.e., general, commander, director, defense minister) in the state's security forces; (d) allow antagonists to remain armed (i.e., settlement does not specify any disarmament measures); (e) allow antagonists to retain their own armed forces.

Economic power sharing. Score as "1" if the civil war settlement includes either of the following provisions: (a) specification of a pattern of resource distribution by the state to disadvantaged groups, either on the basis of a percentage of resources to be allocated to those groups or on a financial amount to be directed to those groups; (b) specification of policies to be used to direct economic assets toward groups on the basis of their group membership or geographic location (i.e., policies associated with provision of land; control or administration of natural resources; scholarships and admissions to schools, training centers, colleges; creation and/or set-asides of jobs, promotions; transfer of factories, capital, and credit; provision or creation of licenses to operate commercial enterprises and to practice professions or trades).

Third-party enforcer. Score as "1" if an outside power sends troops to separate or protect civil war antagonists from one another or at least promises to do so if the security situation calls for such action. If troops are neither sent nor such promises are made, score as "0." The annual Yearbook of the Stockholm International Peace Research Institute (SIPRI), *Keesing's Contemporary Archives*, the texts of the negotiated settlements, tables in Chantal de Jonge Oudraat (1996), and case study material were used to code this variable.

Conflict duration. The duration of the conflict is based on the length of the conflict in months. This number was then logged. In the majority of the cases, the month and year the conflict started and ended is based on those identified in the Correlates of War (COW) civil war database. Where there were questions regarding the dates identified in the COW database or the conflicts were too recent to have been included in that database, *Keesing's Contemporary Archives* and case study material were used to identify the start and end dates of the conflict.

Conflict intensity. The number, in thousands, of war-related deaths was divided by the duration of the conflict in months (from the sources indicated in the previous variable). This number was then logged. In the majority of the cases, the number of civil war deaths was drawn from the COW civil war database. These data were checked against those of Sivard (1996). Where discrepancies between the two sources existed, the annual *SIPRI Yearbook* was consulted and case study material was used.

Stakes of the conflict. Score as "1" if the primary issue at stake in the conflict was ethnic, religious, racial, or linguistic; score "0" otherwise. In the majority of the cases, the coding for the conflict issue was based on Licklider's (1995) coding of the variable. In those cases in which the settlements post-date Licklider's study or case study material raised questions regarding Licklider's coding of the material, statements by the parties to the conflict regarding the issues they believed to be at stake in the conflict were drawn on, as well as consulting Wallensteen and Sollenberg (1997), *SIPRI Yearbook* summaries of civil war cases, and case study materials.

Previous regime type. Score "1" if the country had an authoritarian regime in place prior to the outbreak of the civil war and "2" if the regime was either semi-democratic or democratic. Coding for this variable was based on Mark Gasiorowski (1996) and, for those conflicts ending after 1992, Freedom House's "Annual Survey of Freedom Country Scores" (2000). Because there were no cases in which the previous regime type was "democratic," we collapsed this category together with "semi-democratic."

Although we did not use the Polity III data set because of a number of missing data entries, we should note that the correlation between Gasiorowski's measure of democracy and Polity III's measure of democracy is .85 while the correlation between Polity III and the political rights element of the Freedom House measure is .92.

System structure. Score "0" if the settlement was concluded during the Cold War years from 1945 to 1989 and "1" if the settlement was concluded in the post–Cold War period from 1990 onward.

PART II

Institutional Choices for Peacemaking and Democracy

5

Territorial Decentralization and Civil War Settlements

David A. Lake and Donald Rothchild

Political decentralization along territorial lines is emerging as a key element in contemporary civil war settlements. In Bosnia, the Dayton Agreement rests on a new federal structure to build the peace. In Kosovo, the Western powers used force against Serbia ostensibly to restore regional autonomy for the ethnic Albanians. In the Philippines, state leaders experimented with territorial autonomy as a solution to the decades-old conflict in Mindanao. And in Ethiopia, the Peoples' Revolutionary Democratic Front established an ethnically based federal structure after assuming power from the hegemonic regime of Mengistu Haile Mariam. Territorial decentralization now appears to be an institution of first resort for domestic or international actors in their attempts to bring peace to war-torn societies.[1]

Territorial decentralization is supported by peacemakers because it recognizes the political and spatial realities on the ground, especially the division of territory won on the battlefield and at the negotiating table. By granting each group a state-within-a-state, peacemakers aim to mitigate fears of political exploitation and intergroup violence and, at least in part, to

We are grateful to Philip G. Roeder, the other participants in this project, and an anonymous reader for comments on this chapter.

1. *Territorial decentralization* allocates authority over policy domains to different subnational governmental entities that are, themselves, defined in terms of territory, with municipalities, provinces, and the central government each responsible for different services and policy domains. As mechanisms of representation, these layers also structure the aggregation of interests, defining how lower-level political communities are represented at the political center. We prefer the term territorial decentralization to the more common word "federalism" because it is more generic. *Federalism* is a de jure form of territorial decentralization explicitly organized into a fixed number of levels of government, whereas territorial decentralization can be de facto and vary in the number of levels by policy area. On federalism and decentralization more generally as intermediate forms of political hierarchy, see Elazar 1998, Lake 2003, Rector 2003, and Riker 1964.

satisfy local demands for cultural and religious autonomy. At the same time, decentralization maintains existing external borders, and thus does not challenge the principle of territorial integrity central to contemporary notions of sovereignty (see Zacher 2001). In short, decentralization is believed to address the political insecurities and desire for self-determination that lead to conflict while respecting the principle that, if at all possible, sovereignty should not be dismantled.

We argue in this chapter that, in the short run, territorial decentralization can be a valuable tool in the transition to peace because it can serve as a costly signal of moderation by the political majority and, when offered, can help allay minority fears about its likely treatment in the future.[2] The evidence presented by Matthew Hoddie and Caroline Hartzell in Chapter 4 underscores this role in the negotiation of peace settlements. Yet it is not decentralization itself that mitigates conflict, we stress, but the *offer of decentralization* that reveals information about the moderate intentions of the majority.

More generally, we question the longer-term viability of this short-term solution—particularly once the primary task has shifted from initiating a transition from civil war to consolidating the peace. On the one hand, there are few successful cases of actual implementation of territorial decentralization after civil wars to substantiate the high hopes of contemporary proponents. Although Hoddie and Hartzell find several instances of provisions for territorial power sharing in peace settlements, we find no evidence of successful institutionalization of these provisions in any postwar constitutional order. Recent experiments should be regarded as just that—experiments with unknown outcomes. On the other hand, drawing on evidence from most nearly comparable cases, we expect that the conditions for successful territorial decentralization are extremely limited, casting doubt on the likely future of present efforts. As peace settlements are implemented over an extended time horizon, the trend is likely to be toward greater political centralization, even in cases where some form of decentralization is initially used as a costly signal of majority intent. Peace consolidates majority power, and, over time, this group (or coalition of groups) uses its political strength to centralize state authority and resources into its own hands. Alternatively, the political minority group, fearing the consequences of centralization, may continue to push for full independence, and the possibility of ongoing or renewed violence persists. In this trajectory, stability returns only with secession and separation. In this event, conflict is likely to become internationalized. Territorial decentralization is likely to prove a stable and effective

2. The terms "majority" and "minority" are used loosely to refer not to absolute numbers of individuals in each group but, respectively, to groups that hold power at the political center and those that do not.

long-term solution only under an extraordinary conjunction of conditions—where multiple groups cohabit the same national space; none can achieve decisive control over the state; each is led by moderates willing to accept the desires of others for cultural, linguistic, and religious autonomy; and democracy is robust. These conditions are unlikely to be present at the end of contemporary civil wars. We cannot point to any case of clear-cut success in the years since 1945, demonstrating just how rare is successful territorial decentralization after a major civil war.

External actors can play either a positive or negative role in promoting territorial decentralization. Whether they be states, international organizations, or private actors, advocates of decentralization can promote peace settlements only when a mutually hurting stalemate creates incentives to negotiate and when the warring parties are prepared to divide state power on an autonomous basis. In this case, external advocates reinforce the decentralization of power likely to be agreed on by the parties themselves. Here, sanctions against violators of agreements or the deployment of external peacekeepers can facilitate political stability, but they cannot create stable decentralization by themselves. Conversely, for reasons we develop, placing too much pressure on groups to decentralize can be counterproductive. When the warring factions perceive themselves as relatively stronger, and each retains some hope of success on the battlefield, insisting on political decentralization is likely to promote continued violence. The stronger party, with greater prospects of victory, will welcome external efforts to preserve the shell of the unified state—one that they are likely to organize and control with time. Here, the external advocates of peace and political decentralization become, perhaps unwittingly, the de facto allies of the more powerful actor group—but one that could not, nonetheless, achieve mastery of a unified state on its own. The weaker party, with fewer prospects of victory but greater fears of exploitation over time, will be spurred on to new and heightened efforts in the conflict, either to extract a better deal at the negotiating table (i.e., even greater autonomy, more effective safeguards against centralization, a preferred formula for allocating resources, and so forth) or to obtain complete independence. Under these circumstances, the external advocates of decentralization may further an enduring partition or, if conflict becomes endemic, act against the long run interests of the very parties (commonly minorities) they are ostensibly trying to help.

Throughout this chapter the dependent variable is the success—that is, adoption and durability—of territorial decentralization as an institutional arrangement that is increasingly being pressed on states seeking to initiate a transition from civil war to peace. This chapter proceeds in four main steps. First, we examine the historical record since 1945. Since we find no cases of territorial decentralization following a civil war, we turn to states "born decentralized" as most nearly comparable cases and identify two standard trajectories for the subsequent development of these experiments with territorial decentralization in ethnically divided societies—the first toward greater centralization, the second toward disintegration. Second, we explain why parties to a civil war might agree to decentralization at the end of a civil war by examining both the short-term role of decentralization in transitions to peace and the longer-term benefits of decentralization in creating more efficient government. Third, we explore three political dilemmas of institution-building in divided or postconflict countries and explain why decentralization in ethnically divided societies tends to be an unstable arrangement that typically ends in either centralization or fragmentation. Fourth, we analyze the implications of our arguments for current policy.

The Fate of Territorial Decentralization

To focus our discussion and motivate the inquiry in the rest of this chapter, we begin with two striking empirical regularities. First, since 1945, warring factions have never realized full political decentralization along territorial lines as part of a civil war settlement. There have been approximately 55 civil wars since 1945 that have reached a successful settlement, either by the decisive victory of one side over the other or through a negotiated agreement. As Table 5.1 shows, in no case has full territorial decentralization been implemented with the peace.

There have been nine instances of partial or semi-decentralized institutions being constructed after a war, but the majority of these cases come from the late 1980s or early 1990s and it may still be too early to assess their long-term effects. There is also the case of Bosnia, excluded from the table because it is not covered in the sources from which we draw the data. Significantly, its new federal institutions were imposed from outside, reflecting more the current emphasis of the international community on territorial decentralization rather than any belief among the warring factions that federalism as a system of shared power is likely to produce a viable state over the long run.

The absence of any implemented decentralization accord should make all of us skeptical of federalism as a panacea for implementing durable peace after civil wars. There is no basis in the historical record to judge whether territorial decentralization is a possible foundation on which to build stable post–civil war relations. Indeed, the absence of attempts to create full territorial decentralization after civil wars suggests that the warring parties may know something that policy enthusiasts in the West have yet to learn.

Second, territorial decentralization is a fragile political institution that, even when tried outside a civil war, is often quickly abandoned by dominant political groups and regions in favor of centralization and by weaker political groups and regions in favor of full political autonomy or secession. Most

Table 5.1. Territorial decentralization and civil war outcomes (cases exclude civil wars still unresolved as of December 31, 1999)

Centralized states	Semi-centralized states	Decentralized states
Greece (1944–49)	Argentina (1955)	None
China (1946–50)	Sudan (1963–72)	
Paraguay (1947)	Nigeria (1967–70)[g]	
Yemen Arab Rep. (1948)	Cambodia (1979–91)[h]	
Costa Rica (1948)	Mozambique (1979–92)[i]	
Colombia (1948–62)	India (1985–93)[j]	
Burma (1948–51)	Sri Lanka (1987–89)[k]	
Indonesia (1950)	Burundi (1988)[l]	
Philippines (1950–52)	Tajikistan (1992–94)[m]	
Bolivia (1952)		
Indonesia (1953)		
Guatemala (1954)		
Indonesia (1956–60)		
Lebanon (1958)		
Cuba (1958–59)		
Iraq (1959)		
Vietnam (1960–65)		
Congo (1960–65)		
Laos (1960–73)		
Algeria (1962–63)		
Yemen Arab Rep. (1962–69)		
Rwanda (1963–64)		
Dominican Rep. (1965)		
Uganda (1966)[a]		
Guatemala (1966–96)		
China (1967–68)[b]		
Burma (1968–80)		
Cambodia (1970–75)[c]		
Jordan (1970)		
Pakistan (1971)[d]		
Sri Lanka (1971)		
Burundi (1972)		
Zimbabwe (1972–79)		
Pakistan (1973–77)		
Lebanon (1975–90)		
Iran (1978–79)		
Nicaragua (1978–79)		
El Salvador (1979–92)		
Chad (1980–88)		
Uganda (1980–88)		
Iran (1981–82)		
Nicaragua (1982–90)[e]		
South Yemen (1986)		
Liberia (1989–94)		
Rwanda (1990–94)[f]		

Sources and definitions: Civil wars are from Walter 2002. Countries classed by degree of centralization according to six variables. *Centralization*, defined by degree of decisionmaking authority vested in local or regional governments, is from Polity III data set and ranges from zero to two (Gurr 1989; Jaggers and Gurr 1995). All others from Database of Political Institutions (as described in Beck et al, n.d.), and take the form of questions: *Auton* = "Are there autonomous regions?" (0,1); *Muni* = "Are the municipal governments locally elected? (0–2); *State* = "Are the state/province governments locally

Table 5.1. *Continued for Notes*

elected? (0–2); *Author* = "Do subnational governments have extensive taxing, spending, or regulatory authority?" (0,1); *Stconst* = "Are the constituencies of the senators the states/provinces? (0,1).

Note: Data missing for centralization for Romania (1989), Croatia (1991–92), and Bosnia (1992–95).

[a] Uganda was a decentralized state prior to the civil war.

[b] When DPI begins its series in 1975, auton = 1, muni = 2, state = 2; centralization = 0 from 1968.

[c] Centralization and auton = 0, when coding began in 1980, muni and state = 1.

[d] Pakistan was decentralized prior to the war.

[e] Centralization, auton, muni, state = 0 before 1995, auton = 1, muni = 2 beginning in 1995.

[f] Muni = 1 in 1995, but auton and state = 0.

[g] Nigeria was decentralized or semidecentralized before the war, semidecentralized immediately afterward and became decentralized in 1977.

[h] Muni and state = 1, centralization and auton = 0.

[i] Muni = 1, state = 1, fed, auton and author = 0.

[j] State, author, stconst = 1, auton = 0, centralization and muni are missing.

[k] Muni = 2 and state = 2, centralization and auton = 0.

[l] Muni = 2 and state = 1, centralization and auton = 0.

[m] Auton = 1, other variables missing.

commonly, central governments quickly increase their power at the expense of regions and groups within the state. Less frequently, central governments unravel, ultimately leading to the disintegration of the state and the fracturing of the national territory into several sovereign pieces—each of which then tries, when possible, to centralize political authority within its own domain.

Given the absence of cases of territorial decentralization after civil wars, it is difficult for us to validate some of our positive claims below on the conditions for successful decentralization. The determinants of success cannot be known without significant achievements to draw on. As a result, we turn to the most nearly comparable cases of new states and ethnically divided states. Even in the absence of a civil war, however, we find territorial decentralization to be a fleeting institution.

Table 5.2 lists all states that either possessed decentralized institutions as of 1815 or adopted such institutions at the time they were first created. Presumably, there was something about the size of the country, the political interests at stake, the ethnic diversity, or the nature of other political institutions that made territorial decentralization attractive to the founders of these states. One can infer, therefore, that decentralization would be especially likely to succeed in these cases. Of the countries that were "born" decentralized, only half—including Australia, Czechoslovakia, India, and the United States—maintained this form for more than 20 years. For the others, decentralization proved ephemeral. Argentina, Nigeria, Pakistan, Venezuela, and other early decentralizers either moved steadily toward a more centralized posture or cycled from one form to the other and back again. Only one country, Malaysia, successfully moved from the semi-decentralized (at time

Table 5.2. States "born" decentralized

Stable	
Decentralized	**Semi-Decentralized**
Australia (1901–)	*Azerbaijan (1991–)*
Belgium (1831–)	*Botswana (1966–)*
Canada (1867–)	*Georgia (1991–)*
Czechoslovakia (1948–1991)	*Lesotho (1966–)*
Germany (1871–1945)	
Germany, Federal Republic (1949–)	
India (1950–)	
Papua New Guinea (1976–)	
Switzerland (1848–)	
United Arab Emirates (1971–)	
United States (1815–)	
Unstable	
	Direction of Change
Afghanistan (1920–1924)	Decentralized to Centralized
Argentina (1825–1829)	Decentralized to Centralized
Cameroon (1961–1971)	Decentralized to Semi-Decentralized (1962) Semi-Decentralized to Centralized
Cyprus (1960–1973)	Decentralized to Centralized
Libya (1952–1963)	Decentralized to Centralized
Malaysia (1957–1963)	Semi-Decentralized to Decentralized
Mexico (1822–1833, 1919–)	Decentralized to Centralized Centralized to Decentralized
Mongolia (1924–1928)	Semi-Decentralized to Centralized
Nigeria (1960–1993)	Decentralized to Semi-Decentralized (1966) Semi-Decentralized to Decentralized (1979) Decentralized to Semi-Decentralized (1984) Semi-Decentralized to Centralized
Pakistan (1947–1970)	Decentralized to Centralized
Sierra Leone (1961–)	Decentralized to Semi-Decentralized (1970)
Somalia (1960–)	Decentralized to Semi-Decentralized (1969)
Thailand (1815–1867)	Semi-Decentralized to Centralized
Turkey (1815–1919)	Decentralized to Centralized
Uganda (1962–1965)	Decentralized to Centralized
Venezuela (1830–1869, 1961–)	Decentralized to Semi-Decentralized (1858) Semi-Decentralized to Centralized Centralized to Decentralized

Source: As measured by the Centralization variable in the Polity III data set; see Gurr 1989 and Jaggers and Gurr 1995.

Note: Italics indicate semi-decentralized.

of its "birth") to the decentralized category. Even under what might be regarded as the most conducive circumstances, territorial decentralization proves to be unstable.

Decentralization also moves in the opposite direction, not toward greater centralization but unraveling into separation and secession. Table 5.3 iden-

Table 5.3. Decentralization and secessionism

Decentralized state with strong secessionism	New state that emerged (year of independence)	New state regime: decentralized or centralized?
Czechoslovakia	Czech Republic (1992)	Centralized
	Slovakia (1992)	Centralized
Ethiopia	Eritrea (1993)	Centralized
Indonesia	East Timor (1999)	Centralized
Malaysia	Singapore (1965)	Centralized
Pakistan	Bangladesh (1971)	Centralized
Yugoslavia	Bosnia and Herzegovina (1991)	Decentralized
	Croatia (1991)	Centralized
	Macedonia (1991)	Centralized
	Slovenia (1991)	Centralized
	Serbia and Montenegro (1991)	Decentralized
USSR / Soviet Union	Armenia (1991)	Centralized
	Azerbaijan (1991)	Centralized
	Belarus (1991)	Centralized
	Estonia (1991)	Centralized
	Georgia (1991)	Semi-decentralized
	Kazakhstan (1991)	Centralized
	Kyrgyzstan (1991)	Centralized
	Latvia (1991)	Centralized
	Lithuania (1991)	Centralized
	Moldova (1991)	Centralized
	Russian Federation (1991)	Decentralized
	Tajikistan (1991)	Centralized
	Turkmenistan (1991)	Centralized
	Ukraine (1991)	Centralized
	Uzbekistan (1991)	Centralized

Sources: Gurr 1989; Jaggers and Gurr 1995; Economist Intelligence Unit 2001; Cicciomessere 2001; United States Central Intelligence Agency 2000; Atlapedia Online 2001.

tifies decentralized states with strong secessionist movements that subsequently disintegrated. This is not a full sample of all decentralized states, nor does it compare secessionism in decentralized and centralized systems. As a result, we cannot evaluate the propensity of decentralized states to disintegrate relative to centralized states. But the table does illustrate clearly the second trajectory. Decentralized states that do not consolidate tend to disintegrate into multiple states, which are—in a way consistent with our first trajectory—then more unified.

Although the empirical regularities are striking, specific cases illustrate the two trajectories more concretely. South Africa has followed the first and more well-tread path of increasing centralization. In the transition to majority rule, African National Congress (ANC) negotiators made concessions on the powers of the provincial authorities to secure minority (Inkatha Freedom Party [IFP] and Afrikaner Volksfront) support for the 1993 draft constitution. Legislative and executive authorities were established in the nine provinces and, within the limits set by the central legislature, given power to levy taxes and surcharges. Although the central government had overriding legal competence and financial capacity, the provincial legislatures were nonetheless vested with the authority to make laws for their provinces in such fields as agriculture, health services, housing, public transport, roads, tourism, and traditional authorities. The precise responsibilities of the provincial assemblies were left over until after the transfer of power and were to be determined by an elected, majority government. This procedure opened up the possibility of future controversy on this issue. At that time, ANC negotiators did hold out an olive branch to their opponents, indicating that they were prepared to negotiate over additional powers and increased representation in the central legislature (Rothchild 1997, 56–57).

With the move to majority government, the ANC, concerned mainly with responding to the legitimate claims of its constituents for greater economic and political opportunities, played down the issues of full federalism and minority safeguards. Although a number of responsibilities were transferred to the provincial authorities, the central government maintained control through its dominant position in the areas of taxation and grant disbursement. Inkatha leader Chief Mangosuthu Buthelezi, who headed the government in KwaZulu-Natal, recognized the trend toward centralization and therefore insisted that the final constitution give the provincial governments "significant powers" (*Africa Research Bulletin*, April 1–30,1995, 11822). Some indication of what he meant by this emerged several months later, when the hard-line IFP members at a constitutional affairs committee called for exclusive powers over all constitutional, legislative, judicial, police, and financial matters in the province and for the creation of a provincial army, "with the right to refuse intervention in the province by the South African National Defense Force" (*Africa Research Bulletin*, September 1–30, 1995, 11987). The dispute was ultimately brought before the Constitutional Court in September 1996. In a separate ruling on this matter, the Court refused to approve the provincial constitution drawn up by the KwaZulu-Natal legislature, contending that it far exceeded the powers that the provincial legislature could rightfully claim (*Africa Research Bulletin*, September 1–30, 1996, 12397). Buthelezi continued to fight a rearguard action, threatening to call for international mediation on the issue; however, the Constitutional Assembly approved the final constitution and the trajectory toward centralization became clear for all to see.

This same pattern of increasing centralization is found throughout the developing world. In Ghana and Kenya at the time that independence approached, for example, the dominant parties reluctantly agreed to quasi-federal compromises in an effort to allay minority misgivings and to smooth the way to decolonization. Then, with independence in hand, they quickly dismantled the concessions on regional autonomy and centralized political control over their societies (Rothchild and Curry 1978). In fact, there have been precious few examples of successful decentralization since World War II; most countries seem unable to defy the seemingly inexorable forces pushing them toward greater centralization.[3] Certainly Indian, Nigerian, and Ethiopian federalism stand out as exceptions in the developing world, but it is important to stress that these are still relatively centralized forms of government that are marked by considerable central-state control over revenue extraction and allocation. The successes of Nigeria and Ethiopia in maintaining federalism, moreover, do not conceal the same tendencies seen elsewhere toward the aggregation of power (particularly in regard to fiscal politics) by the political center (Suberu 2001, 44, 56; Keller and Smith, chap. 11). In India, under the Congress party, the highly circumscribed autonomy granted to the subunits—often termed "quasi-federalism" (Verney 1995)—was whittled down by constitutional interpretations and political practices.

Illustrating the second trajectory, a territorially decentralized Yugoslavia under intense ethnonationalist pressures was unable to make the transition to a united, democratic state and splintered into pieces after 1989. Led by a former communist ruler, Josip Broz Tito, this state was federal in form but unitary in practice. Under the 1974 constitution, the state devolved limited political powers to the six republics and two autonomous provinces. Interregional conflicts took place largely behind the scenes, especially at the central cabinet level where representatives of the main nationality groups met behind closed doors to advance their interests and those of their constituents. "The result of this *de facto* confederalisation was a weakening of central federal power" (Vejvoda 1996, 15).

This federal-type relationship survived as long as Tito managed the hegemonic exchange relationship (Rothchild 1986). With his death in 1980, however, the centrifugal forces at work increased and the hold of the center weakened noticeably. As the republics became more and more identified with their heartland nationality group and their administrations and party organizations gained separate ethnoregional identities, the glue uniting Yugoslavia cracked. Assisted by international recognition, the leaders of the separate republics moved in the early 1990s to assert their political autonomy and independence. Elections at the republic level facilitated this process of separation, bringing strong and determined leaders to power who emphasized the interests of their republics at the expense of the Yugoslav federation (Cohen 1995, 163).

National and regional pressures also triumphed over federal ties in the former Soviet Union. In an effort to restructure the USSR in the 1988 to 1991 period, Mikhail Gorbachev, then secretary-general of the Communist party, initiated a series of reforms that devolved greater powers to the fifteen

3. On the generally pessimistic prospects for decentralization, see Mawhood 1984.

union republics. This effort at political liberalization provided an opening for new nationalist demands for political autonomy. "Insisting that Soviet federalism be reformulated," Gail Lapidus and Edward Walker write (1995, 80), "political elites in the fifteen union republics grew increasingly assertive in their demands for greater autonomy from Moscow and centralized Soviet power." With Gorbachev unable to react to this deteriorating situation in an effective manner, the federation fragmented and the fifteen union republics became sovereign states in 1991. As was the case with Yugoslavia, federal ties proved no match for nationalist and regionalist pressures in the former Soviet Union, although elite responses to state deterioration were to prove less contested and therefore less violent in the breakup of the Soviet Union. What is most revealing in terms of the trajectory set out in this chapter is that the process of disintegration did not stop with the breakup of the Soviet Union. Shortly after the Russian republic declared its sovereignty, various autonomous republics within the Russian Federation, including Tatarstan, Checheno-Ingushetia, North Ossetia, and Tyva, called for a further devolution of sovereign powers and, in some cases, for full independence (Lapidus and Walker 1995, 81–84).

A trajectory of disintegration was also evident in federations in developing countries. Despite apparent success in crafting a structure of ethnic federalism in contemporary Ethiopia, the autonomy left to the provinces under the federal relationship still did not dissuade the Eritreans from using the opportunity of a referendum to go their separate way and become a sovereign state. In post-independence Sudan and Pakistan, leaders at the political center, deeply concerned over their loss of control over events in the periphery, took military action in an effort to strengthen the federations' capacity for governance. In both cases, regionalist leaders resisted these efforts to enhance the influence of the federation and brutal warfare ensued. In Pakistan, the regionalist conflict had greater finality, for the country of Bangladesh seceded and gained international recognition. Within what remained of the Pakistani federation, on the other hand, the trajectory was toward a high degree of central control and Punjabi domination (Ali 1997; Burki 1996; Etienne 1994). Until recently the parties to the ongoing civil war in the Sudan found no formula of accommodation such as a redesigned federation or separate sovereignties (Danforth 2002). Although the Sudan government and the Sudan People's Liberation Movement/Army accepted a framework agreement in 2004, they deadlocked in the following months regarding a comprehensive peace agreement. This impasse is possibly explained by the complexities of the negotiating process, by Northern fears that success in the negotiations with the South might contribute to a further upsurge in autonomy demands in Darfur and other Northern enclaves, and by increasing doubts in the South that the Sudan government would honor its future commitments (*Africa Research Bulletin*, May 1–31, 2004, 15770). In 2005 Northern and Southern negotiators reached a settlement but left the question of Southern self-determination to be decided in a referendum six years later.

Territorial decentralization has never been implemented after a civil war. In new states and ethnically divided societies, in turn, decentralization has been unstable, leading either to centralized power or continued secessionism. Alone and together, these empirical regularities bode poorly for current experiments with territorial decentralization. The federal compromise adopted under the Dayton Agreement in Bosnia is fragile; the Bosnia Serbs, in particular, reject federalism and desire to become part of greater Serbia. After peacekeeping forces withdraw, the Bosnian government must consider either centralizing political authority and asserting control over its disputatious republics or accepting separation. The attempt by the United States and Europe to create regional autonomy within Yugoslavia for Kosovo is also likely to fail. It is unlikely that the dominant ethnic Albanian majority in the province will, at some future date, vote for continued autonomy within Serbia. The choice today is between recentralization of authority under Serbian rule or complete independence for Kosovo. The maintenance of a compromise on regional autonomy over the long term is the least likely outcome of this tragic conflict.

The (Potential) Benefits of Decentralization

Territorial decentralization is not an end in itself but is employed by societies around the globe and recommended for many more because it is viewed as an effective means of sustaining the territorial integrity of the state while permitting minorities greater autonomy over cultural, economic, and social policies of intense concern. Territorial decentralization should benefit both the political majority, who gain from a unified state, and the political minority, who desire greater local control over important issues. These are what we refer to as the long-term benefits of decentralization. In addition, territorial decentralization can in the immediate aftermath of civil war serve as a costly signal of moderation by the majority. In this way, offers of territorial decentralization, if not decentralization itself, can contribute to the acceptance of peace accords. This costly signal is the short-term benefit of decentralization. We take up the long- and short-term benefits in order to pose the quetion: If there are so many potential benefits, why does decentralization so often fail?

Long-Term Benefits

A central building block of our analysis in this chapter is that territorial decentralization is at least as efficient as unitary states—and typically more efficient—in translating the preferences of citizens into effective public policy. It is also at least as efficient—and, again, typically more so—than division into separate sovereign states. "In principle," as Patrick Bolton, Gérard Roland, and Enrico Spolaore (1996, 698) conclude in a survey of the relevant literature, "any decentralization that is achieved with multiple nations could be replicated within a federal state by implementing the desired degree of subsidiarity." In short, anything that a centralized state or multiple individual states can do, decentralization can do equally well if not better. Any rules or interactions that can be constructed within a single, centralized state or between independent states can be duplicated in a decentralized political system, but decentralized systems can produce welfare gains that are impossible in the alternatives. As a result, decentralization is a more efficient mechanism for organizing politics and delivering goods and services that satisfy the needs and wants of citizens.[4]

Decentralization facilitates the efficient production of public goods (such as defense, public education, and clean water) in three ways. First, decentralization allows each good or service to be produced at its optimal scale. Defense from foreign predation, for instance, is typically characterized by large economies of scale: As area increases more rapidly than borders, it is often cheaper (per capita) to defend a larger rather than smaller territory (Bean 1973). Under many circumstances, then, the optimal area in which the good "security" can be produced is relatively large, at least compared to other public goods. Protection against fires, on the other hand, typically possesses small economies of scale: The good "protection" declines rapidly with distance from fire stations. Thus, where national defense appears properly located at the level of the central government, fire safety is most appropriately achieved at the local level (Stevens 1993, 332).[5] There is no reason to assume that all public services are produced best at the same scale by a single political entity with a fixed and limited territory.

Second, decentralization allows for a closer fit between policy and the preferences of citizens for different public goods.[6] A central problem for all governments is that public goods are, in fact, public; that is, a single good is produced that all citizens consume. By disaggregating the single countrywide basket of public services, decentralization permits individuals with heterogeneous preferences to pick and choose from a diverse array the particular services that best suit their needs and brings policy into closer conformity with citizen demands. Often the rationale that underlies the claim to auton-

4. If local autonomy is valued for its own sake, and valued highly enough, decentralization may not be superior. See Rothstein and Hoover 2000.

5. Scale economies can differ for reasons other than distance and area, including the degree of natural monopoly, technology, geography, and more.

6. Our argument here rests on models of public finance inspired by the work of Charles Tiebout (1956). See also Alesina and Spolaore (1997, 2003).

omy by the minority, decentralization can benefit the majority as well if individual preferences are not entirely homogeneous.

Third, decentralization breaks the monopoly power inherent in the state's specialized production of public goods and services. Given their comparative advantage in providing public goods, states acquire the ability to earn rents at the expense of their societies. Democracy is one instrument to regulate this monopoly power (see Lake and Baum 2001). Decentralization and the competition between fiscal jurisdictions this implies is another powerful tool (Qian and Weingast 1997). By creating multiple political entities all producing similar public goods and services (albeit in differing quantities and mixes), citizens create fiscal competition and constrain the monopoly power of their central governments.

In short, territorial decentralization should allow both the dominant political majority and minority to benefit. The majority retains the advantages of an integrated state, gaining from the more efficient production of public goods at their optimal scale and greater competition between levels of government. Minorities, in turn, acquire autonomy over policy areas of intense concern to themselves, even while sharing, perhaps, in the benefits of more efficient government. The resources saved from more efficient government can be used to lower rates of taxation, for additional goods and services, or for redistribution. Decentralization is an institution that, when properly designed, can potentially benefit both political minorities, who can be induced or compensated not to secede from the state, and political majorities, who can expand services, gain countrywide acceptance of state institutions, and possibly even reduce the overall burden of government on themselves. If territorial decentralization fails, therefore, it is not because it lacks value to both the majority and minority, but because of *strategic problems* (see below) that make reaching an effective bargain between groups difficult.

Short-Term Benefits: A Costly Signal of Intent

Territorial decentralization also provides more immediate benefits in post–civil war settings as a costly signal of moderate intent. Central to nearly all civil wars is fundamental uncertainty about the preferences of one or more parties to the conflict.[7] Particularly important, the minority is often uncertain whether the majority will be "moderate" and willing to share power in a spirit of amity and accommodation or "extremist" and seek to impose its authority and political preferences on others. Given that a civil war has occurred, the political minority is more likely to hold the latter belief—and

7. On the role of uncertainty and fear in ethnic conflicts, see Lake and Rothchild (1996, 1998).

the war itself may have done little to moderate the majority or alter this perception. Post–civil war settlements are likely to remain fraught with uncertainty over the intentions of the former combatants. In such a setting, offers of territorial decentralization by the political majority to the minority can have beneficial effects, especially in the short term, even if it remains uncertain that they will endure in the long term.

Territorial decentralization is a costly and possibly effective signal of the majority's political moderation. In South Africa, for example, the African National Congress's willingness to concede a measure of territorial decentralization reassured whites and some more conservative blacks about their ability to influence policy at the subregional level in the future, and therefore acted as an incentive for them to agree to the new contract (Rothchild 1997). By the same logic, the failure of majorities to accede to minority demands for, say, local police powers can signal that the majority is more likely to encroach on their interests and safety in the future. It is not that territorial decentralization safeguards the rights and interests of a minority. Rather, it reveals crucial information about the intent of the majority and how it is likely to rule when it does centralize power into its own hands.

Effective signals require that a moderate sender incur some cost that an extremist sender would not be willing to pay. By accepting this cost, the moderates, in the language of game theory, "separate" themselves from possible extremists. Territorial decentralization can be extremely costly to the otherwise centralizing majority because it enhances the political capabilities of the minority, at least in the short run. Internal autonomy often enhances the organizational capacity of the weaker group and allows legitimate leaders to emerge and gain greater political experience. By recognizing the political dominance of a group within a particular region and giving its leaders a political vehicle through which to strive for greater political power, territorial decentralization allows for the more effective articulation of regional demands, facilitates the development of a regional identity, and—at the extreme—enhances the ability of the group to press for secession. It is perhaps no coincidence that all successful secessions since 1945 have occurred along previously determined internal administrative boundaries (Zacher 2001). The minority can use the greater leverage produced by territorial decentralization to claim greater material benefits for itself, to thwart the centralizing tendency of the dominant majority, or to ensure appropriate safeguards for minority interests. Territorial decentralization thus shifts a degree of political power and influence from the ruling majority to the minority.

This shift in political power, in turn, is exactly the cost that the dominant majority pays by decentralizing authority along territorial lines. The minority is now more influential, and the majority less influential, at the political center. Moderates may be willing to pay this cost to signal their accommodative preferences, but extremists are unlikely to do so willingly.[8] Precisely because it increases the minority's ability to mobilize and exert political influence at the center, territorial decentralization is an offer that extremists intent on dominating the minority will normally be unwilling to make. Thus, by offering territorial decentralization, majorities are able to signal effectively that they are, indeed, moderates. Observing such an offer, therefore, the minority can be more confident that it is, in fact, dealing with a moderate majority.

The true effect of territorial decentralization can be seen best when it is offered willingly and sincerely by majorities in preconflict situations. Devolutions of political authority to subnational units prior to the outbreak of significant political violence, as in India, can help stabilize societies and prevent the outbreak of major internal wars. Even though political authority will typically be recentralized over time, the institutionally specific assets or vested interests in decentralization accumulated during the early years (see the discussion of the governance problem below) may be sufficient to maintain the credibility of the commitments previously extended to the

8. But because it carries such a high cost, the majority may be less willing to offer territorial decentralization than is preferred by many would-be peacemakers. Some signals may be too costly to send, even when moderate majorities are otherwise committed to sustainable peace settlements. As a result, territorial decentralization will be infrequent relative to other means of group accommodation—as the historical record since 1945 attests. Conversely, administrative decentralization along communal lines is less costly and therefore may be a more frequent form of conflict management (Deng and Morrison 2001, 2; Danforth 2002, 29). Through administrative decentralization, the state grants its minority communities special rights to arrange and oversee the cultural, linguistic, and religious affairs of their members. Granting political authority to communal groups strengthens group identity and thereby gives leaders greater power at the political center. Nonetheless, communal decentralization does not create the exit option available to groups under territorial decentralization. Individuals may migrate or flee as refugees, but in the absence of a territorial base, secession is less feasible. As a result, administrative decentralization along communal lines does not shift political power to the minority to the same degree as does territorial decentralization. Extremists bent on nationalist purity or hegemony will oppose communal concessions to other groups, and thus will resist such a decentralization of authority; an extremist majority, therefore, is unlikely to offer communal concessions to others. Moderates, however, are typically not disturbed or threatened by demonstrations of cultural difference, and may, as a result, offer communal concessions. Moderate majorities will pay some political price for this action, once again losing political power at the center; the concession is thus costly and therefore a potentially credible signal of their intent. Nonetheless, the cost to the majority is lower than that for territorial decentralization, and thus communal concessions can be more readily made by moderate groups. This suggests that communal concessions may allow moderate groups to distinguish themselves more frequently from extremists and thereby to demonstrate their accommodationist desires to other groups more successfully. Thus, where territorial concessions are so costly that even moderates are unwilling to pay this price, communal concessions may be sufficiently costly to prevent extremists from attempting to masquerade as moderates but not so costly as to prevent moderates from being able to offer them. At the same time, since communal decentralization is less costly to the majority, it sends a less clear and effective signal of moderation.

minority. More important, however, the offer of decentralization reveals the moderate nature of the political majority, indicating that it is willing to bargain and establish constructive relations with the minority.

Yet it is important not to be misled here. It is not the territorial decentralization itself that contributes to a sustainable peace in the short term, but the costly offer of decentralization that gives the minority greater confidence that it is negotiating and sharing a state with a moderate majority. This is a key attraction of territorial decentralization, and one of the reasons, perhaps, why it is so strongly advocated by scholars, diplomats, and others seeking to bring peace to war-torn areas. In our view, this is the principal contribution that territorial decentralization can make to sustainable peace settlements.

The Instability of Decentralization

Despite its potential benefits for the parties, both long- and short-term, territorial decentralization fails because of at least three intractable bargaining problems that are especially acute in post–civil war settings. Since no states have implemented territorial decentralization after civil wars, our argument and supporting evidence in this section necessarily draws heavily on the experience of territorial decentralization in states that have not undergone a civil war. Nonetheless, we explain why we expect at least as much (and probably more) instability in cases of post–civil war decentralization as we observe in cases of non–civil war decentralization.

The Governance Problem

The *governance problem* emerges when the political rules of the game are insufficiently rooted in—and supported by—the society (Gourevitch 1999). To some extent, this indeterminacy exists in some form in all political systems, but it is particularly severe in the initial phases of constructing a new political system after a civil war. The effect of the governance problem is to make all postconflict political institutions unstable.

There is a potential for institutional instability in all political systems. In any policy space of two (or more) dimensions, there may be no determinant equilibrium. Whenever two issues are on the table for decision, there may not be a stable policy outcome under majority rule. In Richard McKelvey's (1976) influential chaos theorem, alternative majority coalitions may cycle through the entire two-dimensional issue space, with coalition *AB* v. *C* being replaced by *BC* v. *A*, and so on. It is sometimes argued that institutions induce equilibria (Sheplse 1979) or create stable outcomes. This important insight drives much contemporary analysis of political institutions. William Riker (1980), however, demonstrated that if policy is unstable, and institutions are influential in shaping policy, then institutions themselves will fall prey to cycling: The battle over alternative policies will simply shift to a battle over the institutions that shape policy choice.[9]

In most political systems, what keeps institutions from falling into chaos are social investments that are premised on particular institutions—what might be called *institutionally specific assets.* Once individuals expect a particular set of institutions to endure, they begin to make a host of private investment decisions—not only financial but also investments in educational, social and cultural attributes, political associations, norms of political behavior, and so on—on the basis of expected policy outcomes. Anticipating that institutions will produce policies that protect private property, for example, individuals can then safely acquire such property. Or, as David Laitin (1998) has shown, expecting different language practices to emerge on the basis of varying institutions and norms, Russians in the near abroad are reaching different decisions on whether to invest in acquiring the titular language of the new countries in which they are living. Where they make such investments, individuals create a vested interest for themselves in preserving these particular institutions. If enough individuals expect the institutions to endure, the institutionally specific assets that are acquired may be sufficient to solidify the otherwise transient political system. Key here is the expectation of stable political institutions held by a sufficiently large number of individuals. As Laitin again leads us to expect, this is a quintessential tipping game: If enough people expect the institutions to be stable, they are likely to gain predictability.[10]

The governance problem will be found in all nascent political systems—until the accumulation of sufficient "vested interests" locks in a particular set of political institutions. In nascent political systems, crises periodically arise that disturb the equilibrium and make politics "plastic" (Gourevitch 1986). To the extent that subnational groups have more homogeneous preferences over policy than all the citizens of a polity, the governance problem may be easier to solve in smaller states that reflect their preferences (Alesina and Spolaore 1997, 2003). As a result, groups may prefer secession and complete independence over continuing political instability in larger, more heterogeneous states.

The governance problem will also be particularly acute in the aftermath of civil war. Following internal violence, many issues are on the table, ensuring that the actors face a multidimensional policy space. Existing political institutions have often been destroyed, leaving the actors to set rules and policies without a clear script. Cycling through policy and institutions is very

9. For an application of the general cycling problem to federalism, see Filippov, Ordeshook, and Shvetsova 2004.

10. Also see Kuran 1991 and Lohmann 1994.

likely. In turn, many previously acquired assets have been destroyed or depreciated by the conflict; there are fewer vested interests in any political order, and thus lower expectations of future stability. Under these conditions, any set of political institutions that is formed is likely to be highly unstable.

In addition, expectations of the future are colored by hostile political memories and deep distrust between the previously warring factions. Each region or group expects the other to act opportunistically whenever circumstances permit. With fragile—indeed, often pessimistic—expectations of the future, individuals have little incentive to invest in institutionally specific assets.

The conditions that promote instability are, thus, particularly acute in post-conflict situations in ethnically divided societies. This explains why institutional solutions to violent internal conflicts, like territorial decentralization, are so seldom implemented in a meaningful way, and when tried why they so often break down. Postconflict political institutions will be more stable and effective in moderating conflict the fewer the dimensions of policy being contested (e.g., when the conflict is arrayed along a single left-right political dimension), the greater the number of preconflict institutions that are preserved, the less extended the social distance between the adversaries, and the less destructive the conflict (i.e., the fewer assets destroyed or depreciated). In general, however, nearly all postconflict situations are likely to be characterized by some polarization and underlying suspicion and uncertainty.

The Problem of Incomplete Constitutions

All political constitutions, like all contracts, are incompletely specified, but especially so in decentralized political systems at the end of a civil war. Constitutions simply cannot cover all future contingencies that might arise and so must leave to some single authority the power to resolve conflicting interpretations of the constitution. The ultimate authority for determining jurisdictional disputes is typically vested in the central government, inevitably creating a centripetal force in politics.

Although constitutions distribute rights and responsibilities across layers of government, they cannot define appropriate procedures or the division of authority under all conceivable future contingencies. There must therefore be some entity, such as a constitutional court, to resolve disagreements over the rules of politics as conditions evolve and unforeseen contingencies arise. In decentralized systems, multiple authorities may contribute to conflicting interpretations of the rules. As a result, there are distinct advantages to vesting powers of interpretation in a single entity at the political center. Thus, in the United States, the Supreme Court is charged with the ultimate power to interpret the meaning of the federal constitution, including deciding which political units actually possess what rights over what policy issues.

When the center is an explicitly political actor, especially in an authoritarian regime, its interests in aggrandizing its own power are clear: Politicians at the center can best ensure their own political survival by controlling the primary levers of authority and resources, thereby enabling them to satisfy their interests and those of their support groups more easily. Even when the central arbitrator is a judicial actor and less overtly partisan, there are strong incentives for its members to aggrandize the power of the political center. This has been demonstrated most clearly in the centralizing decisions of the U.S. Supreme Court and, most recently, in the centralizing interpretations of the European Court of Justice (see Alter 1998; Garrett, Kelemen, and Schulz 1998; Mattli and Slaughter 1998). Whether politicians or judges are the ultimate arbiters, branches of the central government may be limited by what the other, lower levels of government are willing to accept, and judges may be further constrained by norms of precedence and judicial behavior. Nonetheless, they can be expected to expand the residual rights of the central government much of the time. Consequently, there is a built-in institutional motor that drives states over time toward greater political centralization.[11]

It is the problem of incomplete constitutions that makes groups, especially political minorities that are likely to lose if policy is recentralized, oppose agreements short of complete independence. Knowing that strong centripetal forces are likely to exist, groups seeking autonomy and counting on decentralization to protect them from majorities at the political center will hold out for the guarantee of independence normally ensured only in a sovereign state of their own.

The Transient Majority Problem

In politics, no present majority can bind a future majority. Territorial decentralization offered today can be retracted tomorrow. This is a universal problem of all majority rule institutions, but is likely to be particularly acute in the case of territorial decentralization. As Friedrich (1968) argues, federalism is an ongoing, evolving process, not a static encounter between the leaders of different tiers of government. A political majority at the center can seize authority formerly enjoyed by lower levels of government. In an extreme case, even ultimate rights of secession, such as those provided under the former Soviet and current Ethiopian constitutions, can be revoked by the center. Although in principle the self-enforcing nature of a constitution could be used for either greater decentralization (pressures in Canada or Belgium) or greater centralization (South Africa or Pakistan), in practice

11. On juridical federalism, see Bednar, Eskridge, and Ferejohn 2001, 231–233.

this is generally a one-way process: As the authors of the second U.S. constitution recognized, it is easier to create a single majority at the political center to approve a change in the rules than majorities in a majority of the lower levels to block a proposed change. Thus, even though a majority at the center might be committed to decentralization and willing to pay the cost involved today, this commitment can be—and, if the historical record is any judge, is likely to be—overturned in the long run (see Bednar, Eskridge, and Ferejohn 2001).

Since majorities are transient and decentralization is likely to erode over time, minorities may choose to hold out or continue fighting today for full independence. International recognition of sovereignty is not, of course, a guarantee of continued independence nor an indication that the center is prohibited from intervening in the now "internal" affairs of the new state. But the norm of juridical sovereignty, coupled with the norm that sovereignty should not be eliminated by force, means that it is harder to revise a recognized international border than the sometimes slippery boundary of authority between majority and minority within a state. Knowing that their rights can never be permanently safeguarded within a unified state, minorities may hold out for the more robust guarantee of full independence and sovereignty.

The conditions under which significant measures of territorial decentralization are likely to emerge as a stable solution to the problem of transient majorities are extremely limited. Territorial decentralization is likely to be a credible protection of minority rights and status only when it reflects the true capabilities of the domestic political actors. Three factors matter: (1) the relative capabilities of the regions or groups, (2) the costs of continued or renewed fighting, and (3) the expectations of future treatment. Democracy may also reinforce the credibility of decentralization (Wantchekon and Simon 1998).

When there is a single dominant majority, significant forms of political decentralization will typically fail to promote a durable peace. Decentralization will be rejected by the majority, which does not want to give up politically sensitive powers to subnational units. If imposed from the outside, decentralization is likely to lack legitimacy and, given the strategic interactions of elites, can be expected to evolve relatively rapidly into a centralized system of rule. If the political minority fears a future genocide or other catastrophe under central rule, it may choose to resist and, depending on the costs of continued fighting, hold out for complete independence. In most cases, however, it will simply acquiesce to centralization as the least bad alternative.

Where there are a small number of powerful regions, each of which has some realistic chance of victory and future dominance, the parties will also be wary of decentralization, as was the case with the peace agreements in Sri Lanka (Bose 2002). Fearful of future centralization, each may choose to continue fighting now for dominance or complete independence tomorrow, depending on the costs of war and the probability of success. The greater the likelihood that the opponents will exploit one another upon victory, the stronger are the incentives for each side to reject decentralization and seek full independence. In these circumstances, continued conflict is the most likely outcome.

Territorial decentralization is likely to be most stable and effective when there are multiple regions with numerous crosscutting political cleavages and relatively balanced capabilities. That is, decentralization is most viable when no one region is sufficiently strong that it is likely to achieve dominance. These are, of course, the conditions normally associated with stable pluralist political systems. Here, regions combine and recombine in a domestic balance of power and are naturally checked and balanced. In this case, decentralized political institutions reflect the political equipoise between regions. Decentralization may reinforce this equipoise, but again it is the balance between the regions and not the institutions themselves that lead to stability. Decentralization will emerge naturally in these circumstances for all of the reasons addressed above. It will be more efficient, particularly allowing a closer fit between regional demands and policy, and it will help mitigate fears of future exploitation and violence. Decentralization can, in these circumstances, be a real force for peace because it conforms to the balance of political power between regions.

External Intervention and Implications for Current Policy

As noted, political decentralization along territorial lines is emerging as one of the international community's preferred solutions for dealing with deeply divided societies. Decentralization is believed to respond to the need for both state unity and societal diversity. It is thus seen to contribute to internal state stability while avoiding the potential spread of turmoil and insecurity to the wider region.[12] Not surprisingly, therefore, it is the centerpiece of the Dayton Agreement on Bosnia and featured prominently in the proposed Rambouillet agreement for Kosovo. Throughout the world, constitutions featuring different forms of autonomy arrangements are in effect or under consideration. Thus, constitutional provisions allowing for various degrees of regional autonomy are present in the basic laws of Ethiopia, Nigeria, the United Kingdom, and the Philippines. Moreover, such formulas have been proposed as solutions to the ongoing stalemates or wars in Cyprus, Sri Lanka, and the Sudan.

12. For a provocative treatment of nationalism and the potential of federalism, see Hechter 2000.

Our standard trajectories and our theoretical explanation for the paths outlined above both suggest that territorial decentralization is subject to strong centripetal and centrifugal pulls and therefore often fails over the long run. It has, to be sure, survived since independence in India and Russia. In Nigeria, President Olusegun Obasanjo, calling for "a return to true federalism," has declared that his regime will "redress the imbalance of power between the centre and the grassroots level, ensure devolution of power and reduce marginalisation" (Agbaegbu 1998, 21). However, in most cases, decentralization has failed, quickly giving way to greater centralization or secession.

External actors can facilitate efforts at effective decentralization by pushing regions and groups in the right direction, but stability ultimately depends on what the local actors believe will happen when the outside parties and possibly the peacekeepers leave. It is the credibility of promises made by each group to respect the rights and safety of the others that matters in the end. Unless each is confident of its security, regions and groups may continue fighting or may take up arms again (as in Angola) once the interest of external states wanes and the peacekeepers plan their departure (see Lake and Rothchild 1996, 1998). Stability rests on the domestic conditions facing the parties.

External actors can be most helpful in transition periods. As noted above, the governance problem is solved by the creation of vested interests in a particular political order—the accumulation of specific assets that lock in institutions. This process typically unfolds over a number of years—although since stability depends on anticipated effects, expectations of stability can become a self-fulfilling prophecy even in the short run. External actors can facilitate stability by guaranteeing a particular political order, but this also depends on the expectations of the local actors that the external parties will enforce this guarantee until such time as sufficient vested interests have accumulated. As always, it is not the actions of the external parties today that really matter, but it is expectations of their future behavior that influence political stability in war-torn societies. During these transition periods, external financial and economic assistance can be important. By restarting growth and increasing public and private investment, external aid can accelerate the process of vesting interests in the new political order. The more political actors have at stake in the new regime, the more likely they are to defend it against new or renewed internal challengers.

In encouraging territorial decentralization, however, external pressure can be counterproductive. Decentralization works in part by distinguishing moderates from extremists. If external actors force a majority into making territorial concessions, the information normally conveyed by such an action is lost: If the external pressure is great enough, even extremists might make concessions and therefore the minority cannot infer anything about the intentions of the majority. External actors can cajole and encourage majorities to make territorial concessions, but bludgeoning majorities through force or sanctions to offer concessions they otherwise would not make may undercut their effectiveness (Kuperman 1996). In this case, less external pressure is usually preferable.

In sum, the trajectories toward greater political centralization or disintegration that we see occurring in many countries today gravely complicate the task of fostering a creative balance between conflict and stability in post–civil war contexts. The majority imperative to centralize control augments minority insecurities and consequently undermines a sense of common purpose. Bargaining and reciprocity become increasingly complicated. Although various forms of territorial decentralization have some capacity to moderate conflict after civil wars, there are no reliable safety nets. Peace will likely occur because of a general fatigue with war, the development of a commitment to resolve disputes through bargaining and reciprocity, and the emergence of respect and good will among the parties. Only as such conditions emerge can decentralization gain the ability to structure relations between former adversaries in a constructive direction. The international community does have a role to play in encouraging decentralization, but this policy is only likely to succeed if it reflects real conditions on the ground and is employed with full sensitivity to the message that moderate majorities must convey to their beleaguered minorities.

6

Managing Diversity and Sustaining Democracy: Ethnofederal versus Unitary States in the Postcommunist World

Valerie Bunce and Stephen Watts

As David Lake and Donald Rothchild note in Chapter 5, there are few if any cases of a successful transition from civil war to democracy with federal institutions. This makes it hard to draw conclusions about how the institutional design of the state affects both interethnic relations and the introduction and consolidation of democratic politics. In this chapter, we address this relationship in a different context and draw insights for the dilemma of power sharing. In particular, we compare a group of new states that are ethnically diverse, but that diverge from one another in three ways: the design of the state (unitary versus ethnofederal), relations between majorities and minorities, and the introduction and course of democratic politics.

Background: Democracy and Diversity

The Western historical ideal of one state, one nation is the exception not the rule for new democracies. At the same time, the capacity of new democracies to emulate the Western historical practice of a rationalizing state bent on constructing a homogeneous nation has contracted sharply since the French, for example, carried out their nationalizing mission in the nineteenth century. This is largely because of differences in developmental sequencing. To return to the French case: The modern version of nations and nationalism made its debut after the state was consolidated and both before and on behalf of democracy. By contrast, outside the West (and even in the "south" of the West such as Italy) nationalist consciousness preceded statehood and, indeed, was foundational for state formation. At the same time, the introduction of democracy did not usually follow state building.

Instead, the struggle for democracy often accompanied the establishment of state sovereignty.

One important consequence of these contrasting sequences was that majorities versus minorities in these new states and new democracies have interpreted the Western experience—that is, the idea of the nation-state—in eminently logical but nonetheless diametrically opposed ways. For majorities, the self-serving understanding has often been that each state should have one nation. Thus, with statehood comes the responsibility, quickly seized by representatives of the numerically dominant nation, to homogenize the national community in their own image, a process often characterized as nation building. This is invariably at the cost of alienating minority populations. By contrast, for minorities, the common interpretation of the Western model, and one that is again relatively self-serving, is that each nation should have its own state (Csergo 2000). These competing variations on the Western theme of the nation-state place majorities and minorities on a collision course. They also remind us of a more general point. Since the rise of nations and nationalism, ethnic, religious, and linguistic conflicts usually have been built into the state enterprise. This seems to be the case particularly under two common conditions: when the nations making up the state are geographically concentrated (Horowitz 1985; Bunce 1999b; Saideman et al. 2002), and when democracy and the state are new and simultaneous political projects. The key issue, then, is really one of management; that is, whether under such adverse circumstances compromises can be forged that maintain the integrity of both democracy and the state (see, especially, Karklins 2000).

Two other considerations have contributed to the escalation of interethnic conflict in new democracies and new states.[1] First, states outside the West often lack the administrative capacity to construct single nations within their borders and face considerable resistance from minorities when they pretend otherwise. The irony of the situation is inescapable. Competing national identities weaken new states, at least potentially, yet they often serve as the rationale for governments in power to pursue homogenization of the nation. This is all the more likely to happen when the nationalist movement that led to independence defined the nation in ethnic terms and failed to embrace the full diversity of the public.

Second, the fate of nations, democracy, and the state are closely intertwined. If membership in the nation is contested, then the state is necessarily weakened because the nation serves as the major mechanism by which states extract compliance. Without such compliance, states forfeit the spatial monopoly over authority that the very notion of a state requires (Herbst

1. To streamline the discussion in this chapter, we will use the phrase *interethnic conflict* to refer to all political conflicts that are based on ethnic, linguistic, and/or religious differences.

2000). In addition, weak states—or states that fail to define and defend borders and project authority within those borders—cannot guarantee what democracy requires: civil liberties and political rights, accountable and transparent government, and rule of law, with laws applied consistently across time, space, and circumstances (see Bunce 2001a, 2001b).

What can follow is one of several scenarios. Violence can break out within secessionist regions, given competition among local elites and growing insecurity among local populations not belonging to the dominant regional group. What can also happen is that elites representing the majority can decide to punish minorities through political exclusion and violence, and they can decide, more generally, to use what is simultaneously a crisis of space and authority to suspend the democratic rules of the game. It is far from accidental, then, that in heterogeneous national settings, especially in the early stages of democratization and state building, three problems often go together: weak states, minority rebellions, and democratic breakdown (see Gurr 2000, 83, 151; Hartzell, Hoddie, and Rothchild 2001; Herbst 2000; Rothchild 2002; Saideman et al. 2002; but see Suberu 2001 for a different view based on the Nigerian case).

Often, however, is not always. Some new, multinational democracies have managed to maintain the integrity of the state, promote peaceful resolution of interethnic conflicts, and stay the democratic course. This occurs even when the state is new. What factors, therefore, facilitate the sustainability of democracy and the state, when both are new, populations diverse, and minorities large and geographically concentrated? In short, how can democracy survive and prosper in what are by all accounts unusually hostile political circumstances (see, especially, Karklins 2000)?

The purpose of this chapter is to provide a preliminary answer to this question. We will do so by assessing how the institutional design of the state affects interethnic relations and, with that, the course of democracy. Specifically, we will focus on the effects of one key institutional choice confronting divided societies undergoing democratization—whether the state should be unitary or ethnofederal in form. A *unitary state* has indivisible sovereignty. By contrast, like all federal systems, *ethnofederalism* features (1) territorially defined subunits; (2) dual sovereignty, where the center and the subunits each have their own spheres of responsibility (see Aslund 1999; Dent 1995); and (3) a relationship between the center and the subunits that combines autonomy and coordination, rather than the unitary practice of subordination (Stepan 1999, 2000; MacPherson, 1994). What is distinctive about ethnofederalism, however, is that many, if not all of the subunits are composed of (and understood to represent) geographically concentrated minority communities (see Easterly 2001; Mastny 2000; Simeon and Conway 2000; Stepan 1999, 2000; Verney 1995). To provide some examples of these two options: Israel, Estonia, and Peru, along with virtually all of Latin America, are unitary states, whereas India, the Russian Federation, Spain, Belgium, and Nigeria are ethnofederations.

While most scholars agree that state design is critical (but see Bunce 1997; Easter 1997) they diverge in how they see its relationship to interethnic relations and democracy (see, for example, Bednar, Eskridge, and Ferejohn 2001; Horowitz 1985; Lijphart 1977, 1990b, 1996; MacPherson 1994; Murphy 1995; Roeder 2000, 2001a, 2001b; Saideman 1998; Simeon and Conway 2001; Smith 1995; Stepan 1999, 2000; Weingast 1998; Williams 1995; and Chapter 1 of this volume). On the one hand, it has been argued that ethnofederalism has the benefits of legitimating difference and empowering minority communities. As a result, ethnofederalism is thought to generate trust and provide minorities with a stake in both democracy and the state. In this way, the security dilemma, so common in multiethnic systems, is eased (see Fearon 1998; Posen 1993). At the same time, ethnofederalism provides a reasonable solution to a second problem characteristic of federalist systems: a center bent on expanding its powers and thereby compromising the federalist project. In multiethnic contexts, therefore, ethnofederalism may counter two temptations—of minorities to defect and majorities to dominate (see Bednar, Eskridge, and Ferejohn 2001; Lijphart 1990b; Weingast 1998). For these reasons, scholars have written in relatively favorable terms about ethnofederalism in the Indian, Spanish, South African, and Canadian cases (Bajpai 1997; Corbridge 1995; Gagnon and Laforest 1994; Guibernau 1995; Lijphart 1996; Sen 1999; Stepan 1999).

However, there are equally persuasive arguments against ethnofederalism. The key insight here is that there is a fine line between legitimating difference and undermining commonality (see, especially, Bunce 1999b; Hicks 1978; Karklins 2000; MacPherson 1994; Roeder 2001a, 2000). It is by now the received wisdom that nations are constructed and identities are fluid. By drawing tight linkages among the nation, territory, and political power, ethnofederalism can lock in differences and identities. This can limit interaction and prevent cooperation among communities, given the absence of common identities, political projects, and economic activities (see Varshney 2001). Such arrangements can also give minorities the institutional resources and leadership they need to press for independence—a position all the easier to embrace given the plausible impact of ethnofederalism on group isolation, intergroup distrust, and heightened competition among local elites unable to build careers outside their region and in search, therefore, of local issues they can use to mobilize support and outflank their competitors (see Horowitz 1985; Roeder 2001b). Finally, the center can weaken, which encourages local leaders to engage in ethnic outbidding to expand their power and central-level leaders, representing the majority nation and resentful of the gap between large numbers and limited representation, to expand their power by using violence against minorities and suspending the democratic experiment (see, especially, Bunce 1999b on the Yugoslav case).

At the very least, then, ethnofederalism can be understood as a way station to, if not the cause of, a decline in the quality of democratic politics and the territorial integrity of the state. This line of argument has been used, for example, to critique ethnofederalism in Belgium and Canada (see Martiniello 1995, 1998; Murphy 1995; Simeon and Conway 2001; Williams 1995). It has also received empirical support in comparative studies of dictatorships as well as some new democracies (see Bunce 2004a, 1999b; Treisman 1997) and in one statistical analysis focusing on the causes of increasing levels of interethnic violence in heterogeneous systems (see Roeder 2000). To turn an earlier conclusion on its head: Critics of ethnofederalism argue—particularly given its consequences for the state and the preferences and resources of majorities and minorities—that this approach to state design can push minorities out, encourage majorities to be aggressive, and construct a state that serves as a mere bystander to both developments.

Comparing Postcommunist Ethnofederal Legacies

This chapter brings comparative evidence to bear on this debate by examining the relationship between the design of the state and the course of democratization in postcommunist Eurasia. This region is ideally suited for such an assessment. First, it is composed of a large number of new democracies of varying quality and durability. Second, the domestic context of democratization in the postcommunist region could not be more inhospitable given (1) large and territorially concentrated minorities in these states; (2) the absence in virtually every case of a well-established democratic tradition; (3) the simultaneous construction of democracy, the state, and capitalism, a process that is both historically unprecedented and inherently destabilizing; and (4) significant economic decline in at least the early years of the transition to capitalism (see Bunce 1999a).

Finally, the countries that make up postcommunist Eurasia exhibit similarities and differences that are particularly helpful for assessing whether and, if so, how the design of the state influences the course of democratization. On the one hand, all of these countries share a communist past and, as already noted, recent and unusually prolonged economic stress and an authoritarian tradition that predates the communist era. These similarities reinforce the earlier claim that we are dealing with unusually improbable democracies; they also hold constant some plausible factors that could account for democratic performance. On the other hand, the regimes in this region show enormous variation—across country and over time—with respect to a host of factors: for example, democratic performance, the design of the state, level of economic development, the size of minority groups, and relations between majority and minority communities during and after the collapse of socialism (for the importance of these factors, see Horowitz 1985; Przeworski et al. 1996).

We begin the analysis by comparing the 13 postcommunist regimes that represent the intersection among three sets of particular interest to us in this chapter: new states that are also new democracies and that feature in addition sizeable and territorially concentrated minority populations.[2] States included in this analysis are Azerbaijan, Croatia, Estonia, Georgia, the Kyrgyz Republic, Latvia, Lithuania, Macedonia, Moldova, Russia, Slovakia, Ukraine, and Yugoslavia. The purpose of this comparison is to assess, at the most general level, whether the design of the state is associated in any systematic way with variations in majority-minority relations and the quality of democratic life.

Correlations are one thing, however, and causality another. In the remainder of this chapter, we explore the causal linkages between state design and democratic performance in divided societies. We do so, first, by assessing whether some other factors, just as plausible as state design, might account for the patterns we have uncovered. They do not. We then compare two cases drawn from our original group of thirteen regimes that represent the extremes: Estonia, a unitary state, and Georgia, an ethnofederation. They are extreme because their minority populations are unusually large and unusually distinctive with respect to language, ethnicity, and religion (see Fox 1997; Goltz 2001; Gorenburg 1999); at least some of their minority groups are shared with neighboring states (see Kaufman 2001; Roeder 2000); and state formation followed in both instances the mobilization of large nationalist movements, dominated by the majority nation. Despite these similarities, however, in Estonia, majority-minority relations have been peaceful and the quality of democracy has improved over time. By contrast, Georgia has witnessed war, de-democratization, and the disintegration of a unified political and economic space (see King 2001a, 2001b)—problems that have remained to a large extent even after the fall of Eduard Shevardnadze in late 2003 and the rise of a seemingly more democratic government.

Both our macro and more detailed comparisons lead to the following conclusions. First, when communist party hegemony and the state were unraveling, the ethnofederal republics were more likely than their unitary counterparts to feature growing conflicts between majority and minority populations. Second, once these republics became states, the contrasts between the unitary and the ethnofederal approaches continued. Thus, the ethnofederal states were far more likely to be weak, to feature violent conflicts between majority and minority communities, and to experience a

2. We left Bosnia out of this analysis because the current design of the state was imposed by the international community, beginning with the Dayton Agreement of 1995. Thus, ethnofederalism in this instance originated in quite different circumstances than our other cases and is affected, moreover, by a host of factors specific to third-party enforcement.

decline in the quality of democratic governance. Third, while it seems to be advantageous for new states (in postcommunist Eurasia at least) to inherit a unitary rather than an ethnofederal structure, adding ethnofederal features to a unitary system can be helpful in improving strained majority-minority relations and in sustaining democratic governance—as the cases of Ukraine and Moldova suggest.

Finally, while there are good reasons to doubt the advisability of beginning democratization with an ethnofederal state in place, it does not then follow that the unitary approach constitutes an ideal solution to democratic governance in divided societies. Its success depends on whether it is combined with some other key characteristics, such as guarantees of minority rights and cultural autonomy, and separation of powers and proportionality in electoral systems. This formulation seems to provide (in the postcommunist context at least) the most workable solution to the three problems built into political projects that combine new states, new democracies, and diverse populations: keeping minorities in the state, constraining majorities (but not to the point where they are tempted to violate democratic norms), and building a capable state that creates incentives for interethnic cooperation and supports democratic governance.

General Patterns

In Table 6.1, we present a comparison of our 13 cases with respect to: (1) the design of the state (and the constitutional order); (2) the national composition of the population; (3) state capacity; (4) the development of secessionist movements; (5) levels of violence; and (6) democratization over time. Several patterns emerge. First, despite their similarities, these regimes evidence nonetheless a clear contrast with respect to the strength of the state. While all of the ethnofederations are weak states, virtually all of the unitary states are, objectively and by comparison, relatively strong (with the Kyrgyz Republic an exception). More detailed studies of these cases point to a clear reason for this contrast (see, for example, Barbarosie 2001; Cerovic 2001; Crowther 1997a, 1997b; Derluguian 1998, 2001a, 2001b; Lapidus 1998; Lieven 1998, 2001; Pula 2001; Skvortsova 1998; Solchanyk 1994). During the communist era, when these states were still republics within Czechoslovakia, the Soviet Union, and Yugoslavia, the internal boundaries of the ethnofederal republics had the effects of building strong national identities within each ethno/geographical/administrative subunit; of providing majorities and minorities with both their own leadership and significant institutional resources; and of segmenting cultural, political, social, and economic interactions along ethnoadministrative lines. The ultimate effect was to generate conflicts between two groups within these republics that subsequently

Table 6.1. Postsocialist states: Demography and democracy

Country[a]	State form	Demographics[b]	State capacity[c]	Secessionist movements	Violence	Democratization[d]
Azerbaijan***	Federal	82.7% Azerbaijani 5.6% Russian 5.6% Armenian	Low-Medium	Yes	High	6.3 Declining
Georgia***	Federal	68.8% Georgian 9.0% Armenian 7.4% Russian 5.1% Azerbaijani 3.2% Ossetian 1.9% Abkhazian	Low-Medium	Yes	High	4.5 Declining
Russia***	Federal	82.6% Russian	Low	Yes	High	4.1 Declining
Yugoslavia**	Federal	63% Serb 17% Albanian 5% Montenegrin 3% Hungarian	Low	Yes	High	6.1 Improving
Croatia***	Unitary	78.1% Croatian 12.2% Serb	High	Yes	High	4.0 Improving
Estonia*	Unitary	65.2% Estonian 28.1% Russian	High	No	No	2.0 Improving
Kyrgyz Republic***	Unitary	52.4% Kyrgyz 21.5% Russian 12.9% Uzbek	Low	No	Low	4.9 Declining
Latvia*	Unitary	55.7% Latvian 32.3% Russian	High	No	No	2.1 Improving
Lithuania**	Unitary	81.4% Lithuanian 8.3% Russian 6.9% Polish	Medium	No	No	1.4 Improving
Macedonia*	Unitary	66.5% Macedonian 22.9% Albanian	Medium	No[e]	Low	3.8 Declining

Slovakia*	Unitary	85.6% Slovak 10.5% Hungarian	High	No	No	2.1 Improving
Moldova*	Mixed	64.5% Moldovan 13.8% Ukrainian 13.0% Russian 3.5% Gagauzi	Low	Yes	Medium	3.9 Improving
Ukraine***	Mixed	72.7% Ukrainian 22.1% Russian	Low	Yes	No	3.5 Declining

[a] The countries in the table are the only ones in the postcommunist region to meet three conditions: (1) democratizing, (2) new states, and (3) presence of one or more sizable minorities that are territorially concentrated and that together constitute at least 15 percent of the population. The first criterion is based on Freedom House designations, with these countries receiving a score of "free" or "partly free" in at least half of the years since politics were liberalized. For the Yugoslav case (Serbia-Montenegro-Kosova-Vojvodina) we included the rankings for the last two years of the former Yugoslavia along with rankings after the breakup of the state. See www.freedomhouse.org. The third criterion was drawn from studies of each of these cases, along with data provided by the *Europa World Yearbook*, 2000. Finally, the asterisks in this column refer to regime structure, with one asterisk (*) a parliamentary system, two (**) mixed presidential-parliamentary, and three (***) presidential. Our thanks to Timothy Frye for providing these rankings.

[b] All ethnic minorities composing over 5 percent of the country's total population are included, as well as select minorities below 5 percent. All figures are based on the *Europa World Yearbook*, which makes use both of official data and occasionally unofficial estimates. The census or survey data for each country was obtained in the following years: Azerbaijan 1989, Czech Republic 1991, Estonia 1999, Georgia 1989, Kyrgyzstan 1989, Latvia 1999, Lithuania 1996, Macedonia 1994 (the proportion of Albanians has increased significantly since 1994, although it is highly contested by how much), Moldova 1989, Russia 1989, Ukraine 1989, Yugoslavia (Serbia-Montenegro) 1991. Note that these figures are often highly contentious; they are included here not as precise representations of the true ethnic composition of the countries listed, but simply as illustrative and largely accurate "snapshots" of the respective countries.

[c] Our rankings on state capacity are drawn from EBRD 1999, 24, 116; Bunce 2004a.

[d] These are the average scores on civil liberties and political rights combined, taken from the last three years of surveys by Freedom House (1999, 2000, 2001). The scores vary from one—meeting all democratic criteria—to seven—no evidence of democratic politics. The labels indicate recent trends (improvement, decline, or stable over the past three years). Note that these scores differ somewhat from our selection criteria for inclusion as a case; the selection criteria are based on scores from independence until 2000/1 (see footnote a above). Consequently Azerbaijan and Yugoslavia are included, despite the fact that their scores over the past three years classify them as "not free."

[e] As of the time of writing, the violence in Macedonia remained at relatively low intensity, and official demands by the domestic Albanian population were not secessionist. Note as well that, prior to the crisis of 2000–2001, civil liberties and political rights were expanding there, as were minority rights.

became new states: a titular nation, such as the Georgians, committed to expanding its autonomy from the central state (the Soviet Union) and its control over those minority regions such as Abkhazia within its political jurisdiction versus these minority regions allied with the central state against the titular nation of the ethnofederal republic. What we find, in short, is growing political, social, economic, and cultural differentiation of increasingly resourceful groups along ethnospatial lines, combined with insecure majorities and minorities. When the communist regime and state weakened, two developments ensued: Majorities sought their own state and a new regime they would dominate, and minorities, fearing the loss of protection by the larger integral state and the exclusivist nationalism of the successor majority, demanded autonomy and, when the majority resisted, a regime and state of their own.[3]

Thus, just as the Czechoslovak, Yugoslav, and Soviet ethnofederations unwittingly but systematically built nations together with regimes- and states-in-the-making in each of their republics, so, too, were the same dynamics—also unplanned but just as spatially and politically disruptive—repeated within those republics that were, like these three states, ethnofederal in form. Once the regime weakened, this process spelled the end of the Czechoslovak, Yugoslav, and Soviet states, all of which divided along republican lines (even when, as in most cases, "national lines" were different). At the same time, similar dynamics took place within the ethnofederal republics that achieved independence as a consequence of state dissolution. These successor states were, as a consequence, weaker than their unitary counterparts. What the new, ethnofederal states lacked, in particular, was a consensus about membership in the nation, the boundaries of the state, and the ideological complexion of the new regime. Politics, in short, was at once ideologically, ethnically, and spatially contested within these ethnically defined federations (see, especially, Pula 2001 on Kosova). As a consequence, the ethnofederal successor states found it very hard to command popular allegiance, to build an integrated economic space, to control their borders, and to create a unified legal order. In a time of regime transition, therefore, the costs of ethnofederalism translated quickly and easily into the dismemberment of both ethnofederal states and republics.

A second conclusion that we can draw from Table 6.1 is that minority-based secessionist movements have arisen in both unitary and ethnofederal states, during and after the processes of state disintegration. For example, just as South Ossetia and Abkhazia left Georgia, Chechnya and Tatarstan declared independence within the Russian Federation, and Montenegro and Kosova did the same within Serbia-Montenegro, so similar dynamics have

3. However, not all minorities having administrative status within ethnofederal systems respond in the same way (Bunce 2004b). All we are suggesting in this discussion is that there is a much greater probability of such behavior in ethnofederal versus unitary republican and state contexts.

taken place within some of the unitary states in our group—most notably, Ukraine, Moldova, and, largely because of external forces, Bosnia (from 1991–1995), and more recently, Macedonia (see Friedman 1996 and Rossos 2000 for helpful historical insights into Macedonia). However, these similarities should not obscure two important distinctions. One is that such demands have been far more common for ethnofederal states. Indeed, all of the ethnofederations have had to contend with such demands, whereas this situation is far less common in unitary states even though minorities within these states are no different than minorities in unitary states with respect to their size and geographical concentration; how much they differ from the majority (whether language, ethnicity, religion, or all of the three); and their relative levels of economic and social development.

The other distinction has to do with violence. Majority-minority interactions in ethnofederal states are far more likely to be violent than in unitary states. Here, it is important to recognize that (1) violence usually occurs because the majority, having rejected out of hand relatively moderate demands on the part of the minority, then responds violently to their subsequently escalating demands for independence, and (2) the contrast in violence holds up, even when we focus solely on those minorities within both state contexts that demand independence (contrast here, for example, the behavior of the Moldovan and Ukrainian governments in reaction to the demands of their Russian minorities versus the behavior of the Georgian and Serbian governments in reaction to the call for independence by the Abkhazes and the Kosovar Albanians, respectively).

We can now turn to the final column in Table 6.1, where we summarize patterns of democratization over time. Once again, there is a clear contrast between the unitary and the ethnofederal states. Summarized in numerical terms: The average Freedom House scores for the unitary states is 2.9; 5.2 for the ethnofederations; and 3.7 for the mixed cases of Moldova and Ukraine. Simply put, then: the new democracies in the unitary states have been of higher quality and have been far more likely to improve over time than the new democracies in ethnofederal state contexts. At the same time, the unitary states that have faced serious secessionist challenges and that have responded, in every case, by expanding the linguistic, educational, and political autonomy of the dissenting regions, while scoring lower on the democratic scale than other unitary states, nonetheless exhibit stronger democratic performance than their ethnofederal counterparts (all of which have faced similar demands but have responded in very different ways).[4]

4. However, we fully recognize that there are many determinants of democratic performance in the postcommunist region—for example, proximity to Western Europe, economic reform, prior imperial administrative experience, and the development of a strong liberal opposition during the communist period (see Bunce 1999a, 2003; Fish 1998; Kitschelt et al. 1999; Kopstein and Reilly 1999). However, our interest here is with a specific context: new states and new democracies that are also divided societies.

We can now weave together the conclusions we have drawn from Table 6.1. What emerge in this table are two stories. The first, which describes the ethnofederal states of Georgia, Azerbaijan, Serbia-Montenegro, and Russia, is one that combines a weak state, secessionist regions, violence between the center and at least some of the secessionist regions, and, finally, checkered democratic performance. The other story, which describes the unitary states, features greater state capacity, less propensity of minority regions to demand independence, much less likelihood of violent confrontations between the state and minority regions, and transitions to democracy that began early and that were sustained. Here, there are two exceptions: the Kyrgyz Republic and Macedonia (which had evidenced improving democratic performance, including greater political inclusion and representation of the Albanian minority, until developments outside the state in 2000–2001 produced violent conflicts). Moldova and Ukraine, the "mixed" cases on Table 6.1, provide additional support for the contrast we have drawn between the ethnofederal and unitary states. Both were unitary states, but, unlike Estonia, Latvia, the Kyrgyz Republic, and Slovakia, faced powerful secessionist movements when communism and the state were disintegrating (see D'Anieri 1997 on Ukraine; also see Rubin 1998 for helpful insights). However, in contrast to the ethnofederal republics that also became states and that also faced such problems, the leaders of Moldova and Ukraine responded to the concerns of their unhappy minorities by granting substantial, territorially based autonomy. Moreover, there are indications that similar responses are in the making in Macedonia, along with Slovakia—the latter a case where there had been significant discrimination against the Hungarian minority that had produced, not surprisingly, considerable discontent. What this suggests is a more general point. Unitary states may or may not face rebellious minorities, and these conflicts may or may not become violent—though both developments are less likely than in the ethnofederal context. However, if such conditions materialize, the leaders of unitary states seem to be more willing and able to broker the situation in ways that enhance cooperation between majority and minority communities.

Countercausal Claims

It could be countered, however, that the conclusions we have drawn from Table 6.1 are suspect because other factors, aside from state design, may be causing the contrasts among these thirteen countries. In response, we would argue the following. First, our research design has eliminated certain factors from the equation—for example, all of the cases in Table 6.1 are similar with respect to the age of the state and democracy; economic performance is poor overall within the region; and we have limited our study to those cases where minority populations are relatively sizeable and, in most cases, geographically concentrated. Second, the patterns exhibited in Table 6.1 allow us to eliminate some other alternative explanations—in particular, level of economic development and the constitutional design of the regime.

However, this does leave us with three potential problems, all of which shift our attention from state design to other factors that either "caused" state design or accompanied it. First, might ethnofederalism be a response to what are, by the comparative standards of the region, unusually large minority populations that are geographically concentrated? Second, might the decision to establish an ethnofederation be a reaction to a history of ethnic conflicts—an argument prompted by, say, the decision to create an ethnofederation in Czechoslovakia in response to Slovak mobilization from 1967 to 1968? Finally, it is possible that the negative consequences we attribute to ethnofederalism are not inherent in the institution itself but rather a response by majorities to take back the power they have been unfairly denied during state socialism.

These arguments are not persuasive. First, the size of the minority population does not predict the structure of the state. For example, the average size of the minority population is 31.5 percent in the unitary cases; 27.9 percent in the ethnofederations; and 31.4 percent in the mixed cases of Moldova and Ukraine. Second, there is ample evidence to support the argument that the decision during the communist period to create some ethnofederal republics within the Soviet and Yugoslav federations—republics that in all cases subsequently became the ethnofederations listed in Table 6.1—was based on a variety of considerations, the least important of which was a history of interethnic conflict and one of the most important of which was building institutional constraints on potentially hard-to-control republican-based majorities (see Bunce 1999b; also see Pula 2001; Cerovic 2001). For example, just as the Soviet leadership was concerned about their ability to control Georgia (a worry that began in the tsarist period) and decided to constrain Georgian nationalism by investing economically and politically in Abkhazia, South Ossetia, and Adjaria, so Josip Broz Tito had the same concerns about Serbia in particular and therefore created the autonomous republics of Kosovo and Vojvodina (both of which, with the implementation of the 1974 Constitution, received upgraded political status, which lasted until the late 1980s when Slobodan Milošević ended their political autonomy).

One can also note, in this connection, that the decision to ethnofederalize Czechoslovakia after 1968 was not simply a response to fears concerning the dangers of Slovak nationalism. Indeed, this decision seems to have been in large measure a mechanism used by hard-line communist leaders in Czechoslovakia and Moscow to constrain the population in the Czech lands, which had mobilized in large numbers in support of pluralizing the communist order. Thus, to stabilize the communist system (and the Soviet bloc), political leaders in Moscow and in Czechoslovakia catered to Slovak concerns, thereby forging an alliance among Moscow, hard-line domestic communists, and Slovak society. This alliance also had economic consequences, given the remarkable narrowing, beginning in 1969, of the economic gap between the once much richer Czech Republic and Slovakia. When communism departed from the scene twenty years later, it did so with Czechs more committed than their Slovak counterparts to its end and to rapid economic and political liberalization, and with the leadership of the two halves of the country embracing different and, ultimately, irreconcilable visions of the future structure of the state, the polity, and the economy (Bunce 1999b; Wolchik 1994). As with the other ethnofederal experiments during communism, then, the policy of using party and state institutions to divide and conquer was in some sense successful. By tying together the fate of the regime and the state, ethnofederalism extended the life of both, while guaranteeing that the end of the former would be accompanied by the disintegration of the latter.

At the same time, there is little evidence to support the interpretation that the establishment of ethnofederal republics (or states) was a response to the existence of well-defined national identities (though some were in place at the time); a history of minority grievances against the majority; or long-established patterns of majority-minority conflicts. Indeed, what is striking about the decision to introduce ethnofederalism at the state and republican levels in the communist world is not what preceded it but, rather, what followed: the construction of strong, geographically based national identities that often became potent political and economic forces because they were joined with considerable institutional resources; because they simultaneously segmented and nationalized the polity and the economy; and because they produced competing, spatially and nationally defined preferences regarding the state and regime. Ethnofederalism, in short, created multiple and competing regimes- and states-in-the-making. It is far from accidental, then, that all three communist ethnofederations broke up along republican lines; that geographically concentrated minorities with institutional identities and resources were far more likely to mobilize against the communist federations than minorities without such identities and resources (see, especially, Barany 2002); and that such institutional designations became, in turn, a relatively good predictor of whether minorities would mobilize against the new states that formed in the wake of state disintegration (see Beissinger 2002; Bunce 1999b; Treisman 1997).

Finally, our argument must respond to the charge that ethnofederalism itself is not inherently flawed, but that it was biased in the communist context in ways that tempted aggrieved parties, once politics became more malleable, to seek a reallocation of benefits. The problem with such a claim is that the "true" balance of power is probably impossible to determine and is constantly shifting as demographic patterns, economic relations, and other elements of the balance change. Both sides usually feel aggrieved, and such grievances can be exploited by ethnic entrepreneurs in periods of crisis. This is particularly the case when grievances are joined with resources—the latter the "gift" of ethnofederalism. Grievances are rarely sufficient to cause conflict. The province of Kosova before the collapse of Yugoslavia provides one example. During the 1980s, many Serbs resented the fact that Serbia was the only republic of Yugoslavia partitioned by autonomous regions (Kosova and Vojvodina), while Kosovar Albanians overwhelmingly wanted Kosova to enjoy equal status as a constituent republic of Yugoslavia. No reallocation of political influence would have satisfied both groups.

It would seem reasonable to conclude, therefore, that in the postcommunist area at least, the design of the state seems to have important consequences for the course of democracy in divided societies. But this leaves an important question. How does the design of the state affect the preferences of and interactions between majority and minority communities, and how do these dynamics shape, in turn, the evolution of democratic politics? To answer this question, we now move to a comparison of political dynamics in Georgia and Estonia from the communist period through the first decade of independence.

The Case of Georgia

During the Soviet period, several critical developments gave a distinctive stamp to Georgian nationalist politics. One was the decision by the Bolsheviks in 1922 to create an ethnofederal state, with Georgia becoming in 1936 one of its constituent republics. Like most of the other republics, Georgia was a diverse region in ethnic, religious, and linguistic terms, particularly along its perimeters. Georgians comprised about 70 percent of the population, and the remainder was divided among Georgian Muslims (who won autonomy in Adjaria, but limited rights with the reintegration of the state under Soviet rule), Abkhazes, Ossetians, Armenians, Greeks, and Jews. In 1921 and 1922, Abkhazia (where Georgians were easily the plurality) and South Ossetia (where Ossetians were a majority) were given the statuses of a Republic and an Autonomous Region, respectively. Adjaria became an Autonomous Region as well. Thus, during the Soviet period Georgia, like the Russian republic, was itself an ethnofederation nested within a larger ethnofederation—though powers accorded to union republics were greater than those accorded to other ethnically defined units located within those republics.

These different powers, however, should not obscure an important point. Like the republics within the Soviet Union, so administrative units within

Georgia were given the political, social, and cultural institutions, the administrative boundaries, and the local leadership to forge strong identities and to construct claims to becoming potentially sovereign units within the republic (Bunce 1999b). Indeed, in the case of Abkhazia in particular, one can trace the rise, with Moscow's help, of what can only be termed an ethnic machine that privileged the small group of Abkhazes over the much larger group of Georgians within the region (see Derluguian 1998; 2001a; 2001b).

The administrative shifts in Georgia were accompanied during the Stalinist period and after by repeated changes, more generally, in Soviet policies toward minorities. For example, the Soviet leadership introduced and then canceled minority schools, made decisions to give minorities their own alphabets in some cases and the alphabets of the majority within their republic in other cases, and kept changing their minds about their commitments to Russification versus encouragement of minority identities at the republican level and below (see Slezkine 1994). All of this played havoc with the identities, the expectations, the resources, and the security of all those groups that made up the Soviet Union: the titular nations of the republics; the minorities that had administrative identities, albeit not republican, but that easily perceived the benefits of an upgrade; and the minorities that did not have a formal administrative home but might have had one once and surely wanted one in the future. Put differently, the security dilemma was present and nested before the breakup of the Soviet Union (see, more generally, Fearon 1998; Posen 1993).

A long history of geopolitical vulnerability, the brief experience with statehood, Soviet investment in Georgian institutions, isolation from Moscow, and fears of losing hard-won autonomy translated into a nationalism in Georgia that was exclusivist and illiberal. Also critical was that in Abkhazia in particular, the dominance of the titular nation, a dominance supported by Moscow, fed into the construction of Georgian nationalism as a double-pronged sentiment—against Moscow and for the protection of the sizeable Georgian population within Abkhazia. The Ossetians and the Abkhazes, armed with their own leaders, their own quota system in most jobs, and their own educational institutions and media, fearful of losing what little autonomy they had and worried about the weakening of Moscow, the protector of their ethnic machines, responded to Georgian nationalism by mounting parallel and competitive nationalist movements of their own that sought independence from the independence-seeking but assimilationist-minded Georgians.

All of this came to a head in 1988, when Abkhaz communists sent a letter of complaint to the Nineteenth party conference and when Georgians, concerned about discrimination against them at home and within the Federation, took to the streets in huge numbers. The Georgian communists then responded by inviting in Soviet troops—an action that polarized Georgian dissidents, led to subsequent protests by the majority and the minorities, and culminated in the March 1990 declaration of sovereignty by the Georgian Supreme Soviet (with formal sovereignty declared in April 1991) and in the defeat of the Georgian Communist Party in the 1990 elections (in which minorities either supported the Party or boycotted the elections). In mid-1991, Zviad Gamsakhurdia—a radical Georgian nationalist committed to authoritarian politics, withdrawal of minority rights, and violent reconstitution of the state—was elected president. War broke out and he was overthrown by a coup d'etat in January 1992—less than a year after he was elected.

In March 1992, Shevardnadze returned to a Georgia in the midst of war, having lost the state where he had served as foreign minister. Following his return there was precious little improvement in the Georgian situation, despite Georgian admission to the Council of Europe in 1997. Shevardnadze's decision to call on Russian military help to stabilize the country created a difficult situation, especially given Georgia's proximity to other danger zones, such as Chechnya and Nagorno-Karabakh, and the difficulty of reconciling independence from the Soviet Union and Georgian nationalism with a Russian military presence. Georgia may rank third on a per capita basis in receipt of U.S. aid, but the fact remains that Georgia today is neither a state nor a democracy. Corruption still reigns (Transparency International ranks Georgia as the sixteenth most corrupt out of ninety-nine countries around the world); the Georgian economy is about one-third the size it was at the beginning of the 1990s; about 20 percent of the country remains outside the control of the center; and South Ossetia and Abkhazia have their own armies, customs posts, flags, currency (the ruble), school systems, and even time zones. On the democratic side of the ledger, Shevardnadze stayed in power for more than a decade through corrupt elections which, in the late fall 2003, finally produced a massive protest that forced him to hand over power to Mikheil Saakashvili (see Garb 1998; Goltz 2001; Jones 1997; King 2001a, 2001b; Lieven 2001). Whether Saakashvili will succeed in building democracy and reconstituting the Georgian state is questionable, though he has succeeded in bringing one region—Adjaria—back to the fold. Similar developments within Serbia-Montenegro from the fall 2000 to the victory of Boris Tadic in the presidential election of June 2004 have produced the same scenario: a seeming shift from authoritarian to democratic politics that enhances the prospects for the consolidation of democracy and a reconstitution of the state.

The Case of Estonia

Estonia shared with Georgia many similarities during the Soviet era. Both featured above-average levels of educational and occupational achievement (Roeder 1991); cultural institutions under the control of the titular ethnic group; administrative boundaries that largely corresponded to the territory occupied by the titular ethnic group; substantial representation of the titular ethnicity in elite positions (although non-Russified ethnic Estonians never had access to the highest levels of power until well into glasnost); and large ethnic minorities, distinguished by language and religion. Yet Georgia descended into civil war with the disintegration of the Soviet Union, while Estonia shows every sign of having weathered the transition successfully and integrating with Europe. The critical difference lies in their institutions at the point of departure as independent states: Estonia was a unitary republic within the Union of Soviet Socialist Republics (USSR) while Georgia was a federation "nested" within the Soviet federation. When the Soviet Union broke apart, Estonia's ethnic minorities—primarily ethnic Russians—had no indigenous political structures or cultural institutions on which to base resistance to the nationalizing project of the Estonians. While many of the ethnic Russians of Estonia felt threatened by the country's independence, radical actions were isolated and sporadic. Over time, the perception that Estonians had of the possible threat posed by resident Russians began to fade, and with it receded much of the worst of Estonian nationalist politics (see Cichok 1999; Hulburt 2000; Kaplan 1998; Kolstø and Tsilevich 1997; Laitin 1998; Melvin 2000; Park 1994; Raun 1997a, 1997b).

Before its incorporation into the Soviet Union, Estonia had enjoyed a long period of relative ethnic homogeneity (Raun 1997a, 335–336), a much shorter time as a sovereign country, and a yet briefer existence as a democracy. In part due to exceptionally high levels of literacy, however, Estonians had developed a strong national consciousness before its annexation by the USSR (Raun 1997b, 407). This sense of national identity survived both sustained Russification efforts by Moscow and the demographic catastrophes of World War II and Stalinization in which the ethnic Estonian proportion of the republic's population declined from nearly 90 percent in 1934 to just over 60 percent by 1989 (Raun 1997a, 336). As the preceding discussions suggested, Soviet ethnofederal structures were critical in maintaining Estonian identity and ultimately in fostering the resistance movements that would flourish under glasnost (Raun 1997b, 411–412; Steen 2000, 83).

By the 1980s the Estonian sense of cultural distinctiveness began to grow into open resistance. One of the opening salvos in this movement was the "Letter of the Forty" in 1980 in which intellectuals openly addressed issues of ethnic conflict and Estonian cultural identity. Within the political space that glasnost subsequently opened, Estonians began to protest Soviet environmental abuses (Kionka and Vetik 1996, 137). By 1988 explicitly political organizations outside of the Communist Party of Estonia (CPE) began to appear, such as the Popular Front of Estonia and Estonian National Independence Party (ENIP), but equally as important were changes within the CPE itself. By the end of the year the Estonian Supreme Soviet had unanimously passed a declaration of sovereignty. Thus, the "nativization" of the CPE and the capture of ethnofederal resources by indigenous elites proved critical to the transition to independence. Significantly, ethnic Russians within Estonia had no such resources within the republic, given its unitary design. Moreover, the ethnic Russians were also unable to access such resources in their home republic, the Russian Soviet Federated Socialist Republic, because this republic, in contrast to the other 14 within the Soviet federation, was denied its own political, cultural, and social institutions (see Brudny 1998, 2001; Bunce 1999b; Zevelev 2001). Indigenous Russian resistance to the Estonian independence movement was organized by the "Intermovement" (International Movement of Workers of the ESSR), a Soviet state-sponsored, factory-based movement that purportedly represented the ethnic Russians and other Russophones of Estonia. Ultimately the Intermovement proved inadequate to organizing opposition to independence.

In the wake of the failed August 1991 coup d'etat, Estonia gained independence and ethnic Estonian elites began to implement a nationalizing project. The Estonian citizenship law of 1938 was reinstated, transforming nearly all of the ethnic Russian residents of Estonia into noncitizens without voting rights in Estonian national elections. To acquire citizenship, applicants had to demonstrate substantial knowledge of Estonian—a significant hurdle, considering that less than 10 percent of Russian residents could speak Estonian fluently by 1992, while nearly a third had no appreciable Estonian language skills (Park 1994, 74). Consequently, the new Estonian constitution was adopted and the first parliamentary and presidential elections were effectively held without Russian participation.

Various polls of the population suggest that Russian reaction to the Estonian citizenship and language laws and similar discriminatory legislation has been extremely negative. Indigenous Russian resistance to Estonia's "ethnic democracy" (to borrow Graham Smith's term) has nonetheless been sporadic and largely ineffective. There were in practice a variety of political platforms ranging from a "Representative Assembly" of Russophone residents as founded in 1993 to press for the rights of disenfranchised residents to a more radical politics concentrated in the Narva city council (Kionka and Vetik 1996, 143; Park 1994, 80–81). While sporadic strikes and demonstrations have also occurred, none of these amounted to a serious challenge.

What accounts for the political weakness of the Russophone community? It should first be noted that a substantial proportion of Estonia's Russian population supported the republic's independence; the referendum on independence was open to all permanent residents of Estonia, and roughly 30 percent of non-Estonian voters voted in favor (Raun 1997b, 415). Resentments among disenfranchised residents were nonetheless very real, and the size and concentration of the Russian community, and particularly its close proximity to Russia—a large, powerful "ethnic patron"—would seem to have made Estonia a likely case for secession. A number of factors, however, prevented a spiral of ethnic tensions. First, although resources—both in terms of political access and public services—were made available to the Russian minority, opportunities for political empowerment were not concentrated in a particular geographical region as in ethnofederalism. Instead, political representation of the Russophone community was divided among a variety of institutions, both territorial and nonterritorial (Melvin 2000). The first prime minister of independent Estonia, Edgar Savisaar, facilitated the creation of a Representative Assembly in which Russophone organizations could come together to articulate political demands of the Estonian government. Later, President Lennart Meri sponsored a round table to bring together ethnic minorities in a consultative role. Moreover, while the vast majority of ethnic Russians could not vote in the first national elections, noncitizens could cast ballots in the original municipal elections in 1993—although only for candidates moderate enough to be permitted to run for office by the Estonian government.

The plurality of political agendas, the necessity of cooperation with Estonian authorities, and the presence of moderates all worked against the formulation of a single, exclusivist ethnic agenda (Smith and Wilson 1997, 851–852). Moreover, by 1999 an ethnically Russian party became part of the governing coalition of the Tallinn municipal council. This guaranteed the representation of multiple voices in the Russian community.

Finally, within the unitary framework of Estonia there were considerable pressures toward either assimilation or the creation of hybrid identities among the Russian minority. As already noted, the Russians of Estonia lacked their own distinct cultural institutions, either in Russia or in Estonia. This facilitated the development of both a "Soviet-Russian" and a "Baltic-Russian" identity as far back as the Soviet era (Melvin 2000, 137–139), while weakening the power of an indigenous Russian intelligentsia—the key group in the rise of nationalist protests elsewhere in the region (Kolstø and Tsilevich 1997; Smith et al. 1998, 116). The relative success of the Estonian transition and its nationalizing project, moreover, suggest that the gradual assimilation of Russian speakers is the most likely, although hardly inevitable, trajectory of ethnic politics in Estonia (Laitin 1998, 353–359). Because of the relatively mild reaction of the Russian community in Estonia, Estonian elites have come to perceive the Russian residents as relatively nonthreatening. According to a series of polls of elites in Estonia conducted by Anton Steen, the proportion of these elites that expected ethnic confrontation to take the form of "violence and rhetoric" dropped from 44 percent in 1994 to 35 percent in 1997, while by 1997 nearly two-thirds expected confrontation to take the form of rhetoric only (Steen 2000, 77). Such attitudes are in large part responsible for the gradual opening of opportunities for political participation to ethnic Russians. By 1997 Estonia became the first new member of the Council of Europe no longer to require special human rights monitoring by the Council.

In short, Estonia appears to have consolidated its transformation into a democratic, sovereign state without the violence that has plagued Georgia and other ethnofederal states. This is despite the fact, moreover, that the majority comprises a smaller percentage of the population in Estonia than in Georgia (a contrast that would be even sharper for Latvia). In the terminology adopted by Roeder and Rothchild in Chapter 2, a variety of "soft guarantees" provided opportunities for political participation to the Russian-speaking minorities and helped to alleviate their grievances, while a lack of "hard guarantees" helped to prevent the empowerment of minority elites with rigid agendas.

Amendments

Our argument to this point, while parsimonious, can hardly account for the full range of variation in all of the ethnically heterogeneous, democratizing states of the postsocialist world. While a unitary structure at the point of departure for regime and state transition appears to be a necessary condition for sustained democratization, three caveats should be mentioned: the timing of the creation of ethnofederal institutions, the strategies adopted by the majority to protect and accommodate minorities, and the international environment of the democratizing state all influence the political viability of countries that begin their democratic transitions as unitary states.

First, while inheriting ethnofederalism from a previous authoritarian regime provides an inauspicious beginning for a democratizing state, adopting ethnofederalism in the course of transition may provide sustainable structures for ethnic accommodation. The Moldovan case serves as an important example (see Barbarosie 2001; Crowther 1997a, 1997b; King 2000; Skvortsova 1998). Moldova began its transition to sovereignty and democracy with a recent past that was remarkably similar to developments in the ethnofederal republics—for example, politicians pushing for new state language policies that discriminated against minorities and that generated significant protests, attempts to manipulate the structure of the system to serve the interests of the majority, and the rise of a nationalist movement that excluded the Russian and Muslim Gagauz communities. In the early stages of the transition, Moldovan nationalists and elected politicians focused on reunification with Romania—a goal that drove the Gagauz and the Russian minority in Transdniestria in particular to declare independence. This, in turn, led to violence. However, with a change in the government in 1994 came a series of developments that improved both interethnic relations and Moldovan democracy; for example, dropping the demand to join Romania, finally holding a referendum on independence, and passing a constitution that guaranteed minority rights and created substantial regional autonomies.

What this discussion of Moldova suggests is that there is a considerable difference between inheriting ethnofederalism and inheriting a unitary state that then moves toward an ethnofederal system in order to promote interethnic peace. What makes this argument all the more compelling are three examples drawn from outside the region. One is Sri Lanka, where a unitary state has been the site of a long civil war between Sinhalese and Tamils. Here, what is striking is the failure of the Sinhalese elite to respond to the demands of the minority by introducing either a full-scale ethnofederal system or ethnofederal elements into a unitary structure (Herring 2001). As the Moldovan example reminds us, this can be an effective response to minority discontent. It could be suggested, therefore, that the resistance of the Sinhalese leadership to institutional reforms of the state in the direction of power sharing may have contributed to the continuation of what has become a long and unusually violent conflict between the Sinhalese government and the Tamil Tigers.

The other two examples are India and Spain, two countries that introduced ethnofederalism only after they had begun their transitions to democracy—India in 1956 and Spain in 1978. (Spain began its transition to democracy as a unitary state; India began independence as an asymmetrical union of states that had been inherited from British rule with boundaries that did not correspond closely to ethnolinguistic borders.) This sequence can be beneficial for three reasons. First, it avoids the costs of *inheriting* ethnofederalism; for example, the exclusivist nationalism of the majority, a weak state, an "ethnification" of politics (see Kuran 1998), and angry minorities equipped with institutional resources. Second, it reaps the benefits of ethnofederalism—for example, providing the cultural autonomy and political representation that minorities want and that ties them to the state. Finally, when a unitary state serves as the point of departure, there is greater room for political maneuver. While expanding the autonomy of subunits within an ethnofederation could very well mean ending any prospects for a common identity, political project, and economic system, expansion of such autonomy within a unitary context can build on existing state capacity to win more support for democracy and the state from minority communities. Such actions, moreover, create a majority nation that, while less secure in the sense of being required to share power, is more secure in the sense of residing within a more stable democratic order. In this way, the state and democracy are both well-served when unitary states take on ethnofederal features. Indeed, it is precisely for these reasons that the key issue in the early development of Spanish and Indian federalism was not existing units attempting to leave the state but, rather, minorities without such units pressing for them in the context of the existing state.[5]

A second amendment to our general argument concerns the sufficiency of unitary systems to promote interethnic peace and democratic continuity. A unitary state, in and of itself, neither guarantees cultural or political rights to minorities nor necessarily empowers them—though achievement of a full-fledged democratic order guarantees at the least individual rights. Whether unitary states deliver the "minority goods" depends on a variety of factors separate from the design of the state; for example, whether minorities are well-organized, whether majorities are predatory, whether the government is parliamentary or a separation of powers system (with the latter preferable; see Roeder 1999), and whether political leaders use electoral and administrative systems to limit minority representation and, more generally, to divide and conquer. One has only to note here the cases of Macedonia, Slovakia, and Romania, particularly in the early stages of democratization (Csergo 2000). Having said that, however, it is important to recognize that, while the unitary states we have analyzed could do better with respect to cultural autonomy and political representation of minorities, their record tends to be stronger than their ethnofederal counterparts and, just as important, to improve over time. This may reflect differences in nationalist movements and in the degree to which democracy itself is politically contested—differences that, as we argued above, may reflect the historical institutional design of the republic that became a state (and see Abdelal 2001). Put simply, ethnofederal republics, because of their very design, have a high probability of producing contestation over the nation, the regime-in-the-making, and the boundaries of the state—contestation that necessarily undermines both the state and democracy following independence.

Third, this chapter has treated the consequences of institutional design largely as a function of domestic dynamics, but it is clear that international influences play a role. External factors can exercise either a positive or negative influence, and examples of both dynamics are readily apparent in the postcommunist world. Estonia was blessed with an extraordinarily congenial international environment. Its aspirations to join Western institutions such as the European Union and North Atlantic Treaty Organization (NATO) provided Western states and multilateral organizations such as the Organization for Security and Cooperation in Europe (OSCE) considerable leverage in negotiations with the Estonians over minority rights (see for instance Hurlburt 2000). At the same time Moscow urged its tiny neighbor to meet

5. There are, however, two caveats to this conclusion. One is that a longer temporal perspective may reveal increasing weakness of the state and segmentation of politics, culture, and economics—as the Belgian case, for example, suggests. Second, the Spanish and Indian cases share one characteristic that works against the costs of ethnofederation; that is, a public consensus surrounding democracy.

certain minimal standards in the treatment of Russophone minorities—diplomatic efforts lent weight by such factors as Estonia's initial dependence on Russian energy supplies and the necessity of negotiating the withdrawal of troops of the former Soviet Union from Estonian soil (Cichock 1999). Also helpful was the manner in which the Soviet Union disintegrated—in particular, Boris Yeltsin's treaties between the Russian Federation and the Baltic republics, Ukraine, and others that exchanged guarantees of Russian minority rights for continued Russian economic and infrastructural support (Bunce 1999b).

Unfortunately, international factors have not always played such a positive role—as one can see, for example, in Russian interventions in Moldova and Ukraine and, repeatedly, in Georgia. The Macedonian case in particular illustrates the costs of international interference in domestic politics. This is a polity that, despite enduring interethnic tensions, had managed to sustain democratic governance and gradual improvement in interethnic relations over the course of a decade in an extremely unpromising international environment. The violence of the past few years, however, has cast some doubt on Macedonia's future. It is important to recognize, though, that while the ethnic Albanian insurgency in Macedonia has strong domestic roots, it owes a very considerable proportion of its strength to the contribution of trained, well-armed, and highly motivated insurgents based in Kosova (ICG 2001a, 5–9). It is unclear how much of a threat the Albanian insurgents would pose in the absence of such support, especially given the prior record of improved inclusion of minorities into Macedonian politics. In the opinion of some, at least, although the ethnic Albanian National Liberation Army (NLA) "has cleverly tapped into the everyday frustrations shared by the country's one-third ethnic Albanian population, [these grievances] are not generally perceived to be the type of discrimination that drives people to take up arms. . . . Albanians in Macedonia overwhelmingly support the stated objectives of the Albanian guerillas but disagree with their violent methods. It is striking that few intellectuals or elites seem prepared to join them" (ICG 2001a, 5–6).

The Costs of Establishing Ethnofederalism before Democracy

Our comparison among these new and diverse postcommunist democracies seems to suggest that the presence of ethnofederalism at the point of departure for democracy and statehood generates a number of costs. This is, first, because in this regional context at least, ethnofederalism, whether at the level of the state or republics within states, built strong national identities invested with territory and substantial cultural, political, economic, and social resources. In this way, ethnofederalism built microstates and regimes-in-the-making. Second, ethnofederalism created two games within the

Georgian, Serbian, Azerbaijani, and Russian republics. For the institutionally endowed minority nations (such as the Abkhazians) nested within the republics (like Georgia), the enemy was the republic's titular nation (the Georgians) and the key ally was the center (the Soviet Union). These minorities, in short, were strongly committed to the state and often, therefore, to the regime as well. By contrast, the leaders of the titular nation sought to maximize their autonomy from the center, while minimizing the autonomy of the minority-based units within their republics. Thus, prior to the end of socialism and the state, ethnofederalism had created—within the Soviet, Yugoslav, and Czechoslovak states and within the ethnofederal republics inside the Soviet and Yugoslav states—well-defined, compartmentalized, and competitive identities, resources, and political and economic agendas. In practice, this often produced a sequence wherein nationalist mobilization of the majority, invariably exclusivist, often produced countermobilizations by institutionally endowed minorities. Third, the weakening of the regime and the state had predictable consequences. The insecurities of both majorities and minorities increased. At the same time, the stage was set for conflicts between the center and the republics and between majorities and minorities within the ethnofederal republics. These conflicts were at once ethnic, ideological, and spatial. As a result, the ethnofederal successor states, in direct contrast to their unitary counterparts, were weak; their constituent nations unusually conflictual; and their democratic orders compromised from the start and fragile over time.

By contrast, while the unitary republics in the region did face at times secessionist pressures during the break-up of the regime and the state, they were far less likely to confront such problems and, when doing so, far more likely to find accommodation with aggrieved regions and to stay the democratic course. Put simply, then, in a heterogeneous context, unitary states seem to constitute a better investment in democracy; they are far superior in their capacity to avoid violence; and they are more likely to improve over time in their provision of minority rights.

Does it then follow that new democracies that are also new states and that have divided societies should choose a unitary over an ethnofederal system? We do not think that the analysis provided in this chapter leads, necessarily, to such a recommendation. There is little question, of course, that a unitary state seems to be preferable. However, there is some question as to whether such choices are effectively available to states and their leaders given the power of the institutional past. Here, it is important to recall three patterns that were evident in our data. First, institutional legacies tend to stick. Thus, ethnofederal republics invariably became ethnofederal states, and unitary states usually maintained the same structure following independence. Second, some unitary states did add ethnofederal features—in particular, Ukraine, Moldova, Slovakia, and, perhaps in the near future, Macedonia (along with Bosnia, albeit through external intervention). This is a pattern that is also evident in cases outside the region—for example, Nigeria, India, Belgium, and Spain. Third and most important, however, there were no cases within the postcommunist region—and none that we can think of outside the region—where an ethnofederation evolved into a unitary state.

Thus, to argue in support of the advantages of a unitary state for interethnic relations and democracy is not the same thing as recommending that existing ethnofederations become unitary systems. This recommendation does not seem to be realistic because there are considerable constraints on institutional choice—particularly when the direction proposed is one of moving from an ethnofederal to a unitary model. But this reminds us of one more reason to prefer—in theory at least—a unitary model. That reason is greater "wiggle room" in the future, should the need arise. Unitary states seem to be more successful not just with respect to both majority-minority relations and democratization. They also seem to be more open to responding in creative institutional ways to the concerns of their majorities and minorities.

7

Does the Choice of Electoral System Promote Democracy? The Gap between Theory and Practice

Benjamin Reilly

Central to many proposals for power sharing in ethnically divided societies are claims that stable democracy requires inclusive executives, and that the surest way to achieve this inclusiveness is to use proportional representation (PR) electoral systems. Indeed, over the past decade most elections in new democracies—and notably in those following civil wars or international intervention—have used PR in part because of the expectation that this will help to ensure inclusive governments. But is PR the best way to consolidate democracy in divided societies over the longer term? In this chapter I examine the relationship among electoral systems, executive inclusiveness, and stable democracy in both homogeneous and ethnically divided societies. My research indicates some surprising interrelationships among these three variables.

On the one hand, the data on executive formation suggest that inclusive executives, particularly oversized coalitions of different political parties within the cabinet, are common among the world's established democracies. Moreover, in the successful democracies that also have above-average levels of societal pluralism, inclusive governments have been even more frequent than in the more homogeneous democracies. To that extent, the evidence is consistent with the claim that executive inclusiveness increases the prospects for stable democracy in plural societies.

Yet my findings suggest that among the most ethnically divided democracies, this inclusiveness in the executive has not been the result of electoral systems that are designed to encourage proportionality. Rather, a majority of the world's established democracies that also have ethnically divided societies use plurality electoral systems, not PR. This finding represents a challenge to the scholarly consensus on this issue. Accordingly, this chapter concludes by suggesting some reasons for the apparent disjuncture between the empirical record of executive inclusion and the normative claims made for particular electoral institutions, such as the argument that highly proportional electoral systems offer the surest route to power-sharing outcomes.

Electoral Systems for Divided Societies

There is broad scholarly consensus on the virtues of inclusive executives—that is, multiparty and multiethnic coalition executives—for ethnically divided societies (Sisk 1996). At a minimum, some type of government arrangement that gives all significant ethnic groups access to decisionmaking is widely viewed as important both for the transition from authoritarian rule to democracy and for sustaining democracy over the longer term. Inclusion makes all major groups a part of the decision process and encourages moderation by facilitating joint problem solving on important issues. Arend Lijphart (1990b, 505) sees the formation of inclusive multiethnic coalition governments as a crucial factor in sustaining democracy in plural societies. Donald Horowitz (1985, 365–395) argues that multiethnic coalitions are a near-essential element of conflict management for divided societies. There is also widespread agreement among political scientists on the importance of electoral systems in shaping the wider political arena, including power-sharing schemes. However, there is profound disagreement as to which electoral systems are more likely to deliver sustainable power-sharing arrangements in societies divided along cleavages of language, race, religion, and region (see Reilly and Reynolds 1999; Reilly 2001).

Within the main electoral system families, there is a basic division between those electoral systems that lead to majoritarian outcomes and those that are more likely to result in proportionality. *Plurality or majority systems*—including the plurality vote used in the United States, the runoff system of France, or the alternative vote in Australia—are all examples of the former. In each case, the country is divided up into small geographically defined electoral districts, and voters elect in most cases a single candidate to be their representative in the national legislature. Alternatively, *PR systems* allocate seats among contenders in multimember districts based on their respective proportions of the votes. At the extreme, in the highly proportional party-list PR systems employed in Israel and the Netherlands, the entire country forms one electoral district, electors vote for parties rather than candidates, and seats are assigned to parties in proportion to their share of the national vote. In recent years, a third category—"*mixed*" *systems*, as used in Germany and Japan—has become increasingly popular. These combine both principles, with part of the legislature being elected from single-member districts, and the other part by PR. Most transitional elections in the past decade have been conducted under some form of PR—including prominent cases such as

Namibia (1989), Nicaragua (1990), Cambodia (1993), South Africa (1994), Mozambique (1994), Liberia (1997), Bosnia (1996, 1998, 2000), Indonesia (1999), Kosovo (2001), and East Timor (2001).

However, inclusive executives have been more ephemeral in these new democracies. Only Bosnia, in which an inclusive executive is a formal part of the Dayton Agreement enforced by the international community, has maintained an inclusive coalition government. In a number of cases, PR elections have resulted in clear majority rule; Namibia, Mozambique, Liberia, and East Timor are all examples of this. In other cases, such as Cambodia, a short period of inclusive executives was followed by what appears to be fairly entrenched one-party dominance. In two of the most prominent transitions to democracy by ethnically divided states in the 1990s—South Africa and Indonesia—power sharing was an important but temporary phenomenon. In both cases, the first democratically elected governments featured "oversized" cabinets, with all major parties represented. In South Africa, this was a mandatory provision of the interim constitution; in Indonesia, it was the result of political necessity, as President Abdurrahman Wahid came to power via the support of a coalition of Islamic and secular parties. In each case, however, the initial tilt toward an inclusive executive was sharply diluted later. In South Africa, the provisions of the final constitution were much more majoritarian than the interim one, and the governing African National Congress dominated all facets of government. In Indonesia, cabinets were something of a revolving door as a bewildering array of ministers were appointed and then removed by former President Wahid. (He was impeached by the Indonesian parliament and replaced by Megawati Sukarnoputri in August 2001.) In both South Africa and Indonesia, the trend was toward less breadth of cabinet representation and greater centralization of presidential power. Finally, in two other transitions to democracy—Russia and Nigeria—there was very little formal power sharing among the parties in the cabinet; in Russia, most members of the cabinet had no party affiliation, while in Nigeria, the ruling People's Democratic Party has controlled both the executive and the legislature since the return to democracy in 1999.

As this potted survey suggests, there is a great deal of variation in the experience of power sharing around the world. In the analysis that follows, I will show that the link between electoral system choice and inclusive executives has been more complex and less predictable than many political scientists would have anticipated.

Analysis

What is the empirical relationship among electoral systems, inclusive executives, and stable democracy? Any starting point for analyzing this question must begin within the universe of democratic states because it is only in democracies that we can be sure that elections are a significant means of changing and choosing governments. There are numerous cases of autocratic governments that hold elections and form cabinets, but in which the elections are really irrelevant to the choice of representatives and governments. In addition, because power sharing is viewed as a primary avenue by which countries facing deep internal conflicts can create stable politics, many cases of power sharing are introduced in countries that could not be called fully democratic—often countries in the process of transition from authoritarian to democratic politics.

There are today a host of states that have only recently adopted the forms of democracy and in which the new regime remains fragile and open to challenge. This vulnerable group includes most of the putative new democracies of Eastern Europe, Latin America, southern Africa, and Southeast Asia. The political reality of these states as transitional democracies-in-the-making creates problems for comparative analysis of the relationship among stable democracy, electoral systems, and power sharing. When examining the relationship between electoral systems and executive inclusiveness, for example, there needs to be several iterations of the electoral and government-formation process before we can begin to measure the relationship between the two with confidence. But even the most prominent examples of democratization—such as the cases of Russia, South Africa, and Indonesia mentioned earlier—have held only a few elections since their transition from authoritarian rule. In such cases, it may be simply too early to tell whether new democratic procedures are becoming institutionalized, let alone to interpret the effects of different institutional choices.

To understand properly the relationship among electoral systems, executive inclusiveness, and stable democracy we must therefore begin our analysis by examining established democracies—those countries around the world that have a significant and continuous record of democracy. Note that this does not mean Western democracies: although the majority of the world's well-established democracies are located in the West, a range of states from Latin America, Africa, Asia, and the Pacific have also maintained a successful and unbroken record of competitive democracy. There are several good lists and indexes of democratic countries based on variables like the competitiveness of their electoral process, their levels of popular participation at elections, their degree of civil and political rights, and so on, produced by organizations such as Freedom House (2000) and by authors such as Dahl (1971), Powell (1982), Lijphart (1984), LeDuc, Niemi, and Norris (1996), and Vanhanen (1997).

For our purposes, however, the most useful collection of cases comes from Lijphart's 36-country study of established democracies, *Patterns of Democracy*, published in 1999. This work (destined, I think, to be a classic) systematically compares and analyzes data on cabinets, legislatures, parties, elections, and other key elements of democratic governance among all the countries Lijphart classifies as "established" democracies—states with a population of more than 250,000 that have held free elections for over 20 years. These criteria result in the following list of 36 established democracies: Australia, Austria, Bahamas, Barbados, Belgium, Botswana, Canada, Colombia, Costa Rica, Denmark, Finland, France, Germany, Greece, Iceland, India, Ireland, Israel, Italy, Jamaica, Japan, Luxembourg, Malta, Mauritius, Netherlands, New Zealand, Norway, Papua New Guinea, Portugal, Spain, Sweden, Switzerland, Trinidad and Tobago, the United Kingdom, the United States of America, and Venezuela. In some cases—Colombia and Venezuela in particular—Lijphart possibly errs on the side of inclusion, but with the exception of a few microstates that were omitted from his analysis, this group deserves to be seen as a comprehensive collection of the world's successful long-term democratic regimes.

Nine of Lijphart's established democracies are also ethnically divided countries, or what Lijphart classifies as "plural societies": Belgium, Canada, India, Israel, Mauritius, Papua New Guinea, Spain, Switzerland, and Trinidad and Tobago. All of these countries are divided along a powerful ethnic cleavage, and indeed all except one (Trinidad and Tobago) are linguistically divided societies, although most have other strong cleavages—racial, regional, religious—as well. Each of these countries is thus unequivocally a divided society in ethnic terms, and nearly all of them have also experienced ethnonationalist political violence—although the incidence of this varies widely from contemporary secessionist civil wars in places such as India and Papua New Guinea to much more muted or historical violence in Belgium and Switzerland. Despite this, all of these countries also have a significant record of continuous democracy. As such, they provide an important subuniverse for assessing the relationship among electoral systems, executive inclusiveness, and stable democracy in divided societies.[1]

Despite this, it is important to acknowledge up front some of the limitations of this data set as well. Because Lijphart's data set is restricted to suc-

1. By contrast, Lijphart's other categories—"semiplural societies" and "nonplural societies"—are more contentious. His *semiplural* category includes relatively homogeneous countries such as Austria, Finland, Luxembourg, and the Netherlands. The United States—the plural society par excellence—is also classified as *semiplural* despite a degree of societal heterogeneity that far outstrips most of the others. The *nonplural* category includes states such as Australia, which has the highest per-capita proportion of immigrants of any Western country; New Zealand, a bicommunal society with a distinct and politically active (15 percent) ethnolinguistic Polynesian minority; and the United Kingdom, the site of a decades-long ethnoreligious conflict in Northern Ireland. I would argue that all of these cases are incorrectly classified, and that New Zealand and the United Kingdom, in particular, deserve to be categorized as *plural societies* by any reasonable definition of the term—including the fact that both have ethnically based political parties and have suffered ethnopolitical violence (although at vastly different levels).

cessful democracies only, it can tell us little about the relationship between elections and power sharing in new democracies or in those making the transition from authoritarian rule. On the other hand, as an exploratory investigation, the focus on established democracies is useful in highlighting those factors that these varied success stories share in common.

Measuring Executive Inclusiveness

There are several ways to achieve executive inclusiveness. The most overt is to make power sharing a formal constitutional requirement, as in Bosnia's Dayton Agreement constitution, Lebanon's pre– and post–Ta'if Accord government arrangements, South Africa's interim 1994 constitution, or Fiji's 1997 constitutional settlement. In all of these cases, power sharing is (or was) a mandatory legal requirement for forming government.

In most established democracies by contrast, the inclusiveness in government that takes place is not mandated by law but results from voluntary arrangements among parties (Belgium and Switzerland are the exceptions). Sometimes these executive arrangements are underpinned by strong cultural conventions and long historical use, but they remain essentially voluntary agreements to forge multiparty governments, build broad-based coalitions, include minority representatives in cabinets, and the like. Mandatory power-sharing provisions, in which groups or parties are required to share power across ethnic lines, remain relatively unusual.

This raises the crucial question of how we *measure* the inclusiveness of executives. Lijphart (1999, 90) argues that "the breadth of participation by the people's party representatives in the executive branch of the government . . . can be regarded as the most typical variable in the majoritarian-consensus contrast: the difference between one-party majority governments and broad multiparty coalitions epitomizes the contrast between the majoritarian principle of concentrating power in the hands of the majority and the consensus principle of broad powersharing." Following this reasoning, his indicator of broad participation is the proportion of governments that were oversized coalitions—that is, those where the government was not a single-party or minimal-winning coalition, but included more parties than was necessary simply to form a majority.

Lijphart's measure of these data are summarized in Table 7.1, which shows the average percentage of all governments that were oversized-coalition cabinets in each of the nine ethnically divided established democracies compared with the average for the 27 other, more homogeneous, democracies. As this table suggests, there is a clear relationship between ethnically divided societies and inclusive executives across all 36 established democracies. Among this group, the ethnically divided societies have oversized coalition cabinets almost twice as often as the more homogeneous cases.

Table 7.1. Executive power sharing in ethnically divided democracies

Country	Oversized coalitions (percent of all cabinets)[a]
Switzerland	95.9
Israel	89.2
Mauritius	86.0
Papua New Guinea	77.0
Belgium	62.5
India	47.5
Average for 27 homogeneous democracies	*35.5*
Spain	27.0
Canada	9.0
Trinidad and Tobago	0.9

[a] An oversized coalition is any cabinet that is not a minimal-winning or one-party cabinet.

Electoral Systems and Executive Inclusiveness

What does Lijphart's index tell us about the relationship between electoral systems and executive inclusiveness? First, across all 36 established democracies, there is a clear link between PR electoral systems and executive inclusiveness. Among all established democracies, the average proportion of governments that were comprised of oversized coalitions was 40.4 percent. Nineteen countries were above this average, and 17 were below. As Table 7.2 shows, fully 71 percent of the democracies that used PR were above this average. By contrast, only 27 percent that used a plurality or majority electoral system had above-average rates of oversized coalition cabinets. This difference is especially pronounced if we look at the 27 more homogeneous democracies. In this group, the rates of oversized coalition cabinets were 71 percent in PR systems and only 10 percent in plurality-majoritarian systems. At first glance, therefore, the evidence from Lijphart's data points toward proportional representation being an important aspect of executive inclusiveness.

What of the relationship between proportional representation and executive inclusiveness in our subgroup of ethnically divided democracies—the nine established democracies of Belgium, Canada, India, Israel, Mauritius, Papua New Guinea, Spain, Switzerland, and Trinidad and Tobago that are also plural societies? Given the expectations about the heightened need for power sharing in these societies, we would expect these cases to exhibit a higher degree of executive inclusiveness than the more homogeneous democracies. This is indeed the case: 55 percent of the governments in divided democracies featured oversized, multiparty coalition cabinets, compared with 36 percent in the more homogeneous democracies (see Table 7.1).

Table 7.2. Proportion of 36 established democracies with above-average rates of oversized governments, by electoral system and level of ethnic diversity

Electoral system	All democracies	More homogeneous democracies	Ethnically divided democracies
Proportional representation	71% (15 of 21)	71% (12 of 17)	75% (3 of 4)
Plurality or majoritarian	27% (4 of 15)	10% (1 of 10)	60% (3 of 5)

Moreover, the greater the degree of societal diversity, the more likely these democracies were to have an inclusive executive. One way of measuring this relationship, given that our nine divided democracies are all (with the exception of Trinidad and Tobago) divided along a linguistic cleavage, is to look at the extent to which power sharing is related to a country's degree of linguistic fragmentation.[2] Increasing linguistic fragmentation is positively correlated with the rate of oversized-coalition cabinets ($r = 0.49$), although this is not statistically significant at the .05 level. When a dummy variable controlling for British heritage is added to the equation, on the grounds that British-linked countries are more likely to have minimal-winning-coalition governments of the classic Westminster variety, the relationship between the rate of oversized-coalition cabinets and linguistic fragmentation strengthens considerably ($r = 0.71$) and becomes significant at the .01 level.

Yet, this reliance on power sharing in the executive does not appear to be a consequence of the type of electoral system selected. There is a much weaker relationship between PR and inclusive executives in this group of ethnically divided democracies than among the more homogeneous democracies. As Table 7.2 shows, among these divided democracies, three that used PR and three that used a plurality or majority electoral system had above-average rates of oversized-coalition cabinets.

Among the ethnically divided democracies as a whole, the striking pattern in terms of electoral systems is the slight predominance of majoritarian, not proportional, electoral institutions. Of the nine ethnically divided democracies, a majority—Canada, India, Mauritius, Papua New Guinea, and Trinidad and Tobago—use plurality elections, not PR.[3] This includes two countries that are near the top of the oversized-coalition cabinet index—Mauritius and Papua New Guinea—both of which use plurality-majority,

2. I used Siegfried Muller's (1964) index of linguistic fragmentation from Taylor and Hudson (1972).

3. If the United Kingdom and New Zealand are added to the list of ethnically divided societies, as I suggested in footnote 1, then the prevalence of majoritarian institutions is still more pronounced. Note, however, that New Zealand moved from plurality to PR in 1993 in part to encourage a greater degree of minority representation.

rather than proportional, electoral systems.[4] In sum, among the world's ethnically divided countries that have a long duration of unbroken democracy, there is a compelling relationship with patterns of executive inclusiveness, but not with the adoption of PR electoral systems.

Failed Democracies

To explore further the relationship of executive inclusiveness to democratic stability we can also look at the experience of *failed democracies*—those countries that were considered to be "established democracies" at some time in the past, but have since fallen out of this category. Examination of all Freedom House (2000) rankings since 1972 reveal only two countries that maintained a ranking of "free" for more than 10 years before falling out of this category—Sri Lanka and Fiji.

Significantly for our purposes, both of these cases represent ethnically divided states in which there was a deliberate rejection of an inclusive executive in favor of majority domination of the government (by the Sinhalese and indigenous Fijian populations, respectively). In both countries, the failure of attempts to create an inclusive executive appears to have been directly associated with their democratic failure. Sri Lanka until the 1980s was one of the strongest democracies in the developing world. However, the devastating ethnic conflict that has arisen in Sri Lanka since 1982 reflects, in part, the failure to bring Tamils into the executive and the failure of democracy to reduce the intensity of conflict. Fiji, another divided society, fell victim to an ethnic coup in 1987, following the election of a government seen as being too close to the country's Indo-Fijian minority. The election of an Indo-Fijian prime minister under revised constitutional arrangements in 1999 resulted in another coup in 2000.

In both cases, moves toward inclusiveness after conventional democracy had collapsed proved too little, too late. Negotiations were unable to find any institutional formula that was mutually acceptable. Proposals for more formal power sharing, when they came, failed to satisfy all parties. The adoption of PR and a revised form of semi-presidential government in Sri Lanka in 1978, for example, proved to be both inadequate and insufficient to meet growing Tamil demands for independent statehood after the conflict had degenerated into a bloody ethnic civil war. In Fiji, revised constitutional arrangements introduced in 1997 explicitly provided for an inclusive executive. However, these provisions were eschewed by the main indigenous Fijian party after the 1999 election, which chose to remain in opposition to

4. Mauritius uses a variety of plurality elections in multimember districts known as the block vote. Papua New Guinea used plurality elections in the period 1975–2002, and a majority system (the alternative vote) before and since then.

the government (an option made possible by the loosely worded power-sharing provisions of the constitution that made participation in a government of national unity optional, not mandatory, for all parties with more than 10 percent of the seats). An ethnic coup followed a year later.[5] In both Sri Lanka and Fiji, then, the introduction of power-sharing proposals did little to contain a conflict that was already spinning out of control.

Discussion

Overall, the results of this empirical inquiry underline the importance of executive inclusiveness to the consolidation of democracy in ethnically divided societies, but they also call into question the supposedly essential role of PR as a means of facilitating this inclusiveness. It is ironic that data derived from a study by Arend Lijphart, who has done so much to promote the virtues of consociational democracy featuring executive power sharing and PR, should call into question one of his core normative recommendations.

Lijphart has argued that consociational institutions and PR are "clearly superior to the plurality method" of election for divided societies. He says that "the optimal PR system for plural societies is list PR in relatively large districts," because such systems are most likely to deliver highly proportional outcomes and thus enable all politically significant ethnic groups, including minorities, to gain access to legislative representation (Lijphart 1990a, 12). Majoritarian prescriptions, by contrast, are "deeply flawed and dangerous" (Lijphart 1994, 222).

If these conclusions were based on the empirical record of democracy in divided societies, we would expect to see them reflected in our established-democracy country cases. As stated earlier, while PR is empirically associated with governmental inclusiveness across most long-term democracies, this relationship does not hold for the most ethnically divided cases. Moreover, examination of the geographical location of the relevant country cases suggests that the relationship between PR and power sharing is driven in part by the preponderance of multiparty executive governments in the mostly homogeneous democracies of northern Europe—not by the most plural societies. The large-district form of PR recommended by Lijphart and other consociationalists appears to have no empirical relationship with either executive inclusiveness or democratic longevity in the nine most divided democracies (among this group, only Israel combines PR with large districts.)

Regional, historical, and demographic patterns appear to be more important in explaining choice of electoral systems and their relationship to

5. This issue was revisited after the 2001 elections, when the victorious Fijian prime minister, Laisenia Qarase, refused to invite the Indo-Fijian parties to take up the cabinet positions available to them under the Fijian constitution's power-sharing provisions, precipitating another constitutional crisis.

executive inclusiveness and democratic stability in these ethnically divided societies. Of our nine ethnically divided democracies, only two countries in continental Europe—Switzerland and Belgium—might be described as consociational, and Switzerland makes use of such direct majoritarian institutions as the initiative and referendum. Most of the rest use majoritarian political institutions such as Westminster parliaments and plurality elections. With the exception of Israel, the only examples of PR among the ethnically divided democracies occur in continental Europe—Belgium, Switzerland, and Spain. No ethnically divided democracy of longer duration outside the developed world uses PR, although PR has been a common choice in new democracies in the last decade. The successful cases of established democracy in divided societies outside Europe are more likely to use less proportional systems with smaller districts than the national PR systems recommended for plural societies by consociationalists.

Because they are based on the experience of established democracies only, these findings could be dismissed as being too limited to generalize from when examining the many new democracies that have emerged in the past decade. But studies of new democracies have also confirmed this pattern. Robert Bohrer (1997), for example, found that survival rates among new democracies were higher among those countries that used less proportional electoral systems than those that had adopted full-fledged PR. In another study of electoral system choice in new democracies, André Blais and Stephanie Dion (1990, 262) found a similar pattern, concluding that "the single-member district plurality system performs better than proportional representation with respect to the consolidation of fragile democracies." The tendency of highly proportional PR to promote the presence of small extremist parties and undermine effective governance was cited as a recurring problem, particularly in the most highly proportional PR systems in countries such as Israel. Finally, in a broad survey of electoral systems in divided societies, Ben Reilly and Andrew Reynolds (1999, 29, 31) found: "While large-scale PR appears to be an effective instrument for smoothing the path of democratic transition, it may be less effective at promoting democratic consolidation. . . . [I]f consociational structures are entrenched in plural societies which do show potential for the withering away of ethnic voting, then the very institutions designed to alleviate tensions may merely entrench the perception that all politics must be ethnic politics."

How do we explain this curious disjuncture between the theory of consociationalism and the empirical record? One factor is the often neglected issue of the interaction between electoral systems and ethnic demography. One of the basic assumptions about PR is that it will lead to a greater proportion of minority groups gaining representation in the legislature, thus maximizing prospects for governmental power sharing. But this assumption is itself based on presumptions about the nature of ethnic demography that do not always hold up to scrutiny. Because ethnic groups in many developing countries tend to be geographically concentrated, single-member systems may actually do a better job of representing minorities in some cases than proportional ones (see Barkan 1995). Because of this, majoritarian systems can work successfully to manage conflicts and promote inclusive executives in societies where there are a multiplicity of ethnic groups (as in India and Papua New Guinea) or where ethnic groups are sufficiently regionally concentrated to make the combination of plurality elections and federalism a realistic power-sharing package (as in Canada and India).

The importance of ethnic group demography is illustrated by the case of Papua New Guinea, the most linguistically diverse of all our ethnically divided democracies. Papua New Guinea ranks sixth (out of 36 established democracies) on the index of oversized-coalition cabinets despite using a nonproportional, plurality electoral system. Papua New Guinea is on some indicators the most fragmented society in the world, with 852 different language groups and thousands of small ethnic micropolities (see Reilly 2000/2001). In such situations, recommendations for proportional elections as a way of facilitating minority representation become almost meaningless. The legislature itself would have to be eight times larger just to represent all languages spoken—a "parliament of a thousand tribes" to quote the title of one work on preindependence Papua New Guinea (White 1972).

Another example of the importance of ethnic structure comes from India, the world's largest democracy. As the influence of the Congress Party on Indian politics has declined, the pattern of government formation in India has changed radically. Where single-party, minimal winning cabinets were once the norm, shifting multiparty coalitions have replaced the Congress Party as the dominant force in Indian politics since 1996. In late 2001, India's executive government was a broad multiparty coalition that comprised no less than 24 political parties, including a host of minority representatives—making it perhaps the most extreme version of an inclusive executive seen in any established democracy. But this extraordinary executive formation was prompted not by the application of PR elections, but by the operation of a Westminster parliamentary system and plurality elections in a regionally, religiously, and linguistically diverse society.[6]

Conclusion

As these examples suggest, any recommendations for electoral engineering and power sharing in divided societies need to be cognizant of the gap between theory and practice, and of the way different kinds of structural factors, such as ethnic demography, affect political outcomes. I would argue

6. See "The trouble with coalitions," *The Economist*, November 24, 2001, 67.

that the contrast between the normative appeal of highly proportional, large-district PR systems but their limited application in the real world, and the normative rejection of plurality systems despite their successful application in a number of divided societies, is one example of the disjuncture between theory and practice. One clear issue is the problem of generalizing from the small and relatively homogeneous democracies of northern Europe to the much more heterogeneous and complex ethnic demographies of the developing world.

This is most apparent when we examine our group of divided democracies. Of the nine seriously divided societies around the world that have nonetheless managed to maintain continuous democracy, only four use PR—the three European cases, plus Israel. There are no examples of an ethnically plural long-term democracy outside the developed world using PR. These patterns represent a challenge to the case for formal power-sharing institutions. The analysis from which these conclusions are drawn is based directly on Lijphart's own data set—thus representing a particularly serious challenge to consociational claims.

The available evidence therefore suggests that electoral system choices to promote power sharing are highly context-specific, both in terms of the technical aspects of the electoral system and also in relation to a country's broader sociopolitical variables such as the party system, political culture, political history, and demographic factors. Any sustainable strategy for electoral system design in divided societies needs to view these variables as the starting point for a coherent and sustainable electoral system design, rather than adopting a one-size-fits-all model.

8

Fiscal Politics in "Ethnically Mined," Developing, Federal States: Central Strategies and Secessionist Violence

Eduardo Alemán and Daniel Treisman

Does fiscal power sharing exacerbate or alleviate tensions in ethnically divided states? Do particular patterns of central fiscal policy associated with power sharing—including fiscal decentralization, fiscal proportionality, and fiscal appeasement—affect the likelihood of violent bids for secession? Many experts on power sharing would include fiscal decentralization and proportionality rules in their toolbox of devices for avoiding ethnic conflict. In this chapter, we study four noted cases, hoping to understand better whether or not such devices belong there.

The four cases—India, Pakistan, Nigeria, and the former Yugoslavia—are ethnically divided in a specific way. Between 1945 and the early 1990s, the world contained 10 federal states in which (for at least part of the period) at least one ethnic group was both a majority within one of the constituent units and a minority within the federation as a whole (Table 8.1).[1] We call such groups "local-majority/countrywide-minority ethnicities" or simply "majority/minority ethnicities" and the states that contain them "ethnically mined federations," since the demographic facts would seem to plant a mine in their foundations. In other countries, an embittered minority might hope to carve out an independent territory for itself through civil war. But in ethnically mined federations, a majority/minority ethnicity could possibly split off one of the country's subunits, using the state's own internal architecture

We are grateful to Ashutosh Varshney, Valerie Bunce, Amit Ahuja, Caroline Hartzell, David Lake, Mikhail Alexeev, Phil Roeder, Donald Rothchild, and other participants in the San Diego Workshop for valuable comments and suggestions.

1. We use a relatively broad and loose concept of *ethnicity* in this chapter, encompassing religious, linguistic, and racial distinctions and decide which of these seems most salient in particular cases.

Table 8.1. "Ethnically mined" federations, 1945–1990

Federation	Majority/minority states	Majority/minority ethnicity
India	Jammu and Kashmir	Muslim
	Punjab	Sikh
	Meghalaya	Christian
	Mizoram	Christian
	Sikkim	Christian
	Nagaland	Christian
Pakistan		
1947–71	East Pakistan	Bengali
1971–90	Sindh	Sindhi
	NWFP	Pakhtun
Nigeria		
As of 1960	Eastern Region	Igbo
	Western Region	Yoruba
After 1960	*See tables in text*	
Switzerland	Geneva, Jura, Neuchâtel, Vaud, Valais, Fribourg	French
	Ticino	Italian
Canada	Quebec	Québecois French
Spain	Galicia	Galician
	Catalonia	Catalan
	Basque Country	Basque
Belgium	Walloon Region	French
USSR	Belarus	Belarusan
	Ukraine	Ukrainian
	Moldova	Romanian
	Lithuania	Lithuanian
	Latvia	Latvian
	Estonia	Estonian
	Azerbaijan	Azeri
	Armenia	Armenian
	Georgia	Georgian
	Uzbekistan	Uzbek
	Tajikistan	Tajik
	Turkmenistan	Turkmen
	Kyrgyzstan	Kyrgyz
Yugoslavia	Slovenia	Slovene
	Croatia	Croat
	Montenegro	Montenegrin
	Macedonia	Macedonian
	Kosovo	Albanian
Czechoslovakia	Slovak Republic	Slovak

Sources: United States Library of Congress; United States Central Intelligence Agency 2000; Szayna 2000.

Note: *Ethnically mined federations* are those in which the ethnic majority in at least one state or province is in the ethnic minority nationwide. Several additional states joined this category in the 1990s: Russia and Bosnia became independent states and so qualified; Ethiopia adopted a federal structure in its 1994 constitution.

to dismember it. Such states should reveal the politics of secession in particularly vivid form.

Our focus is not on the aftermath of civil wars and the immediate problem of restoring peace, but on the longer-term challenge of consolidating a nonviolent order. Two of our four countries were formed from a civil war (India and Pakistan in 1947), one disintegrated in one (Yugoslavia), and all experienced secessionist violence along the way, as well as periods of relative calm. Violence varied not only over time but also across regions: In each, some groups sought to secede, while others remained loyal to the center. We consider how this record of unrest and quiescence fits with the history of fiscal institutions and policies.

Available data on fiscal systems are sketchy at best, far from exhaustive, and not fully comparable. We do not attempt to reconstruct all fiscal flows systematically, but limit ourselves to relatively straightforward observations that accord with the work of country specialists, on whose careful efforts our analysis relies. We were also forced to adopt an imperfect approach to operationalizing our dependent variable, secessionist violence. By *secessionist violence* we mean acts of force causing bodily harm to others, aimed at making possible the creation of an independent political unit. Lacking systematic data to quantify this cross-nationally, we do not attempt to do so.[2] Rather, we present brief historical narratives for each country, emphasizing moments when major ethnic violence coincided with articulated demands for secession. We leave it ultimately to the reader to agree or disagree with our characterizations. Our aim is to open a conversation about the relevant historical events.

We focus on three fiscal strategies used by central governments: fiscal decentralization (or centralization), proportional distribution, and appeasement. To preview our tentative conclusions, these cases offer little reason to place faith in fiscal power sharing as a means of reducing ethnic conflict. It is not at all clear that either decentralizing state resources or distributing them proportionally among ethnic groups will help. The opposite may be true. In a number of cases, central policies of fiscal appeasement—disproportionately favoring "local-majority/countrywide-minority regions"—seemed to reduce secessionist violence. Yet there were a few counterexamples, where even generous aid apparently failed to induce more moderate politics.

2. We considered various sources of data but could not find any that appeared both sufficiently reliable and focused specifically on what we call "secessionist violence."

Fiscal Politics and Secession

How might fiscal power sharing affect the level of secessionist violence? To answer this requires both a definition of fiscal power sharing and a theory of what causes secessionist violence. By *fiscal power sharing*, we mean the way in which fiscal resources are extracted from and redistributed to the ethnic groups within a state. Strategies include decentralization, proportionality, and appeasement. By *fiscal decentralization*, we mean reducing the scale of central redistribution and allocating a large proportion of fiscal resources directly to subnational governments. More precisely, we measure the degree of fiscal decentralization as the proportion of aggregate subnational government expenditures that is financed from noncentral sources.[3] Whereas this strategy refers to the *scale* of central redistribution, the other two focus on the *pattern*. *Fiscal proportionality* means allocation of central fiscal resources to majority/minority regions in proportion to their share of the country's total population. *Fiscal appeasement* means allocation of central fiscal resources to favor the regions most likely to secede.

How fiscal *decentralization* affects secessionist violence will depend on the true motives of those demanding secession. Such demands may be either sincere or strategic. In the first case, those demanding secession—often called nationalists—believe they would be better off in a separate state. By contrast, strategic demands are made by those who only pretend to desire secession as a means to some other end. There are three common motives. Some strategic secessionists—autonomists—hope, by threatening secession, to win greater authority to set local policies within the existing state. Other strategic secessionists—opportunists—hope, by threatening secession, to extort a greater share of central resources. A third set—local ethnic entrepreneurs—attack the center, politicize ethnic difference, and demand independence as a way of rallying local support. Of course, in reality, motives are often mixed. Why do such demands turn violent? Sincere secessionists might simply believe that the expected benefits of fighting for independence outweigh the expected costs. Strategic secessionists might push conflicts to the point of violence if they do not bear the costs of violence themselves, if they believe violence will convince the center to give them what they want, or if backing down would undermine their local popularity (Fearon 1994).[4]

3. We refer to the degree of fiscal decentralization of a particular subnational government—as opposed to the statewide aggregate—as that government's "subnational fiscal autonomy."

4. The more puzzling question is why a central government would *not* accommodate and preempt violence in such circumstances. In many cases, it would seem rational to appease. Violence might nevertheless occur in settings where (1) information is asymmetric and violence conveys information, (2) contracts between regional and central leaders (for central benefits in return for no secession) are not enforceable, (3) central leaders are self-interested and do not bear the dead-weight costs of violence, (4) central leaders suffer personal political costs if they back down, or (5) central leaders have been listening to the advocates of proportional allocation.

Fiscal decentralization should affect secessionist violence differently, depending on the nature of the secessionists. If demands are sincere, then fiscal policies should have little or no effect. If demands are made by strategic autonomists, fiscal decentralization may help to satisfy them. If education, say, is fiscally assigned to regional governments, then regionally concentrated ethnic communities can set syllabi and levels of education financing to suit their tastes.[5] If demands are pressed by opportunists, fiscal decentralization might reduce the size of central funding pools over which the opportunists compete. This might lower the incentive to make secessionist demands, although there are no guarantees. If the "secessionists" are local ethnic entrepreneurs, however, fiscal decentralization may give them greater resources to press their demands, without reducing their incentive to do so. Fiscal decentralization may also reduce the leverage of unity-oriented central politicians over the local secessionists. Thus, depending on what one assumes about the motives of ethnic politicians, one might derive opposite hypotheses about whether fiscal decentralization reduces or increases secessionist conflict. We treat these motives not as assumptions but as facts to be discovered through empirical investigation.

Given the degree of fiscal decentralization, countries differ in the *pattern* of central fiscal redistribution. In most states, some regions receive larger central transfers, loans, and other forms of aid than others. How might this affect secessionist unrest and violence? Scholars in the consociational school have argued that "proportionality in . . . the allocation of public funds" is an essential element of successful power-sharing arrangements among ethnic groups (Lijphart 1977; 1993, 188–189).[6] By "proportionality," scholars usually mean allocation of central fiscal resources to regions or ethnic communities in proportion to their share in the population. The underlying argument seems to be that allocations proportional to population are a natural compromise position, most likely to be acceptable to leaders of the competing ethnic segments and to seem self-evidently just to their members.

Some suggest, by contrast, that the most effective strategy to preempt secession is to design central transfers to appease the most likely separatist regions. Some regions are more likely to demand secession (sincerely) because their benefits from union are low. Increasing the benefits by pro-

5. This is an application of the famous argument of Wallace Oates (1972). Of course, any education policy that the region enacts could in theory be mandated by the central government, so decentralization is not necessary for differentiated policies (see Breton 2000). However, centralization will leave regions vulnerable to change. If fiscal decentralization is hard to reverse, this will render the center's commitment to respecting subnational desires more credible (Przeworski et al. 1995). There are no guarantees that fiscal decentralization will lead to a better match of local tastes and public goods. As Bardhan and Mookherjee (2000) and Tanzi (1995) note, local governments are often captured by local elites, who may not share the tastes of the local majority.

6. However, Lijphart adds that: "A possible variant of strict proportionality is deliberate minority overrepresentation." On such strategies, see below.

viding larger central transfers may alter the calculus. Certain regional leaders may demand secession (strategically) because the local population is primed to support an anticenter appeal (Treisman 1999b). Giving such leaders resources to buy local support in other ways may persuade them to put away the ethnic card.[7] In ethnically mined federations, the majority/minority regions will tend to have the greatest separatist potential, so this implies that secessionist violence should be lower when these regions are preemptively appeased.[8]

In sum, the existing literature suggests several hypotheses about how fiscal politics might affect secessionist unrest and violence in ethnically mined federations.

Hypothesis 1a (*the decentralization hypothesis*). There will be *less* secessionist violence if fiscal decentralization is greater.
Hypothesis 1b (*the central-control hypothesis*). There will be *more* secessionist violence if fiscal decentralization is greater.
Hypothesis 2a (*the proportionality hypothesis*). There will be *more* secessionist violence in majority/minority regions that receive less than their proportionate share of transfers and tax shares.
Hypothesis 2b (*the appeasement hypothesis*). There will be *less* secessionist violence if transfers and tax shares are allocated disproportionately to regions with greater separatist potential (majority/minority regions).

Note that the proportionality hypothesis and the appeasement hypothesis are related. Discrimination against a given regional unit is simultaneously a failure of proportionality and a failure of appeasement. However, the appeasement hypothesis is stronger: It contends that proportional allocations to the regions with greatest secessionist potential are not enough. To distinguish these empirically, we need to look for cases in which proportional allocations are associated with secessionist violence.

India

Since independence in 1947, India has been a federally structured, parliamentary democracy.[9] The population of 1.01 billion (as of the 2000 census)

7. Treisman (1999a) argues that in Russia in the early 1990s, central policy directed disproportionate fiscal benefits to regions with the greatest demonstrated resolve to threaten the constitutional order, and that this helped to reduce subsequent secessionist demands.

8. However, asymmetric overaccommodation of minority regions is sometimes thought to exacerbate tensions because of the perceived unfairness. Regardless of justice, a strategy of rewarding regions or groups thought to have greater separatist potential might encourage others to seek a reputation for anticenter activism. For a more detailed analysis, see Treisman (2002).

9. The possible exception is 1975–1977, when Prime Minister Indira Gandhi imposed emergency rule.

is today divided among 26 states, six centrally administered union territories, and the federal capital of Delhi. India constitutes a religious and linguistic mosaic. As of the early 1990s, 82.4 percent of Indians were Hindu, 11.7 percent Muslim, 2.3 percent Christian, and 2.0 percent Sikh. The constitution recognizes 15 major languages, the most widespread of which—Hindi—is spoken by 31.3 percent of the population.

The Congress Party, which evolved from the Indian National Congress of Mohandas Gandhi and Jawaharlal Nehru, dominated politics through most of the post-independence period, winning a comfortable majority in all elections up to 1989, except for a protest vote against Indira Gandhi's emergency rule in 1977. From 1989, it has been challenged by the Janata Dal and Bharatiya Janata Parties at the center and by a number of rising regional parties in the states.

If religion is taken as a marker of ethnicity, six Indian states qualify as local-majority/countrywide-minority regions. In the northern, mountainous Jammu and Kashmir, Muslims were 64 percent of the total population as of the early 1990s. Sikhs made up 63 percent of the population of neighboring Punjab state. The four northeast border states of Meghalaya, Mizoram, Sikkim, and Nagaland have Christian majorities (India, 1991). If, on the other hand, ethnicity is defined by language, then as of the 1991 census only 6 of the 24 states had Hindi-speaking majorities (Bihar, Haryana, Himachal Pradesh, Madhya Pradesh, Rajastan, and Uttar Pradesh). Since this would put almost all states in the majority/minority category, and since language has been less politicized than religion in India, we focus here on the latter.

India's Fiscal Politics

In India most taxes are levied and collected by the central government; revenues from some of these are fully assigned to the states, and others are shared with the states.[10] There are three main channels of center-state financial transfers.[11] First, the constitution requires the president to appoint a Finance Commission every five years, which determines what shares of income tax and central excises will go to each state, and also establishes levels of grants-in-aid. These transfers are intended mainly to meet fiscal needs of

10. Fully central taxes include customs duties, corporation tax, most excises, and property taxes (except on agricultural land). The central government must share revenue from income tax (on nonagricultural incomes) with the states, and may share excises. Fully state taxes that are centrally collected include estate duties (except on agricultural land) and sales taxes on subjects of interstate commerce. The states levy, collect, and retain taxes on agricultural income, estate and property taxes on agricultural land or buildings, taxes on mineral rights, excises on alcohol and narcotics, and sales taxes (except on interstate commerce) (Singh 1987).

11. See, for instance, Gandhi (1999), Gulati and George (1988), Rao (1998), and Thimmaiah (1985).

the states and correct for spillovers. Second, a Planning Commission, first established in 1950, makes recommendations for additional grants and loans, aimed mainly at supporting development and helping to finance projects in the states' plans. These transfers are determined annually, and sometimes within the year. Third, since the nationalization of banks in 1969, much of the distribution of commercial credit has been indirectly controlled by the central government. In addition, loans from the Life Insurance Corporation, the Agricultural Refinance and Development Corporation, and the Rural Electrification Corporation support development. These are often considered a third channel of "institutional finance," flowing from center to states.

How great is the fiscal autonomy of the (religious) majority/minority states in India relative to other states? How has their fiscal autonomy changed over time? Answering these questions is difficult given the limited fiscal data available. Answers may differ depending on whether one focuses on states' current or total (current and capital) expenditures. The ratio of the states' "own current revenues"—that is, revenues raised locally—to their current expenditures fell from 68.9 percent in 1955–56 to 57.1 percent in 1994–55 (Rao 1998, 90). However, the ratio of the states' own current revenues to *total* expenditure remained relatively stable—48.5 percent in 1955–56 and 48.9 percent in 1994–55. Lacking data for total expenditure for individual states, we present figures for own current revenues as a share of own current expenditures. We were able to calculate this ratio for local-majority/countrywide-minority states in three periods: 1961–65, 1990–93, and 1996–99 (Table 8.2). Among the majority/minority states, Punjab was the most fiscally autonomous throughout this period, while the other five states had extremely low fiscal autonomy, relying on external sources to finance 80 percent or more of their current spending in the 1990s. The degree of fiscal autonomy appears to have dropped for Punjab (slightly) and Jammu and

Table 8.2. India: State's own current revenues as percentage of its current expenditures

	Average		
	1961–65[a]	1990–93	1996–99
Meghalaya		16.83	17.39
Sikkim		20.23	13.95
Nagaland	2.83	8.51	5.00
Mizoram		7.40	6.25
Jammu and Kashmir	51.10	16.21	12.99
Punjab	82.66	67.42	67.41
All states[b]	67.16	56.17	54.24

Sources: India 1965, 2001.
[a] Nagaland just 1964–65.
[b] 16 states in 1961–65; 25 states in 1990s.

Kashmir (a lot) between the 1960s and the 1990s. The level stayed about the same during this period for Nagaland.

What about the pattern of central fiscal redistribution? While reasonably comprehensive figures were available for Finance Commission and Plan transfers (Table 8.3), we could only find estimates of institutional finance flows for the period 1969–76 (Table 8.4), so the picture we can offer is incomplete. We were also unable to find any data for Mizoram.

What do these figures suggest? The level of combined Finance Commission and Plan assistance for Punjab started higher than that of the median region in the late 1950s and early 1960s. In the late 1960s, however, it dropped below that of the median region, and fell further and further behind until the early 1980s (the last period for which data on plan transfers and loans were available). Whereas in the late 1950s, Punjab received 2.5 times as much as the median region in central government aid via these channels, in the early 1980s the state received only 86 percent of the median state's allocation. Finance Commission transfers continued to drop relative to the median in the late 1980s, but recovered somewhat in the 1990s.

During the one period for which data were available (1969–1976), Punjab received a very high level of institutional capital flows, mostly in the form of credit from the centrally controlled commercial banks. This, if included with the other transfers, would have left Punjab considerably better off than the average region during this period. However, the impact of commercial bank lending on demands for secession may be different from that of central grants or tax devolution. Commercial bank loans are supposed to be repaid: The opportunity to renege on such loans in the event of secession might make such a choice more rather than less attractive. The large credits to Punjab probably reflected a policy of support for agriculture; after 1969, banks were required to make 40 percent of loans to this sector.

Finance Commission and Plan transfers to Jammu and Kashmir were consistently much higher than the median. The trend was clearly upward for both series from the late 1950s. However, Plan transfers fell quite sharply in the early 1980s and Finance Commission transfers—after increasing dramatically in the late 1980s—also fell in the early 1990s. Institutional financial flows were somewhat below the median in the early 1970s. One other relevant point is that the share of loans in central aid increased in the 1970s, so that by the 1980s a large share of current spending was going toward debt service (Prakash 2000, 2053).

Nagaland showed a similar pattern of Finance Commission and Plan aid to that of Jammu and Kashmir: an increasing trend in both, with a drop in Plan transfers in the early 1980s and then in Finance Commission transfers in the early 1990s. The main difference from Jammu and Kashmir was that Nagaland's level of transfers per capita was consistently far higher than the former's very high level. From the mid-1960s to the early 1980s, Nagaland

Table 8.3. India: Center-region transfers (rupees per capita)

	Planning commission transfers and loans						
	First plan 1951–56	Second plan 1956–61	Third plan 1961–66	Annual plans 1966–69	Fourth plan 1969–74	Fifth plan 1974–79	Sixth plan 1980–85
Meghalaya							
Sikkim							
Nagaland			280.51	420.33	790.06	1595.86	357.85
Jammu and Kashmir	30.21	56.19	76.41	153.88	352.02	1131.04	644.43
Punjab	151.73	84.59	111.49	72.09	65.65	115.26	86.34
Median	21.98	27.81	63.01	39.68	63.93	94.49	88.26

	Finance Commission Transfers (tax-shares and grants)								
	II FC 1957–62	III FC 1962–66	IV FC 1966–69	V FC 1969–74	VI FC 1974–79	VII FC 1979–84	VIII FC 1984–89	IX FC 1989–94	X FC 1994–99
Meghalaya					748.03	1008.65	2858.62	1447.34	1787.68
Sikkim						1474	3301.35	1227.25	1531.74
Nagaland		18.23	2164.08	1562.98	2188.23	3341.53	6806.03	3790.66	4378.35
Jammu and Kashmir	71.76	61.08	185.62	231.42	436.62	625.02	1870.08	1088.8	1175.9
Punjab	51.13	29.05	28.32	65.8	114.09	259.93	384.86	135.25	1725.48
Median	26.48	32.08	64.7	76.1	162.73	315.69	585.25	150.87	1928.5

	Planning Commission + Finance Commission Assistance (note the slight divergence in dates)					
Meghalaya						
Sikkim						
Nagaland		298.74	2584.41	2353.04	3784.09	3699.38
Jammu and Kashmir	127.95	137.49	339.5	583.44	1567.66	1269.45
Punjab	135.72	140.54	100.41	131.45	229.35	346.27
Median	54.29	95.09	104.38	140.03	257.22	403.95

Sources: Thimmaiah 1985; calculations from Gandhi 1999.

Table 8.4. India: Institutional financial flows, 1969–76 (rupees per capita)

	1981 Population (in millions)	Commercial banks			LIC[a]	Term lending to industry	ARDC[b]	REC[c]	Total institutional
		Credit	Investment	Total					
Meghalaya	1.3	37	64	101	66	6		13	186
Sikkim	0.3								
Nagaland	0.8	25	145	170	60	21	2	7	260
Jammu-Kashmir	6.0	73	35	108	15	9	2	18	152
Punjab	16.8	346	47	393	32	18	28	11	482
All states	683.3	121	32	153	22	25	9	6	217

Sources: Adapted from Gulati and George 1998, 114–115; "India: A Country Study" in U.S. Library of Congress.
[a] Life Insurance Corporation
[b] Agricultural Refinance and Development Corporation
[c] Rural Electrification Corporation

had the highest level of transfers of any state for which data were available. And Nagaland even had institutional financial flows in the early 1970s that were above the median—and above those of Jammu and Kashmir. The only data available for Meghalaya and Sikkim were for Finance Commission Transfers from the early or late 1970s. These showed a pattern similar to that of Nagaland and Jammu and Kashmir with levels somewhere between the two and far above the median.

Secessionist Violence in India

In Punjab, major violent unrest occurred during the 1980s (Dasgupta 1995, 290). "Extensive violence connected with a militant separatist movement for a Sikh homeland claimed more than twenty thousand lives between 1981 and 1992." The violence died down after 1992, as "resident Sikhs . . . gradually opted for normalcy, and the electoral institutions registered increased effectiveness through several elections at the state and local levels from 1992 to 1994." Before the 1980s, secessionist voices were largely marginalized. The exclusively Sikh Akali Dal party was repeatedly defeated in the five state assembly elections before 1985 by the Congress Party, which appealed to lower class and caste Sikhs. The Akali Dal party during this period collaborated with the Congress Party and even the Hindu Jana Sangh party.

In the early 1980s, the older Akali Dal party elites were challenged by younger activists from the dominant Jat Sikh caste who were "confessionally purist, socially exclusionary, politically militant, and increasingly well-armed" (Dasgupta 1995, 291). These separatist insurgents made armed sanctuaries out of Sikh temples, including the Golden Temple in Amritsar, until the Indian military forced them to leave in 1984. This military action led to the assassination of Indira Gandhi by her Sikh bodyguards and waves of militant and countermilitant violence, most of the victims of which were poor Sikhs. In the midst of the crisis, an Akali Dal government was elected in Punjab in 1985. But by 1992 the mood had changed, and the Congress Party was returned to power in the state assembly election of that year.

If the 1980s were the decade of violence in Punjab, the 1990s could claim this distinction in Kashmir. The Kashmir problem has been deeply influenced by external intervention. Pakistan, which claims the territory, has fought three wars against India—in 1947, 1965, and 1971. By the late 1980s, the end of the Afghanistan war had left Islamic guerrillas in Pakistan searching for new targets, and weapons and militants infiltrated across the border into Kashmir. Tensions between India and Pakistan over the future of Kashmir escalated dangerously in 2002, creating the possibility of a nuclear war.

Given Pakistan's interest in stirring up unrest, it is surprising how *little* secessionist violence Kashmir has seen until recently. The 1965 Pakistan invasion did not receive significant support in the region. In the late 1980s, however, a growing Islamic coalition began to challenge the state's established, increasingly corrupt Muslim leadership. Protests broke out over a rigged election in 1987,[12] and Kashmir activists organized a boycott of the 1989 election. Protests escalated after this, and the Delhi government imposed central rule, backed by military force. Since 1989, thousands of civilians have been killed in confrontations between militants and Indian security forces (Prakash 2000).

The territories that became Nagaland and Mizoram saw periodic secessionist violence during the post-independence period. Violence first broke out in Nagaland, then an area within Assam, in the 1950s. The demands of separatists from the Naga tribe were supported by the population, which engaged in a tax revolt and campaign of sabotage (Dasgupta 1995, 289; Encarta 2001). In response, the Indian government created the state of Nagaland in 1963. However, violent opposition continued and continues today, organized by guerrilla bands that retreated into Burma or China to regroup.

In Mizoram, an insurgency lasted from the 1950s to 1986, when the Mizo leader, Pu Laldenga, negotiated an agreement with the central government upgrading the territory's status to that of a state and emerged as the new state's chief minister. Peace has been maintained since then, and Mizoram is viewed by some Indian leaders as an example of successful negotiation to end secessionist challenges (Mehta 2001). Meghalaya, which became a state in 1972, did not experience any significant secessionist violence. Sikkim was annexed by India in 1975. We could not find references to any secessionist violence within the state.

Impact of Indian Fiscal Policy on Secessionist Violence

To what extent does this experience fit our hypotheses? The impact of fiscal decentralization on secessionist violence is unclear. Secessionist violence occurred in one state with high (Punjab), one with low (Jammu and Kashmir), and one with very low fiscal autonomy (Nagaland). The time trend might be important: Violence flared up in Jammu and Kashmir after the state's dependence on central resources increased. It appears that the same may have been true for Punjab, but we lacked data from the 1980s to check. Overall, there seems to be no clear evidence that the level of fiscal decen-

12. The ruling party of Farooq Abdullah was disqualified by the Indian government on the grounds of corruption.

tralization mattered one way or the other. The evidence supports neither the decentralization hypothesis nor the central-control hypothesis.

The pattern of fiscal distribution appears more closely related to the incidence of violence. The major outburst in Punjab occurred after Finance Commission and Plan allocations had been falling progressively further below the median for a decade. Jammu and Kashmir also seems to provide evidence of an inverse relationship between fiscal appeasement and secessionist violence. The relative lack of violent uprisings in the province until the 1980s—despite support for militants from across the border and even several Pakistani invasions—fits with the pattern of increasingly generous Finance Commission and Plan transfers through the late 1970s. The sharp drop in Plan allocations (and slight drop in combined transfers) in the early 1980s may have helped prepare the ground for the protests of 1989. And the major decrease in Finance Commission transfers in the early 1990s—if not offset by an increase in Plan transfers—would help to explain the flare-up of violence during that decade. The proportionality and appeasement hypotheses both receive some support, although the evidence does not distinguish between them.

From the appeasement perspective, the very generous aid provided to Sikkim and Meghalaya could help to explain their quiescence through the late 1980s. But the drop in the 1990s, pushing both beneath the median level of combined Finance Commission and Plan transfers by the end of the decade, might have been expected to provoke some increase in violence. Either the appeasement hypothesis fails in these cases, or some violent incidents lie ahead. Finally, the very high level of central support for Nagaland alongside continuing secessionist violence seems to contradict the appeasement hypothesis.

In short, the proportionality hypothesis and the appeasement hypothesis do a good job of explaining the two major cases of secessionist violence in Indian postwar history. But there is one exception and some other anomalies. The decentralization and central-control hypotheses do not fit the Indian pattern of events.

Pakistan

After the British left in 1947, the newly created Pakistan consisted of two noncontiguous areas, East and West Pakistan. In the East, Bengalis were in the majority, while Punjabis were in the majority in the West. East Pakistan had 54.2 percent of the country's population, while West Pakistan had better economic assets and controlled the civil service and the military. Because of the West's control over fiscal policy, and more generally over the economic and political systems, we have chosen to classify Bengali East Pakistan as the majority/minority state. Since the end of the 1971 war and partition, Pakistan has been composed of four major subunits[13]: Punjab (majority Punjabi, the dominant ethnicity nationwide), Baluchistan (multiethnic), Sindh (majority/minority Sindhi), and the Northwest Frontier Province (NWFP; majority/minority Pakhtuns).

After the 1947 partition of India and Pakistan, a government of Mohammed Ali Jinnah's Muslim League assumed power. The civil service, allied with the military—which was dominated by the Punjabis and to a lesser extent Pakhtuns—played a central role in the transition period. The 1956 constitution, drafted by an indirectly elected constituent assembly, reorganized the federation under the so-called one-unit rule, which replaced the existing five provinces with only two states, East and West Pakistan, and set up a unicameral legislature with equal representation for each subunit. The new constitution provided little autonomy to the provinces and gave the indirectly elected president the power to oversee all national expenditures and to veto provincial bills (Ahmed 1997).

As the first national elections approached, the military staged a coup in October 1958. The military government further centralized power by enacting a new constitution in 1962, which gave the executive the power to appoint and dismiss provincial governors, who in turn were responsible for hiring and firing the provincial cabinets. In 1969, as part of a democratization plan that included the first national elections, the one-unit rule was abolished and the five provinces of Punjab, Sindh, Baluchistan, the Northwest Frontier (NWFP), and East Pakistan were reestablished.

During the 1970 election campaign, the opposition in East Pakistan proposed radical administrative and economic reforms. The election results favored East Pakistan's Awami League, which won the right to form a government. This outcome threatened the role of the army, which feared losing defense funds, as well as the political and economic privileges of those ethnic groups overrepresented in the army, the civil service, and business. When the military, with the support of the Pakistan People's Party (PPP), decided to postpone the transfer of power, this triggered widespread unrest in the East. The military increased coercive measures and sent troops to repress opposition. The civil war between the East and the West led to the Indo-Pakistan War of 1971, after which the Bengali-led party declared independence and Bangladesh was born.

After the secession of East Pakistan, power in the West was transferred to a civilian government under Prime Minister Zulfiqar Ali Bhutto of the PPP,

13. It also included the smaller tribal areas, northern areas, and the federal capital. The ethnic composition (circa 1996) was 56 percent Punjabi, 17 percent Sindhi, 16 percent Pakhtuns, 6 percent Muhajir, 3 percent Baluchi, and 2 percent other ("Pakistan: A Country Study" in U.S. Library of Congress).

who enjoyed military support. In this new Pakistan, the Punjabis, who dominated civil and military bureaucracies, became the largest ethnic group. As differences increased between the center and the provinces, the Bhutto government dismissed the provincial administrations of NWFP and Baluchistan. After the 1977 election, opposition forces claimed electoral fraud and began mounting antigovernment protests. In July, a military coup deposed Bhutto and General Zia ul-Haq established an authoritarian regime. The government arrested and executed Bhutto for murder, suspended the constitution, introduced an Islamic penal code, and began to further concentrate power in the hands of the federal government. President Mohammad Zia and several of his commanders were killed in a plane crash in 1988.

Elections were held that year, resulting again in victory for the PPP, this time led by Prime Minister Benazir Bhutto (the daughter of the earlier Prime Minister). The president dismissed her in 1990, accusing her of corruption, and appointed instead a prime minister from the Islamic Democratic Alliance party. As unrest around Sindh became widespread, the government lost military backing and fell in July 1993. The PPP won a slim majority of votes in the October 1993 elections, but soon after, in November 1996, the military intervened again. In 1997, the Pakistan Muslim League, under Nawaz Sharif, won a sweeping election victory. Finally, in October 1999, Nawaz Sharif was ousted from power by yet another military coup after attempting to fire his army chief of staff, General Pervez Musharraf, who became Pakistan's new president.

Pakistan's Fiscal Policies before Partition in 1971

Very limited data exist on public finances and tax structures for the first post-independence decade (Pasha and Fatima 1999). During this period, state power was centralized, and the provinces had little financial autonomy. The increasing role and buildup of the Punjabi-dominated military establishment diverted significant resources to national defense.

Center-provincial financial arrangements under the 1962 constitution followed the 1956 constitution's one-unit rule, which established juridical equality between East and West Pakistan. To make up for the inelasticity of the two provinces' independent tax sources, the 1962 constitution entitled them to a share in the proceeds of certain federal taxes (Wheeler 1970, 183). A National Finance Commission (NFC), established by the constitution and appointed by the president, was in charge of making recommendations for the distribution of shared taxes and grants-in-aid, as well as the principles governing borrowing by governments. Divisible pool revenues were allocated on the basis of population, 54 percent to the East and 46 percent to the West. Sales tax proceeds were allocated 70 percent based on population and 30 percent based on incidence. Before 1962, 62.5 of revenues from export duties on jute, a main source of foreign exchange, went to East Pakistan, the major producer. In 1962, the system was changed to allocate all export duties to the province of collection, but in 1964–1965 this was modified again to reflect exclusively population proportions (Wheeler 1970, 184). During the first post-independence years, customs duties were the main revenue source (71 percent of total taxes in 1949–1950), but their share declined continuously through the 1950s and 1960s, with a corresponding rise in the share of excises (Pasha and Fatima 1999).

Table 8.5 shows the total revenues received by the two regions, the share of provincial revenues contributed by their share of central taxes, and the share from central government grants-in-aid from 1950–1951 to 1970–1971. An additional major source of finance came from the annual development programs. These funds were part of central planning policies designed to foster regional development, and according to the constitution were supposed to ensure greater equality between the two provinces and among different areas within each. The levels and distribution of these funds appear in Table 8.6.

How high was fiscal autonomy? East Pakistan relied on central transfers more than West Pakistan. Between 1962 and 1968, central government transfers—taxes and grants-in-aid—rose to equal more than half of total revenues in the East. In 1968–1971, the share dropped to about 45 percent. The share of central resources in revenues of the Western government varied between about 19 and 43 percent of the total.[14]

Did the pattern of central transfers tend to favor the local-majority/countrywide-minority region? East Pakistan was not favored over the West, as can be seen in the last two rows of Table 8.5. On average, the share of central taxes distributed to the two provinces was roughly equal. Since the population of the East was 54.2 percent of the total, the East's share of distributed central taxes was less than its population share in every year (for which we have data) from 1958 to 1971. Until 1970–1971, right before the East's secession, the share of grants-in-aid going to the East was far below that going to the West, although the East's share rose over time. East Pakistan also received a smaller share of development grants than its population share (Table 8.6).

Several authors have offered evidence of what seemed to be skewed government economic policy favoring the West over the East. Samina Ahmed (1997, 93) has argued, "The Punjabi-Muhajir central bureaucracy, responsible for formulating economic planning and for disbursing developmental expenditures to the provinces, adopted policies that favored their ethnic constituents in urban Sindh and Punjab. While one of the main sources of

14. Decisionmaking autonomy was lower than these numbers would suggest. Provincial governors were centrally appointed, giving the federal government leverage over finance and development expenditures.

Table 8.5. Pakistan: Total revenue from central government, by region, 1950–1971

	1950–51	1958–59	1962–63	1965–66	1966–67	1967–68	1968–69	1969–70[a]	1970–71[a]
East Pakistan									
Total Revenue (in 10 millions of Rs.)	*18.2*	*52.28*	*74.52*	*117.94*	*130.42*	*141.52*	*146.27*	*162.51*	*178.91*
Share from central taxes (%)	36.7	32.8	49.5	45.68	47.31	40.48	39.09	38.18	38.96
Share from central government grant-in-aid (%)	0	2.12	9.19	5.95	4.21	11.73	6.78	5.87	6.19
West Pakistan									
Total Revenue (in 10 millions of Rs.)	*35.98*	*88.09*	*134.93*	*178.36*	*179.98*	*182.71*	*197.37*	*218.48*	*187.77*
Share from central taxes (%)[b]	16.6	22.1	26.23	29.79	33.73	29.86	28.75	28.23	34.44
Share from central government grant-in-aid (%)	2.81	5.56	16.48	10.82	8.36	12.71	8.1	7.03	3.81
East Pakistan's share of total									
Central Taxes allocated to Provinces (%)	52.8	46.8	51.0	50.3	50.4	51.2	50.2	50.1	51.9
Central Grants-in-Aid to Provinces (%)	0.0	18.5	23.6	26.7	26.7	41.7	38.3	38.3	60.7

Sources: Total revenues and share from central taxes from 1950 to 1963 comes from Wheeler 1970, 186; all other data from the Pakistan Ministry of Finance 1969–70 and 1970–71.

Note: East Pakistan's share of population was approximately 54 percent.

[a] Budget estimates for 1969–70 and 1970–71; actual figures for prior years.

[b] Since end of "one unit" share of province's revenue from central taxes: NWFP 48.36, Punjab 33.32, Sindh 28.05, Baluchistan 49.24.

Table 8.6. Pakistan: Allocation of central government development programs, 1960–1961 to 1969–1970

Region	1960–61 to 1964–65	1965–66	1966–67	1967–68	1968–69	1969–70
Total (in 10 millions of rupees)	1,403.0	342.0	513.7	570.0	640.7	500.5
to East (percent)	36.6	43.0	44.8	46.2	46.3	46.2
to West (percent)	40.4	40.9	37.0	37.2	37.3	38.0
to Center (percent)	23.0	16.1	18.2	16.6	16.5	15.9

Source: Pakistan Ministry of Finance 1964–65, 1969–70.

foreign exchange, for example, was the sale of East Bengal's jute, the proceeds were spent on developing the industry of the west wing, based in Karachi, as well as the agricultural infrastructure of central Punjab." In regard to differences in regional development, Joseph Stern and Walter Falcon (1970, 5) wrote, "The physical separation of the two provinces and the continued domination of the central government by West Pakistanis have led to charges that the widening of the income differences stems not only from economic causes but from deliberate policy. The use of scarce foreign exchange earned by the East Pakistan to finance rapid growth in West Pakistan, and the fact that the preponderate share of investment resources was allocated to West Pakistan have exacerbated this issue." Omar Noman (1990, 41) wrote about the economic policies of the military government: "Bengali resentment was fueled by the growing disparity between the two regions. At the time of Ayub's coup, there was a difference of 30 percent in per capita incomes of the two regions. By the end of the second five-year plan (1965), the disparity of per capita income had risen to 45 percent. By the time of Ayub's departure, the gap had risen to 61 percent. Although there is considerable controversy over the precise magnitude of interregional resource transfer, there is no dispute about the relative decline of East Pakistan under the Ayub regime."

Secessionist Violence in Pakistan Prior to 1971

Incidents of ethnic and separatist violence in Pakistan before 1971 fall into two groups: those within the borders of West Pakistan, particularly involving the center against the Sindhis, the Pakhtuns, and the Baluchis; and the separatist unrest that emerged in East Pakistan, the majority/minority state in question.

Within the West, conflicts appeared to increase after the imposition of the one-unit rule. In the northwest, the predominantly Pakhtun party Khudai Khidmatgar (KK) had opposed the division of Pakistan from India, and many

Pakhtun nationalists had called for the formation of a separate state in the NWFP and Pakhtun-inhabited regions of Baluchistan. After independence, the KK's successor, the National Awami Party (NAP), became more moderate in its demands and restricted its aims to greater autonomy. The government responded by centralizing control over the NWFP by means of co-opted chief ministers, and using force, particularly in tribal areas that experienced the greatest unrest (Ahmed 1997).

In Baluchistan, intermittent armed conflict between the army and Baluch tribal groups ended in 1969 with a ceasefire and the repeal of the one-unit rule (Noman 1990, 66). A rebellion in Baluchistan served as the pretext for the military coup of October 1958, but the main motivation of the Western leadership appeared to be its fear of losing to the East Bengalis in the upcoming elections (Ahmed 1997, 96). In Sindh, the apparent control of Punjabis and Mohajirs over the political and economic system prompted ethnic tensions. Nationalist mobilizations increased following the announcement of government plans to eliminate Sindhi as a medium of instruction in schools (Pattanaik 1998).

Demands for greater regional autonomy in East Pakistan were common from the time of independence, and grew intense after the imposition of the one-unit rule. In 1954, the center intervened to dissolve the increasingly confrontational local assembly. Opposition to the military regime of General Ayub grew throughout the 1960s (Noman 1990, 32). In December 1968, the political parties of East Pakistan called a successful general strike. As protests mounted, the military decided to remove the sitting executive, Ayub, and replaced him with Army Commander-in-Chief, Yahya Khan.

In 1971, after the army refused to transfer power to the Bengali dominated coalition, the civil war began. The West first launched a military offensive against the East. But soon after, the Bengalis, with crucial help from India, were able to win independence.

Impact of Pakistan's Fiscal Policy on Secessionist Violence Prior to 1971

How does Pakistan's experience prior to 1971 relate to our hypotheses? Fiscal autonomy was quite low in East Pakistan and in the former provinces subsumed by the one-unit rule until 1969. The East's dependence on central grants and tax shares increased between the late 1950s and early 1960s, from about 35 to 59 percent of total revenues, and then dropped to 44 percent by 1969. Thus, the period of gradually growing secessionist unrest in the late 1960s coincided with a period of increasing fiscal autonomy. The slow increase in unrest in the East became a full-fledged separatist movement after the military's decision not to honor electoral results. Several authors have associated the period since 1956, after the withdrawal of political and financial autonomy from the former provinces of West Pakistan, with greater nationalist unrest (Ahmed 1997, Pattanaik 1998). This might suggest an association of lower fiscal autonomy with greater unrest. Thus, overall, there seems to be no clear relationship to support either the decentralization hypothesis or the central-control hypothesis.

The pattern of central transfers to East and West Pakistan did not follow population proportions and benefited the West. We found a consensus in the literature on Pakistan that perceived unfairness of the revenue allocation mechanism contributed to secessionist unrest in the East. Disproportionate allocations favoring the dominant region may well have helped to prompt the autonomy demands, political conflicts, and violence that culminated in the civil war. This pattern is consistent with both the proportionality hypothesis and the appeasement hypothesis (an absence of appeasement contributed to civil war), but does not permit us to distinguish between these hypotheses.

Pakistan's Fiscal Policies after Partition in 1971

After East Pakistan's secession in 1971, differences between Punjab and the other provinces within rump Pakistan became contentious. The period between the civil war and the early 1990s has been seen as one of overwhelming federal dominance of public finance (Sato 1994). Federal taxes and excises were allocated to the provinces according to NFC recommendations made in 1974 and not revised until 1991.

Allocations from excise duties and royalties on natural gas went to the two provinces of origin, Baluchistan and Sindh, and continued after the 1991 revisions. The federal government kept 20 percent of divisible pool revenues, while the provinces shared the other 80 percent. Provincial shares from federal taxes and excises, excluding special grants and subventions, are shown in Table 8.7. Under the 1974 NFC award, 96 percent of these federal transfers were distributed according to population; the share decreased to 75 percent with the 1991 award (IPS 1992, 53).

During the 1970s and 1980s the provinces' own resources became inadequate to meet their increasing expenditures, and the central government began making discretionary grants to fund their current account deficits (IPS 1992). These "revenue-deficit" grants financed about 30 percent of provincial governments' current expenditure between 1977 and 1979. In addition, specific subventions were allocated to the NWFP and Baluchistan as block grants, along with grants for the maintenance of strategic roads.[15]

15. The central government also provided grants and loans to help finance the provincial development programs. Although discretionary, these funds appear to have been shared more or less according to the distribution of population (Sato 1994). Another smaller set of special development programs included a grant for underdeveloped regions such as Baluchistan as well as discretionary funds for projects recommended by members of the National Assembly.

Table 8.7. Pakistan: Federal transfers to provinces since the 1970s (percent of total)

Province	1974 Award	1991 Award	Population	
			1981	1998[a]
Punjab	55.6	45.2	57.9	55.6
Sindh	23.9	22.4	23.3	23.0
NWFP	13.0	19.2	13.5	13.3
Baluchistan	7.5	13.2	5.3	5.0
	100.0	100.0	100.0	96.9

Sources: Adapted from IPS (1992, 53) and information from Government of Pakistan, at http://www.pakistan.gov.pk/finance-division/publications/economic-survey-13.pdf.

NWFP = Northwest Frontier Province.

[a] Excludes population living in the federal capital, Islamabad, and Federally Administered Areas.

Table 8.8 details provincial current revenues from 1970 to 1989, including development grants. Table 8.9 shows the distribution of central grants, including revenue deficit, foreign aid, and development grants.

How high was fiscal autonomy? As of the early 1970s, all provinces were relatively dependent on federal allocations: Punjab and Sindh financed a little more than half of total revenues from their own taxes and other local sources, while the NWFP's and Baluchistan's own revenues came to respectively 42 and 33 percent of the total. For all provinces, fiscal autonomy dropped precipitously over time. The proportion of the provinces' own revenues in total revenues fell from 53 to 19 percent for Punjab between the early 1970s and late 1980s; from 58 to 14 percent for Sindh; from 42 to 8 percent for NWFP; and from 33 to 4 percent for Baluchistan.

Did the pattern of transfers tend to favor local-majority/countrywide-minority regions relative to others? Shares from federal taxes correlated roughly with population throughout the 1970s and 1980s (Sato 1994; Table 8.8). The data on central grants tell a different story. The share of central grants in provincial current revenues increased rapidly for all four provinces. But the total increase was greatest in Baluchistan and NWFP, followed by Sindh and Punjab. The pattern does suggest appeasement of nondominant provinces, although the problematic, ethnically mixed Baluchistan was favored even more than the two provinces with a single non-Punjab dominant ethnicity. The NWFP and Baluchistan also received subventions and grants for the maintenance of strategic roads, as well as all the allocations from excise duties and royalties on natural gas.

Considering the shares of total grants (Table 8.9), Punjab received considerably smaller shares of each than its population. NWFP received larger shares of the largest grant category—revenue-deficit grants—and of development grants than its share of Pakistan's population. Sindh also received disproportionate development grants, but less in other categories than its

Table 8.8. Pakistan: Composition of provincial current revenues, 1970–1989 (as percentage of total provincial current revenues)

Province	Year	Provincial share of federal taxes and excises	Provincial tax revenues	Provincial non-tax revenues	Revenue-deficit grants	Total development grants	Foreign-aid development grants	Federal development grants	Total grants
Punjab	1970–73	42.8	30.5	22.9	0.3	—	—	—	0.3
	1979–81	54.9	16.9	13.2	1.9	12.8	0.8	12	14.7
	1981–83	60.4	16	14.9	3.3	5.4	0.5	4.9	8.7
	1983–85	49.8	15.2	14	20	0.8	0.3	0.5	20.8
	1985–87	35.6	11.1	12.3	35.7	5.1	0.2	4.9	40.8
	1987–89	32.9	9.2	9.4	31.6	16.7	0.3	16.5	48.3
Sindh	1970–73	38.8	36	21.8	0.4	—	—	—	0.4
	1979–81	46.6	21.8	9.6	5.5	13.3	1.6	11.7	18.8
	1981–83	52	20.2	12.3	3.3	8.2	0.8	7.4	11.5
	1983–85	45.6	16.3	9.4	20.8	4.9	0.4	4.5	25.7
	1985–87	34.5	10.4	9.5	36.1	7.7	0.3	7.5	43.8
	1987–89	30	7.7	6.3	34.7	19.4	0.2	19.2	54.1
NWFP	1970–73	51.3	18.5	23.5	6.8	—	—	—	6.8
	1979–81	40.2	6.8	10	26.6	15.4	1.2	14.2	42
	1981–83	40.1	6.5	9.1	36.1	7.1	0.5	6.7	43.2
	1983–85	34.3	6.9	8.2	48.7	5	0.4	4.7	53.7
	1985–87	25.9	5.1	5.6	59.5	2.7	0.2	2.5	62.2
	1987–89	21.6	3.6	4.7	54.1	14.6	0.15	14.5	68.7
Baluchistan	1970–73	53.7	13.9	18.8	13.6	—	—	—	13.6
	1979–81	20.1	1.9	5.6	57.9	15.1	2.8	12.3	73
	1981–83	20.1	1.4	3.5	59.4	14.7	2.5	12.2	74.1
	1983–85	23.4	2.1	4.1	57.6	11.3	1	10.3	68.9
	1985–87	18.3	2.1	3.4	67	8.6	0.9	7.7	75.6
	1987–89	15.1	1.4	2.9	57.5	22.5	0.9	21.6	80

Source: Adapted from Sato (1994, 88).
NWFP = Northwest Frontier Province.

Table 8.9. Pakistan: Allocation of central grants to provinces, 1976–1989 (percent of total)

Grant type		1976–79	1979–81	1981–83	1983–85	1985–87	1987–89
Revenue-deficit	Punjab	30.0	8.5	11.7	34.5	42.8	40.1
	Sindh	13.7	9.5	5.1	17.2	20.0	21.4
	NWFP	27.9	35.9	42.6	28.5	22.7	23.9
	Baluchistan	28.4	46.3	40.6	19.7	14.4	14.4
Foreign-aid	Punjab	—	33.2	35.5	42.9	39.7	39.4
	Sindh	—	29.3	24.8	21.5	19.9	15.2
	NWFP	—	15.1	10.3	11.9	10.6	12.9
	Baluchistan	—	22.3	29.3	23.6	29.7	32.4
Development	Punjab	—	50.5	36.8	9.7	45.7	46.7
	Sindh	—	22.4	27.6	46.7	33.1	27.6
	NWFP	—	17.7	15.5	1.6	8.3	14.0
	Baluchistan	—	9.4	20.2	42.0	13.1	12.1

Source: Adapted from Sato 1994.
NWFP = Northwest Frontier Province.

population would merit. Baluchistan consistently received a much larger share than its population for all three categories of grant.[16]

In short, the data suggest a clear attempt by the government to appease NWFP and Baluchistan with discretionary grants. But the absolute level of these changed over time in ways that are difficult to assess.

Secessionist Violence in Pakistan after 1971

During the 1971–1977 civilian government of Zulfiqar Ali Bhutto, himself of Sindhi origin, separatist unrest was mainly confined to Baluchistan and parts of the NWFP. The 1970 local elections had resulted in victories for the proautonomy National Awami Party (NAP) in both the NWFP and Baluchistan, and in 1972 NAP leaders became chief ministers in both provinces for the first time. In 1972, Bhutto dismissed both assemblies and sent troops to Baluchistan, officially to control tribal unrest. The military intervention grew, and federal officials accused the provincial government of supporting secessionist dissidents. The military's counterinsurgency battle continued until at least 1975. The violence seems to have been mostly concentrated in Baluchistan rather than the NWFP.

In Sindh, which had remained relatively calm during 1972–1979, nationalist conflict increased with the return of the military. In autumn 1983 a full-

16. However, the time trend is also interesting (see Table 8.9). NWFP, after receiving large shares of grants in the early 1980s, tended to lose ground afterward. Baluchistan also received very large deficit grants in 1979–1983, before seeing a reduction afterward; its development grants peaked at a high level in 1983–1985. Sindh's trend in these two categories was opposite: a drop to a low level of deficit grants in 1979–1983, followed by a significant increase; and a big increase in development grants after 1983.

scale rural uprising developed, mostly in certain rural areas of the province's interior. The movement began with a series of unauthorized demonstrations, but later developed into a large-scale uprising that threatened the economic prosperity of Punjab. At this point, the president decided to send army divisions to quash the uprising (Rakisits 1988). According to one observer (Ahmed 1997, 108), "As Sindh dissent spread, the military launched anti-insurgency operations in the Sindhi countryside; hundreds were killed and thousands were arrested and tried by summary military courts, run by military administrators. When force alone did not contain Sindhi dissent or weaken the PPP's base, the military adopted discriminatory policies aimed at excluding the politically suspect Sindhis from the state apparatus." Unrest was also noted in Sindh in the early 1990s. In NWFP, agitation for an independent Pakhtunistan had died down by the late 1980s, but a violent revolt in the mid-1990s erupted over the demand that Islamic law be implemented in the province (Weiss 1999).

Impact of Pakistan's Fiscal Policy on Secessionist Violence after 1971

The relationship between fiscal autonomy and secessionist violence in Pakistan since 1971 is unclear. Fiscal autonomy decreased dramatically for all regions in the 1970s and 1980s. The 1970s witnessed major unrest in Baluchistan and the NWFP, and the 1980s saw similar unrest in Sindh. However, the unrest in Baluchistan and parts of the NWFP in the early 1970s seems to have preceded the noted drop in fiscal autonomy; it actually coincided with greater, but still limited, financial independence associated with the end of the one-unit rule. Although financial dependence increased for all provinces in the 1970s and 1980s, when the Sindhi rebellion occurred in 1983 Sindh had the largest internal revenue base, close to one third of total revenue. Neither the decentralization hypothesis nor the central-control hypothesis can account for these patterns.

The experience of Pakistan seems to offer qualified support for the notion that either proportional treatment or appeasement of minority/majority states decreases separatist unrest. After the military came to power, grants, which had until then been a relatively small proportion of revenues, increased dramatically; these were directed disproportionately at the problematic provinces of NWFP and Baluchistan. Beginning in 1979, the government adopted a new policy which combined a reduced military presence with more development resources for these provinces. While grants in 1979–1981 made up 15 and 19 percent of revenues in Punjab and Sindh, they jumped to 42 and 73 percent of revenues in NWFP and Baluchistan. These two provinces' shares of total deficit grants during this period were respectively 2.7 and 8.7 times their shares in the population. It is notable that the unrest of the 1970s in these two provinces mostly died down in the

1980s. The Soviet invasion of Afghanistan—and the subsequent influx of refugees into the NWFP—may also have helped cool the desires of Pakistani Pakhtuns for merging with their northern neighbor (Noman 1990, 198).

The experience of Sindh also fits the proportionality and appeasement hypotheses. Although fiscal mechanisms do not seem to have been used to benefit Sindh disproportionally, there appears to be a consensus that the Sindhi benefited from government policies during the Bhutto administration (Ahmed 1997, Burki 1980).[17] (It is not clear if these benefits reached the Sindhi rural population or if they were directed toward the non-Sindhi urban centers.) The advent of the military government in 1979 reduced the influence of Sindhi politicians and administrators in federal decisionmaking. Making matters worse, grants to Sindh were reduced quite sharply in the early 1980s—from 18.8 percent of total provincial current revenues in 1979–1981 to 11.5 percent in 1981–1983, a larger drop of the share than in any other province. Sindh's share in deficit grants dropped to just 5 percent in 1981–1983, compared to a population share of 23 percent.

This was followed by the Sindhi rural violence of 1983. The local leaders of the PPP, which had been in power until 1979, led the rebellion in many districts. Demands for a separate Sindhi nation-state were common during the 1983 rebellion (Noman 1990, 195). As noted, the government responded with military force. But it also attempted some financial appeasement, deciding to significantly increase development funds allocated to the province's interior, where Bhutto's support was strongest (Rakisits 1988, 87). Total grants jumped to 44 percent of current revenues in 1985–1987. Sindh's share of deficit grants rose from 5 to 20 percent of the total in 1985–1987; and its share of development grants jumped from 28 to 48 percent of the total in 1983–1985. This may have helped stabilize the situation in the late 1980s.

Nigeria

Nigeria became independent in 1960, inheriting from the British a federal structure with three major subunits: the Hausa-Fulani-dominated Northern Region, the Yoruba-dominated Western Region, and the Igbo-dominated Eastern Region. The mostly Muslim Northern Region included about three-quarters of the country's territory and over half the population. Nigeria's socioeconomic center lay in the more modernized South, which was largely Christian and animist. From the 1960s, the economy began to depend increasingly on oil production, largely concentrated within the Midwest and Eastern regions. Other ethnic groups of different sizes are clustered around

17. The new government after the war changed language policies and put in place some quotas for employment and other preference-based policies.

the three major ones, accounting at independence for about one third of each region's population (Suberu 1999).

Since independence, the country's constituent regions have been subdivided repeatedly. A Midwest Region was carved out of the West in 1963. In 1967, the military regime in power divided the 4 existing regions into 12 States, precipitating a civil war. In 1975, the number of states was increased to 19. It grew again in 1987 to 21, then to 30 in 1991, and 36 in 1996. This complicates the determination of which regions or states are majority/minority units in a given period.[18]

Brief periods of democracy have alternated with longer ones of military rule. The First Republic lasted from independence until 1966. Political parties were organized regionally and represented the major ethnic groups. For the first few years, a Northern and Eastern alliance dominated the federal government. This government declared a state of emergency and took over the administration of the Western Region in 1962. The North-East coalition broke down soon after, with the Northern party retaining power and both parties courting competing Yoruba factions from the West. In 1965, local elections were held in the West. When it became clear they had been rigged in favor of the North's regional partner, the region "erupted into popular rebellion" (Diamond 1995, 427). The federal government was about to intervene when the Prime Minister and other political leaders were killed in a coup in January 1966 led by a group of mainly Igbo officers.[19] The coup was defeated by other army factions, and the chief of the armed forces, an Igbo who had refused to join the plotters, became head of the new military government. When it proceeded to abolish the autonomy of the regions and appointed military governors indigenous to their respective regions, this provoked a second coup, led this time by Northern officers.

The second coup was followed by massacres of Igbos in the North, and an exodus of more than one million Igbos to the Eastern Region (Diamond 1995, 428). To counter secessionist threats from the East, the federal government divided the Eastern Region into three states as part of a restructuring of the country into a 12-state federation. Under the new scheme the Igbos were a majority in only one state. On May 31, 1967, three days after this announcement, the government of the Eastern Region declared independence in a new state christened "Biafra." A week later, a civil war broke out, which lasted until January 1970, when the federal government prevailed and forced the Igbos back into the federation.

18. To decide this, we have combined information offered by Osaghae (1986) and Graf (1988) about the dominant regional ethnicity.

19. It seems they were mainly concerned with ethnic issues inside the military and within the federation at large. The Igbos, over-represented and with better education than the northern majority, were hurt by the imposition of a quota system for recruitment in 1962. (Diamond 1995, 427).

The postwar period of military rule witnessed an oil-fueled economic boom and a flowering of corruption. Government policies appear to have further alienated the Igbos despite a federal campaign for national reconciliation. In July 1975, reform-minded officers overthrew the previous military government in a bloodless coup and reorganized the 12-state federation into 19 states, 10 in the North and 9 in the East and West. They also drafted a new presidential constitution and prepared the way for a return to electoral politics, which took place in October 1979.

The return to democratic government coincided with a sharp drop in world oil prices, reducing oil revenues from $24 billion in 1980 to $10 billion in 1983 (Diamond 1995, 438). When brazen vote-rigging, mostly by the incumbent Northern-based National Party of Nigeria, marred the 1983 elections, violent protest erupted, killing more than one hundred people in the predominantly Yoruba states (Diamond 1995, 440). Three months later, the military staged another coup. Military rule, under Generals Muhammadu Buhari, Ibrahim Babanginda, and Sani Abacha, lasted until May 1999, when Olusegun Obasanjo, a military ruler from the late 1970s, was elected president. The number of states had grown to 36.

Nigeria's Fiscal Politics

Under the revenue system adopted after independence, taxes were either federal, regional, or mixed. Part of the regional share in these taxes was allocated on a derivation basis—that is, returned to the region in which it originated; the rest went into a Distributable Pool Account (DPA), and was allocated to regions according to a formula.

The DPA represented the main channel of center-regions fiscal distribution. The allocation shares prior to the 1966 coup were: Northern Region, 42 percent; Eastern Region, 33 percent; Western Region, 19 percent (25 percent before 1963); Midwest Region, 6 percent (since 1963). The shares of an enlarged DPA, agreed on before the coup and implemented the first two years afterward were: Northern Region, 42 percent; Eastern Region, 30 percent; Western Region, 20 percent; and Midwest Region 8 percent.[20] From 1971, the shares were changed, giving the combined North 51.8 percent and the combined West just 12.7 percent. The formulas for DPA allocation were based in part on equality of the states, so the creation of more states in the North than elsewhere increased its aggregate share. The federal government also provided grants and loans. Federal grants came to about 4 percent of total state revenues in 1968 (Offensend 1976). After the civil war, however,

20. In addition the regions were to receive a new annual grant to be shared as follows: Northern Region, 53.3 percent; Western Region, 16.0 percent; Midwestern Region, 9.3 percent; Eastern Region, 21.3 percent.

these apparently increased. Loans came to be distributed according to the DPA formula (Offensend 1976).

How great was the fiscal autonomy of local-majority/countrywide-minority regions during the post-independence period? As Table 8.10 shows, in the early 1960s all regions were heavily dependent on the central government. Table 8.11 shows the degree of fiscal decentralization for all states in the 1970–1992 period. There were clear waves of centralization under the military regimes (1970–78 and 1986–92) and decentralization under the democratic Second Republic (1978–84). But throughout, the average state financed no more than one third of its expenditures with its own revenues. We have also reviewed figures for individual states for four years of the Second Republic (1980–83). These reveal a great deal of cross-state variation: while Lagos financed about 41 percent of its expenditures independently in 1983, the figure for Gongola State in the North was only 3.7 percent.

Table 8.10. Nigeria: Statutory appropriations from the federal government to regions (as percentage of each region's total revenues)

Region	1959–60	1960–61	1961–62	1962–63	1963–64	1964–65	1965–66
Eastern	63.00	63.17	59.44	61.63			
Northern		77.81	74.19	71.82	70.62	73.62	73.27
Western				69.28	69.10	68.50	64.57

Source: From official estimates of each regional government presented in Adebayo 1993.
Note: Statutory appropriations include Distributable Pool Account funds and tax-share allocated on derivation basis.

Table 8.11. Nigeria: The fiscal position of state governments, 1970–1992

Year	Total revenue (Nm[a])	Independent revenue (percent)	Revenue from federal sources (percent)	Total expenditure (Nm[a])	Independent revenue as percent of total expenditure
1970	232.2	29.3	70.7	247.5	27.5
1972	454.2	26.4	73.6	593.0	20.2
1974	503.2	35.7	64.3	953.0	20.7
1976	2,139.8	19.7	80.3	2,223.4	13.2
1978	2,575.9	8.2	91.8	3,201.1	6.6
1980	5,456.3	24.3	75.7	7,234.4	18.4
1982	4,335.4	25.1	74.9	10,680.5	12.3
1984	4,160.3	33.2	66.8	4,776.2	28.9
1986	4,704.4	39.5	60.5	5,774.7	32.2
1988	10,360.1	21.0	79.0	10,778.5	20.2
1990	19,116.5	14.3	85.7	18,105.5	15.1
1992	31,870.5	16.3	83.7	35,586.0	14.7

Source: Data from the Central Bank of Nigeria reported in Anyanwu 1997, table 10e.
[a] Nm = millions of Naira.

To what extent did central policy discriminate in favor of or against the majority/minority regions? Table 8.12 presents data on total statutory allocations (tax shares allocated from DPA plus those based on derivation) in the pre–civil war period. The West, East, and Midwest appear to have received shares of appropriations larger than their population shares (except perhaps for the East in 1967–68 when the civil war had broken out). The North, by contrast, received a little more than one third of appropriations, although its population was probably greater than half the total. However, the time trends are also worth noting. Appropriations for both the North and the East (the two members of the ruling coalition) increased somewhat up until about 1964 or 1965, before falling back again. The share of appropriations to the Western Region fell precipitously—from 40 percent of the total in 1960, to about 21 percent in 1966–67. In part, this represented a drop in total allocations to the original Western region; in part, it reflected the loss to the West from the creation of the Midwest Region.

We next have figures for statutory appropriations between 1970 and 1975, the years in which the oil boom took off (Table 8.13). Between 1970 and 1974, oil revenues increased from 26 to 82 percent of total government revenues. The federal government aimed to capture part of the oil-producing states' windfall profits for itself and the non–oil-producing states. It asserted the sole right to rents and royalties from offshore oil, and reduced the share of revenues from on-shore oil allocated on the basis of derivation from 50 to 20 percent of the total. Despite this, we see the oil-producing Rivers and Midwestern States' shares of total appropriations more than doubling. The Lagos and East-Central majority/minority states had roughly stable allocations. But the Yoruba Western State suffered a sharp decline in its share, from 17.5 to 7.1 percent of the total, although absolute values muted some of the cut in shares. With the return of democratic rule in 1979, 7 of the now 19 states were majority/minority regions.

Table 8.14 shows total statutory and nonstatutory allocations (including central grants and loans as well as tax redistribution). With a few minor exceptions, the shares of each majority/minority state in 1979–85 look quite stable. The Oyo State in the west suffered a sharp drop in 1985, but we lacked data to see if this was just a one-year irregularity. The oil-producing Bendel State in the midwest lost about one third of its allocation between 1980 and 1985. This may have been due to falling oil prices rather than explicit government policy. Though these figures are not directly comparable with those in Table 8.13, the trend of the early 1970s toward a much larger share for the oil-producing state appears to have been reversed.

Secessionist Violence in Nigeria

Throughout the post-independence period in Nigeria, ethnic unrest has broken out periodically among smaller ethnic groups. One of the first cases

Table 8.12. Nigeria: Total statutory appropriations to region and state governments, 1960–68 (regional shares as a percentage of national total)

Region	1960–61	1961–62	1962–63	1963–64	1964–65	1965–66	1966–67	1967–68	Est. pop. share (%)
Northern	33.56	34.93	34.16	36.43	38.53	36.19	35.43	33.55	53 to 56
Eastern	26.00	29.79	29.83	28.18	28.34	30.82	29.94	23.12	21 to 24
Western[a]	40.44	35.28	36.01						20 to 26
Western[a]				28.88	23.19	22.14	21.14	28.65	16 to 20
Midwest				6.51	9.94	10.85	13.49	14.68	4 to 6

Source: Adapted from Adebayo 1993.

Note: Population share estimates include the upper and lower bounds from censuses taken in postwar period. While the absolute population figures from these censuses were the subject of extreme controversy, the population shares of the different regions changed very little.

[a] The Western Region was divided in 1963 into the Western Region and the Midwest Region.

Table 8.13. Nigeria: Postwar statutory appropriations to state governments, 1970–75 (regional shares as a percentage of national total)

Original region	States	Majority/ minority makeup[a]	1970–71	1971–72	1972–73	1973–74	1974–75
Northern	North-Western	~	6.7	7.1	7.2	6.1	5.0
	North-Central	~	5.9	6.0	6.1	5.1	4.3
	North-Eastern	~	8.5	8.5	8.6	7.3	6.1
	Kano	~	8.5	7.9	8.1	6.2	5.2
	Benue-Plateau	~	6.0	6.1	6.2	5.4	4.5
	Kwara	~	4.7	4.9	4.9	4.2	3.5
	Total		*40.3*	*40.5*	*41.1*	*34.3*	*28.6*
Eastern	East-Central	Igbo	9.0	9.4	9.8	10.0	8.7
	South-Eastern	~	7.2	5.8	6.5	6.2	4.2
	Rivers	~	7.9	10.1	9.5	13.1	19.6
	Total		*24.1*	*25.3*	*25.8*	*29.3*	*32.5*
Western	Lagos	Yoruba	4.9	4.8	4.3	3.6	3.9
	Western	Yoruba	17.5	15.8	14.3	9.3	7.1
	Total		*22.4*	*20.6*	*18.6*	*12.9*	*11.0*
	Midwest	Edo	13.4	13.6	14.5	23.5	28.0
Total (Nm[b])			*286.0*	*326.6*	*321.8*	*361.9*	*833.4*

Source: Adapted from Adebayo 1993.

[a] In regard to the difficult issue of state ethnic makeup, we have classified as majority/minority states those that both Osaghae (1986) and Graf (1998) specifically identify as such. The ethnic identity of the majority is shown in the column.

[b] Nm = millions of Naira.

involved the Tiv, a minority in the Hausa-Fulani–dominated Northern Region. About two thousand people died and thousands more were imprisoned during one uprising in 1964 (Nnoli 1995). Since these groups did not constitute majority/minority ethnicities, we do not consider them in this chapter. Another major conflict engulfed the Western Region in the early 1960s but stemmed mainly from fights among competing Yoruba factions and did not appear to be explicitly related to secession.[21]

The first major threat of secession came in 1963 and was associated with the census, which became politicized because of its implications for the allocation of federal resources and parliamentary seats. When, amid widespread allegations of fraud, census numbers were reported that favored the North, followed by the West, political leaders in the Eastern Region protested vigorously and threatened to secede. Violence appears to have been common,

21. As noted, electoral fraud during the Western regional elections of 1965 precipitated an uprising that rendered the region ungovernable for months, with widespread factional killings. The federal government intervened and suspended the constitution in the West (Nnoli, 1995, 108).

Table 8.14. Nigeria: Statutory and nonstatutory allocations of revenue to state governments, including local government areas, 1979–85 (regional shares as a percent of total)

Original region	States	Majority/minority makeup	1979	1980	1981	1982	1983	1984	1985
Northern[a]	Niger	~	3.3	3.2	3.7	3.2	3.2	2.9	3.0
	Kano	~	6.9	6.7	6.9	7.7	7.5	8.0	8.3
	Bauchi	~	4.2	4	4.6	4.5	4.4	4.5	4.5
	Kaduna	~	5.7	5.6	5.9	6.2	6	6.3	6.5
	Sokoto	~	5.7	5.5	6.4	6.5	6.4	6.3	6.5
	Gongola	~	4.2	4.3	4.8	4.7	4.6	4.5	4.6
	Borno	~	4.6	4.7	5.5	5.1	5.0	5.2	5.2
	Benue	~	4.7	4.8	4.6	4.6	4.5	4.4	4.3
	Plateau	~	4.1	3.9	4.3	4.0	3.9	3.6	7.2
	Kwara	~	3.8	3.8	4.2	3.8	3.7	3.7	3.8
		Total	47.2	46.5	50.9	50.3	49.2	49.4	53.9
Eastern	Anambra	M/M-Igbo	5.6	5.4	5.3	5.7	5.6	5.6	5.6
	Imo	M/M-Igbo	6.5	6.6	5.9	6.0	6.0	5.4	5.7
	Cross River	~	5.6	5.5	5.2	5.5	5.4	5.4	5.2
	Rivers	~	8.1	8.9	7.0	6.3	6.1	6.2	5.6
		Total	25.8	26.4	23.4	23.5	23.1	22.6	22.1
Western	Ogun	Yoruba	3.4	3.4	3.6	3.6	3.5	3.7	3.5
	Ondo	Yoruba	4.5	4.4	4.6	4.9	4.8	4.4	4.4
	Oyo	Yoruba	6.7	6.6	6.6	7.1	6.9	7	4.4
	Lagos	Yoruba	3.5	3.5	3.4	4.2	4.1	4	4.2
		Total	18.1	17.9	18.2	19.8	19.3	19.1	16.5
Midwest	Bendel	Edo	8.8	9.3	7.3	6.6	6.5	6.7	6.3
Total (Nm[b])			2,903.5	3,812.9	4,910.6	4,258.4	4,236.7	3,926.6	4,671.7

Source: Central Bank of Nigeria, 1981–1985.

[a] The predominant ethnic group in the Northern Region was Hausa-Fulani.

[b] Nm = millions of Naira.

although we lack precise measures. After the 1966 coup, the government's decree centralizing power led to massacres of Igbos in the North and the already-noted exodus to the East (Nnoli 1995). The military governor of the Eastern Region began to expel immigrants from the North and West. The civil war broke out in mid-1967 and lasted two and a half years.[22]

For all the post–civil war Nigerian regime's problems, the country does not seem to have suffered significantly from violent secession threats. Ethnic conflicts continued but rarely had a secessionist character. Many ethnic minorities continued to agitate for a separate state in the federation but the two main majority/minority ethnic groups of the prewar era, the Igbos and Yoruba, did not embark on any visible attempt to separate.

Impact of Nigeria's Fiscal Policies on Secessionist Violence

Little evidence relates the degree of fiscal autonomy to the incidence of secessionist violence in Nigeria. All states were highly dependent on federal financial aid in the 1960s when an ethnically based civil war for secession broke out. This might seem to support Hypothesis 1a, the decentralization hypothesis. However, the states appear to have been even more dependent on federal aid in later decades, with no major secessionist incidents arising. The decentralization hypothesis is not confirmed. The generally low level of secessionism since the early 1970s may confirm the central-control hypothesis.

What about the pattern of central redistribution? Consider first the period leading up to the civil war. Both the East and the West seem to have received larger DPA shares per capita than the North (reflecting their greater wealth and the partial influence of the derivation principle). From the appeasement perspective, the sharp drop in the West's share of appropriations should stimulate secessionist unrest. As discussed, serious, violent unrest did occur in the Yoruba West during this period, directed largely against the perceived abuses of the Hausa-Fulani–dominated central government. But it did not appear to follow a secessionist track.

The East's allocation share in 1960–1966 conflicts with the appeasement hypothesis. However, a broader view of the context would be more supportive. The incident that provoked the Biafran declaration of independence was precisely the central government's announced decision to split the East into three states. Of these, the Igbos would dominate only one—and they would lose control over the East's major oil reserves, located in the new Rivers State.

22. Early 1966 also saw the beginning of a violent campaign for the creation of a separate Delta People's Republic out of a portion of the Eastern Region. This small secessionist movement lost most of its appeal after the military government reorganized the federation the following year and created the new Rivers State.

Given the remaining importance of the derivation principle in allocating revenues, this would represent a major revenue loss to the Igbo elites.[23] The declaration of independence might be seen as a forward-looking response to a deliberate central refusal to appease the Igbo. This is a qualified success for the appeasement hypothesis.

Thus, the evidence from this period is not easy to interpret. It is possible to see some confirmation of the importance of fiscal appeasement. This would fit with the apparent consensus in the literature on fiscal federalism in Nigeria, which emphasizes the centrality of revenue allocation in the conflicts among different regions of the country during the pre–civil war era (Adebayo 1993; Ikein and Briggs-Anigboh 1998; Rothchild 1970; Suberu 1999). In the 1970–1975 period, the appeasement view might explain the lack of secessionist violence in the Midwest. In the West, shares dropped sharply, but the absolute value of funds transferred also increased markedly with the boom in oil revenues, reducing the impact of a reduction in shares. The relative stability of allocation shares in 1979–1985 would be consistent with an appeasement hypothesis—as well as with the hypothesis that fiscal allocations did not matter. The fall in the share of the oil-producing Bendel State of the midwest should have increased secessionist pressures, although Bendel continued to benefit from oil and was still better off than most other states.

In short, fiscal autonomy does not seem to explain much about the pattern of secessionist violence in Nigeria. Fiscal short-changing of the Western Region in the early 1960s may have helped create conditions for the ethnic and political violence that broke out there, although this violence did not take a secessionist turn. The central attempt to rob Igbo elites of their main resources by carving out the Rivers State—certainly the opposite of an appeasement strategy—seems to have precipitated the civil war of 1967. But appeasement policies are not so clearly related to the relative lack of secessionist violence in the period since 1970. A more plausible explanation is the center's success at disorienting potentially secessionist ethnic minority elites by continually redrawing the administrative map, in the process undermining some and empowering others. The division of the Yoruba among many states—and the isolation of the Igbo elite in a small, resource-poor region—seems to have been effective at rendering secessionist projects unappealing. It may be that Nigeria's experience indicates not the irrelevance of central appeasement but the possibility of using other mechanisms—in this case, reengineering administrative divisions—to achieve the same ends. It

23. Donald Rothchild (1970, 522) provides evidence that Eastern demands for secession were strengthened by the sense among Eastern elites that they were being despoiled of their oil revenues by the federal government. In 1966–1967, of £29 million pounds in total oil revenues, £17.7 million went to the federal government, while £8.2 million went to the East.

may also be the case that more secessionist unrest lies in store, for instance in the Bendel.

On the surface, the experience would also seem to give some support to the proportionality hypothesis—proportionality (plus the perceived costs of a secession attempt) may have been enough to contain new secessionist violence. Distribution of tax resources has largely deemphasized the derivation principle, and emphasized allocation proportional to population. Simultaneously, the incidence of secessionist violence appears to have fallen.

Yugoslavia

After the end of World War II, Yugoslavia was organized as a federation of six republics (Slovenia, Croatia, Bosnia-Herzegovina, Serbia, Montenegro, and Macedonia) and two autonomous provinces (Vojvodina and Kosovo, both within Serbia). Serbs constituted the largest ethnic group nationwide (about 36 percent as of the 1981 census) and the largest ethnicity in Serbia and Vojvodina. Bosnia-Herzegovina was multiethnic, with Muslim, Serb, and Croat minorities. Slovenia, Croatia, Montenegro, Macedonia, and Kosovo all represented local-majority/countrywide-minority regions.

To incorporate these diverse populations, Josip Broz Tito organized the country after the war as a socialist federation. A North-South divide separated the more economically developed regions of Slovenia, Croatia, and Vojvodina from the less developed southern Serbia, Montenegro, Macedonia, and Kosovo. The communist party tried throughout the postwar era to reduce these interregional inequalities. Foreign aid and loans were channeled to increase industrial growth in poorer regions. Liberalizing economic reforms and Western-oriented trade were introduced in the 1960s, and in 1965 considerable political power was devolved to the members of the federation. Yet, despite the initial growth this fostered, the gap between Northern and Southern regions increased (Plestina 1992, 82).

Reforms after 1967 increased the republics' autonomy. The two provinces within Serbia (Vojvodina and Kosovo) gained full control over their parliaments, budgets, and judicial systems. Each republic's party controlled its own cadres, and republic-level elections and party congresses preceded federal congresses (Woodward 1995). In Croatia, the liberal faction of the party pressed for greater control over its finances in the early 1970s. While republican governments were economically independent, they nevertheless depended on federal funds, particularly those of the most underdeveloped members of the federations.

By the late 1970s and early 1980s, a mounting economic crisis—with rising foreign debt, unemployment, and strikes—was complicating interrepublic relations. In May 1980, Tito died. A deep economic recession and conflicts between Albanians and Serbs in Kosovo—where the economic situation was particularly severe—followed (Plestina 1992, 114). The federal government attempted to recentralize some of the powers it had devolved, such as control over foreign exchange operations, in order to meet conditions for an International Monetary Fund (IMF) loan. This angered Slovenia and Croatia, the main exporters. Both republics protested federal tax levels and what they perceived to be a waste of funds redistributed to the country's less developed South. At the same time, the Serb leader, Slobodan Milošević, fought a strike in Kosovo using force.

In 1988, relations between Serbia and Slovenia began to deteriorate rapidly. Late in 1989 the Slovenian leadership amended the constitution to assert their republic's economic and political sovereignty and its right to secede (Burg 1993). Serbia and Slovenia broke economic relations. In early 1990, electoral victories of independence-oriented coalitions in Slovenia and Croatia and former communists in Serbia deepened divisions. In December 1990, a referendum in Slovenia revealed overwhelming support for independence. The Yugoslav defense minister threatened force to preserve the federation, but by the end of 1990 Croatia had also enacted a new sovereign constitution. In June 1991, Slovenia and Croatia declared independence. The military sent troops into both, starting a war that later spread to Bosnia and Kosovo.

Yugoslavia's Fiscal Politics

In the fiscal system that emerged from the decentralizing reforms of the early 1960s, most taxes were collected by the republics, which made annually negotiated contributions to the federal budget (Bookman 1992). Until the late 1980s, such contributions accounted for a large fraction of federal revenues. But sizable flows also went in the opposite direction, in the form of federal investments, subsidies, loans, and grants. Subsidies and grants to republics came in two forms: disbursements of the Federal Fund (FF) and budgetary grants. The Federal Fund, established in 1965, received a uniform percentage of the social product of the social sector of each region (total social product included the social, industrial, and agricultural sectors). Between 1960 and the early 1980s, this percentage ranged between 1.85 and 1.97 percent. Money from the Fund was allocated to the less developed regions of Bosnia-Herzegovina, Kosovo, Macedonia, and Montenegro and administered locally. The federal budget allocated transfers for social services.

Regional contributions to the Federal Fund are shown in Table 8.15, and distributions to underdeveloped regions in Table 8.16. In the 1980s, decreases in FF disbursements and other resources meant that for the 1980–1988 period total investment in the less-developed regions was falling by an average of 10.7 percent per year (Plestina 1992, 121).

Table 8.15. Yugoslavia: Participation of republics in the Federal Fund (percent of national total)

	Population		Contributions to federal fund			
Republics/provinces	1971	1980	1960	1965	1971	1982
Serbia proper	25.5	25.4	24.5	24.3	24.4	27.4
Croatia	21.5	20.9	28.0	27.2	27.4	23.6
Vojvodina	9.5	9	10.6	11.1	10.9	11.4
Slovenia	8.4	8.2	16.8	16.5	16.9	12.7
Bosnia-Herzegovina	18.3	18.6	12.8	12.2	11.3	15.1
Macedonia	8.1	8.3	4.4	5.0	5.4	5.6
Kosovo	6.1	7	1.4	1.8	1.8	1.9
Montenegro	2.6	2.6	1.5	1.9	1.9	2.3
Total	100.0	100.0	100.0	100.0	100.0	100.0

Sources: Population figures from Yugoslavia Federal Statistical Office 1986; data for 1960–71 calculated from World Bank 1975; shares for 1982 from Bookman 1992.

Table 8.16. Yugoslavia: Distribution of federation resources to underdeveloped republics and to Kosovo (region's percentage of national total)

	1966–70		1971–75		1976–80		1981–84	
Republics or province	Federal fund	Total federation resources	Federal fund	Total federation resources	Federal fund	Total federation resources	Federal fund	Total federation resources
Bosnia-Herzegovina	30.7	31.7	32.4	31.4	30.6	28.7	26.4	26.0
Macedonia	26.2	29.0	22.9	20.7	21.6	17.6	20.2	16.5
Kosovo	30.0	25.3	33.3	33.6	37.0	40.8	44.3	47.0
Montenegro	13.1	14.1	11.4	14.3	10.8	13.0	9.1	10.5

Sources: Yugoslavia Federal Statistical Office 1986.

However, FF transfers and budgetary grants were just two of several channels of redistribution (Dubravcic 1993; Kraft 1992; Kraft and Vodopivec 1992; Mihaljek 1993). Evan Kraft and Milan Vodopivec identified a number of such channels—taxes and subsidies, extension of credits at negative real interest rates, investment funds, the inflation tax, implicit taxation through price regulation—and estimated the size of total flows for 1986 (Table 8.17). Adding up all flows, they found that Slovenia lost by far the most per capita from redistribution, while Montenegro and Kosovo were the biggest winners. Croatia and Serbia both came out about even.

Several circumstances worsened Slovenia's situation in the late 1980s. The republic ended up contributing a larger relative share to the FF (its share rose from about 16 percent to 24 percent between 1984 and 1989). In the late 1980s, the central bank was issuing money at inflationary rates, in large

Table 8.17. Yugoslavia: Estimated interrepublican redistribution, 1986 (as percent of Yugoslav gross social product)

	Disbursements from federal fund[a]	Net subsidies including gains/losses on money	Estimated loss due to administrative pricing[b]		Total transfers (1+2+3)	Total transfers per 10 million residents (percent of Yugoslav GSP per 10 million)	Republic GSP as percent of Yugoslav GSP[c]
			p_1	p_2			
Bosnia	0.4	2.3	–0.5	–0.3	2.2 to 2.4	4.9 to 5.4	13.5
Montenegro	0.1	0.7	–0.2	–0.1	0.6 to 0.7	9.4 to 11.0	2.0
Macedonia	0.2	0.8	–0.6	–0.4	0.4 to 0.6	1.9 to 2.8	5.7
Kosovo	0.6	1.2	–0.3	–0.2	1.5 to 1.6	7.7 to 8.3	2.3
Slovenia		–0.9	–0.9	–0.3	–1.8 to –1.2	–9.2 to –6.2	18.1
Croatia		1.1	–1.3	–0.5	–0.2 to 0.6	–0.4 to +1.3	24.7
Serbia[d]		1.2	–1.6	–1.7	–0.4 to –0.5	–0.5 to –0.6	33.7
Total	1.2	6.8	–5.4	–2.4	2.6 to 5.6	1.1 to 2.4	

Sources: Kraft 1992; Kraft and Vodopivec 1992; Yugoslav Federal Statistical Agency 1988, 469; 1990, 496.

[a] Federal Fund for the Crediting of the Development of the Less-Developed Regions.

[b] p_1 and p_2 represent two different assumptions about the degree of price distortion.

[c] Gross Social Product (a communist-era measure of economic production).

[d] Includes Vojvodina.

Table 8.18. Yugoslavia: Access to concessionary loans and money creation, by Croatia, Serbia, and Slovenia, 1987

	Croatia	Slovenia	Serbia
Percent of increase in concessionary loans for agriculture	23.6	6.1	57.0
Percent of increase in concessionary loans for exports	33.5	17.9	29.0
Share in total money creation	19.7	7.5	38.8
Share in gross national product	25.3	16.8	37.3
Share in population, 1980	20.9	8.2	41.4

Sources: Adapted from Dubravcic (1993, 266) and *Yugoslavia 1945–85, Statistical Review*, Federal Statistical Office, 1986.

part to provide concessionary loans to support agriculture and exports. Despite Croatia and Slovenia's leading export position, they received smaller shares of these loans than their share in gross national product (GNP). Serbia, by contrast, got a larger share of loans than its share in GNP (Table 8.18).

In sum, we do not have data to assess the level of fiscal autonomy precisely, but it appears to have been relatively high in the more developed provinces. Fiscal redistribution seems to have advantaged the poorer southern republics at the expense of Slovenia and Croatia in particular. In the late 1980s, the more developed republics reduced contributions to the FF. But the pattern of disbursement of inflationary central bank loans and losses due to administrative pricing seem to have continued to hurt Slovenia and Croatia.

Secessionist Violence in Yugoslavia

Three periods of secessionist violence stand out: the Croatian crisis of 1970–1971; the conflicts in Kosovo during the 1980s; and the struggle for independence, leading to civil war, in Croatia and Slovenia in 1989–1991. The problems in Croatia began as a protest over economic grievances, specifically about the handling of foreign exchange. The nationalist demands escalated, and following a student strike in November 1971 troops were sent into the province. The opposition leadership was arrested, and the liberals were purged from the communist party. In Kosovo, the unrest began in March 1981 with a series of student strikes protesting the deteriorating economic situation. In following months, the strikes spread to coal miners and other businesses (Plestina 1992). Dozens were reportedly killed and as many as one thousand injured during the demonstrations that followed (Irwin 1984). Yugoslavia declared its first state of emergency since World War II, sent federal forces to control the unrest, and sealed off the province for two months in the summer of 1981. (We discussed the unrest in Croatia and Slovenia in the late 1980s in the background section.)

Impact of Yugoslavia's Fiscal Policies on Secessionist Violence

We lacked precise data to assess the fiscal decentralization and central-control hypotheses. However, the reforms of the 1960s, which increased the republics' fiscal autonomy, preceded the various cases of ethnic unrest mentioned. Fiscal autonomy was undoubtedly higher in Slovenia and Croatia than in most other republics and provinces; this did not save them from major secessionist unrest in the 1970s (Croatia) and late 1980s (both). These patterns would seem to be consistent with the central-control hypothesis.

A fuller accounting of all financial flows over time would be needed for reliable conclusions about the role of fiscal appeasement in Yugoslavia. However, the tentative conclusions we draw tend generally to fit both the proportionality and the appeasement hypotheses. The Croatian crisis in the early 1970s was prompted by the republic's demand for greater control over the foreign exchange the republic earned. Croatia was among the regions least favored by interregional redistribution of development funds. The growth of sentiment favoring independence in the two northern republics in the late 1980s also seems to have been fueled by central policies that favored southern republics at their expense (for example, the disproportionate flow of inflationary central bank loans to Serbia) (Treisman 1999a).

However, the Kosovo crisis does not fit. Kosovo was among the regions most favored by redistribution of development aid, and its share in federal fiscal transfers increased throughout the late 1970s and early 1980s. This aid did not succeed in fostering economic development, and economic grievances prompted the strikes. Thus, in Yugoslavia a central policy of fiscal appeasement was not always effective at containing unrest.

Conclusion

This chapter requires more than the usual caveats. Our characterizations of the history of secessionist violence may overemphasize or underemphasize certain incidents. We did not attempt to quantify our dependent variable. We also interpreted our main hypotheses in a somewhat ad hoc manner, looking for evidence both cross-sectionally (was a particular region favored over others at time *t*?) and longitudinally (was a region's treatment improving or worsening?), rather than committing ourselves to one or the other perspective. Were we able to control for contextual factors and nonfiscal causes, we might reach more confident conclusions. For example, does appeasement work because it "buys off" government elites? Are increased transfers to the general public also required? Must fiscal aid increase the level or quality of public goods and services? Must it fuel economic growth? More precise hypotheses might find stronger statistical support.

But our goal here was to open a conversation with those expert in different parts of the story we examine and to illustrate the rewards of exploring what we believe has been a neglected subject in political science—the fiscal sociology of developing countries. The chapter represents a plausibility probe rather than a true test of competing hypotheses. In this spirit, we offer a few tentative conclusions to those considering including fiscal arrangements in the design of power-sharing institutions (Table 8.19).

In the four cases we examined, we did not find any evidence that the degree of fiscal decentralization to ethnic minority regions affected the frequency of secessionist violence. Secessionist unrest broke out in some states with high levels of fiscal autonomy (Indian Punjab), in some with medium levels (East Pakistan), and in some with minimal levels (Nagaland). Cases occurred during periods when fiscal autonomy was increasing (Croatia, East Pakistan) and decreasing (Kashmir). A high level of dependence on central fiscal transfers was neither necessary nor sufficient to provoke secessionist unrest. The same was true of a high level of fiscal *in*dependence. More systematic examination with better data and a large number of cases might turn up some correlations, but based on this exploration we doubt that they would be strong. For the moment we conclude that neither the decentralization hypothesis nor the central-control hypothesis successfully explains the pattern of secessionist violence.

We did find some stronger—although far from unequivocal—support for the appeasement hypothesis in all four countries. In some cases, a strategy of fiscal appeasement seemed clearly to reduce secessionist tensions; conversely, in some other cases fiscal discrimination appeared to exacerbate a crisis. The Pakistani leadership's fiscal neglect of East Pakistan in the 1950s and 1960s laid the ground for the secession of Bangladesh. The Yugoslav federal government's disregard for economic interests of Slovenia and Croatia in the late 1980s hastened that country's disintegration. Flare-ups of secessionist unrest in India's Punjab and Jammu and Kashmir in the 1980s and 1990s respectively may also have been fueled by decreasing central aid in preceding years. Increases in central fiscal aid may have helped stabilize ethnic unrest in post-1971 Pakistan.

However, there were also a few counterexamples in which either appeasement failed to prevent conflict or the lack of appeasement did not provoke it. In Nagaland and Kosovo secessionist violence occurred *despite* fiscal support. And Nigeria's Yoruba-dominated West in the early 1970s and its Edo-dominated Bendel State in the early 1980s remained quiet despite central neglect. In general, Nigeria suggests the need to view fiscal appeasement as just one of several possibly effective central strategies for dealing with ethnic demands in a federal state. The particular instability we study in "ethnically-mined federations" stems from the control by a local-majority/countrywide-minority ethnicity of a subunit within the federal state.

Table 8.19. Summary of results by majority-minority region

Country	Majority/minority region	Fiscal decentralization	Central transfers	Secessionist violence
India	Punjab	High	Started high, dropped by 1960s, still lower by 1980s[a]	1981–92
	Jammu-Kashmir	Low	High, but probably falling in 1980s and 1990s	From 1989
	Meghalaya	Low	Very high	No
	Sikkim	Low	Very high	No
	Nagaland	Low	Very high and increasing; maybe lower in 1980s, 90s	Periodic 1950s to present
	Mizoram	Low	n.a.	Periodic 1950s–1986
Pakistan				
Pre-1971	East	High	Low (until 1970–1), but grants rising	1960s leading to 1971 civil war
Post-1971	Sindh	Quite low	Moderate, but increasing. Fell 1981–3, then rose.	1983, died down in late 1980s
	NWFP	Low	High, increasing	1970s, died down in 1980s
Nigeria				
1960s	East	Low	High, increasing till 1965, then falling	1966–67
	West	Low	High, falling sharply	Violence, but not secessionist
Early 1970s	East-Central	n.a.	Stable	No clear cases
	Lagos (West)	n.a.	Moderate fall	No clear cases
	Western	n.a.	Sharp fall	No clear cases
	Midwest	n.a.	Sharp increase	No clear cases
Early 1980s	Anambra (East)	n.a.	Stable	No clear cases
	Imo (East)	n.a.	Slight fall	No clear cases
	Ogun (West)	n.a.	Stable	No clear cases
	Ondo (West)	n.a.	Stable	No clear cases
	Oyo (West)	n.a.	Stable (drop in 1985)	No clear cases
	Lagos (West)	n.a.	Increase	No clear cases
	Bendel (Midwest)	n.a.	Drop	No clear cases
Yugoslavia	Slovenia	Prob. high	Very low, worsening in late 1980s	1989–91
	Croatia	Prob. high	Low, worsening in late 1980s	1970–71, 1989–91
	Macedonia	Prob. lower	High, falling 1970–84	No
	Montenegro	Prob. lower	High, falling 1975–84	No
	Kosovo	Prob. lower	High, increasing	1980s

n.a. = not applicable.
[a] Does not include bank credit.

Instead of appeasing such a unit with fiscal aid, central governments could try—as did successive Nigerian regimes—to engineer their way out of the crisis. By redrawing regional boundaries, central officials can eliminate majority/minority states or at least reduce their size and disorient their leadership. Such policies can, of course, backfire, as in the Biafran civil war.

Is proportionality—rather than appeasement—sufficient to stabilize ethnic tensions? Determining this is extremely difficult because of the rareness of cases in which perfect proportionality is achieved. In Nigeria after the civil war, relative ethnic stability might be attributed to fiscal proportionality. However, given the radical constitutional engineering occurring simultaneously, the role fiscal policy played is unclear.

Our reading of this mixed and complicated evidence is that central fiscal appeasement can at times preempt or contain crises in ethnically mined federations. But, like any tool, its effectiveness will depend on how—and in what context—it is used. Deeper understanding, in our opinion, will require more context-rich theories; a better attempt to control for other important factors; a search for more precise and reliable data; a more detailed examination of the mechanisms by which central fiscal aid influences public service provision, economic performance, and public opinion; and rigorous thinking about how fiscal strategies interact with the redrawing of internal administrative boundaries. Meanwhile, examination of these cases offers meager support for those tempted to include fiscal decentralization or proportionality as elements of civil war settlements.

PART III

Where Power Sharing May (or May Not) Work

9

Power Sharing in Lebanon: Foreign Protectors, Domestic Peace, and Democratic Failure

Marie-Joëlle Zahar

"This little country that is so important."
Clemens Metternich

Lebanon's experiment with power sharing dates back to 1861. In the 140 years since then, foreign powers and Lebanese leaders have devised four different power-sharing "regimes" for the country. Although Lebanon has experienced violent crises, including two civil wars, none of the attempts at crisis resolution has altered the fundamentals of the Lebanese power-sharing institutions. At most, these institutions have been recalibrated to address changes in the domestic and international context. As one of the most enduring power-sharing experiments, one that has lasted for over a century under shifting domestic and international conditions, the Lebanese case sheds light on the relations between power sharing on the one hand and the durability of domestic peace and the transition to democracy on the other.

My argument is twofold: First, power sharing has brought long periods of peace, but this has depended on external protectors. When there have been foreign protectors, peace has lasted, but the withdrawal of an existing protector or the intervention of new would-be protectors has often brought significant turmoil to the country. Second, even though all three regimes

The author wishes to thank Donald Rothchild and Philip Roeder for their invaluable insights and support in writing this chapter. I am particularly indebted to Valerie Bunce, Ashutosh Varshney, David Lake and Bassel Salloukh as well as to participants in the Power Sharing and Peace Making workshops sponsored by the University of California's Institute on Global Conflict and Cooperation (IGCC) for their many useful suggestions and comments.

established since the end of the Ottoman Empire have been based on the notion that Lebanon must make a transition from power sharing based on religious affiliation to "one citizen, one vote" democracy, power-sharing institutions have thwarted the country's transition to democracy.

"A House of Many Mansions"[1]

To the casual observer, the unity of Lebanon appears inexplicable. Contemporary Lebanon officially boasts 17 religious sects, commonly referred to as *confessions*. The country's political system and civil administration are a delicate exercise in proportional balancing of elected representatives of these confessions. To complicate the task of proportional balancing, Lebanon's only official census was conducted in 1932. It showed that Maronite Christians enjoyed a slight numerical majority over the next largest confession, the Sunni Muslims. Yet they made up only 32 percent of Lebanon's overall population. Other relatively large confessions in Lebanon included the Christian Greek Orthodox (followers of the Russian Orthodox church), Greek Catholics (followers of the Vatican), the Shia Muslims or Shiites, and the Druze (an offshoot of Islam). Lebanon was—and remains in spite of demographic changes that have decreased the overall proportion of Christians in the population—a country of minorities.

Not only is Lebanese society divided along confessional lines, these divisions were for most of the twentieth century concomitant with class divisions. At the start of the century, the rich urban merchant classes tended to be Sunnis and Greek Orthodox. The rural farmers tended to be Maronites and Shia, but Maronites were on the whole more prosperous than their Shia counterparts. The Druze, initially the ruling political class and the feudal landlords of the Ottoman Empire that controlled Mount Lebanon, lost their privileged status under the French mandate (1920–1946).[2] Maronites prospered under French rule.

Although each confession had its share of well-to-do strongmen and rich landlords, it is reasonable to describe Lebanese society as exhibiting reinforcing rather than crosscutting cleavages. Confessions have tended to concentrate in distinct geographical regions, although there are a few mixed regions and many areas with substantial minority clusters. The territorial concentration of confessions has grown as a result of sectarian acts of violence committed by all sides during the civil war.

1. The expression comes from the title of Kamal Salibi's (1988) book.

2. A number of factors including internal power struggles within the Druze community, the arrival of Greek Catholic communities from Syria that joined the Maronites and swelled their ranks, and Maronite economic ascendancy account for Druze decline.

Lebanon's Power-Sharing Regimes

This section reviews the historical conditions that led to the emergence of the four power-sharing regimes and the details of power-sharing arrangements in each (Table 9.1). The discussion summarizes a rich and complex history and highlights factors leading to stability and instability in each period. I also focus on reasons that led to the decay of each regime under study and assess their ability to maintain domestic peace and initiate a transition from power sharing to full democracy.

The 1860 Civil War and the *Règlement Organique*

The first recorded autonomous political entity in what became modern-day Lebanon dates back to the early seventeenth century and the establishment of the Mount Lebanon *Imarah* (principality) within the Ottoman Empire.[3] The *Imarah* rested on a feudal society that linked the primarily Druze feudal landlord class (although there were also Druze peasants) to the primarily Maronite peasantry (even though a few Maronite families had become members of the elite). Religion was not a factor in the principality's politics until the late eighteenth century (Harik 1968, 40). Feudal ties formed the basis of social order. Rank was the marker of elite status, and, within the elite, family alliances transcended differences of faith (Makdisi 2000, 35). The principality's autonomy was premised on subservience to its Ottoman masters; the *Emir* (prince) was required to maintain social order and deliver required taxes and other obligations to the Sultan in Constantinople.

Religious communal identities emerged with a tax revolt in 1820. Maronite peasants rebelled against landlords using religious identity to call into question the relationships that underlay the social order. The revolt resulted in a new power configuration. The Maronite Church, which sided with the peasants, became a prominent challenger to the lords. Large and wealthy, the Church advocated the establishment of a Christian emirate (Harik 1991, 125; Aulas 1987, 11). Things came to a head in 1858 when Maronite peasants in the northern district of Kisrawan rose up against their lords (Abraham 1981; Kerr 1959). The conflict spilled over into southern Mount Lebanon where Druze lords played the communal card to rally the Druze peasantry. By July 1860 the Druzes were victorious. The death toll on the Christian side stood at eleven thousand.

It was against this background of communal violence that the first power-sharing arrangement was devised. The *Règlement Organique* (Organic Law)

3. Lebanon's foremost historian Kamal Salibi dates the consolidation of the *Imarah* to 1627.

Table 9.1. Lebanon's four power-sharing regimes, 1860–2002

	Règlement Organique (1861–1920)	1926 Constitution (1926–1943)	National Pact (1943–1975)	Ta'if Agreement (1989–)
Historical context	Communal violence (1858–1860)	French mandate	Preparation for independence	Civil War (1975–1990)
Power sharing	Christian governor Administrative council (12 mems, proportional representation) Territorial subdivisions	—	Maronite President (strong presidency) Sunni Premier Shia Speaker PR in Cabinet PR in Parliament (6:5 Christian-Muslim)	Maronite President Sunni Premier (strong cabinet) PR in Cabinet PR in Parliament (1:1 Muslim-Christian)
Constituent groups involved in negotiations	None (1861) Indirect (1864)	Maronites Sunnis	Maronites Sunnis	Maronites Sunnis Shia Druze Other confessions[a]
Direct or *indirect* foreign involvement in negotiations	Ottoman Empire, France, Great Britain, Russia, Austria, Prussia	France	*France, Syria*	*Saudi Arabia, Syria*[b]
Success in maintaining domestic peace	High	Medium-High (political instability, no violence)	Low (repeated crises; violence in 1969, 1971, and 1973; civil wars in 1958 and 1975–1990)	Medium (political stability, low-level violence)
Reason for regime's end	Dismemberment of Ottoman Empire	End of French Mandate	1975 civil war	—

[a] Other confessions represented by parliamentary representatives
[b] No non-Lebanese representatives were present at the Ta'if conference.

was announced by the Ottoman Empire, backed by a consortium of European powers, on June 9, 1861.[4]

Following the violence of 1858–1860, various foreign brokers stepped in as a consortium to contain the conflict because of its negative impact on their strategic interests (Hourani 1966, 22). While the Ottomans sought to restore the disrupted social order, European ambassadors used their "concern" for Christian communities as a pretext for intervening in the Ottoman Empire's affairs. The French were mainly concerned for Maronite safety, and the British—who backed the Druze to check French influence among Maronites—were worried about growing French influence. The result was 32 weeks of negotiations between France, Great Britain, Austria, Russia, Prussia, and the Ottoman Empire. Through French initiative, an international commission representing the five European guarantors of the agreement was established to "fix responsibility, determine guilt, estimate indemnity, and suggest reforms for the reorganization of Mount Lebanon" (Khalaf 2002, 6).

The Règlement Organique transformed Mount Lebanon into a fully autonomous Ottoman province with political institutions based on power sharing among its various sects under an Ottoman-European consortium protectorate. The Ottoman governor, a non-Lebanese Catholic, was appointed by Constantinople with the approval of the five foreign guarantors. Each of the six major communities was allotted two seats on the twelve-member administrative council that helped the governor rule.[5] According to article 11 of the Règlement, all members of the administrative council and of judiciary councils as well as local officials of smaller counties were to be "nominated and chosen, after agreement with the notables, by the leaders of the respective communities and appointed by the government" (Khalaf 2002, 278). The province was subdivided into six districts. Each had a dominant religious community and was ruled by a local mayor chosen by members of that community.

The Maronites looked unfavorably on these arrangements. With a numerical majority, they wanted representation to reflect their preponderance (Khalaf 2002, 279) and rejected equal representation with sects, such as the Shia, who made up less than 6 percent of the population.[6] By 1864, tension between the Maronites and the Ottoman governor required substantial modifications to the arrangement. Once again, the foreign brokers stepped in,

4. The *Règlement Organique* was preceded by another attempt at organizing the policy along sectarian lines, but that attempt, known as the *double qa'immaqamiyya*, sought to separate communities and give them exclusive spheres of influence rather than introduce power sharing per se.

5. The six major communities were the Maronite, Greek Orthodox and Catholic Christians and the Druze, Shia, and Sunni Muslims.

6. In the 1860s, Maronites made up almost 60 percent of the population.

and over time they redesigned the administrative council to consist of four Maronites, three Druzes, two Greek Orthodoxes, one Greek Catholic, one Sunni Muslim, and one Shia Muslim. Proportional communal representation thus became the norm (Meo 1976, 34).

The 1864 settlement introduced by the Ottoman-European protectors brought almost a half century of communal peace to Mount Lebanon. Although political instability and tension occurred between local notables seeking increased autonomy and the Sublime Porte (the Ottoman Empire's government) attempting to maintain control over these Ottoman territories, there was no major violence among Mount Lebanon's religious communities. The settlement lasted until 1920 when the victorious Allies dismantled the Ottoman Empire, which had sided with Austria and Germany in World War I.

Power Sharing under the French Mandate

Upon the dismemberment of the Ottoman Empire, the victorious Supreme Allied Council met in San Remo on April 28, 1920, and entrusted France with a mandate over present-day Syria and Lebanon. On September 1, 1920, the French High Commissioner, General Henri Gouraud, proclaimed the creation of Greater Lebanon (*Grand Liban*), which would include the territory of Mount Lebanon, the towns of Beirut, Tripoli, Sur (Tyre), and Saida (Sidon), the regions of Baʿalbak and the Biqaʿ, and the districts of Rashayya and Hasbayya (Figure 9.1). Expansion of Lebanon also increased the country's religious heterogeneity. From 80 percent of the population of the Mount Lebanon province, the Maronites fell to a bare 51 percent majority in the new polity (Zamir 1985, 98). For their part, the Druze lost their position as the dominant Muslim sect to the Sunnis. Yet Maronites and Greek Catholics enthusiastically backed the creation of Greater Lebanon; other communities were ambivalent.

From 1920 to 1926 the political situation in Greater Lebanon remained unsettled. From 1920 to 1922, four successive French governors administered Lebanon. A 17-member consultative council, representing the different Lebanese confessions and selected by General Gouraud, assisted the governors. Council members continued the tradition of the administrative council of Mount Lebanon, which had tended to defend local interests against the Ottoman governor. In March 1922, the French High Commissioner sought to establish a more permanent representative body and decreed the institution of a Lebanese Representative Council. The Council, inspired by the experience of the *Mutasarrifiyya* (the Arabic term for the power-sharing regime), would comprise 30 deputies elected by general (male) suffrage for a period of four years. It was based on "confessional representation in proportion to the size of each community as recorded by the

Figure 9.1 Lebanon: Confessional communities (population distribution as of June 1982)

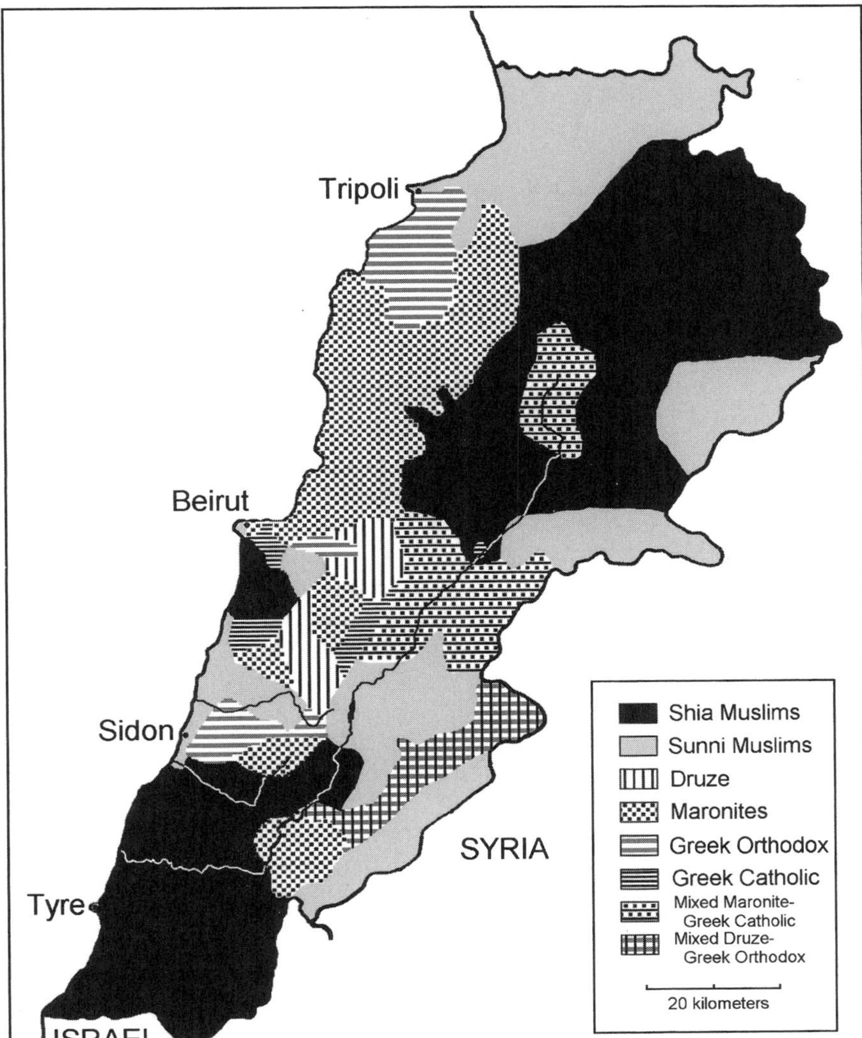

census of 1921" (Zamir 1985, 142). Predicated on a belief that only sectarian representation could stem the tide of sectarian strife and bring about intergroup cooperation, its design reinforced sectarianism and increased the power of sectarian leaders (Hourani 1946, 181). The Council was limited to an advisory role. The High Commissioner and governor had a final say in all matters and could overturn any decision of the Council; they also had the authority to adjourn or dissolve the Council.

Between 1920 and 1926, France's inability to develop proactive policies toward the Syrian Arab nationalist movement entangled Lebanon in the growing French-Syrian confrontation and hindered the development of a Lebanese national identity. Maronites sought to secure Lebanon's gains in terms of political autonomy; several other sects (mainly the Sunnis) refused to acknowledge the country's independence and considered it a part of Greater Syria.

Against this background of mounting communal tensions, France ended the six-year transition by establishing Lebanon's second power-sharing regime. A new constitution transformed Greater Lebanon into the Republic of Lebanon in 1926 and enshrined confessional politics throughout all levels of governance. The 1926 constitution vested legislative powers in two houses—a senate and a chamber of deputies. Both houses enjoyed widespread powers including the election of the president, voting confidence in the government, and approval of the yearly budget. The two houses elected the president, who also enjoyed wide-ranging powers for a three-year term, with the possibility of renewal. Article 95 guaranteed sectarian representation (Zamir 2000, 30). Although this was supposed to be a temporary arrangement on the way to an integrated Lebanese nation-state, these institutions actually made realization of this objective more difficult. Power sharing increased the influence of a small group of prominent Christian families in Beirut and the region known as the Mountain, of Shia and Sunni landowning feudal families on the peripheries, and later—when Sunnis decided to accept the independence of Lebanon from Syria—of Sunni notables in the coastal towns. According to Meir Zamir (2000, 31):

> Despite religious, sectarian, regional and national differences, members of this dominant class [of Christian, Shia, and Sunni notables] cooperated with each other because they shared a similar interest—exploitation of the institutions of the new state to strengthen their positions and increase their wealth. Indeed, they used sectarianism more as a tool to exact privileges for themselves, their relatives and their clients than to protect the interests of the communities to which they belonged. . . . Only politicians predisposed to these methods were able to succeed in the Lebanese political arena. Those who genuinely strove to transform Lebanon into a democratic, pluralistic and equitable society either had no influence or were forced out of the system altogether.

These squabbles among political hopefuls jockeying for power and relative advantage would leave two legacies for politics in post-independence Lebanon. First, they altered the balance of power among the president, government, and parliament. With French backing, this shifted toward the president. Parliament became "a mere forum for debate, rather than a sovereign authoritative body" (Zamir 2000, 245). The government became unstable, and the prime minister dependent on the president. The Maronite presidents came to exercise significant clout, which would later jeopardize the delicate intercommunal balance on which Lebanon's stability depended. The second legacy was the introduction of political feudalism in the political system. This tendency of political elites to seek access to state institutions and wealth under the disguise of serving community interests can be credited in part for the growing intensity of sectarian politics that would ultimately bring about the collapse of the "Lebanese miracle."

After establishing Greater Lebanon in 1920, the French deployed their political and military power to defend the young state's autonomy and territorial integrity against both internal and external threats. Several Lebanese communities, notably the Sunnis, were hostile to Lebanon's independence. Similarly, Syria rejected the separate existence of the young state. The French role was part of a historical continuity. It was, as Zamir (1985, 97), notes, "an international guarantee for the independence, territorial integrity and Christian character of Greater Lebanon, recalling the guarantees of the six European powers, headed by France, for the existence of the autonomous Sanjak of Mount Lebanon more than half a century before."

France helped to consolidate the new Lebanese state. French representatives prevented Maronites from completely dominating state institutions, tempering the opposition of the Sunnis and other communities to Lebanese independence (Zamir 2000, 241). However, these short-term solutions had longer-term destabilizing consequences. First, although they maintained a balance among the various communities, the power-sharing policies of French officials left Lebanon vulnerable to political sectarianism, feudalism, and clientelism. Old and new elites managed to strengthen their control over the state by portraying themselves as guardians of their communities' rights (Zamir 2000, 245). Second, France's policies in Lebanon and toward the Greater-Syrian Nationalists in Syria invited Syrian intervention in Lebanese politics. The Syrians exploited sectarian, factional, and personal divisions against France.

The National Pact of 1943

In 1941 the French presence in the Middle East was seriously weakened by the German invasion of France. The end of the Mandate was on the horizon—and would terminate in 1946. On the eve of independence, three major nationalist positions could be discerned in Lebanon. Christian nationalists sought to retain French tutelage. Arab nationalists sought Lebanon's incorporation into Syria. Lebanese nationalists accepted Lebanon's independence within the 1920 frontiers, provided the country followed a policy of real independence and cooperated closely with the Arab world (Hourani 1946, 298).

The National Pact (*al-Mithaq al-Watani*) of 1943, which was an informal agreement between representatives of the largest Christian and Muslim communities, reflected a compromise based on the Lebanese nationalist position. It provided a framework to reconcile the interests of the Maronites and Sunnis and confronted the French with a united Lebanese position for an end to the mandate. Led by a prosperous merchant class, the Maronites wanted to control the machinery of government in their own interests and settled for a formal break with France; the Sunnis, led by Arab nationalists, sought independence from the French mandate and were willing to settle without a formal tie to Syria (Hourani 1966, 27). The unwritten pact would supplement the formal constitution of the country. It enshrined three principles:

1. *Segmental proportionality:* representation of the communities in government in proportion to their demographic weight;
2. *Segmental autonomy:* a guarantee of the communities' rights to conduct religious, educational, and cultural affairs with no state intervention; and
3. *Foreign policy "neutrality":* an agreement by the Sunnis not to seek union with Syria in return for a pledge by the Maronites not to steer the country toward the West.

From 1943 to the eruption of the civil war in 1975, Lebanon's political institutions sought to preserve the autonomy of the country's 17 religious groups while guaranteeing their proportional representation in the central government. True to what by then had become a long-standing tradition, the distribution of political offices was a delicate balancing act. The Maronites held the Presidency of the Republic, an office endowed with extensive powers and privileges.[7] To counterbalance Maronite presidential prerogatives, the Sunnis were given the office of the premiership. Cabinet posts provided representation for the largest religious communities relative to their importance. The Ministry of Finance was shared almost equally between the Sunnis and the Maronites (Salem 1967, 501). Christians held the offices of Deputy-Premier (Greek Orthodox) and Minister of Foreign Affairs (Maronites/Greek Catholics). Muslims held the ministries of the Interior (practically always held by the Sunni Premier), Defense (Druze), Agriculture (Shia or Druze), and Post and Telegraph (Crow 1962, 496).

The 1943 National Pact fixed the ratio of Christian to Muslim representatives in Parliament at six to five, the number of seats per community being set by law. Later the post of Speaker was assigned to the Shia, and the office

7. These powers included ultimate control over the Lebanese Army, veto over legislation passed by Parliament, and an informal say in the choice of the premier.

of Deputy-Speaker to the Greek Orthodox. But the constitution also intended Parliament to serve as an instrument of national integration, and members were elected on the basis of a "common roll" that represented electoral constituencies rather than specific communities (Crow 1962, 494).[8] Yet, after 1943 the Lebanese electoral system failed to fulfill its unifying role. Traditional leaders used intimidation and patronage to secure the election of their lists. Candidates on the list did not have to worry about building support across communities (Salibi 1988, 189). The legislature turned into a private club as leaders promoted their protégés. The elites almost secured a monopoly of representation. Hence, patronage politics did not bode well for legislative responsiveness to popular demands.

In the mid-1950s, the Muslim community increasingly called into question the arrangement that had produced a decade of peace among communal groups (Hourani 1988, 3–10; Hudson 1988, 226–234).[9] A host of factors was transforming the sociodemographic structure of Lebanon. Economic growth focused on the service sector at the expense of agriculture. This triggered an exodus of impoverished Shia farmers from South Lebanon to the slums of Beirut's southern suburbs while the country was experiencing its economic golden age and the rich, mostly Sunnis and Christians, were getting richer. This deepened the rift between the center (Beirut) and the periphery, the elites and the masses, and created a never-before experienced socioeconomic gap that closely mapped onto religious affiliation. The Maronites were on top of the heap and the Shia at the bottom.

Yet, the decisive problem was the absence of a foreign protector to maintain the rules of power sharing, to prevent confessional groups from seeking outside allies, and to exclude competitive foreign interventions into Lebanese affairs. Despite their agreement to share power, the two "founding" communities continued to disagree on the country's identity. Despite their apparent compromise to maintain neutrality in foreign affairs, Lebanese communities drew outsiders into domestic politics to redress internal inequalities or to counter perceived threats from one another (Khalaf 1997; Azar 1988). The result was recurring crises and episodes of civil war in Lebanon's third power-sharing regime.

While domestic socioeconomic developments increased Muslim popular disenchantment, competitive foreign intervention rocked the foundations

8. Within a single constituency, where ordinarily there are several seats of varying religions, the electorate forms a common roll with each voter voting for all seats including those denominations other than his own. Thus electoral contests turned into intrasectarian struggles, and candidates, to be acceptable, could not solely count on the approval of their co-religionists.

9. Both Michael Hudson (1988) and Albert Hourani (1988) see the failure of "power-sharingism" as a result of growing regional/political and internal/socioeconomic pressure that the system failed to absorb.

of the National Pact. U.S. foreign policy sought to drum up support for regional stability by including conservative Arab regimes in the Baghdad Pact. Egypt's President Gamal Abdel Nasser challenged this U.S. policy, advancing instead a message of pan-Arab unity. President Camille Shamʿun's decision to join the Baghdad Pact in 1958 was strongly opposed by the Lebanese National Movement (LNM), which was influenced by the discourse of Arab unity (Tuéni 1982; Hudson 1988; Khalaf 1997).[10] Disagreement over Lebanon's foreign policy developed into a crisis over the extensive prerogatives granted by the constitution to the Maronite president. The opposition demanded political reforms to prevent the Maronite vision of Lebanon from dominating. Syrian intervention only worsened matters.[11] Upon creation of the United Arab Republic (UAR) on February 1, 1958, an event that was met with feverish enthusiasm among Lebanese Muslims, UAR radio broadcasts urged the LNM to use violence and overthrow the Lebanese government (Anonymous 1958, 370). The political and military support that Syria and Egypt provided to the mobilized Muslim populace forced elites to shed their moderation and adopt a radical tone for fear of losing support at the ballot box. Opposition leaders thus allowed themselves "to become prisoners' of their own followers' extremism . . . and [proved] more interested in their own personal political status than in the country's welfare" (Khalaf 2002, 124). This led to a brief civil war, a small U.S. intervention, and a slow return to the status quo ante by the end of the year.

This was the first of three major crises that brought the National Pact to an end. Second, following the establishment of the Palestine Liberation Organization (PLO) in 1964, the Palestinian armed presence in Lebanon became a major bone of contention among the various communities. Maronite leaders argued that commando operations launched from Lebanese territory exposed Lebanon to the danger of Israeli retaliation and threatened national security and stability. The Maronites also saw the Palestinians "as a Trojan Horse which the radical parties in the country . . . were already making expert use of to subvert the Lebanese system" (Salibi 1976).[12] This provided the backdrop to the 1969 crisis between the Lebanese Army and the Palestinian guerrillas (Hudson 1978, 262–267; Sirriyeh 1976, 78–79; Salibi 1976, 26–43; Brynen 1990, 46–48).[13]

10. The Lebanese National Movement was an umbrella organization of all the opposition parties during the 1958 crisis headed by Progressive Socialist Party and Druze feudal leader Kamal Junblatt.

11. As early as 1949, the Syrian Nationalist Party, a Lebanese party favoring the creation of a Greater Syria, attempted a coup against the first post-independence Lebanese government.

12. Camille Shamʿun's National Liberal Party, Pierre Jumayyil's *Kataʾib* and Raymond Iddah's National Bloc formed the Triple Alliance (*al-Hilf al-Thulathi*) in view of the upcoming 1968 parliamentary elections. Their stance on the Palestinian question was openly backed by Maronite Patriarch Maʿushi.

13. On April 23, 1969, clashes erupted between the Lebanese Army and the Palestinian guerrillas.

Following clashes in April 1969 and again in August, President Nasser of Egypt mediated between the parties. The Cairo Agreement, signed by Lebanese and Palestinian representatives on November 3, 1969, granted the PLO wide autonomy within the Palestinian camps and limited freedom of movement outside the camps. It deepened divisions among the Lebanese. Muslims for whom Christian political ascendancy was a "sort of domination" considered the Palestinian commandos a source of security and an embodiment of their cause. While Muslim leaders showed impatience with the PLO, they were caged in by the masses (Salibi 1976, 54). Maronites regarded the agreement as an unwarranted betrayal of Lebanese sovereignty and exerted pressure on their own leaders not to give in to the demands of the Muslims.

Once again, Syria's intervention made matters worse. Between 1969 and 1973, Al-Saʿiqa, a Syrian-financed and supported Palestinian militia, acted to extend Syrian influence in Lebanon (Brynen 1990, 57). It and other Syrian-backed Palestinian groups were instrumental in instigating Lebanese-Palestinian clashes in April and October 1969 (McLaurin 1977, 257). In a small crisis in 1973, Syria sided with the Palestinians and closed the Lebanese-Syrian border to pressure the Lebanese government into containing the conflict. The Maronites considered this an infringement on Lebanon's sovereignty.

Against these mounting competitive pressures within and outside Lebanon, the National Pact's third armed crisis began: April 13, 1975, marks the beginning of the Lebanese Civil War. Dissatisfaction with the power-sharing formula that privileged the Christians was a major cause. The two warring factions are often labeled Christian and Muslim, but it is more accurate to describe them as pro– and anti–status quo.[14] The powerful traditional elites (mostly Maronites) fought to maintain their privileges while socioeconomically disadvantaged groups (mostly Shia) fought for more power and access to state resources. However, domestic political issues might have been resolved differently were it not for the inside-outside dialectics that linked developments within the Lebanese political system to wider international issues.

The Ta'if Accord of 1989

In 1989, members of the Lebanese Parliament met in Ta'if, Saudi Arabia, to negotiate an end to the war that had begun fourteen years earlier. They produced the Ta'if Accord. Although the basic power-sharing nature of Lebanon's institutions remained unaltered, reforms changed the powers of

14. The mainly Christian, pro–status quo forces came to be known as the Lebanese Front. The Front included political forces associated with Maronite traditional political families in addition to the militias of Maronite religious orders. The anti–status quo forces revolved around the mainly Muslim Lebanese National Movement and some Palestinian guerrillas.

the presidency and council of ministers and the composition of parliament. By 1991 the war had ended, and most parties had accepted or acquiesced in the terms of the Ta'if Accord.

The impetus to reach agreement was the imminent collapse of the Lebanese state. Until 1988, some state institutions, notably the Central Bank, the Foreign Ministry, and the Presidency of the Republic, had remained active. In August 1988, however, the presidency became formally vacant. Under the constitution, no president could serve beyond his term. When the constitutional deadline for the election of a new president passed without elections, the outgoing president had to step down. Two parallel governments emerged when outgoing President Amin Jumayyil appointed Army Commander General Michel ʿAwn to head a cabinet of transition, while Muslim leaders recognized the outgoing prime minister, Salim al-Huss, as government leader. Arab mediation efforts in early 1989 failed to resolve the deadlock. Against this backdrop, a confrontation between the troops of General ʿAwn and Syrian armed forces heightened concern in the Arab world for the survival of Lebanon. In May 1989, Arab mediators formulated a truce plan according to which a ceasefire would come into effect on August 29 followed by a meeting of the Lebanese parliamentarians in Ta'if.

The parties to the conflict were not the main negotiators who designed the power-sharing arrangement of the post-conflict Lebanese state. Lebanese members of parliament, who had been elected in 1972 and who for the most part had been spectators rather than actors in the civil war, negotiated the agreement (Maila 1994, 37). The Ta'if Accord maintained the broad outlines of the older power-sharing system but redistributed domestic political power among the major confessions—Maronite, Sunni, and Shia. It curtailed the powers of the Maronite president (Harik 1991, 45–56), entrusted most executive powers to the confessionally mixed Council of Ministers (thus yielding significant power to the Sunni prime minister), and increased the power of the legislature and especially that of the Shia house speaker. Ta'if replaced the old 6:5 distribution of seats in parliament by an equal distribution between Christians and Muslims; it also increased the number of seats in parliament from 99 to 108 and eventually to 128.[15]

Ta'if also provided for Syrian Army assistance in helping the legitimate Lebanese forces extend state authority. This provision recognized the role of a hegemon to maintain the peace and legitimated military intervention

15. Christians argue that the extensive powers of the president are a security guarantee. The prerogatives are considered by many Maronites as an essential political tool to implement their "vision" of Lebanon. Safeguards were built in to prevent any community from establishing de facto control of the executive. A two-third majority in government was required to decide major issues including the state of emergency, war and peace, general mobilization, international treaties, the budget, comprehensive development and long-range plans, the dissolution of parliament, the election law, the naturalization law, and personal status law.

to assist in the implementation of power sharing. The agreement also clarified the nature of relations between Lebanon and Syria: Ta'if stated that the two countries have "distinctive relations which derive their force from the roots of propinquity, history, and common filial interests," but it stipulated that any agreements between Syria and Lebanon shall "realize the interests of the two filial countries within the framework of the sovereignty and independence of each" (Salem 1991a, 171). In addition, Ta'if sought to introduce a number of reforms—including administrative decentralization, a new electoral law, the establishment of an economic and social development council, reform with a view toward reinforcing national integration and identification of education and teaching, and regulation of the media—and to reassert the objective of liberating Lebanon from Israeli occupation.

As was the case with the 1926 constitution and the 1943 National Pact before it, the Ta'if Accord emphasized confessional compromise and intercommunal cooperation as temporary measures to facilitate transition to an integrated, nonconfessional democracy; however, no steps were taken in the direction of a nonconfessional regime. Rather, confessionalism became deeply institutionalized once again. Ta'if sought to replace the rule of individuals by the rule of institutions; thus, executive powers were taken away from the presidency and placed in the hands of the government. In practice, however, the country was ruled after 1989 by a troika whose members perceived themselves as representatives of their respective communities.[16] This "three-man show" consisted of the President of the Republic, the "president" of the Council of Ministers, and the "president" of Parliament.[17] Far from working to eradicate confessionalism, Lebanese leaders used customary practices to challenge the provisions of the new constitution and each attempted to enhance his own power at the expense of the others (Krayem 1997, 426–427). For instance, President Ilyas Hrawi insisted on attending all the meetings of the Council of Ministers to assert his control over the executive branch (Mansour 1993, 204–207).

The stability of the power-sharing arrangement owed much to Syria's newly recognized role as protector. Jockeying for predominance among the confessional leaders might have been destabilizing were it not for Syria's role as an arbiter among the president, the prime minister, and the speaker of parliament. Yet, this drew the Syrian authorities deeper into domestic politics in Lebanon. Much as the French presence had affected the realities of power sharing during the Mandate, so the Syrian presence affected the reality of power sharing after 1989. First, like the French presence that had

16. The word *troika* (drawn from the Russian for a vehicle drawn by three horses but meaning a tripartite leadership) has made its way into the Lebanese political lexicon.

17. The titles of prime minister and house speaker respectively translate from Arabic into English as president of the Council of Ministers and president of Parliament.

strengthened the hands of Maronite leaders in earlier decades, the Syrian presence strengthened the hands of Syria's political allies among the community leaders. These favored leaders had less reason to compromise with the leaders of other communities or with challengers within their own communities. Second, much as the French presence had strengthened the hands of the president, the Syrian presence strengthened the government. Third, much as France had been in a position to change the rules of the game as long as it remained a hegemon, Syria's protectorate allowed it to reinterpret major clauses of the Ta'if Accord, such as the provision that required a full Syrian military withdrawal prior to the first postwar elections (Zahar 2002). In 1992, despite a provision that major changes in the rules required a two-thirds majority in the government, the executive with Syrian backing passed a new electoral law that totally disregarded the opposition of Christian ministers. In summer 2004, Syria pressured the Lebanese Parliament into amending the constitution to extend the term of President Emile Lahoud, a Maronite close to Damascus, by three additional years.

Despite Syrian favoritism toward Lebanon's Muslims, Christian forces did not react violently to what amounted to a forced renegotiation of the power-sharing arrangement. This stability owed much to Syria's determination to quash opposition. In 1989, no sooner was the Ta'if Accord disclosed than General ʿAwn and his supporters rejected it, contending that Ta'if did not commit the Syrian armed forces to a rapid and complete withdrawal from Lebanon. They also rejected the proposed political reforms as unable to solve fundamental political problems (Salem 1991b). Bolstered by popular support, ʿAwn urged other Christian political forces to take sides. Disagreement among the Christian leaderships followed and led to a military confrontation that left them weakened and vulnerable. The Syrian Army took advantage of this vulnerability and on October 13, 1990, with a quick strike, defeated ʿAwn's troops and paved the way for implementation of the Ta'if Accord as Syria interpreted its terms. By so doing, the Syrian forces demonstrated their willingness to use force in their dealing with spoilers. This deterrent message was not lost on the Lebanese Forces in 1992.

Conclusions to be Drawn from Lebanese Power Sharing

Power sharing has brought extended periods of peace to Lebanon, including the 50 years under the Règlement Organique (de jure 1861–1920, de facto 1864–1920), the decade and a half under the 1926 constitution (1926–1943), and the first dozen years under the National Pact (1946–1958). Yet, as popular participation in politics has grown and deference to traditional elites has waned, the length of each successive period of peace has declined. More important, peace has depended on a stable foreign protectorate and has thwarted the transition to a nonconfessional democracy.

Power Sharing and Domestic Peace

External factors are paramount in explaining the varying degrees to which power-sharing regimes have succeeded at maintaining domestic peace in Lebanon. The pattern over time is quite clear: When a foreign protectorate—particularly a multilateral protectorate—has been in place, Lebanon's power sharing has brought peace. When there was no protector, violent crises in the power-sharing system were more likely. The likelihood of violence began to rise as one protector weakened or began to withdraw. In a transition between protectors, the danger of violence continued into the early stages of establishing a new protectorate. Other factors, such as changing elite-follower relations, played a secondary role to this. The Règlement Organique successfully stemmed communal violence in Lebanon. In spite of the widespread massacres that accompanied the events of 1857–1860, quiet was restored relatively quickly in Mount Lebanon. The 1926 constitution was also relatively successful, with no intercommunal violence reported throughout the period of the Mandate: During the political crises of the 1920s and 1930s, the French authorities often used the threat of force to deter Lebanese politicians and their followers from pressing what were considered "unacceptable" demands, yet none of the political demonstrations involved more than low-level rioting. In contrast, the 1943 National Pact, despite its first dozen years of peace, must be considered a failure in light of the numerous violent and nonviolent politico-military crises that beset Lebanon as early as 1958 and culminated with the 1975 civil war. Finally, the Ta'if Agreement seems to have reduced the level of intercommunal violence. The heavy-handed Syrian military presence in the country and the repression of opposition forces have lowered the level of intercommunal violence (Zahar 2002).

In the Lebanese case, a foreign protectorate has been necessary—and perhaps sufficient—to secure domestic peace and stability, even without the support of all Lebanese communities. It is interesting to note that the most stable period in Lebanese history remains the period following the Règlement Organique. Peace was restored relatively soon after the violence; it endured even beyond the dismemberment of the Ottoman Empire. Key to understanding this stability is the congruence in the interest of all foreign powers to maintain stability and order in the region and prevent large-scale violence. In the same vein, the post-1990 domestic peace in Lebanon is in no small part a function of Syria's interest in the stability of Lebanon. In contradistinction, Lebanon's most unstable period, 1943–1975, saw no international guarantees of the power-sharing regime.

Multilateral condominiums appear to have led to more durable power-sharing arrangements than have single-state protectorates. First, multilateral agreements included provisions to abstain from competitive intervention. The Règlement Organique, the mandate system, and the Ta'if Accord all included such multilateral guarantees. Presumably, it is more difficult to achieve consensus among a larger number of foreign protectors, yet this was precisely the constellation that secured domestic peace for the longest period.

The history of foreign efforts to end Lebanon's most recent civil war is telling in this respect. Of the many conferences, summits, and agreements organized to end the Lebanese civil war of 1975–1990, all those set up solely by one foreign player failed—as evidenced by the many Syrian-sponsored peace agreements and the ill-fated Israeli-Lebanese agreement of 1983. The Ta'if Accord, in contradistinction, had drummed up support from all quarters (the Arab world, the United States, France, and the Vatican).

Second, the numbers of guarantors was also important for the stability of domestic peace in one other way. The larger the number of guarantors, the less likely it was that one player's withdrawal from the agreement would endanger the stability of a power-sharing regime. Thus, the Ottoman Empire's disengagement did not affect the situation in Mount Lebanon. However, one can only wonder about the impact that an abrupt end to the French mandate would have had on Lebanese politics in the 1920s and 1930s. Finally, Syria's withdrawal may well put the stability of the post-Ta'if second Republic in jeopardy. Given the essential Syrian role in the implementation of the Ta'if Accord—including the repression of political opponents and the silencing of counterelites—a Syrian military pullout would be likely to reopen the Pandora's box of civil violence.

Alternatively, the intervention of new external actors to challenge a declining protectorate or to create a new protectorate has undermined the stability of power-sharing arrangements. Foreign intervention in the periods before 1860 and in the periods 1920–1926 and 1943–1975 contributed to the political crises that rocked the country. French meddling in the affairs of the Ottoman Empire fueled growing Maronite demands for expanded political rights that led to communal violence. Syrian meddling during the Mandate period encouraged Sunni opposition to French rule and support for the idea of Greater Syria. It fueled the Maronites' relentless pursuit of guarantees, which involved controlling key executive and military positions in the new state. In the newly independent Lebanon, Syria's political and military support of the LNM was a critical factor in the violence of 1958.

From late 1975 to 1990, Syria began to play the role of protector that would ultimately support a new power-sharing arrangement, but the transition to this new protectorate and power-sharing regime was accompanied by extreme violence. Looking to avoid a partition of Lebanon that could further weaken the Arab world in its conflict with Israel, the Syrian government sought to stabilize the situation militarily by contributing heavily to the Arab League's peacekeeping mission in Lebanon, the Arab Deterrent Force. It also tried to forge an alliance between the Lebanese Front and the LNM (Brynen 1990, 91–92).[18] This attempt failed, but it highlighted a shift in the Syrian involvement in Lebanon as it got closer to actually establishing a protectorate: Syria's new role as a mediator among the various factions. In 1976, the Syrian authorities helped produce the Constitutional Document, a proposal that conceded some internal reforms to the Lebanese power-sharing formula in return for guarantees that the PLO would respect the terms of the 1969 Cairo Agreement.[19] Damascus was involved in 1980 in the elaboration of the Fourteen Points for Reconciliation that sought the reestablishment of Lebanese sovereignty, an equilibrated system of power sharing, close cooperation with Syria, and Lebanese support for the Palestinian cause.

In 1984 Syria mediated among the Lebanese factions in the civil war at national reconciliation conferences in Geneva and Lausanne, Switzerland. The talks resulted in proposals for a slightly modified power-sharing formula, including the redistribution of parliamentary seats and a curtailment of presidential powers. In a major departure from the neutrality provisions of the National Pact, the talks asserted Lebanon's full affiliation with the Arab world (Khalidi 1989, 379). Later that year Syria sponsored the Tripartite Accord, a peace deal negotiated and signed in Damascus, which introduced significant changes to the terms of Syrian-Lebanese relations. The 1984 accord severely limited presidential prerogatives and planned a sweeping deconfessionalization of Lebanese politics. Although these mediation efforts ultimately failed, they usually coincided with lulls in the fighting. In sum, while Syrian intervention on behalf of one side in the conflict was usually associated with an increase in the level of violence, Syria's growing role as protector and attempts at mediation were on the contrary associated with a decrease in the intensity of conflict.

The Illusory Hope of Transition to Democracy

Since the end of the Ottoman Empire, all power-sharing regimes have included provisions that stipulated that these institutional arrangements were to be only a transitional mechanism that would lead Lebanon toward

18. According to the semi-official *Al-Ba'ath* newspaper: "Lebanon's security, interests and Arabism are an essential part of Arab national security and interests, especially after the retrogressive Egyptian-Israeli agreement which is firmly linked with what is going on in Lebanon."

19. Although the Constitutional Document did not alter the confessional character of the top decisionmaking elites, it promised sweeping reforms in Parliament, the civil service, and education.

a nonsectarian democracy. Yet none of these provisions was able to transcend sectarianism. On the contrary, at the end of each regime the sectarianism in politics was stronger and more firmly rooted. This may in part have been a result of incentives created by power sharing, but the role of foreign protectors and the alternation of peace and conflict associated with the rise and decline of each protectorate increased these incentives. Indeed, protectorates had five unintended effects on the bargaining among communal leaders that increased the incentives for sectarianism and thwarted the development of a nonconfessional democracy.

First, in designing power-sharing arrangements, protectors introduced procedural measures to convert politically charged issues into technically tractable matters; yet, this deliberate avoidance of the hard issues of Lebanon's statehood did not make these go away. (This tactic was also used in a number of other peace negotiations, including the Israeli-Palestinian peace talks and the Northern Irish process, where the different groups postponed decisions on the statehood issue.) Instead, the parties agreed on procedures about which their interests coincided and avoided issues that might have led to breakdown of negotiations. This aptly describes the dynamic of interelite cooperation under French rule where elites with diametrically opposed objectives (Lebanese autonomy and the creation of a Greater Syria) managed under French pressure to cooperate by focusing on the details of power sharing without addressing the ultimate identity of the country that they were building. Yet, the festering statehood issue continued to give rise to severe crises that threatened to tear apart or extinguish the Lebanese state.

Second, the presence of a protector encouraged mutual intransigence on many issues by decreasing the painful consequences associated with hardened positions. A good illustration of this dynamic is provided by the particularly unstable Lebanese politics under the French mandate. Aware that the French presence in Lebanon presented a guarantee against a descent into anarchy, the various Lebanese elites did not feel compelled to display a spirit of compromise in their dealings with one another on difficult overarching issues. Rather than creating incentives for cooperation, the protector-backed power-sharing arrangements increased the tendency of sectarian elites to engage in the type of extortionate threats that tore Cyprus apart.

Third, the presence of the protector created winners and losers, and once the protector began to weaken its hold, the losers were likely to seek a fundamental revision in the distribution of powers and invite in outside challengers to back their demands. Thus, under the French mandate, the Presidency of the Republic acquired so many prerogatives that "after 1943 Maronite presidents would wield considerable clout, with a detrimental effect on the delicate balance between the communities. The presidency thus became a means for the Maronites to maintain their dominance"

(Zamir 2000, 245). Under Syria's tutelage, disagreement over the design of electoral institutions served to rekindle sectarian politics. In the same vein as the 1926 constitution, the Ta'if Accord sought to encourage moderate multiconfessional voting, by holding elections on the basis of the *muhafaza* (governorate). Instead, as a result of extensive electoral gerrymandering, the *muhafaza* was replaced with the more homogeneous *qada'* (district).[20] Although Ta'if provided for a new electoral law that required the support of two-thirds of Lebanon's cabinet members—effectively allowing a dissenting minority to exercise a veto—the law was adopted in total disregard of the Christian leaders' opposition to its content. The electoral debacle resulted in a Christian boycott of the first postconflict parliamentary elections. The Syrian-backed Lebanese government disregarded the boycott and went ahead with the elections, leaving Christian political forces with little to no access to the formal structures of power. The Christian population worried that the behavior of Muslim political elites indicated their intention to achieve in peace the victory that they had been unable to achieve in war. The Syrian bias toward some Muslim communities reinforced sectarian cleavages in the country (Bahout 1993; Krayem 1997).

Fourth, the presence of a protector permitted Lebanese elites to focus on cementing their respective political monopolies. The leaders focused on the manipulation of specific institutional arrangements to benefit their own position within their communities at the expense of other politicians. Within their respective communities this reinforced political feudalism and blocked challenges to the elites' power. With the backing of the protectorate, these elites could quell all challenges to their own power in the guise of a defense of the power-sharing peace accord.

Fifth, the perceived bias on the part of the protector and the heightened insecurity among losers left the latter less willing to forgo power sharing for a nonconfessional democracy. Rather than the growing trust that Timothy Sisk and Christoph Stefes find in South Africa (Chapter 12), power sharing backed by a protector heightened suspicions and fed demands for still stronger power-sharing guarantees. For example, after 2000 Christian elites felt threatened by the terms of the Ta'if power-sharing arrangement. An expression (*al-ihbat al-Masihi* [Christian hopelessness and discontent]) was even coined to describe the situation of Maronites specifically and Christians

20. The *muhafaza* was adopted only in regions where there was no doubt on the political loyalties of the would-be parliamentarians. Where the elections were expected to be contested by anti-Syrian forces, or where Syria sought to reward one client over another, it was abandoned in favor of the *qada'*. Thus in 1992 and 1996, a special status was accorded to the Druze in the predominantly Maronite governorate of Mount Lebanon to secure the election of Syrian ally, Progressive Socialist Party (PSP) leader Walid Junblatt. Mount Lebanon, a stronghold of Christian opposition, was divided into a number of constituencies to decrease the electoral chances of opposition candidates.

more generally. Under such conditions, Christians rejected any moves toward deconfessionalization and a transition to full democracy in favor of locking in guarantees through power sharing. This is not unlike the situation in 1958 when the foreign policy of President Camille Sham'un was seen as a breach of the National Pact by Muslim communities and elites. The result was retrenchment behind the defenses of sectarian politics and political feudalism. Power sharing also paralyzed any move toward democracy.

Thus, there has been a perverse resilience to Lebanese power sharing. Although the Lebanese Civil War prompted a reformulation of the power-sharing formula, it did not question its fundamental logic. Indeed, in spite of the many political and military crises that rocked Lebanon in the past century, power sharing endured. Lebanese elites renegotiated the terms of the power-sharing arrangement after each major conflagration. The renegotiated agreements differed only slightly from previous ones. None was able to make the step to democracy.

10

Antecedent Nationhood, Subsequent Statehood: Explaining the Relative Success of Indian Federalism

Amit Ahuja and Ashutosh Varshney

Can power sharing be an institutional device for stability and peace? The contributions to this volume by David Lake and Donald Rothchild (Chapter 5) and Philip Roeder (Chapter 3) serve as a cautionary tale. Against the rising international trend toward power sharing, they pitch evidence of the overall failure of such decentralization since the end of World War II. They discover an important and disconcerting paradox. To achieve peace and political stability, the diplomats and intellectuals of the world appear increasingly to rely on dividing powers between the units and subunits of a state, or between communities; but the evidence that such power sharing has worked in the past is remarkably thin. Normatively, the world is progressively embracing power sharing as an idea; empirically, the catalog of power sharing is blotted with failures. Indeed, power sharing, argue Lake and Rothchild and Roeder, may do more harm than good. Instead of facilitating peace, it may instigate greater violence.

Why might that be so? The crux of their argument is that in the developing world, or in countries coming out of a civil war, there is typically no stable equilibrium between the majority and minority communities. Credible commitments cannot be made. The arrangement over a period of time tips either toward centralization (and defeat of minorities) or toward secession. Power sharing, in short, is a highly unstable political arrangement. It leads, according to Roeder, to "a knife-edge equilibrium," but the power-sharing arrangement itself increases the fragility of this equilibrium. Decentralization is unstable, argue Lake and Rothchild, because the minority fears for its future or the majority finds it difficult to commit credibly to maintaining this institutional form.

Our chapter is not about whether this argument is on the whole correct. We assume that as a statement of the central tendency of the institutional landscape of the developing and ex-Communist world, their argument is right.[1] Our chapter will concentrate on what appears to be an exception, India, and single out one part of its power-sharing design. There are other power-sharing practices in India as well,[2] but we will focus on federalism. It is central to how the most powerful units of Indian politics—the center and the states—have interacted with each other. It is also in many ways central to the analytic enterprise of this volume.

Over five decades old by now, the Indian federation has worked reasonably well. Though it cannot be called a perfect example of a smoothly functioning federal system, it has survived its crises and moved further along. Problems have come from both sides. States have sometimes seriously challenged central authority, and there have also been periods in India's political life when the top central leaders proposed greater centralization as a solution for the country's many problems and tried to translate such beliefs into action. However, rebellious attempts have on the whole not succeeded, and centralizing periods have been short-lived.

More than anything else, two enduring continuities—geographical and constitutional—sum up the overall success of Indian federalism. Since independence, India has not experienced a secession, though it has witnessed a few secessionist movements here and there; there has been no replay of the terrible partition of 1947. India's constitutional continuity also calls our attention. The federal features of India's constitution, debated over several years in the constituent assembly and promulgated in 1950, remain intact. The constitution has gone through several amendments, but no amendment has altered the basic outlines of center-state relations permanently in favor of the center. Indeed, the current situation is the obverse of a centralizer's dream. If anything, the polity is becoming more and more decentralized. In the 1990s a third layer of government at the local level was added to the two-tier governmental system that had consisted of a center and mostly linguistically based states; de facto, if not de jure, powers of state leaders and governments have manifestly increased; and several new states have been carved out of the existing ones, with a clear possibility that some more may emerge before long.

Such developments would have alarmed a leader like Indira Gandhi, India's prime minister for about 15 years between 1966 and 1984 and its principal centralizer after independence. "The stronger the states, the weaker the nation" was often her argument. Over the last 10 years or so, no important political force—the states, the center, the political parties, the bureaucracy—

1. For a different view, see Bermeo 2002.

2. Most of them are summarized in Lijphart 1996 and Lijphart 1999. We do not, however, draw the conclusion Lijphart does; namely, that India's power-sharing practices make it a consociational democracy. In our view, India is a majoritarian democracy with some strong power-sharing features.

has made a powerful case and mobilized opinion in favor of centralization. The Bharatiya Janata Party (BJP), a party that used to favor a much more centralized polity when it was out of power, also became an advocate of greater federalism during its first terms in power (1998–2004). For all practical purposes, federalism has become the routine commonsense of Indian politics.

What accounts for such a state of affairs? Several arguments are available in the existing literature (Dasgupta 2001; Kohli 1997; Manor 2001). Instead of reviewing them, we opt for a different analytic path. Engaging the framework provided by Lake, Rothchild, and Roeder, we wrestle with India's political and institutional history. This combination has generated two arguments. We contend that the applicability of their argument depends on:

1. how far the sense of nationhood, or "nation-ness," has gone before federal arrangements are formally worked out or negotiations over them take place; and
2. whether the ethnic structure is bipolar or multipolar, whether identities are cumulative or crosscutting, and whether, as a consequence, there are permanent majorities and minorities in a country.

India's freedom movement lasted almost three decades (1920–1947), mobilized millions of people, emphasized a nonviolent overthrow of the British, and built links across the various regions. It turned India from a civilization to a nation. To be sure, nation building did not stop in 1947; nor was it fully successful in that a new nation, Pakistan, was carved out of British India. Nation building remains an ongoing political project of independent India, but we argue that the existing sense of Indian nationhood has kept linguistic federalism from producing the consequences predicted for federations in ethnically divided societies by Lake and Rothchild and for ethnofederations by Roeder. It is with the arrival of independence that the actual business of institutional details, including federalism, was negotiated in the constituent assembly. The antecedence of nationhood over state formation, we argue, changed the bargaining framework of the center and states dramatically. In their dealings with Delhi, India's subnational units, with isolated exceptions, have *voluntarily* chosen not to break the nation over the distribution of power and resources. The nation was constructed by India's freedom fighters after a long and arduous struggle launched against the might of the British Empire. State governments take pride in the shared history of that struggle and, in their dealings with the center, have resisted brinkmanship that would jeopardize this.

Moreover, India is multipolar in its ethnic structure, has crosscutting identities, and the country's notional majority community is so internally divided that the term "the ethnic majority" makes little political sense. Given such a situation, the metaphor of "knife edge equilibrium" does not capture the essence of the bargaining problem. For in a multipolar and crosscutting structure, majorities and minorities can be constructed in several shifting ways, "*the majority*" and "*the minority*" do not confront each other in a do-or-die battle, and desperation born of a permanent future loss is easily avoidable.

Though we have a twofold explanation, we would assign primacy to the first one. Our intention is not to imply, or suggest, that the second explanation is reducible to the first. In our analysis, antecedent nationhood is basically an overarching factor. It is like the sun that bathes all trees that come in its way, but the trees are not the sun's creations. Without the prior sense of nationhood, the dispersed and crosscutting identities may not have acquired the meaning they do, but the multipolar and crosscutting ethnic structure is not a product of nationhood.

One more point should be noted before we develop our argument. Though apparently contradictory, our argument does not fundamentally refute the analytic proposals of Lake, Rothchild, and Roeder. This is so for two reasons.

First, their large-*n* studies yield, as most such studies do, arguments primarily about the central tendency, not about the cases that may be located away from that line. Statistically speaking, so long as outliers do not constitute a separate mode, they do not undermine a central tendency. All they suggest is that the central tendency may not be able to summarize—precisely and well—the entire distribution of data points. Until we are proved wrong, India appears to be an outlier. Second, speculating theoretically about the exceptions to their analysis, Lake and Rothchild in chapter 5 tantalizingly suggest that "decentralization is likely to be most stable and effective when there are multiple regions with numerous crosscutting political cleavages." And in contrast to Juan Linz and Alfred Stepan's (1996) focus on the "stateness" problem, Roeder notes that no institutional arrangement is likely to hold together peoples who do not want to live in the same state. That is, prior to state-ness problems, there are a host of nation-ness problems (Roeder 1999). These imaginative theoretical concessions quite neatly anticipate our arguments about India.

Indian Federation: Principles, Form, and Record

Following Stepan (1999), we would like to call India a "holding together" federation, not a "coming together" federation. The United States is the prime example of the latter. Coming-together federations, according to this formulation, involve the participation of formally sovereign units in an agreement that pools their sovereignty for the purpose of collective security and economic gains. The Indian federation, an example of the holding-together model, brought under one roof subunits that did not enjoy complete sovereignty over their affairs, hence their bargaining power in the process of state creation was limited. The Indian union, when it adopted the federal model, did so through an act of the constituent assembly, and not as an agreement between the different composing units. The center is, therefore, envisaged as an enforcer of this arrangement and is typically endowed with more powers than in the case of the coming-together federations such as the United States and Switzerland.

In India, though the powers of states are clearly laid out in the constitution and the state governments can be quite powerful, the center has extensive and constitutionally assigned powers over them. We outline below the basic principles of the federation, the constitutional distribution of powers, and our overall assessment of India's federal record over the last five decades.

The Linguistic Principle

India in 1947 was comprised of three politically and geographically distinct groups of territories: (1) the provinces governed directly by the British; (2) over six hundred princely states of varying sizes, which fell within the British domain but were not directly administered by the British; and (3) the tribal territories, which were also more or less autonomous under British India. Compressing these areas into a single political entity and devising a power-sharing arrangement was never going to be easy. The challenges were addressed in part by creating a federation that included states, whose boundaries would correspond to populations with important cultural similarities.

But which federating logic should be used? India's leaders wrestled with this question. As it turned out, language in most of India and tribe in the seven small northeastern states became the key principle. Of all of India's cultural identities, these two were the only geographically based. Religion and caste tend to be unevenly spread all over the country.

Because language was the rationale for statehood for most parts of India, the federal scheme came to be called linguistic. Each state has its own official language; central government business is conducted either in Hindi or in English.[3] More than 12 languages are spoken by an overwhelming majority of people in their respective states (Table 10.1). Language forms the basis of most Indian states.[4] With the exception of Hindi (which is the lingua

3. The term "official language" is to be distinguished from another term, "national language." An *official language* in India refers to a designated language approved for official transactions of the state mainly at the administrative levels and for formal political communication. A *national language* implies a much wider range of communication.

4. English, Sanskrit, and Sindhi are also included in the Eighth Schedule for political or historical reasons. An additional seven languages are each spoken by more than one million people (Breton 1997, 192–196).

Table 10.1. India: Linguistic profile of the population, 2001

Language	Percentage of population
Hindi	40.2
Bengali	8.3
Telugu	7.9
Marathi	7.5
Tamil	6.3
Urdu	5.2
Gujarati	4.9
Kannada	3.9
Malayalam	3.6
Oriya	3.3
Punjabi	2.8
Assamese	1.6
Other	4.6

Source: *Census of India*, 2001.
Note: The total population of the country on 1 March 2001 was 1,027,015,247.

franca in six states), each of the major languages is both the main language in a single state and is rarely spoken outside that state.[5] (The exceptions to this are located within the northeast—Arunachal Pradesh, Nagaland, and Tripura.)

Major language groups were simultaneously given a direct stake in the Indian system and separated from each other. Their stake came in the form of a politically legitimized regional subnationalism. A political party in the states of Tamil Nadu, Gujarat, or Karnataka, respectively, would be hard pressed to come to power in that state without invoking commonly held notions of Tamil, Gujarati, or Kannada cultural pride. But language groups are also separated because claims supporting Tamil heritage, for example, are meaningless outside the state of Tamil Nadu. Hindus, Muslims, Christians, and castes can be found in most states, but not the speakers of Tamil, Gujarati, or Kannada. Thus, ethnic entrepreneurs could not easily construct

5. The 1951 census reported 845 languages and dialects in India, but the designation of a language or dialect is both subjective and political. The 1961 census mentioned 1,642 "mother tongues" as reported by Indian citizens, but did not clarify the meaning of "mother tongue." Citizens sensitive to the political meaning of language enumeration have used the census strategically. During the 1950s and beyond, upper-caste Sikhs pressed for a revision of the Punjab state boundary such that a majority of the population spoke Gurumukhi (rather, they claimed to write it, for script is the main difference between Gurumukhi and Hindi). In response, Hindus and lower-caste Sikhs who were opposed to the proposed state reported in the 1961 census that they spoke Hindi. For more details, see Brass 1973.

large political coalitions based on shared language across state lines to challenge the federation.

Language made great sense from a regional perspective, but what about language communities that do not speak the state's official language? Each state in India has substantial populations not speaking the state's dominant or "official" language (Table 10.2). First, Articles 29 and 30 of the Indian constitution guarantee that all children may receive primary education in their "mother tongue" and that the state government may not discriminate against educational institutions on the basis of the language of instruction. Second, Article 351 mandates a Special Officer for linguistic minorities who will serve as a watchdog over these communities' social and cultural rights. Despite these cultural protections, great pressure for regional assimilation remains.

From an all-India perspective, multiple languages as a basis of state communication seemed problematic to begin with. For greater national cohesion, Article 351 directs the central government to promote Hindi "so that it may serve as a medium of expression for all the elements of the composite culture of India," and Article 343 provides for English as an official language only for a period of fifteen years. In practice, however, the challenge of several official languages was not as intense as the challenge of quelling social mobilization that followed the hasty attempts to delegitimize regional language groups and introduce Hindi as an all-India language. After the early and adverse experiences, the central government has limited its efforts at Hindi evangelism, and every fifteen years Parliament reinstates English as an official language. Basically, a multilingual India has been accepted as a reality, especially after it became clear that the linguistic formation of states had led to a decline in language-based violence.

The choice of linguistic identities as a basis for statehood in the federation, thus, was not simply an act of far-sighted statesmanship. Many of India's most violent social mobilizations in the post-independence period were organized along linguistic lines. The first linguistic state, Andhra, was created in 1953 following riots touched off by a "fast unto death" by a linguistic promoter.[6] As it finally emerged, the linguistic basis of federalism was a synthesis of principles, pragmatism, and learning through experimentation.[7] Though the Congress Party had agreed in theory that language would be

6. Andhra was comprised of the Andhra-speaking portion of Madras province. It evolved into Andhra Pradesh in 1956, when the Andhra-speaking portion of neighboring Hyderabad was added. That portion, known also as Telengana, was the site first of a violent communist secessionist struggle and then of a violent Muslim secessionist one. Linguistic statehood effectively lowered the Telengana problem to a simmering level, where it has remained—unresolved but, by and large, nonviolent.

7. For a description of Prime Minister Jawaharlal Nehru's vacillations, see King 1997.

Flexibility

Table 10.2. India: Linguistic profile of the population, by state, 1991

	Largest Language Group			Second Largest Group			Third Largest Group		
State	Language	Speakers	Percent	Language	Speakers	Percent	Language	Speakers	Percent
Andhra Pradesh	Telugu	56,375,755	84.8	Urdu	5,560,154	8.4	Hindi	1,841,290	2.8
Arunachal Pradesh	Nissi/Daffla	172,149	19.9	Nepali	81,176	9.4	Bengali	70,771	8.2
Assam	Assamese	12,958,088	57.8	Bengali	2,523,040	11.3	Bodo/Boro	1,184,569	5.3
Bihar	Hindi	69,845,979	80.9	Urdu	8,542,463	9.9	Santhali	2,546,655	2.9
Goa	Konkani	602,626	51.5	Marathi	390,270	33.4	Kannada	54,323	4.6
Gujarat	Gujarati	37,792,933	91.5	Hindi	1,215,825	2.9	Sindhi	704,088	1.7
Haryana	Hindi	14,982,409	91.0	Punjabi	1,170,225	7.1	Urdu	261,820	1.6
Himachal Pradesh	Hindi	4,595,615	88.9	Punjabi	324,479	6.3	Kinnauri	61,794	1.2
Karnataka	Kannada	29,785,004	66.2	Urdu	4,480,038	10	Telugu	3,325,062	7.4
Kerala	Malayalam	28,096,376	96.6	Tamil	616,010	2.1	Kannada	75,571	0.3
Madhya Pradesh	Hindi	56,619,090	85.6	Bhili/Bhilodi	2,215,399	3.3	Gondi	1,481,265	2.2
Maharashtra	Marathi	57,894,839	73.3	Hindi	6,168,941	7.8	Urdu	5,734,468	7.3
Manipur	Manipuri	1,110,134	60.4	Thado	103,667	5.6	Tangkhul	100,088	5.4
Meghalaya	Khasi	879,192	49.5	Garo	547,690	30.9	Bengali	144,261	8.1
Mizoram	Lushai/Mizo	518,099	75.1	Bengali	59,092	8.6	Lakher	22,938	3.3
Nagaland	Ao	169,837	14.0	Sema	152,123	12.6	Konyak	137,539	11.4
Orissa	Oriya	26,199,346	82.8	Hindi	759,016	2.4			
Punjab	Punjabi	18,704,461	92.2	Hindi	1,478,993	7.3	Urdu	13,416	0.1
Rajasthan	Hindi	39,410,968	89.6	Bhili/Bhilodi	2,215,399	5	Urdu	953,497	2.2
Tamil Nadu	Tamil	48,434,744	86.7	Telugu	3,975,561	7.1	Kannada	1,208,296	2.2
Tripura	Bengali	1,899,162	68.9	Tripuri	647,847	23.5	Hindi	45,803	1.7
Uttar Pradesh	Hindi	125,348,492	90.1	Urdu	12,492,927	9	Punjabi	661,215	0.5
West Bengal	Bengali	58,541,519	86.0	Hindi	4,479,170	6.6	Urdu	1,455,649	2.1

Source: Census of India 1991, Statement 3, Paper 1 of 1997—Language

the federal principle as far back as the 1920s, this principle was given concrete institutional and administrative form only following linguistically based social mobilization in the 1950s. And the first round of successful linguistic federalization generated support for additional linguistic states later. By the late 1960s, India's state boundaries had been fundamentally reorganized along linguistic lines. Today India comprises 28 states and 7 union territories (Figure 10.1).

Figure 10.1 India: States and territories, 2002

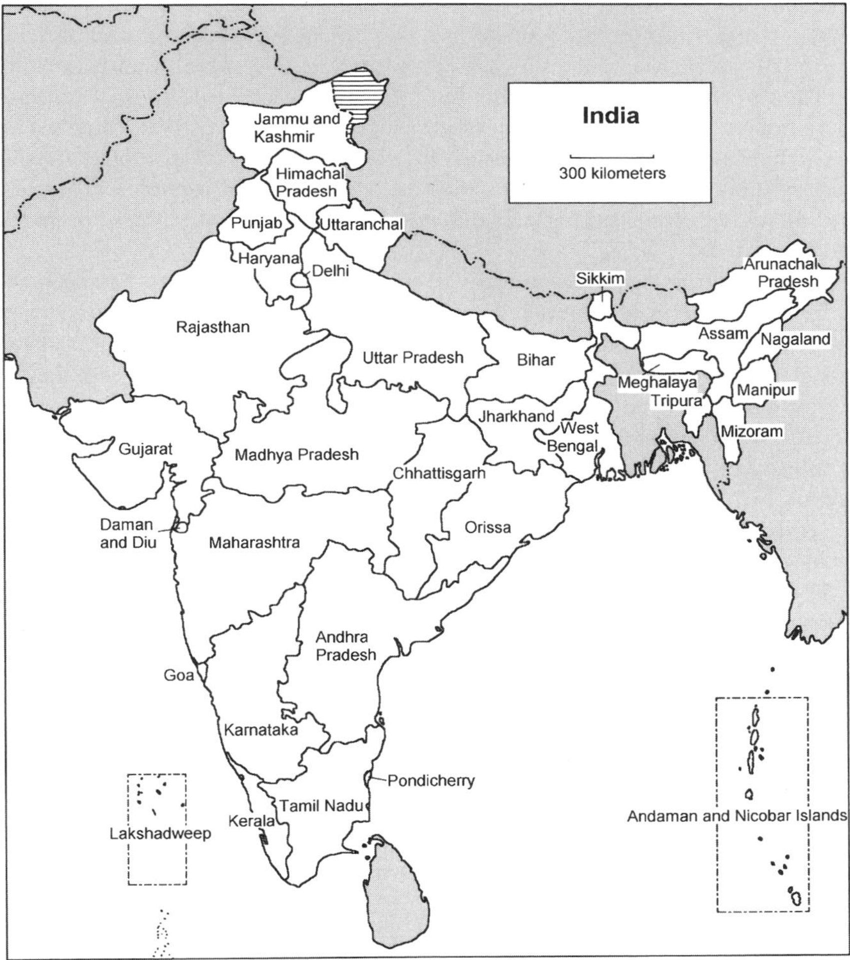

Constitutional Division of Powers

Unlike the debate on the U.S. constitution, the debate in India's constituent assembly showed a fair degree of consensus on the subject of centralization. The horrors of India's 1947 partition—perhaps one million deaths and nearly 15 million displaced persons on either side of the India-Pakistan border—provided the context for such a consensus. Members of the constitutional assembly argued vociferously for the division of powers, but these arguments were more on the techniques and details of division rather than the direction. To cope with the continuing challenge of nation building and the new task of economic development, a strong central government was a necessary prerequisite. The states were denied the right to secede from the union.

The constitution created three lists of powers: union, state, and concurrent. The union list of legislative powers includes 99 subjects and the state list 61, and concurrent powers belonging to the union and the states extend to 52 items.[8] The first list includes defense, external affairs, major taxes, and so forth; the second covers public order, police, agriculture, primary and secondary education, among other powers; and the third includes economic and social planning and higher education. All the residual powers are vested in the center.

The constitution also lays out the division of financial powers between the union and state governments. Taxes that have an interstate base are under the legislative jurisdiction of the union, while those that have a local base fall under the legislative jurisdiction of the states. The constitution vests in the center (or the union) the power to make grants and capital transfers to the states. The union may borrow on the security of the national revenues within such limits as are established by parliament. The state governments may also borrow within limits set by their legislatures, but those legislatures must follow the restrictions imposed by the constitution. A state government, for example, cannot borrow in Euro markets, though the central government can.

The constitution provides only how certain revenues are to be levied and collected, and not how the proceeds from them are to be distributed. This was left for the Finance Commission, a constitutional creation, to decide. There have been nine such Finance Commissions so far, each lasting roughly five years. In each Finance Commission, the center and states have bargained vigorously over how to distribute national revenue. With the exception of the 1980s, the state share of national revenue has been consistently increasing (Figure 10.2).

The most center-oriented provisions of the constitution cover the powers of the national cabinet and parliament over the making and functioning of

8. For a full-length treatment of divisions of powers between central and state governments, see Austin 1999.

Figure 10.2 India: States' share of national tax revenue, 1950–2001

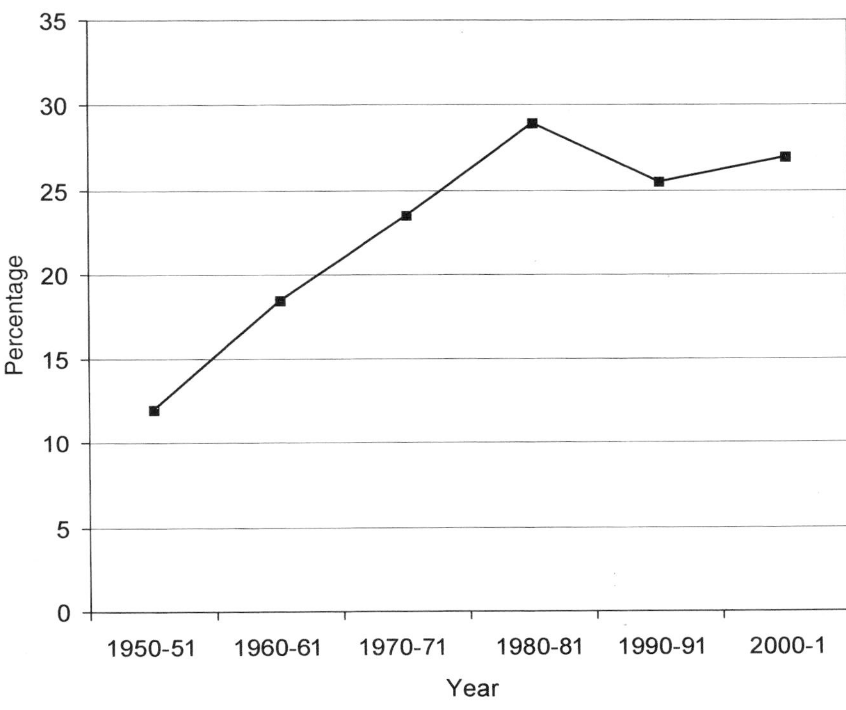

states. The constitution offers extensive formal authority to the national parliament to reorganize states. These provisions enable parliament by law to admit a new state, increase or diminish the area of any state, or alter the boundaries or name of any state. The exercise of these powers requires that the president, a nominal head of government under India's parliamentary system, make a recommendation to this effect and that the president ascertains the views of the legislature of the concerned state.

The part of the constitution that has generated the maximum, and often bitter, debate covers Articles 352 through 360. These are the emergency provisions, when the country begins to function more or less like a unitary state. On taking effect, these provisions concentrate all power in the hands of the center. They can be invoked in situations of national- and state-level emergencies. The national emergencies are broadly defined as financial emergency, external threat to the state, and cases of internal disturbance.

The worst abuse of emergency powers at the national level took place in June 1975 and continued until March 1977. The then Prime Minister Indira Gandhi declared an emergency under Article 352 on the grounds of internal disturbance. During the term of the emergency, the 42nd amendment was passed, which made the constitution more centralized. More than 60 clauses of the document were affected. Later, after the post-emergency electoral defeat of Indira Gandhi and the Congress Party in 1977, the 43rd and 44th amendments corrected the imbalance introduced by the amendments that had been voted in by a docile parliament. The emergency was the only time in India's post-independence history when most of the country's opposition leaders were sent to prison on charges of undermining internal order. India's parliament as well as state governments had become the central executive's rubber stamp.

Under the provision of Article 356, among the most controversial parts of the constitution, the center has at its disposal a most potent instrument for intervening in state politics. In the event of a state-level breakdown of the constitutional machinery, Article 356 allows for the invocation of "President's Rule," whereby the president, on the recommendation of the union cabinet, can assume the normal powers of a state, remove a state government, dissolve the state legislature, and empower the union legislature to exercise the respective state's power for a temporary period.

Over the past five decades, Article 356 has been used on more than a hundred occasions. The Sarkaria Commission, appointed by the government of India to investigate the abuse of this provision found that out of 75 cases until then, only in 26 was its use clearly justified or inevitable. The pattern, however, changed in the 1990s, when the frequency of President's Rule and the use of Article 356 declined significantly. In 1994, the Supreme Court ruled—in the *S.R. Bommai* case—that a proclamation under Article 356 can be judicially reviewed, and the central government would have to reveal to the court the relevant material justifying its decision to exercise its power under the provisions of this article. The president has also of late exercised his constitutional privilege to return to the cabinet the executive request to impose President's Rule on a state. Over the past decade, three such requests have either been denied or sent back for review.

These interventions, by the Supreme Court and president, have seriously reduced the risk of arbitrary central intervention in state politics and begun to restrain central leaders from using exceptional powers for partisan purposes. A political consensus that the use of Article 356 should be minimized is beginning to emerge in India, which appears to have made federalism deeper and more secure.

What Kind of Success?

If we use the criteria of "coming together" federations to judge how Indian federalism has done, the case of Indian success would not be clear-cut. As already stated, the center has on many occasions violated state-level authority, though each such violation has been constitutionally justified in terms of

Article 356. The "coming together" criteria, however, are not the best ones to use here, for Indian federalism is based on "holding together" principles. In this respect, it is quite different from the U.S. model. States did not create a center in India. Rather, it would be more appropriate to say that for efficient and inclusive governance, the center, and a constituent assembly, created the states as they came to be.

On the "holding together" measures, as well as in a comparative third-world perspective (which would include the ex-Communist world today), Indian federalism has on the whole been a substantial, if not a spectacular, success. Consider the following four "indices":

First, India's 1950 constitution, which laid down the federal framework, has not been overthrown, and its legitimacy only occasionally challenged by states. On the central side, Indira Gandhi did seek to challenge the overall principles of federal functioning, but the centralization she attempted has long been reversed (Brass 1991). Her favorite argument, that if states became powerful the nation would be weakened, has disappeared from the political sphere. Central leaders over the last decade have instead argued that the more powerful the states become, the lesser would be the governance problems for the nation as a whole. More new states have been voluntarily created, not resisted, by the center. In 1957, India had 14 states; in 1971, the number had grown to 17, and in 1981 to 23; by 2001, there were 28 states.

Second, language riots, which preceded the formation of linguistic states and continued through the 1960s, have precipitously declined since the emergence of linguistic states (Wilkinson 2000). Language—a source of great conflict in the 1950s and 1960s—is no longer a divisive political force in India.

Third, there has been no serious threat to Indian nationhood since 1947. As explained later, there have indeed been four exceptions—Nagaland and Mizoram in the northeast, and Punjab and Kashmir in the north. But two facts should be noted. First, none out of the remaining states has ever raised the banner of secessionist revolt. Second, at no point did more than two insurgencies rock the polity simultaneously. The worst year was 1990: The insurgency in Punjab had not quite died out when the insurgency in Kashmir burst on the scene. Even at this moment, a mere 3.5 percent of the national population, spread over these two states, was affected. In other instances, the affected population constituted a smaller percentage of the total.

Fourth, dispute resolution mechanisms between the center and states have become institutionalized. The disputes are settled either in the National Development Council, which is the forum for bargaining over investment funds, in the Finance Commission, which is the forum for distribution of national revenue, or in the highest reaches of ruling political parties. If nothing works, all units of the federation have learned to accept the

Supreme Court's judgments. In some institutional arena or the other, disputes get resolved, and problems managed.

After all is said and done, the greatest objective of India's federation was to hold the nation together without giving up the division of powers between the center and states. Whatever its other deficiencies, Indian federalism has certainly achieved its paramount objective.

Nation Making before State Formation

For an analysis of the success of Indian federalism, independence in 1947 is not the right starting point. Of inescapable analytic importance is the freedom movement that preceded independence. The movement was led, foremost, by Mahatma Gandhi and by a political party, the Indian National Congress (Congress Party hereafter), that Gandhi helped transform into a vast, continent-sized, mass-based organization in the 1920s.

Why should we start with India's freedom movement? For the purposes of this chapter, it acquires significance in light of what we know to be the new conventional wisdom in the field of nationalism. Nations are not naturally occurring entities; they have to be politically constructed. The scholarship on nation making in Europe has forcefully brought this point out. Peasants, as Eugen Weber (1976) tells us, were turned into Frenchmen by a conscription army and public schooling. Similarly, Linda Colley (1992) argues that for Britain a common enemy in Catholic France, shared Protestantism, and the empire, turned a highly divided society, especially its English and Scottish constituents, into a British nation over the course of little more than a century (1707–1837).

In the first half of the 20th century, India, an old civilization, was also turned into a nation for the first time in India's history. A *civilization* is by definition a cultural entity, which India had been for centuries. A *nation* is both cultural *and* political, which India came to be only in the 20th century. Nation making, in a formulation often attributed to Isaiah Berlin, is like building a political roof over one's cultural head.[9]

Our argument must commence with India's nation-building history, or at least its most pivotal hour starting in 1920 and lasting until 1947. The political roof over the long-lasting cultural configuration called India was constructed in opposition to the British. Peasant armies, or the public schools, were not the principal institutional vehicles of nation making, as in France.

9. The exceptions, of course, are the so-called ideological nations, where political ideas, not culture, constituted the bedrock of nationhood. The examples are the United States, the former Soviet Union, and the former Yugoslavia. For a brilliant discussion of how ideological nations are different from nations based on culture or ethnicity, see Samuel Huntington 1981, chap. 2.

Rather, the Congress Party played a functionally equivalent role.[10] Two aspects of nation making during the freedom movement had serious implications for the functioning of Indian federation later: *what* kind of nation was built, and *how*? We turn to each in turn.

Imagining the Nation

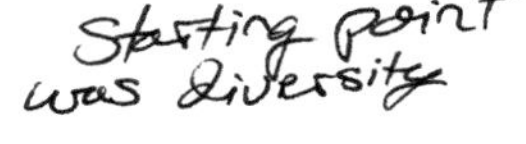

The leaders of India's freedom movement—the founding fathers—recognized diversities as central to India as a nation. They subscribed to what is now known as the "salad bowl," as opposed to the "melting pot," view of the nation.[11] India's leaders, including Gandhi and Nehru, gave it a different name: "unity in diversity" or "composite nationalism."

Indeed, "unity in diversity" became the master narrative of Indian nationhood. It not only guided the freedom movement, but the Indian constitution, born after independence, institutionalized this spirit. Birth in India or naturalization was to be the sole legal criterion for citizenship, and acceptance of Indian culture the only political criterion. To underline the point that accepting Indian culture (not religion or race or language) was all that was required to be an Indian, Mahatma Gandhi presented a remarkable formulation about Indian nationhood: "It is not necessary for us to have as our goal the expulsion of the English. If the English become Indianized, we can accommodate them" (Gandhi 1938, 59). Thus, even the colonizers were welcome if they transformed their cultural condescension for India into an acceptance of it and chose to live in the country.

Caste (a hereditary social status), religion, language, or social background could not be used to deny anyone citizenship rights. The state, on its part, was to operate above these concerns. All religions, caste, and linguistic groups would enjoy equal status and freedoms in the eyes of the law. It is difficult to imagine the effectiveness of the freedom movement and the federal project without calling attention to the public and repeated proclamation of these principles of inclusiveness by India's political leaders. Time and again, these principles have been questioned and challenged in some quarters. However, their survival and continued acceptance bears testimony to their success since their inception.

The rationale for this narrative came from a reading of Indian culture and history, which was explicitly and repeatedly articulated in politics by the

10. Political parties have played this role elsewhere as well. In the former Soviet Union and in Eastern Europe, a political party was engaged in nation making but not on the basis of conciliation and democracy. Because their nation building was based on coercion, it was not clear how deeply a Croat felt for Yugoslavia, or how ardent a Georgian or an Estonian was for the Soviet Union. The principles embraced by India's Congress party were different.

11. For a longer treatment of the ideas about Indian nationhood, see Varshney 2002, chap. 3; and an earlier essay, Varshney 1993.

leaders of the freedom movement. It was not the only reading of Indian history possible, but the leaders elected to concentrate on it, partly because they believed in it and partly because that was the only historical interpretation, which, when deployed in politics, promised unity rather than disunity.[12] Ideas of syncretism, pluralism, and tolerance, they argued, have historically defined Indian society and culture.[13] Several religions—Hinduism, Buddhism, Jainism, and Sikhism—were born in India, and in its history, India also repeatedly received and accommodated "outsiders"—Parsis, Jews, and "Syrian Christians" (followers of St. Thomas, arriving as early as the first century). In the process, and partly as a consequence, contended the founding fathers, syncretistic forms of culture have become part of India. Apart from syncretism, which represents a merging of cultures, pluralism and tolerance have been the other features: different communities, finding their niche in India, fell into mutually acceptable principles of interaction while keeping the core of their identity intact.

In keeping with this salad bowl view of the nation, the freedom movement committed itself to a linguistic Indian federation as early as 1921. It is conceivable that if the leaders had insisted on a "one language, one nation" formula, there would have been as many nations in India at the stroke of British departure as in Europe today. Unlike Europe, language was systematically delinked from the concept of nation. Multiple languages and multilingual leaders were seen as an inevitable part of nation building in India.

Putting the Idea into Practice

How were these ideas about the nation put into political practice? The 1920s were a transformative moment, when mass politics emerged in British India under Mahatma Gandhi's leadership. Before Gandhi, the Congress Party, born in 1885, was for all practical purposes a lawyers club, which made constitutional appeals for more rights from the British in the Queen's English. It did not formulate clear ideas about nationhood.

Upon his arrival on the scene, Gandhi transformed the freedom movement by altering the character of the Congress Party and its agenda. First, he convinced the party that the British were unlikely to be impressed with demands for independence unless they were confronted with a mass movement. Therefore, it was time for the Congress Party to embrace mass poli-

12. Why other ideas could not take root is a fascinating counterfactual. Hindu nationalist ideas, defining India as a Hindu nation, were certainly in the air, but they remained on the periphery of the independence movement, never capturing its heart.

13. The best source for the secular nationalist construction is Nehru's *The Discovery of India* (1990). Syncretism, pluralism, and tolerance are the main themes of Nehru's recalling of India's history.

tics and lead a mass movement. Second, Gandhi emphasized social transformation as an essential accompaniment to political freedom. Hindu-Muslim unity, the removal of *untouchability* (the very low status accorded some castes), and *swadeshi* (think Indian, buy Indian, wear Indian) had to become an integral part of the party's agenda. To these were added other projects, including women's rights, increased attention to tribal areas, labor rights, and prohibition. Not all of these efforts met with equal success, and most of these issues still persist as challenges, but a substantial beginning was made. The initiatives took the form of different organizations and movements between the 1920s and 1940s. A nationwide mass-based movement was launched, and people from many walks of life and most parts of the country came to join it. Slowly but surely, a sense of a distinct political unit began to emerge from what was till then a highly politically decentered country.

The Congress Party was the focal point of the important activities in this period of momentous change. Its growth in stature was accompanied by a widening of its agenda and an increase in its capacity. The party opened district and provincial offices. It spread to small towns and even villages, recruited cadre, attracted local elites and notables, and organized and ran national and local movements. It conducted internal elections for choosing its office bearers and saw itself as an embodiment of the spirit of nationhood. Aware of the diverse cross-section it was trying to attract to its fold, it pitched itself as an inclusive organization, in which even the dissenters were invited and had a place. They could hope to hold office, provided they were prepared to convince the organization to tilt toward their view.

The adoption of this strategy gave the Congress Party a preeminent place in the political arena. It attracted many strands of views, not always complementary. The Congress Party had vigorous and sometimes public debates, but a commitment to inclusiveness and procedures precluded the appearance of any other major national party. The Muslim League did eventually appear as a challenger, but only in Muslim-dominated electoral districts, and there too, not without considerable struggle.

The Congress Party in the last 27 years of the freedom movement (1920–1947) had developed an umbrella-like character. This had a significant bearing on its preparation for federal governance, at least in the crucial early years after independence. The different state units of the party, where it existed, were organized on the linguistic principle, and the party came to be a federation of these units. All this while, the party was learning the difficult process of balancing national-level demands with local ones. It expected to be voted to power after independence, and by the time it did, it was already on its way to learning the art of making the federal game work. A cohort of regional leadership had arisen within the party. They represented both the aspirations of their respective regions and the commitment of these regions to the national project.

Another defining characteristic of the Congress Party's dominance of the freedom movement was its adoption of a nonviolent form of struggle. Gandhi's commitment to civil disobedience and nonviolence, and its adoption as a policy by the Congress party, ensured that even calls for violent response to British repression were never sponsored by the Congress Party. Since there were other groups who took the opposite view, violence, both anti-state and interethnic, did erupt, but the Congress Party was quick to denounce it and often worked against it, even when it sometimes meant opposing the popular sentiment. The outcome of this stance was that, violence was deligitimized as a means of attaining political objectives.

We would like to suggest that a peaceful freedom movement with local power centers is better suited to federal governance than a violent one. In the latter case, organized violence is not unlikely to emerge as a dispute settlement instrument, once the movement has to take on the task of governance. (Afghanistan is faced with this problem today, among other things.) Since power sharing is an ongoing conflict resolution exercise, afflicted with the credible commitment problem, especially in the early stages, having peaceful norms of dispute resolution are a nontrivial determinant of its success. Consider the following counterfactual: If the Congress Party had a military wing, it could have posed a challenge to the authority of the central state as center-state and interstate disputes arose, or certain regional power centers within the Congress Party challenged the authority of the central leadership in independent India. Such outcomes cannot be ruled out in a holding-together system, which is contingent on a stronger center and therefore more prone to political dissatisfaction, even disenchantment, in the states, especially in the periphery. As it turned out, demands for linguistic reorganization were made through the use of agitation politics, not armed rebellion. On the whole, armed rebellions were crushed, and could be legitimately crushed given this prior background, in the first 20 to 30 years of Indian independence.

Finally, a word about India's partition in 1947, especially as it concerns federalism. The partition of the country did not result from the inherently unstable equilibrium of a federal system; it came about because the question of who would legitimately represent Muslims could not be answered in a way that would satisfy the warring parties. Despite its umbrella-like character, the Congress Party was unable to win over the Muslim community fully. In the end, a significantly large proportion of Muslims embraced the Muslim League, which championed the call to create the state of Pakistan.

Indian Muslims were a religiously defined, not a linguistic, group. They spoke the languages of the regions in which they lived. The so-called Muslim Question in British India, therefore, was by definition not a federal question. The Muslim League wanted a federal and consociational democracy; the Congress Party argued in favor of a federal and majoritarian democracy, with a bill of minority rights built into the constitution. The Muslim League claimed the right to be the sole spokesman of Muslims; the Congress argued against a "one-community, one-party" principle, saying it also had Muslim support, and that other parties in the future could gain Muslim support as well. The consociational versus majoritarian struggle evaded a satisfactory resolution, leading to India's partition in 1947 and the birth of Pakistan.

Cleavages: Dispersed and Crosscutting

A second reason for the success of Indian federalism has to do with the country's ethnic configuration.[14] The latter helps federalism for two reasons. India's ethnic structure is *dispersed*, not centrally focused, and the identities *crosscut*, instead of cumulating. Let us draw out the implication of each.

A Dispersed Ethnic Structure

To Donald Horowitz (1985) we owe an important analytic distinction between *dispersed* and *centrally focused* ethnic systems. Identities in dispersed systems are locally based, and there are many such identities; the centrally focused systems have fewer salient identities that, moreover, pervade the entire country. In dispersed systems, generally speaking, ethnic conflict remains localized and does not have a national spillover. This gives the center room to maneuver, for it can deal with one group at a time in one part of the country without worrying about the nightmare of the entire federal system collapsing. It can even mobilize the support of some states while it takes on one of them. In centrally focused systems, because of the nation-wide prevalence of the cleavage, conflict tends to escalate all through the system and stakes go up, saddling federalism, or federal prospects, with the kind of bargaining and credibility problems and the resultant disequilibria that Lake, Rothchild, and Roeder identify (see Chapters 5 and 3).

The Tamil-Sinhala conflict in Sri Lanka, the Malay–Chinese conflict in Malaysia, and the pre-1971 conflict in East Pakistan, it can be argued, have been centrally focused. In East Pakistan, the outcome of the conflict was the breakdown of federalism followed by the disintegration of the country. In Sri Lanka, the different proposals on the possible federal arrangements have met with repeated resistance from the majority community. And in Malaysia, there occurred a significant change in the power-sharing principles following the Malay–Chinese riots of 1969. Here the fear of the dilution of the Malay character of the country led the government to increase the

14. We use the term *ethnic* in its broader sense, by which we mean any cultural *ascriptive* identity, actual or imagined. For why we should have this larger view, see Horowitz 1985.

Malay presence across all arenas, making the arrangement more Malay dominant.

Compare these examples with India, where most ethnic cleavages are regionally or locally anchored. Most languages, as already explained, have a geographical homeland, and, with the exception of Hindi, each language is the majority language in one state only. Linguistic conflicts are thus typically confined to a single part of the country, not threatening the entire country, which means that the center is not necessarily pushed toward centralization as a strategy.

More generally, other kinds of ethnic and religious conflict also have the same localized character. The Sikh-Hindu religious cleavage was restricted to the state of Punjab and to parts of North India. The insurgency in Kashmir has not spilled out of the Kashmir valley to include all Muslims. Many were killed inside the northeastern state of Assam in the early 1980s but not outside. The "sons of the soil" movement, led by the Shiv Sena in Bombay in the 1960s and aimed at limiting employment in the state to those born in the state, did not attract recruits outside the state of Maharashtra; and so on and so forth.[15]

The all-pervading caste system also rules out the appearance of a centrally rooted cleavage. The caste system is national in concept but local in experience. There are no nationwide castes that recognize each other as co-ethnics. When members of a caste group organize and unite, it happens typically at the state or substate level, and more often than not, it generates a counterreaction on the part of other castes in the same state, thereby splitting state politics rather than building a cohesive and united state-level force against the center.

Conflicts never cease to break out in India, sometimes giving the impression that the political system, including federalism, is coming apart. Yet violence goes away before long, the state returns to normalcy, and the center manages to hold. Even when an ethnic party leading an insurgency confronts the central government, the central characteristic of dispersed systems remains. Unable on the whole to mobilize support beyond the state, the insurgents end up facing the central government in its full coercive might. Unlike an escalating conflict in a centrally focused state, in a dispersed system even an insurgency gets bottled up in a fragment of the country. Normal rules of federalism are suspended in the area of insurgency, while the rest of the country continues to function under routine federal processes. The system of federalism as a whole is not gravely threatened.

15. Only lately, in the highly diverse northeastern states, have a half dozen or so small insurgent groups begun to coordinate their activities against the Indian state. However, the support of these movements remains locally based in different tribes. Moreover, in most cases, the demands and bargaining positions of these groups are also different from each other.

Crosscutting Identities

Analytically separable, but equally important for the longevity of federalism, is the crosscutting nature of Indian identities. India has four major attributes of ethnic diversity: language, religion, caste, and tribe. We have already provided an account of the linguistic diversity and its manifestation. Similarly the religious landscape is marked by multiplicity and variety. Indeed, in spite of being a nation with a Hindu majority, India is a land of many religions and faiths (Table 10.3). Even among the Hindus, there is a large diversity of subfaiths and belief systems.

As briefly argued above, the caste system, which is common to almost the entire country, is also defined by subdivisions. There are three metacategories of caste—upper, middle (also called other backward castes [OBCs]), and the Scheduled Castes (formerly called "Untouchables" for their low status) (Table 10.4).[16] The last two, viewed as historically deprived, constitute a majority by a huge margin, but the upper castes have by and large dominated the nation's political, social, and economic landscape. This,

Table 10.3. India: Religious profile of the population, 2001

Religious group	Percentage of population
Hindus	80.5
Caste Hindus	64.5
Scheduled-Caste Hindus	16.0
Muslims	13.4
Christians	2.3
Sikhs	1.9
Buddhists and Jains	1.2
Others	0.6

Source: *Census of India, 2001.*

Table 10.4. India: Caste composition of the population

Group	Percentage of population
Upper Castes (such as Brahmin)	16.1
Middle Castes (or Other Backward Castes [OBCs])	43.7
Scheduled Castes (fomerly "untouchables")	14.9
Scheduled Tribes	8.1
Non-Hindu Minorities	17.2

Source: India 1981, pt. 1, vol. 1, p. 56;
Varshney 2002, 58.

Note: Since no caste census has been taken since 1931, the figures above are best guesses, not exact estimates. They are sufficient to show the overall magnitudes, however.

16. As already stated, caste is essentially a local category, and there are thousands of castes in India. With some qualification, however, they can be grouped together in larger, metacategories. The metaclassification is also known as *varna* classification.

however, has now begun to change, as democratic forces and increased social and economic mobility have taken effect, and the "lower castes" have risen.

Tribes constitute 8.1 percent of the population (see Table 10.4). The tribes in India, like the linguistic groups, are geographically concentrated. Their numbers are the largest in central India and the northeast of the country. There are hundreds of these groups, each with a distinct identity.

Given the geographical concentration of language and tribe, they could in principle provide states with a firm resolve and a source of great power against the center. That does not, however, happen. First of all, in each state, linguistic minorities exist, making a statewide linguistic unity hard to achieve (see Table 10.2). Moreover, as Tables 10.2 and 10.5 show, linguistic and religious groups do not coincide in most states, with some exceptions discussed later. As a result, religion seriously crosscuts the political potential that language (or for that matter, tribe) might theoretically create for brinkmanship on the part of a state. Though census data on caste have not been collected

Table 10.5. India: Religious profile of the population, by state, 2001 (percentage of each state's population)

State	Hindus	Muslims	Christians	Sikhs
Andhra Pradesh	89.0	9.2	1.6	0.04
Assam	64.9	30.9	3.7	0.1
Bihar	83.2	16.5	0.1	0.02
Chhattisgarh	94.7	2.1	1.9	0.3
Goa	65.8	6.8	26.7	0.1
Gujarat	89.1	9.1	0.6	0.1
Haryana	88.2	5.8	0.1	5.5
Himachal Pradesh	95.4	2.0	0.1	1.2
Jammu and Kashmir	29.6	67.0	0.2	2.0
Jharkhand	68.6	13.8	4.1	0.3
Karnataka	83.9	12.2	1.9	0.02
Kerala	56.2	24.7	19.0	0.0
Madhya Pradesh	91.1	6.4	0.3	0.2
Maharashtra	80.4	10.6	1.1	0.2
Manipur[a]	46.0	8.8	34.0	0.1
Meghalaya	13.3	4.3	70.3	0.1
Mizoram	3.6	1.1	87.0	0.03
Nagaland	7.7	1.8	90.0	0.1
Orissa	94.4	2.1	2.4	0.04
Punjab	36.9	1.6	1.2	59.9
Rajasthan	88.8	8.5	0.1	1.4
Tamil Nadu	88.1	5.6	6.1	0.01
Tripura	85.6	8.0	3.2	0.03
Uttar Pradesh	80.6	18.5	0.1	0.4
Uttaranchal	85.0	11.9	0.3	2.5
West Bengal	72.5	25.2	0.6	0.1
Delhi	82.0	11.7	0.9	4.0

Source: First Report on Religion: Census of India 2001.

Note: [a] Excludes Mao Maran, Paomata and Purul Sub-divisions of Senapati district in Manipur. Rows do not sum to 100, for other, smaller religions are not listed.

since 1931, it is well known that caste also cuts across language groups. Thus, both religion and caste often cause splits within a state's boundaries, turning intrastate issues into a more enduring form of politics than a confrontation with the political center.

A typical Indian will almost always stand at the intersections of multiple identities. The first language of a Muslim could be Hindi, Urdu, Bengali or Tamil, depending on which state she lives in. It is the same for a Hindu. Moreover, the Hindus have a number of caste identities, which for the sake of simplicity can be categorized under the first three metacategories listed in Table 10.4. However, castes manifest themselves differently across the states. For example, a North Indian who is a member of the scheduled castes will differ from a South Indian of similar caste designation. The same is true for other castes. Being a Brahmin in North India is very different from being a Brahmin in South India. Caste names, histories, languages, and rivalries all differ as one travels the length and breadth of the country.

In such a diverse landscape, political entrepreneurs use different organizing principles for mobilizing people, and therefore two outcomes become remote. First, the center-state cleavage becomes difficult to activate. Second, cross-state alliances between similar groups do not materialize.

In the few Indian states where identities are cumulated instead of crosscutting, the most serious center-state clashes have occurred, including secessionist movements. Religion, language, and geography coincide in such cases, and caste differences are not as central as they are elsewhere in the country. The majority community of Kashmir is not only Muslim, otherwise a minority in India, but the region of Kashmir is also linguistically different and geographically distinct from the rest of India. Moreover, caste distinctions do not exist among the Kashmiri Muslims—not in any rigid sense at any rate. In the state of Punjab, the Sikhs, a minority in the country overall, constitute a majority and their first language is Punjabi, which also therefore makes them linguistically different from the rest of the country. Moreover, compared to the Hindus, caste distinctions are also minor among the Sikhs.[17] Finally, in northeastern India, some states, especially Nagaland and Mizoram, are not only tribe-based, but those tribes are linguistically as well as religiously distinct from the rest of Indians. Their respective vernaculars are the first languages of Nagaland and Mizoram, not Hindi, and both are Christian-majority states (see Table 10.5).

It is in these states with cumulated identities that the attempts at secession have been made. Note, however, that with the exception of Punjab,[18] the Congress Party during India's freedom movement was not allowed by the

17. Indeed, the Sikh religion was born in 1499 partly in rebellion against the caste hierarchy of the Hindu social system.

18. This makes the 1980s insurgency in Punjab especially analytically complex. For a recent interpretation, see Singh 2000. For earlier history, see Brass 1973.

British system to penetrate these states. The problem thus may be doubly serious, going a long way toward explaining the drive for secession in them. Identities tend to cumulate in Kashmir and the northeastern tribal states, and the nation-making enterprise did not reach them.

Conclusion

If we are right, the framework provided by Lake, Rothchild, and Roeder is applicable to a particular kind of analytic space. It appears to work best when nationhood is either weak or nonexistent, and the ethnic structure of a country is bi- or tripolar and identities cumulate. The strategic problems in such a situation can make federalism an unstable equilibrium, pushing it toward either centralization or secession.

We have argued that India does not belong to this analytic space. First, an embrace of cultural diversities in the very idea of nationhood and a political implementation of that idea through organizations, especially the Congress Party, during the long freedom movement changed the framework within which India's center and states bargained after independence. The same political party ruled both the center and states after independence, and internal federalism was one of its key organizational principles. Rather than a shaky equilibrium, India's federalism developed a cooperative character. Many political battles were fought by the states against the center, but few were taken to the brink of breaking nationhood. Embracing diversities, the center did not generally seek to obliterate the many identities of Indian citizens, regions, or states.

Moreover, the dispersed and crosscutting nature of India's ethnic configuration also contributes to the survival of federalism. Had the identity structure been bipolar—reducible to "the majority" and "the minority"—and had the identities been cumulative in nature, battles over federalism could have acquired deadly political proportions. There are so many ways to construct a majority in India, both in states and the nation as a whole, that remarkable fluidity is lent to the majority-minority framework of politics. In Indian politics, permanent majorities are virtually inconceivable.

This is not to say that problems have not occurred. Where identities cumulate and/or the freedom movement was not allowed to penetrate, demands for succession have arisen. These, however, have remained limited in number and restricted to pockets, and through a combination of elections and coercion, the Indian state has been able to contain them.

11

Obstacles to Implementing Territorial Decentralization: The First Decade of Ethiopian Federalism

Edmond J. Keller and Lahra Smith

Why do plans for federalism after civil wars so often fail to bring about territorial decentralization in ethnically divided societies? Among power-sharing options available to the leaders of deeply divided societies, some form of federalism should ameliorate conflict between and among culturally defined groups (see Horowitz 1985, 601–622). Yet, David A. Lake and Donald Rothchild find in Chapter 5 that no post–civil war arrangements have actually led to decentralized political systems and that in ethnically divided societies decentralized and semidecentralized political systems have not been stable, tending either toward greater centralization or a breakup over time. They focus in particular on the centralizing role of constitutional courts interpreting the incomplete constitutions of these states.

In this chapter we examine the implementation of a federal plan in Ethiopia after 1991—an ethnically divided society that had just emerged from authoritarianism and civil war. We find that the problems of implementing territorial decentralization in ethnically divided societies after a civil war are more complex than Lake and Rothchild describe. Even prior to the emergence of conflicts between center and periphery that might result in constitutional court cases, other immediate constraints—constraints that we would venture to say are typical of ethnically divided societies after civil wars—emerged to limit the implementation of federalism and the decentralization of policymaking.

In sub-Saharan Africa, organizing regional states on the basis of their ethnic composition has rarely been attempted. In this respect, the current Ethiopian experiment with *ethnic federalism* represents a novel approach to power sharing. It provides interesting comparisons with other experiments with federalism, particularly with that in Nigeria, the only other sub-Saharan state to have attempted to implement a federal system. (See Eduardo Alemán and Daniel Treisman's discussion of Nigeria as an "ethnically mined" state in Chapter 8 of this volume).

Throughout its modern history, Ethiopia has been characterized by ethnic tensions. Until 1991, however, successive regimes tried to suppress the unique cultural identities of that country's more than 80 distinct ethnolinguistic groups and to assimilate them into the dominant Amhara culture.[1] In May 1991, following a relatively brief civil war, the Marxist regime that ruled for more than 17 years was displaced by the Ethiopian People's Revolutionary Democratic Front (EPRDF), an umbrella organization comprising six ethnically based opposition groups. On coming to power, the EPRDF decided not to suppress the national aspirations of Ethiopia's ethnic groups but instead to allow them the full expression of their languages and cultures. It decided, in less than two years, that the country would be administratively and politically reorganized, creating what are largely (but not exclusively) ethnically based states.[2] The then-ruling Transitional Government of Ethiopia (TGE) also publicly committed itself to the introduction of pluralist, multiparty democracy. This was significant because until then Ethiopia had never had political parties or pluralist democracy.

The EPRDF government was immediately faced with the problem of managing an ethnically diverse polity. Many in the general population were concerned about the future of their nationality groups. They viewed the decentralization implicit in ethnic federalism as the best way to demonstrate the regime's commitment to social equity and democracy. Democratic principles were eventually enshrined in a well-crafted national constitution in 1994. In addition to the formulation of a constitution that included the principles and institutions of democracy, the new regime introduced public policies designed to devolve administrative authority from the center to regional states. The intention of the new regime was to use a form of ethnic federalism to attempt both to reduce ethnoregional inequalities and to provide an enabling environment for democracy (Keller 1995).

The purpose of this chapter is to identify reasons why the EPRDF government in the first 14 years was unable to implement plans for ethnic fed-

1. In terms of population, Ethiopia is the second largest country in Africa, with a population of almost 73 million. It is populated by between 80 and 100 distinct ethnic groups, who speak more than 70 languages. The single largest ethnic group is the Oromo (32 percent), followed by the Amhara (30 percent). See Ethiopia, Central Statistical Authority 1996.

2. For our purposes, when discussing center-state relations, we use the term *state* to mean regional states. In a federal or quasi-federal system this would be the next level of government below the federal or central government. It should be noted that, in some ways, Ethiopia's public commitment to the principles of ethnic federalism could be considered nothing more than a fiction, since in practice not all states are ethnically based. Four of the nine regional states (Gambella, Harari, Benishangul/Gumuz, and the Southern Nations, Nationalities, and Peoples' Region [SNNPR]) are comprised of several different ethnic groups. Young has shown that rather than this leading to political stability within multiethnic states, federalism has served only to fuel interethnic tensions in those states.

eralism successfully. Although it is too early to call these reforms a failure, Ethiopia after 14 years operated very much like a centralized, unitary state, with most power residing at the political center. Rather than focusing on all aspects of public policy, this chapter is concerned with two purposively chosen policy sectors: fiscal reform and education. Fiscal policy is important because of its role in the distribution and redistribution of resources needed for development. Central to the Ethiopian approach has been a revenue-sharing system that involves the central and regional governments. Education policy is important in the context of ethnic federalism, for educational reforms could send signals to ethnic groups of their rulers' sincerity in pledging to systematically reduce social inequalities throughout the country.

From Empire to Federation

The primary architect of the modern state of Ethiopia was Emperor Haile Selassie I, who reigned for 44 years until his overthrow in 1974. Historians largely view Haile Selassie as a modernizer who fiercely guarded the sovereignty and independence of this northeast African polity. Despite this reputation, Haile Selassie's regime was ultimately toppled by the weight of official corruption, bad governance, and his failure to address the needs of nationality groups (the so-called nationalities question). The emperor had cultivated both at home and abroad a myth that Ethiopia was a multiethnic but unitary nation-state. However, by the early 1970s, Ethiopia's poverty, gross inequalities, and political and economic underdevelopment laid bare the lack of a foundation for such a myth. Even before Haile Selassie was overthrown, evidence of ethnic and regional discontent had begun to surface, and, in the aftermath of the demise of his regime, ethnic tensions emerged as the main challenge to the political stability of the new revolutionary regime (Keller 1988a, 1988b).

Less than two years after the overthrow of Haile Selassie, Ethiopia's leaders committed themselves to "scientific socialism" (socialism based on Marxist-Leninist principles) and proceeded to reorganize society to achieve this end. One of the defining features of Ethiopia's brand of scientific socialism was the illegitimacy of ethnicity as a political organizing principle. Instead, the ruling regime of Colonel Mengistu Haile Mariam thought it best to group the public into mass organizations on the basis of their economic or social roles. In doing this, the Mengistu regime failed to address the national question effectively. In a final effort to legitimize itself and its programs, the regime created the Worker's Party of Ethiopia (WPE) in 1984, and in 1987 constitutionally established the People's Democratic Republic of Ethiopia (PDRE). The new national assembly, attempting to diffuse discontent among regionally based nationality groups, created 24 administrative regions and 5 autonomous regions (Keller 1995).

Rather than enhancing the PDRE's legitimacy, these reforms exposed its vulnerability. Opposition groups, mainly the Tigray People's Liberation Front (TPLF), the dominant partner in the EPRDF, came to control ever-increasing amounts of territory in the north-central part of the country. On May 28, 1991, the Mengistu government collapsed, as the victorious forces of the EPRDF moved in to take control of Addis Ababa, the capital city. Mengistu was forced into exile, ushering in a significant change of regimes.

Federation from Above

The EPRDF initially presented a public image of itself as possessing the political will to address many of Ethiopia's past problems, including the national question. Its leaders moved quickly to fill the power vacuum caused by the collapse of the Mengistu regime, and within a few weeks began establishing a transitional government. A national conference for this purpose was convened in July 1991. This was an attempt on the part of the EPRDF to secure widespread acceptance. It resulted in the signing of a transitional charter by representatives of some 31 political movements, the creation of a Council of Representatives with 87 members, and the establishment of the Transitional Government of Ethiopia (TGE). The EPRDF had the largest single bloc in the Council, with 32 seats, and the Oromo Liberation Front (OLF), until its withdrawal from the government in late June 1992, was the second largest, with 12 seats. The EPRDF's commitment to institutionalizing a system of ethnic federalism was indicated in key planks of the transitional charter, in implementational proclamations, and in the new constitution. The new policy quickly prompted protests among Ethiopian nationalists both at home and abroad who vigorously opposed policies they feared would lead to the balkanization of Ethiopia. The unsettled nature of the transitional period allowed the EPRDF to forge ahead with its plans to administratively reorganize the country along ethnoregional lines. Table 11.1 outlines the key proclamations the EPRDF issued during its first two years.

It appeared to outside observers at the time that Ethiopia might be able to form what Alfred Stepan (1999) has labeled a "holding together" federa-

Table 11.1. Ethiopia: Key proclamations in the implementation of ethnic federalism

Proclamation Number	Year	Provisions
7[a]	1992	Provided details for the ethnoregional states
26[b]	1992	Budget for Ethiopian year calendar 1984 (1991–92)
33[c]	1992	Defined revenue sharing between central and regional governments
41[d]	1993	Defined powers and duties of central and regional executive organs

Sources: [a] Ethiopia, Negarit Gazeta 1992a. [b] Ethiopia, Negarit Gazeta 1992b. [c] Ethiopia, Negarit Gazeta 1992c. [d] Ethiopia, Negarit Gazeta 1993.

tion based on a broad consensus among elites. There are various ways in which federal systems come into being. Stepan, building on the seminal work of William Riker (1964), identifies three main patterns:

1. *Coming-together federations* emerge when sovereign states for security purposes and/or purposes of governmental efficiency decide voluntarily to form a federal system.
2. *Holding-together federations* are the outgrowth of a consensual parliamentary decision to preserve a united country by creating a multiethnic federal system. As discussed by Ahuja and Varshney in Chapter 10 in reference to the Indian federation, this is most often done to avoid or manage divisive ethnic, religious, regional, or other types of group conflict within the polity.
3. *Putting-together federations* are imposed from the center without a broad elite consensus.[3]

Ethiopia began as what appeared to be a holding-together federation in 1991, but quickly became a putting-together federation. The Marxist regime had been eliminated, and ethnic communities were promised that they could exercise their right to self-determination in the *New* Ethiopia—a federation comprised of ethnically based states. All that changed within a year. The center forced federation from above rather than creating it through bargaining. The ruling coalition narrowed as the EPRDF forced out ethnic parties that wanted to assert the right of their regional states to "self-determination up to and including secession" (Ethiopia 1994, Article 39). In their place the EPRDF created so-called People's Democratic Organizations—that is, ethnically based surrogate parties through which it could project the illusion of a multiethnic federal state. As the constitution was in the final stages of being drafted, the EPRDF announced a major policy document outlining its political views and policy objectives on regional reforms (Ethiopia, Office of the Prime Minister 1994). It outlined its intentions to devolve power from the center to the regional states and local governments, but this *devolved federalism* would lack extensive subnational control over technical policies, laws, regulations, and taxes. This putting-together approach contrasted with a system of consensual federalism resulting from bargaining and negotiations among states. Publicly, the EPRDF has consistently claimed

3. The official line of the EPRDF went something like this: "The nations, nationalities, and peoples of Ethiopia have historically been denied their rights to self-determination. This was as true under the imperial regime as it was under the Marxist regime. The New Ethiopia is committed to redressing these historical wrongs and to giving all its peoples the right to self-determination up to and including independence. To insure that the multi-ethnic state remains intact, there will be guarantees of individual and collective rights enshrined in a federal constitution." See *Constitution of the Democratic Republic of Ethiopia*, December 8, 1994, Article 39.

that it is committed to the following objectives: (1) reducing the ethnic conflicts and tensions that have dominated modern Ethiopia; (2) forthrightly tackling social and economic problems to ensure that all ethnic groups are treated equally; (3) building a democratic society; and (4) constructing effective, efficient, and uncorrupt systems of governance (EPRDF 2000). To do this, there would have to be a new social compact. However, rather than negotiating such a compact among elites representing the major ethnic and political groups in society or allowing it to emerge in an organic manner, the EPRDF imposed federalism from the top.

At a very fundamental level, the implementation of decentralization has been a political process intended to keep the EPRDF in the position of being the dominant player in Ethiopia's reconstruction. Initially in the transitional period, as already mentioned, the EPRDF created a broad political pact for the purpose of governing. But the governing coalition narrowed considerably in April 1993, as the EPRDF-dominated government ousted five political groups for endorsing a resolution that called for dissolution of the Council of Representatives. The membership of the Council was reduced to the representatives of the EPRDF and the ethnically based parties it had created (Keller 1998, 114). National, state, and local elections were held after adoption of the constitution, but most opposition parties either chose not to participate or were kept out by official intimidation, and manipulation of electoral rules limited the opportunities for any organized opposition, resulting in a landslide victory for EPRDF candidates.

Institutional Design of Ethiopian Federalism

The Ethiopian Constitution of 1994 proclaims the establishment of the Federal Democratic Republic of Ethiopia (FDRE), consisting of nine regional states and two self-governing, multiethnic cities, Addis Ababa and Dire Dawa. Five of the nine regional states (Afar, Amhara, Oromiya, Somalia, and Tigray) are dominated by a single ethnic group, and four (Benishangul/Gumuz, Harari, Gambella, and the Southern Nations, Nationalities, and Peoples' Region [SNNPR]) are multiethnic states, with no one dominant ethnic group. The Constitution declares that regional states may prepare their own constitutions, decide their own official languages, develop their own administrative systems, establish separate police forces, and collect certain taxes. In the multiethnic regional states, although each group may choose to use its own language on a day-to-day basis, Amharic is the working language. In the others, the working language is usually the language of the predominant group in the state, though this is also subject to variation, as we shall discuss later.

Ethiopia's brand of federalism has five levels of government: the federal, regional state, zone, *woreda* (district) and *kebelle* (local) levels (Figures 11.1

Figure 11.1 Ethiopia: Region-states of the federation (based on information provided by the Ethiopian Government Information Service)

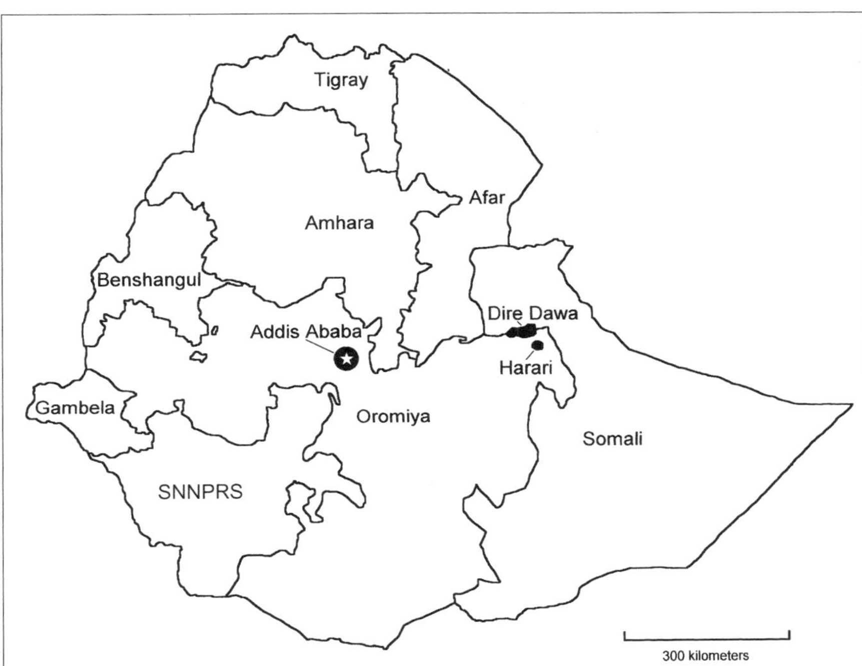

SNNPR = Southern Nations, Nationalities, and Peoples' Region

and 11.2). Each of the levels of government has more or less the same structure, with executive, legislative, and judicial branches. The policies of the regional state governments have the most impact on the citizens of the various regions in that they are the primary implementers of development policies. In fact, very little decentralization has occurred below the regional state level.

The Constitution states in Article 39 that all ethnic groups and nationalities have the right to secede. In order for this action to be taken, however, it must have the approval of at least two-thirds of the members of the legislative council of any nation, nationality, or people, and the action must be ratified in a regional state–wide referendum three years later. Furthermore, before any of this can happen, there are constitutional provisions for a review of the claim to secession by the Constitutional Court and the House of the Federation, a national political and deliberative body of 108, with elected representatives from all regional states (Haile 1996, 25–31).

Figure 11.2 Ethiopia: Organization of the federal hierarchy

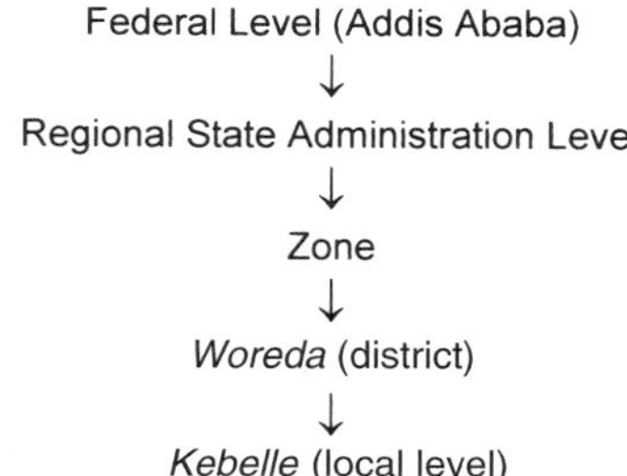

Revenue Sharing and the Implementation of Fiscal Federalism

A central feature of Ethiopia's devolved federalism is a hybrid system of revenue sharing. Under this system the central government shares tax and other revenues with regional states, and much of the sharing takes the form of block grants from the federal to the regional state governments. The authority for this policy is Proclamation 33, which is aimed at (1) enabling the federal and state governments to efficiently carry out their respective duties and responsibilities; (2) assisting state governments in the development of their regions on their own initiative; and (3) reducing uneven development across regions (Ethiopia, Negarit Gazeta 1992c).

The Constitution gives the federal government the power to collect all revenues from trade and most revenues generated by federally owned state enterprises. It establishes the right of state governments to collect taxes from revenues generated by public enterprises they own, to tax personal income of nonfederal or international employees, and to tax unincorporated activities in their domain.

The dominance of the Ethiopian federal government in revenue generation has resulted in state governments relying extensively on transfers from the central government to meet their obligations. Ideally, a federal arrangement would be characterized by a fiscal balance whereby regional governments would have taxing powers sufficient for them to meet their service delivery and governance obligations. However, in Ethiopia, this has not been the case. There have been significant mismatches between the regional-states' expenditure responsibilities and their revenue-generating capacities. For example, in the 1993–1994 fiscal year, out of a total regional expenditure of Birr 3,145 ($39.2) million,[4] only Birr 807 ($9.8) million (26 percent) was generated by the states, with grants and subsidies from the central government accounting for the remainder. Moreover, the expenditure patterns

4. One U.S. dollar is equivalent to 8.2 Birr.

of the states are centrally monitored and thereby controlled (Chipande and Enquobahrie 1997, 23).

As Table 11.2 indicates, the taxing powers of the federal government have far exceeded those of the regional governments. Between 1994 and 1998 Ethiopia's regional states collected only 15 to 18 percent of total national revenues. The poorest regions, Afar, Benishangul, Gambella, and Harari, have improved their revenue-generating capacity, but richer regions such as Amhara, Oromiya, and Addis Ababa have made much more impressive gains than their "poor cousins."

Acknowledging the significant disparity in terms of levels of economic development among the regions of Ethiopia, their widespread poverty and inequality, and the differences in the revenue-generating capacities of the states, the federal government has turned to a form of revenue sharing as a way of implementing an equity-based developmental strategy. Taxes are collected at the center and then sent to the regions according to a formula that seeks to compensate for these disparities and differences among regions.

Only funds designated for the Road Fund are officially earmarked, and the center coordinates the road projects of neighboring states. In principle, block grants to states come with no strings attached. Grants are determined

Table 11.2. Ethiopia: Federal and regional state revenue shares, 1993–98

Regional State	1993–94	1994–95	1995–96	1996–97	1997–98
Afar	$867,073	$1,187,805	$1,353,659	$1,793,902	$1,342,683
Somali	$5,289,024	$5,745,122	$4,902,439	$4,602,439	$5,856,098
Amhara	$11,589,024	$14,686,585	$16,489,024	$19,526,829	$21,648,780
Oromiya	$26,258,537	$30,354,878	$40,445,122	$42,347,561	$41,996,341
SNNPR	$8,941,463	$12,787,805	$17,489,024	$19,215,854	$17,756,098
Tigray	$5,392,683	$7,130,488	$10,514,634	$12,802,439	$10,560,976
Dire Dawa	$2,462,195	$2,231,707	$1,798,780	$2,186,585	$2,198,780
Benishangul	$439,024	$615,854	$664,634	$839,024	$981,707
Addis Ababa	$22,521,951	$31,985,366	$42,532,927	$56,497,561	$65,487,805
Gambella	$481,707	$662,195	$597,561	$880,488	$814,634
Harari	$697,561	$723,171	$942,683	$941,463	$970,732
Regions Total	$84,940,244	$108,110,976	$137,730,488	$161,634,146	$169,614,634
Federal Total	$395,524,390	$612,963,415	$711,801,220	$783,725,610	$866,646,341
National Total	$480,464,634	$721,074,390	$849,531,707	$945,359,756	$1,036,260,976
Regional states as percent of national total	18%	15%	16%	17%	16%
Federal government as percent of national total	82%	85%	84%	83%	84%

Source: World Bank 1998.
Note: Totals include tax and nontax revenue. 1996–1998 is based on revenue estimates. Figures were converted from Ethiopian Birr to U.S. dollars based on rate of US$1 = Birr 8.2.

according to a formula that has been in place since 1995–1996 and has been revised twice.[5] The share of the budget subsidy that is accorded each region is based on such objective factors as the region's population share, its relative level of development, and its relative projected revenue generation capacity (World Bank 1999a, 28). Regions under such circumstances theoretically have the power and authority to identify the policy preferences of their constituents, to formulate their own development plans, and to make decisions about the allocation of their own budgets between sectors as well as between capital and recurrent expenditures (World Bank 1999a, 8). However, state spending decisions most often are heavily influenced by priorities set nationally in the EPRDF Five Year Program. In other words, officials at the state and zone levels, who are generally party loyalists, structure the choices at the *woreda* and sub-*woreda* levels so that they conform to centrally determined priorities.

While there has generally been a policy consensus between states and the federal governments, there have been occasions when intraregional conflicts have emerged over how to allocate the revenues received from the center. For instance, in the Amhara region in 1998 there was an incident where zonal preferences did not match state preferences. One zone wanted to allocate its entire budget to roads, at the expense of such important activities as improving educational infrastructure and instruction, health care, and agricultural programs. Another wanted to use its entire budget to construct a sports stadium. However, each zone was eventually persuaded to change its plans and to follow guidelines set at the federal and regional levels "for a more balanced approach to development" (World Bank 1999a, 70). Such incidents show that there are limits to autonomous decisionmaking on the part of lower levels of administration, especially when they stray too far outside nationally and regionally determined priorities. This is especially true at the *woreda* level. Rather than popular participation being enhanced at that level, it is constrained by the heavy hand of the center and its representatives at the state and zonal levels, as well as capacity limits at the *woreda* level.

In addition to the fiscal imbalance that exists between the center and the regional states, there are also significant differences among the regions themselves. For instance, the city of Addis Ababa finances almost all its public spending from revenues that it generates independently. Addis Ababa, in fact, accounts for an average of 34 percent of the revenues raised by all states

5. Nigeria also has historically used a revenue-sharing formula. Initially, the principle of derivation—that is, the policy of returning a fair share of the revenues generated in a regional state back to the state—dominated the formula. However, since 1981 the trend has been toward fiscal reforms that emphasize population and equality. Critics claim that this practice is without an objective basis and prevents Nigeria's Revenue Allocation System (RAS) from becoming a dynamic and effective instrument of development.

(Table 11.3). The state that collects the next largest percentage of revenues is Oromiya (28 percent), followed by Amhara (12 percent), and the SNNPR (11 percent). The lowest collections tend to be in Gambella, Benishangul/Gumuz, Harari, and Afar (World Bank 1998, I, 44). The regions of Benishangul/Gumuz and Gambella are barely able to finance 10 percent of their public expenditures on their own. A second difference among regions is the sources of the revenues they generate. In Gambella, one of the poorest states, most of the state's revenue comes from personal income tax paid primarily by government employees. Tigray and Afar (another extremely poor state) derive a far larger percentage of their revenue from sales taxes. Richer states such as Addis Ababa derive a larger share of their revenues from taxes on private business activity.

Why Are Ethiopian Finances Still So Centralized?

The guiding role played by the EPRDF in the creation of Ethiopia's putting-together federation is an important part of the explanation for why fiscal federalism is by design highly centralized. Yet even in areas where the regional-state governments have been given fiscal discretion, they have not been able to exercise this fully. The reasons that Ethiopia operates like a unitary state are not limited to the motives of the center but also include problems in the states themselves. Despite an admirable development strategy centered on the principle of revenue sharing, regional states tend not to be able to make any significant headway. The reasons for this include:

1. *The reality of an underdeveloped private sector and a lack of access to credit for this sector.* In most regions except for Amhara, Addis Ababa, Tigray, and Oromiya, the private sector is either at a very low level of development or non-existent (World Bank 1999a, 8–9; Young 1998, 83). This leaves most regions with limited tax bases and few independent revenue sources.

2. *A shortage of administrative capacity, particularly in the poorest regions.* There are significant nationwide shortages and significant regional variation in the availability of skilled administrative and technical staff, and these are major constraints on autonomous development (Egziabher 1998, 41; Cohen and Peterson 1999, 136–137). The shortage is a natural consequence of attempting to implement a federal system under conditions of abject poverty and underdevelopment. Decentralization comes at a high price. It involves the duplication of institutions and functions in a hierarchical pattern from top to bottom. To meet staff needs, regional bureaucracies must either employ individuals who may not be qualified for the positions they hold or force skilled bureaucrats to underutilize existing talents. This problem is particularly acute in the poorest regions. The

Table 11.3. Ethiopia: Regional revenue indicators, 1994–95 to 1997–98

	Tigray	Afar	Amhara	Oromiya	Somali	Ben-Shangui	SNNP	Gambella	Harari	Addis Ababa	Dire Dawa
Share of total state revenues	6.98	0.91	12.12	27.51	4.07	0.48	11.02	0.48	0.60	34.16	1.67
Per capita revenue/GDP	0.05	0.02	0.02	0.04	0.06	0.03	0.03	0.08	0.12	0.36	0.21
1994 Population (millions)	3.14	1.11	13.83	18.73	2.32	0.46	10.38	0.18	0.13	2.11	0.25
Personal income tax	15	26	19	12	11	31	17	47	19	13	12
Business profit tax	13	14	8	28	78	2	19	2	44	16	41
Agricultural income and land fees	10	0	33	25	0	12	25	2	1	0	0
Agricultural income tax	4	0	16	13	0	6	14	1	0	0	0
Rural land use fee	6	0	16	12	0	6	11	1	0	0	0
Sales tax on goods	32	39	4	14	2	2	15	6	0	5	15
Service sales tax	2	0	1	0	1	0	1	0	1	2	3
Urban land lease fee	0	0	0	0	0	0	0	0	0	14	0
Government sale of goods and services	5	8	13	7	1	15	7	21	0	5	9
Stamp sales and duty	6	0	1	1	1	0	1	0	2	11	5
Charges and fees	10	3	7	4	0	3	3	1	4	3	9
All others	9	8	14	9	6	34	13	20	10	33	6

Source: World Bank 1999a.

capacity to absorb shared revenues is quite low in such regions as Afar, Somali, Gambella, and Benishangul/Gumuz, and this serves as a drag on regional development. States are required to give their recurrent needs the highest priority, followed by ongoing noncapital projects, and new investment projects are given the lowest priority. The poorest regions often have administrative capacity to meet only their recurrent needs and nothing for expansion or innovation (World Bank 1999a, 5–6). In an effort to address the problem of low levels of administrative capacity at the regional level, the federal government began to provide state governments with training and technical assistance for capacity building. But this support has been modest relative to the amount of public fiscal resources the states are asked to distribute and redistribute. The record shows that there has not been significant improvement in the efficiency of administration. In most regions basic public services such as drinking water, sanitation, education, public health, and public works are generally unavailable or are available only to limited parts of the population.

3. Problems with making state governments accountable. Ethiopia's federalism is new, and regional and local administrators and politicians have a great deal of discretion to set their own rules on dealing with their constituents. In some cases this has led to serious excesses in administration. For example, although the Constitution guarantees citizens freedom of assembly, this right is not always respected by local administrations. In January 1999, the Coalition of Ethiopian Opposition Political Organizations held a rally in Addis Ababa to announce its political agenda, but its organizers claimed that they could not properly do this because local authorities did not approve a permit for the rally until a day before it was to happen (U.S. Department of State 2000, 18). It has been common for local officials to assume that ethnic federalism means that they are no longer accountable to any higher authority, even to the voters within their own regions.

4. Pitfalls of donor assistance. Donor assistance has reinforced the strong hand of the center. Assistance provided by donors is distributed and tightly controlled by the federal government, and, in theory if not always in practice, subtracted from the amount that according to the formulaic calculations is to be allocated through the revenue-sharing scheme. Moreover, the strings attached and the stringent reporting requirements of many donor-driven projects reduce the autonomy of state administrators.

5. Official corruption. A final obstacle in the development of federalism in Ethiopia is official corruption (Young 1999, 336). In the past, the EPRDF has used *gim gima,* or self-evaluation sessions, to address charges of corruption. As infighting within the ruling coalition and its constituent parties increased in 2001, charges of corruption at all levels of government began to surface. Throughout the summer months, all EPRDF parties were called to their regional headquarters to conduct party congresses whose purpose was aimed in part at rooting out corruption and what was termed "narrow nationalism." An additional anticorruption measure was the introduction in spring 2001 of the Federal Ethics and Anti-Corruption Commission (FEACC). As 2001 drew to a close, several high-profile politicians and businessmen were investigated and tried on corruption charges. However, this process coincided with major purges in the TPLF and other EPRDF-affiliated parties, and some observers have argued that the primary aim of the commission was not to root out official corruption but to settle old scores. Evidence supports such an assertion. For example, the commission appears to have spared individuals close to the dominant faction in the ruling EPRDF. One positive feature of present administrative practices is that responsible bureaucrats are regularly subjected to public reviews of their performance in office. This process in a small way serves to deter some corrupt activities. However, for the time being the costs of corruption to the federal system are significant: An ethic of good governance at all levels of administration has yet to develop.

Education Policy and Power Sharing

Like fiscal reform, educational policy reform is seen as a central feature of the EPRDF's plan to minimize ethnoregional inequalities, reduce the prospects for political instability, and promote consolidation of democracy over the long run. Education serves as the cornerstone of the EPRDF's plan because long-ignored issues of regional educational inequalities were a primary source of the armed conflicts that toppled Ethiopia's two previous regimes (Abbink 1997, 164). Similarly, by increasing access and improving the quality of education, the regime can demonstrate its commitment to redistributing political power and resources to various ethnolinguistic groups. Finally, it is widely understood that improving educational systems is essential to the goal of poverty reduction and achieving higher levels of economic development, as well as the development of a culture of participatory democracy.

The Structure of Educational Reform

The main thrust of Ethiopia's educational reforms begun in 1991 was in line with the overall shift to decentralization. It sought to "improve educational quality and expand access to education, with special emphasis on primary education in rural and under served areas" (Ethiopia, Ministry of Education 1999a). This decentralization was accomplished by shifting authority for many educational decisions, including curriculum content, infrastructural development, choice of the language of instruction, and hiring and training of teachers, down to the lowest feasible levels (EPRDF 2000, 37; Altbach and Teferra 1999, 84). For the first time in Ethiopia's modern history, state governments had direct authority for determining curriculum as well as the use of nationality languages. This has resulted in the use of over 20 nationality languages in schools and regional educational administrations across Ethiopia.

The move toward decentralization also involved the creation of new educational hierarchies, with the Ministry of Education (MOE) in the top position of "supervising and guiding higher education, while the Regional States [were] to supervise and guide education" at lower levels (EPRDF 2000). In this decentralized context, 87 percent of the Education Sector Development Program (ESDP) was to be implemented by the regions and only 13 percent by the Ministry of Education (Ethiopia, Ministry of Education 1999a, 12). As in the case of other countries attempting this type of change, such as Nigeria, educational reforms have "provoked some of the most emotive debates and struggles" in the federal experiment (Suberu 2001, 129–130).

The Ethiopian MOE is responsible for developing the core objectives of educational policy, thereby dictating the focus on primary education, educational quality improvement, and relevance of the curriculum to the needs of the populace (EPRDF 2000, 21; Altbach and Teferra 1999, 85). From its general plan, the Regional Education Bureaus (REBs) are responsible for "the implementation of the curriculum—developing, transcribing, translating, producing and distributing educational materials" and other educational reforms (Altbach and Teferra 1999, 85). The implementing unit is the Woreda Education Office; no fiscal transfers occur lower than the woreda. Since woredas usually have a low tax base, they rely on subsidy transfers from the zone level.

How education reforms are financed is of pivotal importance to the success of the program. Since a number of elements of educational policy, including curriculum development, textbook production, and teacher training, had previously occurred at the federal government level, and since there have historically been regional disparities in the total number of schools and total enrollment rates, the states' ability to achieve desired results is highly variable. In all cases, the creation of additional administrative structures with new and expanded responsibilities necessitated additional funding to support office development, personnel recruitment and training, the writing of textbooks, the building of schools, and the hiring of teachers.

Federal government dominance in revenue generation has resulted in the heavy reliance of states on transfers to fund their various obligations. Presumably, the special budgetary formula, through its inclusion of a variable for educational development, provides regional states with the budgetary supplements needed to support development (EPRDF 2000, 30). Some states are more dependent on such supplements than others. Even with these budgetary supplements, overall funding to education remains well below the needs of the states.

Education-sector development has also been linked with more general capacity-building needs to narrow existing regional disparities. The EPRDF regime has publicly committed itself to "providing assistance to the relatively most backward states . . . [giving] practical support and assistance by assigning to the least developed states its professionals . . . [by] opening experience-sharing forums among states and [by] expanding bilateral relations of cooperation among states" (EPRDF 2000, 29). Focus was put on capacity building in educational administration, procurement, finance management, and monitoring and evaluation (Ethiopia, Ministry of Education 1999a, 10). Budget shares were allocated among the various education levels and support services, including 60 percent of the overall budget of the ESDP to primary education, 11 percent to secondary education, 11 percent to tertiary education, 8 percent to other education, 7 percent to administration, and 3 percent for capacity building and the MOE (Ethiopia, Ministry of Education 1999a, 11). The ESDP Action Plan also outlines the intended administrative framework: Though overall coordination should come from the MOE and the Ministry of Finance (MOF), federal and regional joint donor-government steering committees were to be established to oversee the implementation process (Ethiopia, Ministry of Education 1999a, 11).

In addition to the use of nationality languages as a tool for improving educational effectiveness, regions were supposed to have authority to devise methods and materials suited to the unique needs and goals of their student population. Access issues were to be addressed through widespread construction of new schools, as well as repairs and additions to existing schools. The massive need for teacher training was identified as a high priority. Programs were proposed (and to some extent implemented) for teacher certification, distance learning, and the use of other teaching aids and materials to foster improved teaching. Boarding schools, hostels, and pilot nomadic (mobile) schools were to be constructed and/or organized in regions—including Afar, Somali, Benishangul/Gumuz, and SNNPR—where nomadic children's education has been hindered by lack of access (Ethiopia, Ministry of Education 1999a, 7).

Educational Outcomes

Despite the well-articulated and thoughtful education plan outlined above, educational outcomes rarely met expectations in the first 12 years. By 1999 primary school enrollment was still at 30 percent of all school-age children, less than half the average for the rest of sub-Saharan Africa. Rates in rural areas were as low as 19 percent, and in nomadic and seminomadic areas such as Afar were as low as 8 percent (Figure 11.3). Book shortages, high dropout and repetition rates (only about 50 percent of those who enroll completed primary school), inadequate teacher training (only about 40 percent of teachers in the secondary schools were qualified), high pupil-to-teacher ratios, and poor curricula continued to create significant barriers to educational progress (Ethiopia, Ministry of Education 1999a).

The EPRDF, at least in its policy rhetoric, recognized the need to address historical disparities among regions by providing manpower, training, material, and human resources (EPRDF 2000). A report on education in 2000 noted that "gross regional and gender disparities" were hampering the quality of education throughout Ethiopia (Ethiopia, Ministry of Education 2000, 1). The special budgetary formula mentioned in the previous section is one example of how the government attempted to implement reform in this regard. In its 1999 annual report, the MOE reported spending 13.7 percent of the government budget on education (up from 2.6 percent in 1992–1993). It committed itself to increasing spending on education to 19 percent of the national budget. Of the total education budget, the federal government would finance 73 percent of the programs, with the remaining amounts to come from donors and, to a lesser extent, from regional governments (Ethiopia, Ministry of Education 1999a).

However, as Figure 11.4 shows, recurrent expenditures on education, particularly in poorer regions from 1993 to 1998, remained roughly unchanged. This indicates that the states were either not getting the budget subsidy or were not able to use it effectively to fund various development sectors such as education.[6] The trend in relatively well-off regions seems to indicate a steady rise in recurrent expenditures for education, with dramatic increases in Oromiya and SNNPR. In general, however, there is no evidence of a narrowing of development gaps among regions, and in some of the poorer regions, recurrent expenditures on education declined, particularly in Benishangul, Somali, and Gambella.

Beyond revenue generation itself, human capacity remains a critical element of educational need. This is true in all sectors of teaching and administration. A March 2001 report notes that the most progress has been made in terms of expanding enrollments, without requisite improvements in curricula, construction of schools, textbooks, and teacher training (Ethiopia, Ministry of Education 2001b, 4).

6. It is unclear what happens when a state cannot use their budget subsidy, perhaps owing to inadequate capacity at the regional state level. Does it go back to the central government for redistribution? Is it kept in a fund for the regional state in the future? Additionally, since population numbers and other development indicators are key to determining the budget subsidy, these are a matter of considerable dispute (see Young 1999).

Figure 11.3 Ethiopia: Gross educational enrollment rate, grades 1–8, 1996–2000, by regional state

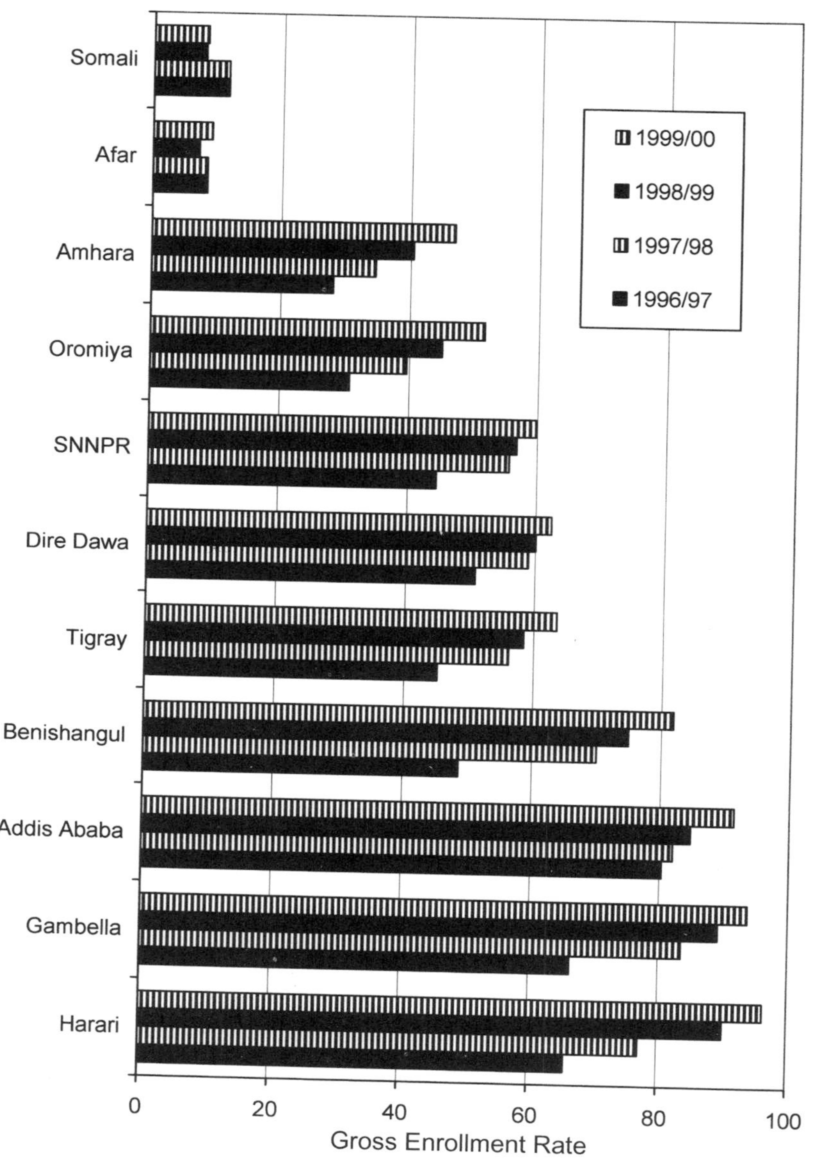

Source: Ethiopia, Ministry of Education 2001a.
Gross Enrollment Rate is the ratio of (1) the total number of pupils (irrespective of age) enrolled in grades 1 through 8 to (2) the school-age population corresponding to grades 1 through 8.

Figure 11.4 Ethiopia: Recurrent expenditures in education, 1993–1998, by regional state

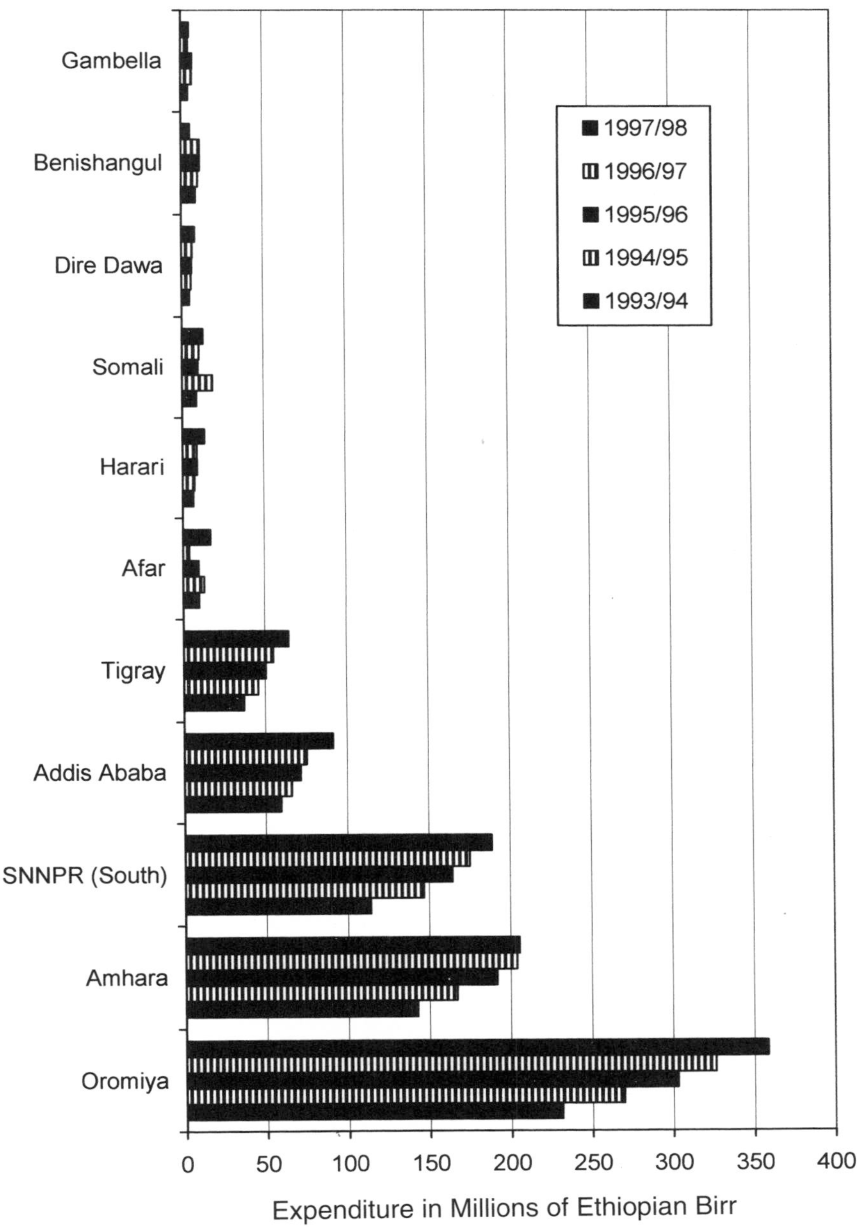

Source: World Bank 1998.

At the school level, there are insufficient numbers of teachers, and high percentages of these lack necessary qualifications. A 2001 Ministry of Education report states:

> At the *woreda* level, there are insufficient supervision visits to schools to support the teaching there. At the zone level, there are too few civil works technicians and qualified accountants to manage school activities. At the regional level, curriculum development, educational planning, budgeting and accounting manpower are in short supply. At the federal level, the professional personnel needed to provide technical support to the decentralized units have been decreasing as the program expands and the need for such personnel grows. (Ethiopia, Ministry of Education 2001b, 8)

There is considerable variation among regional states in terms of the extent to which they are affected by the lack of human resource capacity. Some regional states have a greater human and financial resources base than others. In these regions, one finds competent technical staff in the REB, even if they are in short supply and even if decentralization has not yet extended fully down to the woreda level. In other regions, it is known that there is such a shortage of trained and qualified staff that even the REBs are staffed with members of other ethnic groups, such as Amharas and Oromos working in Gambella. Young also found that "approximately half of Benishangul/Gumuz's bureau heads are outsiders" (Young 1999, 38). It is widely understood that a similar situation exists in other disadvantaged regions such as Afar, and that in regions such as Afar, Somali, Benishangul/Gumuz, and Gambella, decentralization has not occurred below the regional level. As recently as August 2001, Afar and Somali regions did not send representatives from the REB to a national-level conference on a new school-clustering program for teacher training. Their absence was noted to be a consistent feature of many national-level planning meetings. Young has called this a system of "two-tiered federalism" because "the low level of political development in Gambella and Benishangul/Gumuz means that the EPRDF plays a greater role in local administration in these regions (together with the Afar and Somali regions) than in other parts of the country" (1999, 342).

Implementation of Language Policy in Education

In addition to the presence of significant disparities in human and financial capacity among regions, conflicts over language use and curriculum content, particularly in multiethnic states, represent an example of how the power-sharing arrangement in Ethiopia remains contentious. Conflicts over language policy in schools and regional administrations are occurring primarily *within* the regions and between the regional governments and the federal government. Language moved to the center of the political agenda in Ethiopia as a crucial element of the EPRDF's education plan, which gave support to the development and use of nationality languages for all ethnic groups. This support was in part attributable to the fact that language represents a proxy for ethnic identity under ethnic federalism and thus linguistic identity has assumed an elevated level of importance.

Undoubtedly, use of local languages in regional administration and instruction in schools was a critical political issue for a large proportion of Ethiopia's ethnic groups, particularly minority groups and those whose language had previously been banned or suffered from neglect. Under the regime of Haile Selassie, the use of indigenous languages for purposes of instruction and regional administration was illegal, and even the production of private print materials was banned (see Bulcha 1997; McNab 1990, 81). There was a slight change under the Mengistu regime, when the problems of literacy were addressed through the *zemacha*, or national youth work campaigns and were conducted in approximately 15 nationality languages (McNab 1990, 70). Writing in 1990 about the economic costs of the literacy campaign, Christine McNab noted that "the political costs of retreat from this policy (of teaching in 15 nationality languages) may be reckoned to be higher than the costs of pursuing it" (1990, 70). Despite this effort at multilingual education, however, Amharic remained the dominant language of administration and instruction, and in 1991 language rights were a central issue for the EPRDF regime to address.

Use of local languages is a powerful cultural symbol for many citizens of Ethiopia. Regional state leaders have made language choice a central element of their political and social agendas. Over the last 10 years, there has been an increase in the number of regions using nationality languages, and language identity has been the primary basis for creation of new regional states. For instance, as recently as April 2001, the Silte people in the multiethnic Southern Region held a referendum to separate themselves from the Gurage nationality, primarily on the basis of language. This separation has clear political implications for the Silte people and their political leadership, elevating them from a woreda of the Gurage Zone to their own zone and providing direct access to the central government and central resources. Similarly, the political conflict surrounding the introduction of an Esperanto-style language, *Wagagoda*, derived from the four languages of the Wolaitta, Gamo, Gofa, and Dawro ethnic groups, led to their separation into three separate zones—Wolaitta, Dawro, and Gamo-Gofa. Up to 10 persons were killed, hundreds injured, and as many as one thousand arrested in the protests surrounding this incident (U.S. Department of State 2000, 9). Although regional officials had initially objected to the separation of these groups, ethnic leaders persisted with their claims, pointing out that four regional states in Ethiopia had populations smaller than the Wolaitta ethnolinguistic group. Their demands for separation eventually met with success. A similar process is occurring elsewhere in the Southern Region through the creation of "special woredas," administrative units with the same status as zones, but intended for smaller ethnic groups (Ethiopia, Central Statistical Authority 1996).[7]

The economic costs of the multilingual policy in education are massive and have contributed to the overall growth in regional disparities, without necessarily lessening the political conflict over ethnicity. Some smaller ethnic groups in the South have opted to continue the policy of Amharic instruction. They contend that the use of nationality languages is a policy of the ethnic group in power to marginalize minority ethnolinguistic groups, especially in light of the fact that Amharic is the official language of the state and widely used in multiethnic cities such as Addis Ababa.

In the case of those that have chosen to use nationality languages, especially in multiethnic states, a tremendous burden is put on their Zonal Education Office to translate educational materials provided by the REB from Amharic to these languages. For instance, there are presently 12 languages of instruction in Southern Region and more are in the process of being added. Many of these languages have never been written before, requiring local "experts" to select orthographies, develop standardized grammars, and oversee translation. It is unclear who these "experts" are and whether those zones using nationality languages receive additional budgetary supplements to support the translation of Amharic materials into nationality languages. Teachers who have always taught in Amharic must now be instructed in these languages. Authorities report that site visits often find teachers using Amharic, or Amharic interspersed with the nationality language, throughout their teaching despite the written policy. All of these factors affect educational quality, as well as the perceived success of the decentralization arrangement.

Even in the case of considerably larger ethnic groups located in nearly homogeneous regional states, such as Tigray and Oromiya, the costs of standardizing the use of the nationality language, training teachers, and producing supplementary reading materials in that language have contributed to an overall decrease in educational efficiency. Yet the question of linguistic minorities is a source of conflict even within the more homogeneous states. The 1999 U.S. State Department Human Rights Report noted that the decision of the regional government of Oromiya to adopt Oromiffa as the language of instruction "has drawn protests from groups that reside in Oromiya whose mother tongue is not Oromiffa and who believe that their children are now at a disadvantage" (United States, Department of State 2000, 31).

Finally, there are those states such as Afar and Somali where almost nothing is known about the effectiveness of the language policy. For

7. The official definition of some of these terms such as "special woreda" is unclear. These appear to be administrative units for ethnic groups that are numerically smaller than zones, but separate from other woredas in that zone; that is, they have status of a zone without meeting the requisite size requirements. As of September 2001, there were five special woredas in Southern Region and one in Amhara.

instance, Afar Regional State has an official policy on the use of Afarigna as the language of instruction in primary schools, but it is widely understood that Amharic is the language being taught, owing to an absence of qualified teachers and available written materials in Afarigna. With a gross enrollment rate of 9 percent of the age-appropriate children in primary school, such an inconsistent language policy can only be seen as contributing to further negative education outcomes.

Summing Up: Problems of Implementation versus Minority Empowerment

The implementation of Ethiopian federalism in education has encountered obstacles that are probably typical of ethnically divided societies after civil wars—a combination of expensive tasks and limited (and even depleted) resources. A decentralized system of education that accommodates the demands of a culturally divided population places additional costs on government in terms of expanded administration, curricular development, and teacher training. Yet the capacity of Ethiopia to assume these additional costs is limited and has been further depleted by civil strife and the recent war with Eritrea. Four obstacles have prevented state governments from fully exercising the new powers given them in the federal educational program:

1. *Funds.* The dependence of states on funds from the center limits their autonomy.
2. *Personnel.* The shortage of teachers and administrators—particularly of those with the requisite language skills—has limited the development and implementation of separate curricula that respond to the cultural and linguistic diversity of society.
3. *Material.* The scarcity of facilities—particularly in the regions inhabited by nomadic peoples—and of teaching materials in the different languages parallels and exacerbates the shortage of personnel.
4. *New conflicts.* What are often low-scale, but sometimes paralyzing, conflicts between dominant ethnic groups and minorities *within* the new states over language policy have hindered development of state programs.

Although these problems have resulted in less decentralization than originally planned, there is still evidence of limited empowerment fostered by the use of nationality languages. The proliferation of zonal and special woreda units in the Southern Region, the policy of nationality languages in disadvantaged states such as Afar and Somali, and the priority attention given to development of language materials in the more homogeneous regions such as Tigray and Oromiya are all indications of the value attached to the use of nationality languages. Educators and administrators at the regional level, even as they bemoan the economic and efficiency costs of such a policy, indicate they prefer the policy because of its pedagogical effectiveness and political and cultural symbolism. For instance, it is believed that increases in gross enrollment rates in the last decade are in part attributable to this policy, as parents see a greater relevance to their children's education. It is unclear whether this policy is contributing to political empowerment, however, and certainly it consumes significant proportions of regional budgets.

The language policy in Ethiopia is illustrative of the trials of implementing public policy to accommodate political conflict, particularly in the presence of a highly diverse population. Over and over, language choice—both the EPRDF policy and the policies of the various states—are cited by Ethiopian citizens as emblematic of ethnic federalism, both good and bad. It has resulted in the proliferation of administrative units and has consumed a large proportion of regional education budgets, particularly in historically disadvantaged regions already suffering from a wide variety of obstacles to efficient regional budget management. In practice, no states are ethnically homogeneous and since the rights of ethnolinguistic minorities within regional states remain unclear, it is highly unlikely that future conflict will be reduced. In fact, when certain burning issues come to the fore, intraregional communal conflicts could greatly heighten political instability.

There is little doubt that the EPRDF could not have ignored language policy as part of its power-sharing arrangement. This is even truer today, when minority ethnic groups see their political rights best preserved through their membership in ethnic groups, most commonly understood in linguistic terms. What the problems associated with language policy demonstrate most poignantly is that regional capacity variation in Ethiopia is a serious obstacle to successful implementation of a power-sharing arrangement. Conflict, while diminishing somewhat at the federal level in Ethiopia, is elevated at the state and lower levels, particularly as ethnic entrepreneurs pursue an agenda of ethnic identity for their own purposes. Even where autonomy is being exercised under the power-sharing arrangement, particularly in the case of language policy, this appears to be contributing to subnational conflict and also to be producing significant residual costs. In particular, the last dozen years do not seem to have led to anything approaching a narrowing of the disparities among the regions or ethnic groups in Ethiopia, which is one of the key objectives of the policies of ethnic federalism.

Conclusion

Ethiopia is presently involved in attempting to implement what is officially billed as a form of *ethnic federalism*. The government claims that this approach is best for achieving democracy in this multiethnic polity. A central element in this process of creating an enabling environment for democracy is a system of devolved administration giving state and zonal authorities major roles in making decisions relating to socioeconomic development and the building of democratic institutions. In reality what is billed as a unique form of ethnic federalism in Ethiopia operates very much like a centralized, unitary state, with most power residing at the center. As a consequence, while some institutional forms associated with democracy such as political parties and periodic elections with universal suffrage may exist, this is more of a "pseudo-democracy" than anything else (Diamond 1997).

Programs for territorial decentralization are typically expensive—at least when compared to centralized, uniform programs—and these additional costs must be borne by a society with limited resources, particularly after a civil war. The attempt by the central government to keep many powers in its own hands provides part of the explanation for the limited implementation of territorial decentralization. Yet the separate states have been unable to utilize fully the powers they have been given. Revenues collected at the center are shared with regional states, but most of these resources are used to cover the salaries of state, zonal, *woreda*, and local bureaucrats and other recurrent expenses. Most states, because of the lack of resources, are therefore not able to engage in new capital projects. Moreover, there is in most cases a severe lack of skilled administrative capacity below the national and state levels, and this too serves as a drag on democracy and development. Because of the predominance of the central government in revenue generation, regional states tend to be highly dependent on the center and often forced to follow the lead of the federal government in setting and implementing policies. This dependence serves as a drag on the overall effective and efficient implementation of policies at the regional level. In addition to the fiscal imbalances between the center and the regions, imbalances across regions continue to be a problem. In large measure this is because of the historically acute differences in levels of development from region to region. The problem is further exacerbated by the limited administrative capacities of regional states and subregional governments, and growing incidence of official corruption.

In Ethiopia, there have been some improvements in the educational sector, particularly evidenced in the relative expansion of school enrollment rates. However, decentralization of authority in the education sector has been hampered by regional capacity variations, both in terms of human and financial capital, which has proved to be a significant barrier to broad-based improvement in educational outcomes. A decade of ethnic federalism has had limited impact in key areas of educational quality or access. Although providing a significant source of cultural empowerment for ethnolinguistic groups, elements of the policies of ethnic federalism, particularly language policy, have at times hardened group claims, thereby increasing rather than reducing the possibility of ethnic conflict. The long-term implications of this phenomenon are unclear, but in the short term there has been a tendency for increased demands for further autonomy among distinct groups within regions, particularly in multiethnic states.

Our research into the two policy sectors of revenue sharing and education underscores the need for further study of how variations in financial and human capacity have an impact on power-sharing arrangements such as ethnic federalism. For example, between 1997 and 2000 "federally managed programmes [in education] have spent 21.5 percent more than planned . . . whilst Regional States have spent 28.5 percent less." Government analysts attributed this to reductions in federal subsidies to the regions (Ethiopia, Ministry of Education 2001a, 7). Federal transfers are critical to the success of the regionally managed (rather than federally managed) programs. It is the regionally managed programs that represent actual transfers of control to the various regional groups, and any decrease in federal subsidies to allow the implementation of these programs makes their success highly problematic. But the human capacity is necessary to use these funds. In a 1997 report, Graham Chipande and Asmamaw Enquobahrie found that the critical issue is not a lack of authority by relevant actors at the regional and subregional level, but a lack of capacity. Government has continued to build decentralized structures and to move authority down to lower levels of administration. Local capacity to implement policies in terms of human and administrative resources remains critical. "The problem appears to be that of acute shortage of personnel, especially professionals within the Regional Public Service Administration Bureaus (RPSABs), to do the job . . . The distribution of these staff shortages was not uniform, ranging from a shortfall of over 90 percent in the regions of Benishangul/Gumuz and Harari and under 50 percent in the Southern Peoples, Afar and Oromiya regions" (Chipande and Enquobahrie 1997, 49). The authors concluded:

> there seems to be a gap between what regions can do and what they are expected to do during this period of socio-economic and political transformation . . . The disparity in resource availability and the unbalanced distribution of trained manpower as well as the difference in exposure and access to modern development infrastructures and facilities still remains to be considered in attempts to decentralize the management of the economy at the regional, zonal, woreda and community levels. (Chipande and Enquobahrie 1997, 5)

Part of the problem of limited financial and human resources is attributable to the border conflict with Eritrea, which diverted massive amounts of government resources between 1998 and 2000 to the military sector and caused donors to withhold proposed funding for various reform packages.[8]

8. A recent report of the Ethiopian Economic Policy Research Institute estimates that the two and a half year war cost Ethiopia more than $2.9 billion (Bhalla 2001).

For example, rather than achieving the planned levels of government spending on education, spending actually decreased during the 1997–2000 period, from 14.6 percent to 10.5 percent in 1999–2000 (Ethiopia, Ministry of Education 2001a, 7). Government reports note that in many cases the government fulfilled its developmental commitments, but donor funding was much lower than planned. Yet the border conflict was only a small part of the problem.

In sum, ethnic federalism in Ethiopia has proved to be more of an aspiration than a reality. In large measure this is attributable to poorly planned policy and the lack of the administrative, technical, and financial capacities needed for effective implementation. Although this policy has allowed the federal government to divert local pressures from itself to regional and subregional governments in the short run, the benefits of this strategy in the long term would seem to be limited. So long as the federal state is not able to make a credible commitment to social equity across regions as well as across ethnic groups, it is unlikely to reduce the potential for political instability and to create an enabling environment for democracy.

12

Power Sharing as an Interim Step in Peace Building: Lessons from South Africa

Timothy D. Sisk and Christoph Stefes

South Africa's power-sharing experience was remarkable: In the first or initiation phase of the transition from apartheid to democracy, power sharing served as a device to foster practices of ethnic and racial inclusion, compromise, and moderation. For the long term, however, the South Africans agreed on an institutional arrangement that most foresaw would lead to *majoritarian* democracy. In short, South Africans succeeded in resolving the dilemma of power sharing: During the negotiation process, concessions on power sharing by the majority allayed minority fears of being overpowered in a nonracial regime structure in which they would be at an electoral disadvantage. Over a period of six years (1990–1996), South Africa moved to a regime of majoritarian democracy. This guarantees extensive individual rights and facilitates longer-term consolidation of peace and democracy through a careful balance of majority prerogatives and minority cultural, language, and property rights. Formal power-sharing institutions were used during three of these transition years (1993–1996). Throughout this process, compromise and moderation characterized not only politics but civil society as well. These norms and practices have remained in place well after formal power sharing in political institutions ended.

In the light of South Africa's relatively successful experience with power sharing during the initial stages of the transition to full democracy, we ask how it was possible to avoid the dilemma of power sharing that in other societies often traps regimes in institutions that can thwart the consolidation of democracy. We draw lessons that may be helpful for peace building in other divided societies, particularly Northern Ireland and Bosnia-Herzegovina. We argue that the preconditions in South Africa that led spontaneously to a successful transition—one that used power sharing but avoided the dilemma of power sharing—may have been unique to South Africa. Traditions among opponents to apartheid dating back to the Freedom Charter of 1955 stressed inclusiveness, moderation, and compromise but rejected ethnically based institutions, such as assigning posts on the basis of race or ethnicity, in designing the constitution. Yet, the process of transition itself revealed tactics used by the parties that international organizations and foreign powers could encourage in other societies.

Our analysis of these tactics that emerged in the transition focuses on the relationships in South Africa between the initiation and consolidation phases in the transition to democracy and between formal and informal institutions of power sharing. We contend that peace in the short-term and democracy building in the long-term can be facilitated by formal power sharing during the initiation phase that provides a period of confidence building while the process of negotiating majoritarian-democratic institutions for the longer term unfolds. It is important to extend in time the period during which these interim arrangements are in place and negotiations over the new constitution occur. This extension of the initiation phase of the transition during which formal power sharing is in place has two important effects. First, the original parties to the peace settlement have time to test each others' commitment to democratic procedures and particularly the majority's commitment to respect the right of minorities. Second, parties and interests other than the original parties to the peace settlement have an opportunity to enter the negotiations over the new constitutional order and to seek arrangements for the longer term that will permit them access alongside the original parties. The South African process began as elite-centered conflict between the two major protagonists—the black liberation movement represented by the African National Congress (ANC) and the white minority government led by the National Party (NP)—but was later broadened to include a much wider spectrum of political players.

Yet, as the South African experience illustrates, limiting power sharing to formal political institutions described in an initial peace settlement is not enough; practices of inclusiveness, compromise, and moderation must *expand and deepen* into myriad informal bargaining arenas beyond the political elite that negotiate the formal political arrangements. The informal ways in which contending forces in deeply divided societies negotiate their differences is essential to managing the problems of ethnic, religious, or racial tensions over time. Indeed, it is the persistence of what might be labeled "*informal* power sharing" that reaches into society and the economy to include non-elites that has allowed *formal* power-sharing institutions to wither away in politics without threatening moderation and cooperation among members of different ethnic groups. Informal power sharing emerged because of the balance of power favoring the ANC (which opposed consociational features advanced by the NP in negotiation) and because informal power sharing gave all sides political cover from allegations that they were colluding with their political opponents instead of fighting for principled positions.

Between 1990 and 1996 the transition from white minority rule and apartheid to a vibrant multiethnic democracy in South Africa was difficult, violence-ridden, and occasionally prone to breakdown. Nevertheless, the first four years of turbulent negotiations led to elections in April 1994 and the inauguration of formal power sharing in the 1994–1996 Government of National Unity (GNU). For the principal government and opposition parties, the initial period of power sharing grew out of a realization that consensus-based rule was needed to help the country through the volatility and uncertainty of the "founding" elections of 1994. The moderate core of elites who negotiated the transition were all assured of a place at the table in the interim power-sharing order, significantly reducing uncertainty and reinforcing a spirit of national unity in escaping a violent and damaging past. It was also critical to assuring domestic and international investor confidence, which all parties realized was needed to facilitate economic recovery. Although short-lived, the essentially consociational arrangement of the GNU—which ended in 1996 when the NP withdrew from the grand coalition executive two years before its scheduled expiry—provided an important stepping-stone to future peace and to the South Africa democratic constitution adopted in 1996. The NP could withdraw from the coalition government and assume the role of loyal opposition in a majoritarian democracy because it had gained sufficient trust in the ruling ANC that it would respect the newly negotiated constitution with its protection of private property rights and its commitment to minority protections and antidiscriminatory policies.

By the end of this six-year initiation phase of the transition, with its protracted negotiation and subsequent power sharing, a permanent peace agreement was reached in the form of a comprehensive constitution adopted nearly unanimously in 1996. The constitution established a progressive charter of basic human rights, addressed thorny issues on regionalism and local control, and codified the rights of identity groups to cultural, religious, racial, or ethnic autonomy. In addition, civil-society actors, such as many churches and businesses, made considerable strides toward the creation of crosscutting social ties. In this consolidation phase, political violence—which had been endemic prior to and even during the first years of the transition—began to fade from the scene. In the 2004 general elections, there were only three politically related deaths in campaign violence, limited to the still-volatile KwaZulu-Natal province.

Although South Africa's most difficult issues of deep socioeconomic inequality, lingering racism, and meaningful reconciliation for past wrongs remain, the society has made tremendous strides toward peace and democracy in a relatively brief period of time. In sum, in South Africa *flexibility* in institutional design was achieved through continued inclusiveness in negotiations on constitutional reform—made possible by the interim power-sharing institutions—that continued beyond the initial settlement that committed all parties to postconflict democracy.

The *deepening* of moderation occurred through the crosscutting integration of society by informal institutions, such as those that have helped steer economic policy or that linked truth telling and reconciliation. The sense of South African nationhood stems from the opposition to apartheid: because the white minority government's policies of apartheid were based on enforced social division along race and ethnicity, major opposition leaders of many different races and ethnicities reacted by consciously pursuing a vision of national unity. In short, because of the ability to perceive a common destiny into the future, South Africa appears to have found a way to use power sharing for the short term and avoid the dilemma of power sharing that undermines peace and democracy in the longer term. The principal problem it faces 10 years after the transition is the overwhelming dominance of the ANC, which has politically outmaneuvered its rivals. The NP disbanded in 2004, joining the ranks of the ANC after a bruising electoral defeat. This has created concerns that the country is sliding into a de facto one-party state despite the fine functioning of electoral democracy.

In our view, whether Northern Ireland, Bosnia, or other deeply divided societies can move toward a more stable peace depends much on whether the groups in conflict can use formal power sharing as a foundation for renegotiating the design of political institutions for the longer term and to share power informally in both political and social life. Flexibility in the design of political institutions is difficult to achieve because the parties will often demand credible commitments about the future in more concrete and enduring institutions. It also requires that the commitment to democracy must be deepened, and ties that crosscut the deep divisions of society must be forged—also a challenging task. Initiating a transition to peace through a negotiated settlement is a short-term process that may require formal power sharing; consolidating democracy for peace building is a long-term enterprise that requires moving beyond power sharing and deepening integration across the lines of ethnic, racial, or religious divides.

Getting Beyond Formal Power-Sharing Institutions

We believe there is a need in ethnically divided societies to move beyond formal, often called "consociational," power-sharing institutions. Sharing power among contending ethnic groups in a consociational framework has an Achilles' heel that is prone to failure; comparatively, they are not durable solutions.[1] First, a key feature of such power sharing—the *mutual veto*, whereby decisions are taken only with the widest possible consent and only with a near consensus—often leads to the use of "political blackmail." In Cyprus, for example, power sharing failed in the 1960–1963 period because of the workings of the mutual veto.[2] Without consensus among contending social forces, governance stagnates, policy-making drifts, and tensions mount. When power-sharing agreements lead to such political *immobilism* (i.e., the inability to make or implement policy due to protracted disagreement), frustrations emerge, and one or more parties defect from the accord. Violence frequently ensues.

Formal or "consociational" power sharing suffers from a second problem, too. These institutions are based on elite consensus and do not seek to build bridges across the segments of society that are in conflict. While pacts between the leaders of ethnic groups temporarily halt ethnic strife; in the long run, a durable and peaceful solution to ethnic conflict depends on citizens' tolerance and their willingness to cooperate across ethnic lines. As Donald Rothchild (1999, 320–321) elucidates, the underlying causes of ethnic violence are "the intense struggle over economic resources" and "the uncertainty arising from a lack of accurate information regarding the intentions of the adversaries and the profound insecurities that . . . groups feel about their future." An immediate cause that triggers violence "is often the willingness of an elite to exploit the ethnic ties of its clients and the collective fears . . . of their future exploitation and victimization."

Power sharing may be desirable, and necessary, as an immediate exit from deadly ethnic strife. Parties at the negotiating table may demand the fixed representation, the mutual veto, and the hard-and-fast guarantees that formal power sharing offers. However, such institutions are not a viable *long-term* solution to promoting democracy in ethnically divided societies—particularly in those societies that have experienced deep enmity and ethnic violence (as opposed to other multiethnic societies without a history of violence, such as Belgium or Switzerland, where consociationalism seems to work well). Thus, for divided societies emerging from violent conflict, a critical question emerges: What are the ways in which formal power sharing can evolve into more flexible institutions that can foster crosscutting political allegiances and a cosmopolitan national identity?

Our answer focuses on the roles of *formal* power sharing in creating the conditions for negotiation of more durable political arrangements and in

1. Military victories are arguably more unstable than negotiated settlements because they leave grievances among the vanquished unresolved, only to reerupt at the first opportunity when strength has been regathered. For the argument that military victories are more durable than peace agreements, see Wagner 1993.

2. On consociationalism as blackmail in Cyprus, see Jarstad 2001.

setting the stage for broadening and deepening *informal* power sharing in auxiliary political institutions, in society, and in the economy. The initiation phase in which institutions for democracy are negotiated must be extended in time—six years in the South African case—and must be made inclusive by interim power-sharing arrangements. This permits the majority to demonstrate its commitment to a democracy that will not become a tyranny of the majority. It also empowers many more groups—including groups that cut across ethnic lines—in the negotiations to design democratic institutions for the longer term.

In addition, during this initiation phase power sharing must become broader and deeper by embracing non-elites—not only in politics but also in society and the economy—even as it prepares to wither away as a formal political arrangement in the consolidation phase. A broader and deeper foundation of moderation—rooted in informal political institutions *and* social organizations—is essential for sustainable peace and durable democracy. A dense network of informal institutions connecting various ethnic groups strengthens interethnic moderation in four ways. First, if citizens identify not only as Serbs, Pashtuns, Kurds, Abkhazes, or Hutus but also as union workers, parents, and members of certain neighborhoods, interests and grievances are not exclusively identified with and expressed through one's ethnic community. "The intense struggle over economic resources" might then be fought not for one's ethnic group but for all union members irrespective of their ethnic affiliation. In short, by crosscutting societal polarization, institutionalized cooperation among communal groups mitigates ethnic conflict. In South Africa, such crosscutting identities were reinforced as a reaction to the enforced division that was apartheid: Across the political spectrum, those opposed to white minority rule—including many in the white community—advanced a common national identity in contrast to the divisiveness of state-imposed racial segregation. Indeed, the 1955 Freedom Charter (the liberation manifesto), articulates a common nationality as the alternative to apartheid's emphasis on "separate development."

Second, interethnic organizations in the short term monitor and punish those members that violate organizational rules and norms by raising divisive ethnic issues and in the longer term cultivate new values of toleration across ethnic lines.[3] Third, civic groups are important agents of socialization. If organized across ethnic borders, they promote norms and values of ethnic tolerance and cooperation. And a tolerant culture is arguably the best guar-

3. Ashutosh Varshney (2001, 375), for instance, demonstrates that Indian neighborhood peace committees, consisting of Hindus and Muslims, played an important role in preventing ethnic tension from turning into violence. These committees "policed neighborhoods, killed rumors, provided information to the local administration, and facilitated communication between communities in times of tension."

antor for a durable peace among ethnic groups. In contrast, social organizations in societies that are deeply divided along ethnic lines are unlikely sponsors of ethnic peace. If ethnic groups are organized "from womb to tomb" in ethnically exclusive kindergartens, schools, labor unions, and retirement communities, ethnic polarization and isolation is clearly not ameliorated but further increased. In addition, without interethnic communication among members of different communities there are few if any opportunities to overcome the insecurities and prejudices that divide them.

A fourth aspect of expanding and deepening informal power sharing is the cultivation of cooperative links of political and ethnic elites with representatives of multiethnic organizations. John Paul Lederach (1996; 1997) speaks in this regard about an "organic approach" to ethnic peace building.[4] Top-level negotiators have the greatest capacity to influence the peacebuilding process, yet they are often unaware of specific problems that exist in certain local areas. Without cooperation at the middle and grassroots levels, it will be difficult to implement peace accords because leaders at lower levels of the hierarchy are able to upset carefully crafted elite settlements. Lederach (1997, 45) insightfully writes that it is illusory that "the accomplishments at the highest levels will [automatically] translate to, and move down through, the rest of the population."

In sum, the durability of postconflict peace depends heavily on flexibility in the design of political institutions and on the broadening and deepening of power sharing throughout society. How can flexibility in institutional design and a deepening of moderation occur as part of the peace process to end violence and build a durable peace in deeply divided societies? An important part of our answer is extending the initial stage of negotiations over the constitution that is expected to structure politics for the longer term. This is not a purely academic concern. In Bosnia, for example, the ability of NATO's international community to draw down its peace-building mission is premised on the ability of the power-sharing institutions forged in the 1995 Dayton Agreement—now dominated by nationalists—to melt into more moderate and ethnically mixed political institutions.[5] Examining the South African experience may have lessons for other attempts to build flexibility in institutional design and a deeper base of moderation throughout society.

4. Lederach (1996) argues that three levels need to be involved to achieve ethnic reconciliation. At the top level, political and military leaders are involved in high-level negotiations to achieve settlements between rivaling ethnic groups. At the middle level, economic, religious, and humanitarian leaders organize problem-solving workshops and peace committees, and provide training for conflict resolution. At the grassroots level, local leaders and officials organize neighborhood committees and workshops for prejudice reduction.

5. On the practical policy challenges in Bosnia, see ICG 2001c.

Evaluating South Africa's Experience

The transition from apartheid to nonracial democracy that began in early 1990 represented a strategic turn of the political elite to bargaining as a way to exit the escalating conflict caused by apartheid laws and the piecemeal and inadequate reform of the 1980s.[6] The turn to bargaining started at the highest levels. In late 1989 talks between then-President F. W. de Klerk and ANC leader Nelson Mandela established the basic formula for the peace process. Apartheid (i.e., statutory racial separation) would end and a nonracial democracy would emerge as the outcome of talks. At first, there was no agreement on whether the transition would feature power sharing, which the ANC rank-and-file opposed. Indeed, it was the relative balance of power in favor of the ANC that tipped the balance in negotiation toward informal power sharing.

Over time, the high-level talks spread to many other strata of society and eventually to virtually every arena of politics, society, and the economy. South Africa's many facets of conflict were mediated in multiple arenas of bargaining that emerged as informal institutions involving civil-society actors such as businesses, churches, and trade unions to manage and facilitate the transition to majority rule. Continuing inspiration came from the most influential and powerful political leaders, such as Mandela and de Klerk, whose leadership has been widely recognized as reflecting a deep commitment to surmounting even the most difficult and serious issues at the negotiation table. (It is for this reason that the Norwegian Nobel Committee awarded the 1993 Peace Prize to these leaders together.) These attitudes came to be shared by, and in turn helped shape, the attitudes of many rank-and-file political leaders and members of the South Africa public at large. Eventually and for the most part, the bargaining in these multiple arenas overcame the legacies of violence. Despite several crises and nearly 14,000 deaths from political violence between 1990 and 1993, the parties continued to negotiate.

There were broader causes that helped this process along, but, without the pragmatic use of power sharing during the negotiations and without the spread of formal power sharing to informal power-sharing practices throughout society, these broader causes would not have foreordained a democratic outcome. The transition to the "New South Africa" was facilitated by three major factors: (1) a sense of shared and common destiny, (2) a high degree of intergroup economic interdependence, and (3) the abject failure of apartheid's attempts to territorialize and reify race and ethnicity (Sisk 1995). These underlying factors, combined with significant political pragmatism and foresight, no small measure of international pressures and

6. For an analysis of the period leading up to the demise of apartheid, see Price 1990 and Lodge 1983.

incentives (Rothchild 1997), and the need to assure ongoing domestic and international investor confidence, supported the progress in negotiation in 1990s South Africa. Added to these factors is the effective use of symbolic politics, particularly by Mandela, which demonstrated an appreciation for the need to address minority fears about majority rule. These factors still propel moderation in post-apartheid South Africa. Yet, the artful use of power sharing as an interim tool and the deepening of power sharing beyond the political institutions ensured that these opportunities were not squandered in the transition.

Once the parties committed themselves to democracy, they understood that the ANC could impose majoritarian institutions if it chose and that the other parties could probably not prevent this except by the most extreme means. Nevertheless, these other parties could make any decision by ANC to impose simple majoritarianism very costly. They were able to reach a broad-based agreement on formal power sharing in a series of agreements beginning in 1990 and culminating in the 1993 Interim Constitution. These pacts, however, were flexible: The interim agreements created a foundation of political legitimacy through founding elections in April 1994, while an elected Constitutional Assembly (which also acted as an interim parliament) debated a permanent constitution. This constitution was eventually certified by the Constitutional Court in October 1996.

The Interim Power-Sharing Arrangements

South Africa's transition to democracy between 1990 and 1994 was characterized by a *series* of political pacts that established the structure of interim power sharing. In the first two pacts, the Groote Schuur Minute (Pact) of May 1990 and the so-called Pretoria Minute of August 1990, the issues on the table were the release of political prisoners that had been jailed by the apartheid regime and the return of exiles who had fled the country. In subsequent pacts, such as the creation of ANC/Inkatha Freedom Party (IFP) liaison committees, the aim was to help quell political violence that had escalated in the East Rand and KwaZulu-Natal regions. The first pact on substantive constitutional negotiations was the agreement to establish the broadly inclusive Conference for a Democratic South Africa (CODESA I) in December 1991, although this bargaining forum collapsed in May 1992 at the CODESA II conference. Rampant political violence during mid-1990 and throughout 1992 led to yet another pact, titled the National Peace Accord of December 1992, which created national-, regional-, and local-level peace committees; although these committees did not bring down the overall levels of violence, they may have helped prevent the violence from getting worse. In any event, the committees were an important set of forums for deepening the bargaining process; in many local areas, the police, ruling parties, anti-apartheid political parties, and nongovernmental organizations (NGOs) met together for the first time. This series of pacts reached by the parties between May 1990 and July 1993 created both formal, but transitional, power-sharing institutions and informal, extralegal power-sharing practices for bargaining.

The pact-making approach to negotiating democracy in South Africa led, over time, to the all-important "Record of Understanding" of November 1992. This pact formed the essential core of the agreement to share power for the period before and after the 1994 elections. The late 1992 and early 1993 negotiations led to the establishment of the Multi-party Negotiating Process, which met from April to July 1993; in this forum, both the power-sharing institutions for the transitional period (July 1993–April 1994 elections) and for the period of constitution-making through 1996 were negotiated. In this forum as well, the parties reached agreement on an interim constitution that provided for power sharing and set the parameters for the final pact.

Finally, as the deadline for more comprehensive agreements approached, a series of ANC–NP bilateral negotiations (called *bosberaad* or bush-meeting conferences) helped break deadlocks in negotiation, thrashed out the details of the transition, and ironed out a number of constitutional disagreements.

The key elements of the 1993 Interim Constitution Pact, which was essentially a consociational agreement, were as follows:

1. *The GNU.* A Government of National Unity would govern for up to five years, which would include all major parties on the South African scene. Each party winning more than 5 percent of the vote would be entitled to a proportionate number of seats in the 27-person cabinet. Decisionmaking in the cabinet would not be based on majority rule, but instead decisions would be taken in a "consensus-seeking spirit" without formal-legal constraints.
2. *Constitutional Assembly.* Based on the outcome of the 1994 elections, a new 400-member National Assembly and province-derived Senate would sit jointly as a Constitutional Assembly to craft a new, permanent national charter. The decision rule for approval of the new constitution required a supermajority of two-thirds, although the pact included a complicated deadlock-breaking mechanism.
3. *Electoral Principles.* The parties agreed to a list proportional representation (PR) system (amended in February 1994 to include national and regional ballots), full adult franchise, and the creation of an Independent Electoral Commission to oversee the vote slated for April 1994. Proportional representation was seen as a way to alleviate minority fears by assuring their participation in parliament without a strict guarantee of representation through the use of ethnic or racial quotas.

4. *Regionalism.* Nine provinces would be allowed to adopt their own constitutions "consistent with the constitutional principles and national constitution," and these would be certifiable by the constitutional court. The powers and functions of local governments were enumerated. Provision was made for the establishment of traditional authorities and of provincial houses of traditional leaders.
5. *Security.* The constitution provided for the integration of the South African National Defense Force with the armed wings of the liberation forces and the creation of the South African Police Services.
6. *Economics.* Private property rights were guaranteed, but expropriation (especially land) would still be possible under certain rules and with compensation of fair market value. Trade unions were assured of their rights; nevertheless, the Interim Constitution also included a clause that permitted employer lockouts of striking workers.
7. *Constitutional Principles.* The Interim Constitution contained a series of 32 constitutional principles that delimited the parameters of the final constitution, particularly on the powers of the regions. These principles were the most important substantive aspects of agreement that guided subsequent constitution making.
8. *Judicial Review.* A Constitutional Court—appointed by the president—would be established to have wide original jurisdiction to determine the constitutionality of any statute, regulation, or administrative procedure. The Court was empowered to certify that the final constitution was in conformity with the series of 32 Constitutional Principles.

Why did the ANC, clearly garnering the support of a majority of the electorate, agree to share power? Answering this question is key to understanding the origins of power sharing in South Africa and the terms under which it was allowed, even encouraged by both majority and minority interests, to wither away. The basic rationale for ANC acquiescence to power sharing on an interim basis—demanded by the incumbent National Party regime—was outlined in the controversial 1992 ANC discussion document "Strategic Perspectives," authored by former Communist Party leader Joe Slovo.[7] To prevent a counterrevolutionary threat to the new political order emanating from the bureaucracy and security forces, sharing power with the outgoing white minority regime (and implicitly political foes such as the Zulu nationalist IFP) was a self-interested, "strategic" necessity for the ANC. However, these concessions would be limited by a sunset clause that would allow formal power sharing to expire after five years. This "strategic" pragmatism was manifested in the ANC concessions of early 1994 to the Freedom Front and the IFP—potential spoilers of the pact—that brought these parties into the Government of National Unity at the eleventh hour. This averted a bloody show-

7. See Sisk 1995, 221.

Table 12.1. South Africa: Representation in the Constitutional Assembly, 1994

Party	Seats	Percentage
African National Congress	312	63.7
National Party	99	20.2
Inkatha Freedom Party	48	9.8
Freedom Front	14	2.8
Democratic Party	10	2.0
Pan-Africanist Congress	5	1.0
African Christian Democratic Party	2	0.4

Source: South African Independent Electoral Commission.

down at the moment of regime change following the celebrated liberation elections of April 1994. The outcome of the 1994 elections in terms of the number and percentage of seats secured by each party are listed in Table 12.1. (The elections figures are now accepted as an authoritative outcome, although in the troubled KwaZulu-Natal province it is also widely accepted that the results themselves were negotiated when ballot counts were disputed, such that the IFP percentage was raised sufficiently to allow them to become a majority party in that province.)

Why did the other parties agree to participate in an interim power-sharing arrangement with a sunset provision? They saw that they could not prevent the ANC from emerging as South Africa's new governing party, but they might use the negotiations to introduce limits on simple majority rule in South Africa's new constitution. Further limits would include a strong provision on private property rights; the ability of employers to lock out striking labor; a strong judiciary; and provisions for cultural, linguistic, and own-language educational rights in the final constitution. These provisions would be effective in addressing the core concerns of minorities in the post-apartheid order. Moreover, minority opposition parties in South Africa took the long view: The ANC would eventually—almost naturally—lose support over time given the challenges of governance that faced them and the fading of their revolutionary legitimacy that could be anticipated in the future. Strict forms of power sharing would possibly limit the powers of a future—possibly non-ANC—majority (although this possibility has thus far turned out to be a chimera).

The Impact of Interim Power Sharing on Longer-Term Democratic Institutions

Formal power sharing was not permanent, but it had a significant effect on the final shape of the South African constitution adopted in 1996. The National Party's withdrawal from the cabinet in May 1996 occurred earlier than expected because NP leaders were uncomfortable with being the principal opposition party while still being associated with government decisions. However, the participation of the National Party from 1993 to 1996 was essential to the successful completion of a constitution on which most ethnic groups could agree. There should be no underestimating how important it was for stability and a peaceful election that former President de Klerk became deputy president in the post-apartheid order and his erstwhile deputy Chris Stals remained as finance minister in the first ANC-majority government. It was also significant that IFP leader Mangosuthu Buthelezi was given the important Home Affairs portfolio (a powerful cabinet position overseeing citizenship issues).

Constitution-making process. The interim power-sharing agreement set the stage for more inclusive and accommodative negotiations over the terms of the 1996 constitution. Four aspects of the constitution-making process proved to be important for future political relations: First, the proceedings were generally open and transparent, with a very high level of public education on the issues. Public input occurred via mail, meetings, surveys, and contributions on the Internet. There were over 1.9 million submissions to the Assembly during the public comment period, with some of the inputs submitted by NGOs proving especially insightful. Second, agreement was generally reached by consensus. When sticking points arose on specific issues (e.g., the death penalty, appointment of judges, employer lockout clause, competence of regions, and so forth) the differences were ironed out in bilateral meetings between the ANC and the National Party, or with other parties (such as the Freedom Front on the issue of own-language education or the Democratic Party on the appointment of judges). Third, agreement on the formation of a Cultural Commission for the Promotion and Protection of the Rights of Cultural, Religious, and Linguistic Communities resolved much of the concern about "group rights." The Commission is purely advisory, but it has an important "bargaining arena" function. The most important judiciable rights are those relating to nondiscrimination on the basis of race, religion, culture, gender, sexual preference, or national origin. Fourth, the Constitutional Court rejected the initial draft of the charter in May 1996 and sent it back to the Constitutional Assembly to ensure its conformity with the Constitutional Principles and to safeguard the independence of several state institutions (e.g., the Auditor-General and the Public Protector). This proved an important, early indication of the power of an independent judiciary to protect minority interests by enforcing constitutional provisions.

There were, of course, some significant problems during the negotiations. The IFP essentially boycotted much of the formal negotiating process, insisting that agreements made in April 1994 with the ANC on postelection international mediation be upheld (such mediation never occurred). The party also asserted that regional powers were insufficiently protected by the Interim Constitution's principles. Nevertheless, negotiations under formal power sharing came to fruition with agreement on a new constitution for South Africa, which was finalized in October 1996. The constitution was adopted by a vote of 421 to 2, with 12 abstentions. (The IFP did not participate in the final vote.) The new constitution was signed by President Mandela on December 10, the anniversary of the 1960 Sharpeville massacre by government troops that precipitated the first armed uprising against apartheid—a day that is now celebrated as Human Rights Day.

The 1996 constitution. The inclusive constitution-making process softened the majoritarian democracy of the 1996 constitution. This constitution—designed to serve South Africa into the indefinite future—does not include formal or consociational power sharing. The vestiges of Westminster are there—the majority party in the National Assembly chooses the president who chooses the cabinet. There is no grand coalition and no ironclad minority veto. Voluntary executive coalitions are possible, of course, but there is no constitutional mandate that parties receiving a set percentage of the vote must be included in executive decisionmaking. Nevertheless, the new constitution creates no garden-variety, winner-take-all system. As noted below, it incorporates many features to assuage minority concerns and introduces important checks and balances on unilateral ruling-party decisionmaking.

List proportional representation electoral system. First, the double-ballot, list PR electoral system contains strong incentives to act moderately given the spatial distribution of the electorate. Despite the fact that the Democratic Party and IFP have failed to attract significant support beyond their identity bases, the incentives produced by the electoral system have encouraged them to continue trying.[8] So, too, the ANC has an incentive to remain moderate on divisive racial themes because it hopes to continue to attract minority-group votes (Friedman 1996; Southall 1994). This wide-ranging support, in turn, fosters moderation inside the ANC itself. As Donald Rothchild has pointed out, much informal power sharing across ethnic lines occurs within the ANC. That is, the "Charterist" tradition that embraces inclusion of South Africans of all communities remains alive and well within the ANC, and the party has done much to ensure that it is broadly representative of South African society. The ANC must keep this tradition alive to continue to win votes in the minority communities.

8. There continues to be a debate on whether voting in South Africa's 1994, 1999, and 2000 local elections was an "ethnic census." See Johnson and Schlemmer 1996. On the election results, see the Electoral Institute of South Africa's home page at www.eisa.org.za.

Indeed, the ANC has been exceptionally effective in broadening its base over time, with increased majorities in both the 1999 and 2004 national elections.

Cooperative governance. Second, the nine provinces themselves and the upper-chamber Council of Provinces—the manifestations of the concept of "cooperative governance"—have been important to managing complex diversity in post-apartheid South Africa. (Importantly, the provinces do not feature the territorialization of ethnicity, a key provision in many power sharing or consociational arrangements.) The independent elections for provincial parliaments offer minority parties opportunities to control governments—notably in Western Cape and KwaZulu-Natal provinces. In addition, ANC provincial premiers are showing some degree of autonomy, because they articulate provincial interests that are at variance with central party policy. Political decentralization proliferates points of multiethnic negotiations and creates training grounds for intergroup conciliation, especially when territory and ethnic identity do not overlap.

Judicial checks and balances. Third, judicial institutions and processes have been engaged in reconciling the ambiguities in the Bill of Rights, particularly the balance between group self-determination, language, and cultural rights as well as the prohibitions against discrimination and racism. Virtually all observers agree that the Constitutional Court has jealously guarded judicial independence and the rule of law. The Court is designed to be the arena of last resort in translating the vagaries of the constitution into public policy and government practice. Judicial appointments in post-apartheid South Africa have been carefully selected to ensure that this critical institution is balanced on a number of criteria, among them race, ethnicity, region, and gender.

Chapter IX bargaining institutions. The constitution provided for so-called Chapter IX provisions that offered a full range of protections to minorities and a set of bargaining institutions through which future disputes could be resolved. Among the mechanisms to mitigate intergroup conflict are the Pan-South African Language Board, the cultural commissions, and the office of the Public Protector. The national Council of Traditional Leaders provides the government with advice on traditional affairs (although tensions remain over the ability of the Council to exercise more than advisory powers). Although these institutions are yet to be tested, they may potentially be the most important vehicles for managing ethnic conflict. Statutory bodies such as these can be helpful in managing intergroup relations to promote peaceful politics. In June 2002, for example, the Broadcasting Complaints Commission (a Chapter IX body) banned a popular song from the airwaves (Mbongeni Ngema's "A'madiya") because it included lyrics that rallied Africans to stand up to Asian shopkeepers that some feel have exploited their customers. Later, the well-known playwright and author agreed the song's combative tone went too far.

Deepening Moderation: Informal Institutions

Many attribute the strength of contemporary civil society in South Africa to the plethora of organizations that spontaneously sprouted during the difficult years of apartheid. Despite the oppressive, exclusive apartheid state that purposefully sought to keep groups apart through social policies such as separate political enfranchisement, housing, and education systems and in social life through separate religious organizations, progressive anti-apartheid organizations worked against such policies. In neighborhoods and communities, in exile politics and in underground movements at home, civil-society groups were geared toward disproving apartheid's premise that separation, not integration, is the solution to multiethnicity.

During the transitional period, these civil-society groups emerged as critically important because of the legitimacy they secured from their long, difficult struggle against the apartheid state. Although organizations such as the South African Council of Churches or Congress of South African Trade Unions faced enormous problems as they evolved from liberation organizations to partners in negotiation and eventually governance, they were critical to a relatively smooth transition process. In virtually every arena of public policy, parallel civil-society forums emerged as alternative arenas of bargaining in which midlevel and grassroots participants augmented the elite-level bargaining of the formal constitution-making activities.

The report of the Carnegie Commission on Preventing Deadly Conflict, titled *A House No Longer Divided: Progress and Prospects for Democratic Peace in South Africa* (1997a), details the comparatively extensive social integration and the pivotal role that civil-society actors played in supporting, and at times mediating, the formal negotiation process. For example, in June 1992, as the negotiations were on the brink of collapse, the South African Council of Churches stepped in to mediate among the political parties; this initiative is credited with keeping the process on track in the midst of extremely damaging political violence. Another instance of mediation by civil-society actors is the experience with the structures of the National Peace Accord, an agreement reached in late 1991 that set up violence monitoring and prevention committees at the national, regional, and local level. The Peace Accord committees were facilitated mostly by NGOs, and they included a myriad of bargaining arenas in the most troubled areas (such as KwaZulu-Natal and the "East Rand" near Johannesburg) that brought together the police, anti-apartheid neighborhood committees, political parties, church leaders, social workers, and trained mediators. Through the layered peace structures, midlevel elites (particularly the police and local ANC and IFP party activists) had the opportunity to build critical cross-ethnic ties (Gastrow 1995).

Today informal power sharing in the form of ethnically and racially inclusive leaderships, moderation, and compromise occurs in myriad arenas at many levels of civil society and government in South Africa, not least of which are local and provincial governments and the issue-specific (e.g., education, language, arts and culture, housing) consultation forums. In the larger cities, the new municipal governments are the pivotal arenas, and community policing and development forums throughout South Africa are certainly among the more important bargaining venues.[9] The basic structure of local government indicates that the practice of inclusive, collaborative decisionmaking remains critical to public policymaking and implementation in post-apartheid South Africa. These informal practices have fostered conflict amelioration and have avoided ethnic or racial (though not necessarily party-political) hegemony through the ANC and ethnic violence. Power sharing continues in many non-executive, informal political institutions and arenas in South Africa. Even in the government without formal power-sharing rules there has been intermittent inclusiveness involving Zulu nationalists and the New National Party in the ANC-dominated coalition. Some see Zulu nationalist participation in the national government as tokenism or co-optation, whereas others suggest that having the IFP in the cabinet at high levels means that with some parties, at least, power sharing has not fully withered from the South African political landscape. Indeed, in the troubled KwaZulu-Natal province, the ANC and IFP have had a formal power-sharing arrangement since 1998. The ANC has proved astute at informal power sharing by including a wide range of diversity within the cabinet, the bureaucracy, and in key provincial and local government posts. But such sharing of political power is largely voluntary and falls well outside constitutional requirements.

Intergroup bargaining arose during the 1990–1996 transition from apartheid to nonracial democracy and is now deeply embedded in many sectors of South African society. In a remarkably short time, a virtual culture of bargaining emerged that is now found in both formal and informal institutions. The areas of power sharing that lie beyond the formal arenas of politics are myriad and are often seen behind the scenes of public life. Most corporate boards are now racially diverse, and smart companies pitch their products with visibly multicultural advertising themes. In the arena of sport, great strides have been made in integrating training, coaching, and athletic participation. The arts community is vividly multicultural and diverse; South African music, theater, and performance are defined by close attention to inclusion, diversity, multilingual presentation, and fusion of traditions and

9. On local governance in South Africa, see Storey and Woolridge 2001.

styles. The "New South Africa" has moved considerably beyond initial slogans of the "rainbow nation" and is now seen on street corners, in social life, in shops and on the shop floor, and in the country's sports teams and reflected in the country's media and international image. Far from a tourism marketing ploy, the image projected of South Africa as a vibrant, culturally diverse, and tolerant society has become part of the new political culture.

Ethnic and racial conflict clearly remains a long-term threat to this newborn democracy;[10] nevertheless, severe intergroup antagonisms do not now endanger the new democratic order.[11] Balancing the need to keep minorities on board while delivering results to the majority will continue to be a difficult act. As Antoinette Handley and Jeffrey Herbst (1997, 224) write, "Reconciliation, if it is to endure, must move beyond symbols and will mean little if the causes of conflict are not dealt with." Today, South Africa faces acute governance challenges—among them crime, poverty, racism, and disease—yet the presence or absence of power sharing is not the key determinant in whether these governance challenges will be met. Perhaps most important is the further building of basic state capacity, including efficient service delivery, competent public administration, improved policing, and policies that lead to job creation.[12]

Lessons for Northern Ireland and Bosnia-Herzegovina

The successful tactics of the South African transition offer some important insights into why formal power sharing in ethnically divided societies so often fails. These points of analysis and conclusion, derived from our evaluation of South Africa, also point up ways to use formal power sharing as an interim step to promote democracy and peace in these societies. Three lessons stand out. First, it is important to keep the early initiation phase that follows a ceasefire and leads to ratification of a formal arrangement (often in the form of a constitution) a relatively lengthy one. During this initial period the previously warring parties can negotiate the arrangements for the longer term, and other parties and interests can enter the political process. Equally important, it provides time for the *informal* power-sharing arrangements to take root and sustain this longer-term arrangement.

10. As South African political analyst Steven Friedman (1995, 1167) writes, "The post-1948 legacy of violence and racial polarization seems likely to ensure that a South African democracy will be partial, at least for the next decade. South Africa remains a divided society in which pluralism and compromise presented themselves to political leaders as an unavoidable necessity, not a preferred option."

11. For a compelling confirmation of this point in South Africa, see the statement of Deputy President Thabo Mbeki as cited in the report of the Carnegie Commission on Preventing Deadly Conflict 1997a.

12. See du Toit 2001, 177–179.

Second, *formal* power-sharing institutions can play a central role during this early initiation phase, but this must be an interim arrangement. Therefore, the formal power-sharing arrangement must be flexible and not block the development of more durable democratic institutions. These interim formal arrangements often empower all of the previously warring parties in the negotiation of the new constitution. The interim arrangements permit all parties to demonstrate their own commitment and to gauge each others' commitment to democratic procedures. This permits the majority to demonstrate that it is unlikely to abuse the minorities by transforming a future democratic regime into a tyranny of the majority.

Third, the elites empowered by the interim formal power-sharing arrangement must not be permitted to dominate and structure society. In addition to the interim governing institutions and constitutional assembly, government must expand and deepen informal power sharing by drawing in midlevel elites and grassroots support into advisory panels and specialized implementation agencies like local peace commissions. Throughout society and the economy, negotiations must include midlevel elites and non-elites to help shape the transition in such diverse spheres as interdenominational religious cooperation and labor-management relations.

These lessons resonate especially strongly in Northern Ireland and Bosnia, where peace settlements have led to formal power-sharing institutions, but informal power sharing is largely lacking. As a consequence, difficulties have emerged in achieving cooperation through formal institutions. Nongovernmental organizations typically resist interethnic moderation.

Northern Ireland

Despite many differences of context, intensity of violence, and the role of external actors such as the United Kingdom and the Republic of Ireland, the "Good Friday" peace process in Northern Ireland has in some respects been similar to that of South Africa. A turbulent and difficult set of talks has yielded an agreement to share power in the new Northern Ireland Assembly, which is essentially consociational in design and practice. Many suggest that it is the genius of the April 1998 "Good Friday Agreement" that all parties could defend the agreement as containing the elements of what they had fought for all along. Moderate Republicans could claim that the agreement represents the first step toward accession to Ireland; moderate Loyalists could claim that the agreement preserves British sovereignty.[13] The key to power sharing in the Assembly is the implicit understanding that strong nationalist parties, such as the Ulster Unionist Party (UUP), the Social Democratic and Labour Party (SDLP), and Sinn Fein, can divvy up govern-

13. See Darby and MacGinty 2000, 78–79.

ment posts on a proportional (in this case, roughly equal) basis. For example, the First Minister is presently derived from the UUP while the Deputy Minister hails from Sinn Fein (Martin McGuiness).

The Good Friday peace process has been troubled in its implementation from the beginning, with the lack of progress on decommissioning and police reform consistently stifling efforts to achieve a functional power-sharing administration in Belfast. Only in late 2001 and early 2002 did it seem that the logjam on decommissioning had been broken. At times, the British government at Westminster has withdrawn the powers of the Assembly rather than allow its collapse. The difficulties of the Assembly have not generally been attributed to design flaws—indeed some have lauded the choice for centripetalist features such as the use of preference voting (Reilly 2001)—but rather to the absence of political will to share power and consistent extremist outbidding that trumps relatively moderate Unionist politicians.

Yet this lack of will to cooperate and to moderate demands is in part a consequence of the incentives created by the power-sharing arrangement itself. The dominance of exclusive national tendencies has not appreciably waned in light of breakthroughs in the peace process, but instead the fortunes of Sinn Fein and the rejectionist Democratic Unionist Party—representing the Republican and Loyalist tendencies most ardently—have actually improved in the electoral sphere. The mutual veto inherent in the consociational framework reflected in the Northern Ireland Assembly has led to a division of power among the nationalist parties more than any real sharing of power in a collaborative sense.

So, too, in the civil-society sphere, formal power sharing has made it more difficult to engender peace. As Colin Knox and Pádraic Quirk (2000, 50–51) write: "Any progress at the political level therefore needs to be consolidated by government initiatives to bring about equality, promote reconciliation and mutual respect for the separate traditions and cultures which exist within Northern Ireland; in short, to create a community which accommodates peoples' differing beliefs, aspirations and traditions . . . the 'hearts and minds' strategy." Despite considerable funding of such efforts by the United Kingdom and the European Union, the process of encouraging an integrated civil society in Northern Ireland has foundered. These scholars report that in key areas of public policy, notably education, violence management, and employment, Northern Ireland has had unfortunately little success. Notable too is the striking absence of cross-community peace building by the religious communities; indeed, there has been active hostility from the clergy on both sides in opposition to government and civil-society efforts to build bridges across the sectarian chasm.

Continued deadlock in political power sharing, and the persistence of social division in Northern Ireland and parallel, antagonistic blocs in society suggests that formal consociational power sharing will continue to be insufficient for peace building. Unless the kinds of fluidity in constitution-making and civil-society integration seen in South Africa can somehow be emulated, the future does not augur well for Northern Ireland. As David Bloomfield has suggested (1997), what Northern Ireland seems to lack is "complementarity" between the formal, elite political process and the on-the-ground efforts to bridge the communal divide. Even with persistent effort, considerable external support, and dedicated activists at work since the peace process began in the mid-1990s, society remains polarized and separated.

Bosnia

Much the same can be said about Bosnia. The power-sharing arrangements in Bosnia, implemented through the Dayton Agreement, reify ethnic divisions and undermine cooperation between Bosniaks, Croats, and Serbs at both the elite and mass levels. It is therefore unlikely that the country's power-sharing system will wither away in favor of an approach that fosters interethnic reconciliation and moderation.

The Dayton Agreement signed in December 1995 not only brought an end to Bosnia's protracted civil war but also introduced the country's first constitution. This constitution, written mainly by legal experts of the U.S. State Department, structures the political system around ethnic identities. It does so in two ways. First, although the prewar constitution of Yugoslavia recognized the rights of ethnic groups within Bosnia, it did not crudely pair territory and identity within the republic. By tolerating the outcomes of ethnic "cleansing" and by prescribing a federalist system based on ethnicity, the Dayton constitution does exactly that. It divides Bosnia into two Entities: the Bosniak-Croat Federation of Bosnia and Herzegovina and the Republika Srpska (Serb Republic). Both Entities are further divided into numerous municipalities. The Republika Srpska and the municipalities of the Federation are by and large ethnically homogeneous (with the exception of the larger cities, such as Tuzla and Sarajevo). The political center of this federation, representing all three ethnic groups, is extremely weak. The central government has only limited policymaking authority and commands a budget that is significantly smaller than the funding of even some local governments. Decisions that directly impact citizens' lives are primarily made at the Entity and municipality levels (Bieber 2001; Chandler 2000, 66–69; Karatnycky, Motyl, and Schnetzer 2001, 113; Ni Aolain 2001).

Second, the Dayton constitution introduces ethnic veto rights and parity representation in central governmental institutions. The statewide presidency consists of three members each elected from their ethnic constituencies. Each member has a veto right to protect the interests of his or her ethnic group. The legislative branch is divided into two chambers. The upper house (House of Peoples), representing the Entities, consists of five representatives from each of the three ethnic groups that may veto decisions made by the lower house, the House of Representatives. Seats in the House of Representatives are also allocated among Entities—two-thirds of the parliamentarians are elected within the Bosniak-Croat Federation, the other third within the Serb Republic. Similar formal power-sharing arrangements exist in the Bosniak-Croat Federation itself, dividing power equally between the Croat and the Muslim groups (Chandler 2000, 66–69; Karatnycky, Motyl, and Schnetzer 2001, 113).

In the absence of sufficient levels of trust between the ethnic elites, these power-sharing arrangements regularly lead to governmental deadlocks at the federal level and in the Bosniak-Croat Federation. By exercising its right to interpret and implement the Dayton Agreement, the U.N. Office of the High Representative often steps in and imposes legislation on the country. The international community thereby further reduces the incentives for ethnic leaders to find compromises.

Given recurring deadlocks, financial constraints, and limited authority, citizens of Bosnia consider the central and multiethnic institutions as being extremely weak and unable to protect their interests. They therefore rely on regional and local governmental structures, which usually "reflect a single [ethnic] group and are dominated by nationalist parties largely committed to their own communities and not to minorities" (Ni Aolain 2001, 73).[14] Regional and local elites try to advance the interests of their own ethnic groups through official policies but also through extensive patron-client networks that are closely linked to the nationalist parties (Aplon and Tanner 2000, 13). It is therefore not surprising that most citizens still vote along ethnic lines, although the strength of the nationalist parties declined somewhat in the 1998 legislative elections (Karatnycky, Motyl, and Schnetzer 2001, 114).

In sum, the Dayton power-sharing system has not facilitated cooperation among the ethnic elites. In fact, it has done the opposite. While nationalist elites willfully sabotage the federal government of Bosnia through an excessive use of veto power, they focus their political attention and efforts on the ethnically homogeneous Entities and municipalities, rallying their ethnic constituencies behind them. In this situation, only a strong civil society organized across ethnic lines could overcome the reification of ethnic divisions by challenging ethnic elites through alternative channels of information and sources of protection. In the long run, multiethnic organizations could

14. As Florian Bieber (2001, 115) similarly puts it, "The powers of the central state of Bosnia are extremely curtailed, to the advantage of the entities. These essentially ethnically-defined entities provide adequate protection for group members *within* their territory, but are incapable of providing an institutional safeguard for the rights of their group members in another entity."

thereby undermine the support for nationalist parties and induce leaders to assume a more moderate political stance, making Dayton eventually work.

Unfortunately, civil society in Bosnia is generally weak, and groups organized across ethnic lines are almost non-existent. Even more than in other postauthoritarian societies, a genuine civil society, independent from foreign (especially Western) financial and ideological tutelage, has been extremely slow to develop. Although "[t]here has been tremendous growth in the scale and activity of citizen's groups, non-governmental organizations [NGOs], and institutions centered on religious congregations, etc., in the post-Dayton period" (Karatnycky, Motyl, and Schnetzer 2001, 116), these are only loosely rooted in society. Ordinary citizens, especially those living in the rural areas, conceive representatives of the NGOs as elitists. This is not surprising, given that NGO representatives are usually highly educated, of middle-class origin, and from the urban centers. Local leaders of the nationalist parties in Bosnia therefore remain closest to the hearts and minds of the common people (Bieber 2001, 149–153; Aplon and Tanner 2000, 3).

The status of associations organized across ethnic lines is even more deplorable. Only a small number of NGOs (e.g., the Tuzla Citizens' Forum and the Coalition for Return) include members from at least two ethnic groups. These organizations operate mainly in the few remaining multiethnic cities of Bosnia, such as Sarajevo and Tuzla. Outside of these more tolerant centers, the organization of citizens across ethnic lines is almost impossible. Freedom of movement across the physical boundary lines that separate the ethnic groups is sharply restricted. Moreover, representatives of multiethnic organizations face repression by local leaders whose legitimacy they question. Communication across these regional dividing lines is poor, as telephone lines that in the prewar period connected different regions have rarely been restored. Finally, there are no independent media outlets that serve the entire territory of Bosnia. Local newspapers as well as TV and radio stations remain under the control of nationalist party leaders. As Julia Demichelis (1998, 4) summarizes the situation: "In general, basic freedoms stop at these municipalities' dividing lines, which are typically reinforced by land mines. There is no freedom of movement and no freedom of expression against the politicians."

Under these conditions, the future for the development of a multicultural society in Bosnia is not very hopeful. A strong momentum for such a development may originate only in the larger, multiethnic cities of the country. Yet, as Jason Aplon and Victor Tanner (2000, 7) point out, "[e]thnic cleansing forced rural populations into the cities. Resentful, cut off from their environment and their traditions, they form the backbone of popular nationalist support." It might therefore be that ethnic dividing lines will become impermeable even in the cosmopolitan centers of Bosnia.

Impetus for the development of multiethnic NGOs therefore needs to come from foreign and international actors who could focus their financial and technical support on multiethnic organizations to the detriment of monoethnic organizations. In fact, this has rarely been the case. As Roberto Belloni (2001) and Demichelis (1998) show, the international peace-building efforts in Bosnia and Herzegovina have primarily taken the form of channeling funds (designated for promoting civil society) through ethnic elites. This assistance has thereby strengthened the position of these elites and encouraged the formation of clientelist networks along ethnic lines. Belloni (2001, 163) concludes: "By viewing civil society building as a technical task, as a matter of allocating resources and delivering services, the international community misunderstands the struggle to overcome nationalist fragmentation. . . . Civil society's contribution to peace, tolerance, and the reintegration of the country thus has been extremely limited." In conclusion, the rigidity of the Dayton power-sharing system, combined with a society largely organized along ethnic lines, has fortified "the tripartite division of nation, community and individual in the new Bosnia where ethnic identity is all, and the body politic is a fractured soul" (Ni Aolain 2001, 63).

Conclusion

We suggest that South Africa—though still a deeply divided society, governed by a democratic, albeit single-party–dominant, regime—may offer some lessons to societies such as Northern Ireland and Bosnia where formal power-sharing institutions have replaced violent conflict. From South Africa's experience, we see how formal power sharing that was close to the model of consociationalism served as a transitional device on the road to democratic institutions that are essentially majoritarian, but nevertheless contain important opportunities and protections for minority interests. This also created an opening to broaden and deepen power sharing through informal institutions in multiple arenas of bargaining. With the period of national unity government—which resolved much of the deep-seated uncertainty about majority rule for the fearful ancien regime—an extended opportunity for constitution-making allowed South Africa to arrive at a new social contract reflecting the need to integrate political parties and civil society. The inclusion of civil-society arenas in the process of state-building helped to create the social basis for integration, preventing the enduring division of society along lines of historical conflict. This withering of formal power-sharing institutions augurs well for longer-term peace in South Africa.

One method for achieving a subtle but steady movement toward more durable political institutions is to keep the process of constitution-making going well into the postwar period. Peace agreements cannot freeze in time the conditions that pertained when violence was forsworn. Such agreements do need to resolve the war with certainty, but they need to be imbued with provisions that allow for flexibility, continued bargaining, and opportunity for amendment. They need an incentive structure that encourages ongoing bargaining, moderation, and ethnic conflict management (Rothchild 1997). The lesson for countries such as Northern Ireland and Bosnia is clear. At present, it is unrealistic to expect the politicians in Northern Ireland and Bosnia to revisit the terms of the Good Friday agreement or Dayton Agreement on political institutions. However, over time, it will be important to change some of the key institutions so that they provide greater incentives for creating integrative, cross-communal political parties.

In the realm of civil society, the lessons are equally clear. Without progress in this area, power-sharing solutions are likely to get stuck in a pattern of communal stalemate. Perhaps what moderates in Northern Ireland and Bosnia need is simply more time, a great deal of persistence, and unwavering support from abroad. The fluidity of civil society integration in South Africa was facilitated by the fact that underneath the simple black-white division of the apartheid era, the society was in reality much more complex and diverse. In Northern Ireland and Bosnia, by contrast, the ethnic communities are cohesive and have much less social differentiation or complexity. As a result, the ability to form crosscutting coalitions is limited. How much time can pass with formal power sharing in politics but without informal power sharing in society is uncertain. On practical issues, particularly in education and in the economic sphere, cross-community peace building is essential if peace is to be sustained.

Our evaluation suggests that power sharing works best when it can, over time, wither away. Whether in South Africa, Northern Ireland, or Bosnia, in the immediate term power sharing has been a necessary confidence-building device to ensure that all groups with the capacity to spoil a peace settlement can be included in the institutions. Over time, however, postwar societies need to move beyond the mutual hostage-taking that a guaranteed place at the decisionmaking table implies, the *immobilism* it inevitably creates, and the construction of postwar societies around the fixed and unyielding social boundaries of ethnicity. Centripetal democratic solutions have an inherent advantage for peace building, but only if the crosscutting integration in civil society on which they rely can be achieved over time. Seen in this light, peace building requires a much longer time line for the negotiation of formal, integrative political institutions and for a concerted and persistent effort to foster informal institutions that create the social conditions necessary for such political institutions to survive.

13

Conclusion: Nation-State Stewardship and the Alternatives to Power Sharing

Philip G. Roeder and Donald Rothchild

This project began with the title "Power Sharing and Peacemaking" and with the relatively narrow objective of understanding the contribution that power sharing can make after civil wars in ethnically divided societies. More specifically, we sought to understand the role of power sharing in facilitating the peaceful settlement of civil wars, preventing ensuing civil wars, and strengthening democracies as part of a strategy of nation building or regime change. The project focused on the consequences of formal power-sharing institutions. It began with a definition of *power sharing* that emphasized arrangements to achieve inclusive decisionmaking (such as coalition executives), partitioned decisionmaking (such as territorial decentralization, ethnofederalism, or fiscal decentralization), and predetermined decisions (such as proportional allocation of bureaucratic positions or state revenues). It also began by asking whether the consequences of these institutions might vary from the initiation phase of a transition from civil war to the consolidation phase in which peace and democracy become self-sustaining.

Our original agenda was shaped by recent events. Power sharing has become a favored instrument by which the international community has sought to establish peace in ethnically divided societies after intense domestic conflicts like civil wars. Inclusive central governments and regional autonomy serve as the basic pattern for many peace settlements around the world—from Bosnia to Afghanistan, South Africa to Rwanda and Burundi. But is this optimism about power sharing warranted? Is power sharing a pro-

The authors thank our colleagues in this project for their suggestions concerning this concluding chapter. We are particularly indebted to Valerie Bunce, Simon Chesterman, David A. Lake, Ben Reilly, and Stephen Watts for close readings and extensive comments on earlier drafts.

ductive foundation for a stable peace and democracy? Our findings raise a flag of caution, advising extreme care in the use of this instrument for securing a lasting peace.

The focus widened and the label changed as we discovered that in ethnically divided societies and after conflicts such as civil wars there were many experiments, but few long-term successes with power sharing. Our findings point to an alternative strategy for the international community—what we call a strategy of *nation-state stewardship*. This strategy limits power sharing to two tactical roles in the initiation phase: (1) as an offer by a majority to reassure minorities about the peace implementation process and (2) as a principle of proportionality for one-time, pump-priming decisions, such as the initial staffing of new bureaucracies and the armed forces. As we outline its tactics at the end of this chapter, the strategy of nation-state stewardship has three informing principles. First, the prime objective of nation-state stewardship is to construct political institutions that express the shared sentiment of a people that they should constitute an independent state. Where the people share a sense of nationalism or at least do not actively oppose this, the international community can hope to build a state. However, where there are strong sentiments against this among some ethnic groups, partition is sometimes preferable. Second, the shared sense of nationhood also limits the realm of governmental responsibilities. Thus, where there are fundamental disagreements among the former combatants about what a state should do—such as enforcement of religious laws—the state should leave these tasks to civil society and private associations, not to microstates within the state. Third, the international community must avoid privileging the former warring parties—often these are the ruling state coalition and insurgent groups—in the organs of the new state. This typically should mean dividing the powers of government among multiple, independent organs that represent alternative majorities. This may necessitate a long period of international trusteeship in which the international community governs the divided society directly without central governing institutions. In these circumstances international stewards should begin by building multiple, local democratic institutions to replace the power bases of the former warring parties from the ground up.

The Dilemma of Power Sharing

The nation-state stewardship strategy warns of a dilemma in attempting to institutionalize power sharing after civil wars: Although power sharing may be necessary to initiate a transition to peace and democracy from civil war, it is at odds with the consolidation of peace and democracy over the longer term.

Power Sharing in the Initiation Phase

Ironically, power sharing may be most successful at initiating a transition to peace and democracy when it is used by a clearly preponderant party to induce others to come to the negotiating table and sign on to a peace agreement. As a civil war approaches the denouement that all parties can now foresee, the offer by the more powerful party—a promise of conceding some of the powers that it can anticipate from victory—may reduce fears among the weaker parties that the preponderant political actor will abuse them once they lay down their arms. Since this is a voluntary and costly concession of powers by the preponderant party, it is more likely to be viewed as a credible signal of its intent. The irony lies in the fact that these are not the conditions in which either academic or policy communities are most likely to prescribe power sharing.

If a civil war ends with a clear winner, or is approaching a decisive victory, power sharing may be a prudent concession by the (impending) victor to facilitate the initiation of a peace process that avoids the final destructive stages of a "fight to the finish." The authors in this volume identify three closely related consequences of power sharing in the initiation of a transition from civil war: signaling, updating, and negotiating.

First, a majority's agreement to power sharing constitutes a signal that is somewhat more costly for it than simple cheap talk of its intent to treat other parties equitably. In particular, the preponderant parties can use power sharing to reassure weaker parties about their participation in decisionmaking after a negotiated settlement has ushered in peace—even if only a cold peace. As Valerie Bunce and Stephen Watts observe in Chapter 6, the experience of unitary postsocialist states shows that the offer of autonomy to minorities can help end ethnic conflicts, as it did in the Moldova-Gagauz and Ukraine-Crimea conflicts, even if this does not result in actual power sharing.

As Matthew Hoddie and Caroline Hartzell indicate in Chapter 4, fully 97 percent of the negotiated agreements to end civil wars since 1945 have involved promises of at least one of their four dimensions of power sharing: inclusion in the central executive, territorial decentralization, control and staffing of the armed forces, and allocation and control over fiscal resources. In particular, they find that commitments to territorial decentralization and to shared staffing and control of the armed forces strengthen the peace during the initial period after a settlement. These commitments provide greater assurances to the parties to the peace settlement—particularly to those likely to become minorities in the new political arrangements. With the insertion of power-sharing provisions in the peace agreement, the parties will feel more secure and less likely to fear exploitation at the hands of the new central government. In addition, Hoddie and Hartzell find that commitments in the initial settlement for balanced control over economic resources and for equitable governmental fiscal policies will increase the likelihood of timely democratic elections after the peace settlement. These economic provisions are costly signals by majorities to pursue equitable policies toward weaker parties following victory in democratic elections. Significantly, Hoddie and Hartzell find no strong relationship between provisions for power sharing within the central government and either the endurance of peace or the timeliness of democratic elections in the initial transition period after civil war. Hence, only some promises of power sharing can serve as costly signals by majorities about their intention to treat minorities equitably in the future.

Second, the period during which power-sharing arrangements are actually in place provides minorities with increased opportunities to analyze the propensity of the majority to abide by formal rules and not to abuse these at the expense of others. In South Africa, as Timothy Sisk and Christoph Stefes explain in Chapter 12, the transitional power-sharing arrangements gave the racial and ethnic groups a chance to observe the behavior of the African National Congress in power and to conclude that it would, indeed, abide by the rules of full democracy. In brief, it gave ethnic and racial minorities the opportunity to update their information about the ANC's commitment not to create a tyranny of the majority.

Third, the power-sharing framework increases the likelihood that the process of negotiating the institutional arrangements for the longer term will be inclusive and lead to institutional and policy outcomes that are acceptable to more ethnic communities. That is, an initial power-sharing arrangement can provide an environment, such as a constituent assembly and inclusive executive, in which parties can negotiate the shape of institutions for the longer term. (Although, as we discuss later in this chapter, the negotiations over a constitution should not be limited to the parties of the power-sharing arrangement.) As Sisk and Stefes note, the South African Government of National Unity provided leaders of the various racial and ethnic groups a role in the drafting of the new constitution, a document that included wide guarantees of civil rights of all South Africans.

Alternatively, if a civil war in an ethnically divided society ends without a clear victor, the resort to power sharing is likely to be imprudent, even though this may be the only institutional arrangement on which the parties can agree. Although power sharing permits parties to initiate a transition from civil war, new conflicts can be anticipated in the period that follows. New conflicts are particularly likely if power sharing permits all parties to keep alive a myth that they would ultimately have been victorious in the previous war and an expectation that during the peace and through the power-sharing institutions they can improve those chances of victory. Indeed, the terms of the power-sharing arrangements may themselves become objects of conflict almost immediately and delay or block the implementation of the accord. In Lebanon, as Marie-Joëlle Zahar observes in Chapter 9, the initiation of each power-sharing regime was accompanied by considerable shuffling for advantage among the parties. From 1860 to 1864 the Maronites held out for better terms in the power-sharing arrangement under the *Règlement Organique.* From 1920 to 1926 the communities jockeyed for privileges under the French Mandate, delaying adoption of a constitution. From 1989 to 1992 the parties sought to define the relative powers of institutions under the Ta'if Accord, prolonging the civil war by years.

Significantly, none of this points to the conclusion that imposition of power sharing by the international community is a prudent way to end a civil war. This is likely to keep alive incompatible myths and hopes of victory. In addition, if it is forced on a preponderant party, the minorities receive a clear signal that the majority is reluctant to make commitments that protect their interests. In these circumstances minorities are unlikely to see power-sharing institutions as guarantees of their rights.

Conditions Necessary for Consolidation after Civil Wars

Although the parties to a domestic conflict often demand power sharing as a condition for setting down their arms and demobilizing their forces, implementation of such arrangements may be particularly difficult because they create a special need for conditions that are unlikely to exist at the end of such conflicts. This is underscored by the fact that the models of successful power sharing—such as the Netherlands or Belgium—are societies that had not recently experienced civil war before the creation of power sharing. Moreover, the typical lists of power-sharing experiments show that there are few, if any, instances of successful consolidation of peace and democracy through power-sharing arrangements after conflicts such as civil wars. The chapters in this volume highlight two conditions that are essential to consolidation of peace and democracy through the power-sharing approach: an identity constraint and a resource constraint. First, a shared national identity is an important element in power-sharing cases that perform well. Where this condition prevails, ethnic elites are not competing national elites, cross-cutting issues divide citizens in different ways and lower the salience of ethnicity, and the issue of secession seldom surfaces. Second, in the successful cases, the state is strong in the sense that it is viewed as a legitimate authority possessing the capacity to enforce its responsibilities—chief among these being the preservation of national security from domestic challengers—and has an abundance of resources to cover the costs of duplicating administrations for different regions or ethnic groups. At the end of civil wars, however, competing nationalist challenges are often acute and state capacity and resources are limited.

The success of ethnic power sharing in India is particularly instructive because it underscores how unlikely it is that the circumstances that contributed to Indian stability will prevail after a deeply polarizing civil war. In Chapter 10 Ahmit Ahuja and Ashutosh Varshney stress the importance of a shared sense of nationhood, crosscutting cleavages, and the demographic given of ethnic fragmentation rather than bifurcation. In Chapter 12, Sisk and Stefes show that South Africa's successful experiment with power sharing as an interim arrangement on the route to majoritarian democracy confirms these findings. South Africans, whatever their racial and ethnic differences, shared a common sense of nationhood; few proposed dividing the country. South Africa's vibrant civil society was united by an overarching commitment to common values and purposes; although divided by multiple issues, these did not all accumulate around a single racial or ethnic chasm. This common sense of nationhood proved critical in smoothing the difficult transition to nonracial democracy and then, two years later, to a further transition from formal power sharing to majoritarian democracy, with extensive informal power sharing in politics and in civil society. Yet after civil wars, it is unlikely that a strong sense of national unity and crosscutting cleavages will prevail in ethnically divided societies. Indeed, civil wars are often linked to a desire to secede and to create new nation-states among ethnic or confessional groups. If crosscutting cleavages had existed prior to the civil war, as in former Yugoslavia, war itself is likely to destroy these ties across national lines.

These cases—particularly that of India—are also revealing because they underscore that successful institutional arrangements at the end of civil wars seek to avoid privileging the parties to the previous conflict and instead attempt to empower alternative and hopefully crosscutting cleavages. India has avoided introducing formal power sharing between the parties that produced one of the most divisive civil wars in recent history—that between Muslims and Hindus at the time of independence. India was unable to find an institutional arrangement to avoid partition at independence or to end the Muslim-Hindu conflict that has continued within post-independence India. Today there is no formal Hindu-Muslim power sharing in India's central executive, nor separate states for Muslims (except perhaps Jammu and Kashmir), nor proportional allocation of seats and funds for Muslims. Although Muslims account for about 12 percent of the population of India, they hold only 5.2 percent of the seats in the Lok Sabha (the lower chamber of parliament), occupy only about 3 percent of government and public-sector jobs, constitute less than 3 percent of the police and paramilitary forces, and receive only about 3.7 percent of available financial assistance.[1]

1. John Ward Anderson, "India's Muslims Fear New Physical Threat, Militant Hindu Nationalism, Discrimination Solidify Group's Sense of Alienation," *Washington Post* March 12, 1994, A16.

Instead, while avoiding empowering Muslim communities (or other religious communities such as the Sikhs) that might constitute alternative nation-states, power sharing in India has sought to accommodate subgroups within the Hindu-Indian nation. The one exception to this—Jammu and Kashmir—has been a continuing source of secessionist activity and violence. In short, ethnolinguistic power sharing in the India federation gives formal political status to identities that cut across the cleavages most likely to threaten India's unity.

Power sharing also typically demands expanded state capacity and resources at the very moment that resources have been depleted by a costly civil war. In Chapter 11, Edmond J. Keller and Lahra Smith's study of decentralization in Ethiopia underscores that in the conditions that typically prevail after a civil war, implementation of provisions for territorial decentralization are likely to overtax scarce resources. They note the scarcity of trained personnel, materiel, and funds throughout the country, the fiscal imbalance between the center and regions, and the inequalities among the regions themselves as obstacles to implementing decentralization. The effect of this scarcity, imbalance, and inequality is to complicate the achievement of the Ethiopian state's goals on equitable opportunity and development in the country as a whole. They find the gap between promise and reality to be particularly acute when it comes to implementing the state's educational plan. Keller and Smith attribute this failure largely to lack of trained administrative and educational personnel and to a resource-strapped country's inability to provide adequate subsidies to fund educational programs, particularly in the poorer regions.

Problems with Power Sharing in the Consolidation Phase

Even where the conditions for power sharing are present, the nation-state stewardship strategy warns that in the longer term power-sharing arrangements tend to be conflict creating, even increasing the possibility that civil war may resume. Power sharing can in fact become an obstacle to the consolidation of genuine democracy. The authors of chapters in this volume have highlighted three possible consequences of utilizing power-sharing institutions after civil wars: institutional instability, the escalation of conflict, and blocked transitions to democracy. First, power-sharing arrangements tend to be unstable. David A. Lake and Donald Rothchild in Chapter 5 question the longer-term viability of territorial decentralization, once the primary task has shifted from initiating a transition from civil war to consolidating the peace. They note that there are no examples of successful consolidation of peace following civil war with political decentralization along territorial lines as the defining principle. From the evidence of most nearly comparable cases—ethnically divided societies that had not necessarily experienced civil war—they find that over an extended time horizon territorial decentralization has not been stable. Rather it has tended toward either greater political centralization or political fragmentation. They explain the typical failure of territorial decentralization by three dilemmas they see as inherent in the institutional design and context: the governance problem that emerges when the institutions are insufficiently supported by society, the incompleteness of constitutions that requires some central agency to resolve disputes over rules, and the inability of majorities to credibly bind themselves not to seek recentralization once in power. Paradoxically, by failing to create more durable protections, the designers of power sharing that rely on territorial decentralization as the primary means to protect minority rights may leave these rights more vulnerable.

Second, power sharing does not reduce conflict and typically erodes peace in the longer term because it increases the incentives of ethnic leaders to escalate conflict. In Chapter 3 Philip G. Roeder argues that power sharing creates incentives for politicians to make more extreme demands on behalf of ethnic groups and to back these with more extreme forms of coercion. When a power-sharing arrangement is put in place at the end of a civil war, the leaders of the previously warring ethnic groups are brought into the new government and become the gatekeepers who decide on government policies. Anyone who wants to press a policy proposal through the central decisionmaking organs must frame the proposal in terms of the interests of an ethnic group and the interests of the empowered ethnic leaders. Thus, power sharing turns all policy issues into ethnic ones. Crosscutting issues that might moderate ethnic divisions are less likely to reach the bargaining table. Empowered ethnic leaders discourage appeals that might divide the members of their respective ethnic groups; they tend to look for divisive questions that will reinforce the unity of their own ethnic groups and their own privileged positions within them. Moreover, power sharing risks creating a contagion process among ethnic groups that widens conflicts. The escalation of conflict by one ethnic group at the expense of the central government must be matched by other ethnic groups. No ethnic group wants to be left behind as the sucker who upholds the agreement while other ethnic groups secure a larger and larger share of state benefits. As a consequence, power sharing can unravel through a domino effect of cascading defections.

In addition to the incentive for more extreme demands, power sharing increases the incentives for ethnic leaders to back these demands by escalating conflict to more destructive levels of coercion. By giving the separate ethnic leaders parts of the government, power sharing leads to a concentration of institutional weapons in the hands of the parties to the agreement. This can at times involve giving ethnic groups their own autonomous regions or their own armed forces. The effect is to provide ethnic groups with institutional weapons they can use to coerce the central government. Power sharing may attempt to create a balance of power between the leaders of the central government and the leaders of the ethnic groups. As a solution to the credible commitment problem, this is supposed to assure the ethnic groups that they will not be brutalized by the central government once they have surrendered their arms. Yet the institutional weapons in the hands of ethnic leaders also increase the likelihood that they will conclude that they can prevail over the central government should any escalation of conflict occur. Indeed, this type of balance of power system, as Robert Harrison Wagner (1993, 261) contends, keeps "the peace . . . as fragile at the domestic level as at the international one, since many things can happen that will lead antagonists to expect a more favorable outcome from the attempted use of force."

Moreover, power sharing may create new, intense conflicts at all levels of the state. Bunce and Watts find that in communist states ethnofederalism fed conflicts between titular nationalities and their minorities within the constituent republics and only continual intervention from the center to restrain these titular nationalities contained predatory policies by local majorities. Similarly, Keller and Smith find that in Ethiopia the attempt to implement a federal arrangement for education led to new conflicts within states between the locally preponderant majority and local minorities.

Third, power-sharing institutions hinder the consolidation of democracy. Bunce and Watts in Chapter 6 conclude from their analysis of transitions from communism in ethnically divided societies that initiating a transition to democracy with ethnofederal institutions is an inauspicious beginning. These institutions leave the new states much weaker than unitary states because they create microstates and regimes in the constituent autonomies. These constituent states are more prone to conflict, not only between the autonomies and the central government but also between the titular nation of each autonomous unit and their own minorities. Their democratic orders are compromised from the beginning and therefore prove fragile over time.

Benjamin Reilly (Chapter 7) finds a correlation between executive inclusiveness and the consolidation of democracy in ethnically divided societies, but he questions the claims of the power-sharing school about the impact of proportional electoral systems on democratic outcomes. He notes that in ethnically divided societies majoritarian electoral systems, such as plurality elections in single-member districts, are just as likely to lead to inclusive executives and just as likely to be associated with the successful consolidation of democracy. Indeed, in ethnically divided societies that have also been stable democracies, Reilly finds that slightly more than half have had majoritarian rather than proportional electoral systems.

This begs the question: What does power sharing guarantee over the longer term if not peace and democracy? Zahar's study of one of the longest experiments with power sharing suggests an important insight. This arrangement did not save Lebanon from devastating civil war nor did it move Lebanon closer to its professed objective of a nonconfessional democracy. Power sharing, an agreement among ethnic elites to contain political conflict, has instead been most effective at maintaining the political cartel against its challengers. Power sharing has proved to be an institutional arrangement in which an elite has held on to power and resisted democracy.

Dilemmas of International Interventions and Protectorates

The problems that can hinder the implementation of power sharing and the extraordinary conditions necessary for its success have led many analysts in recent years to contend that power sharing requires external protectors in order to provide stability after civil wars (Walter 2002). Yet these interventions on behalf of power sharing do not eliminate its dilemmas and may both exacerbate these and introduce new dilemmas.

External protectors can provide creative support for the initiation of power-sharing arrangements where local parties share common values and look to the external protector to help overcome problems of limited information and credible commitment (Lake and Rothchild 1998). In Northern Ireland, for example, as the Mitchell Report (1996) noted, "the vast majority of the people of both traditions want[ed] to turn away from the bitter past." Nevertheless, it was difficult to overcome the antagonisms of the past and reach across the "peace line" without securing a commitment from the Irish and British governments to protect the internal relationship. Consequently, the provisions in the 1998 Northern Ireland Peace Agreement firmly linking the two external powers to the internal peace process demonstrate a valuable role for outside protectors in initiating a transition to peace.

The evidence in this volume, however, leads us to conclude that intervention of outside powers does not eliminate the longer-term problems of power sharing and may actually further inhibit developments that can lead from power-sharing arrangements to viable institutions for the consolidation of peace and democracy. That is, intervention exacerbates many of the dilemmas of power sharing. In addition, it introduces four new problems that can thwart the consolidation of stable peace and democracy—problems associated with signaling, the temptation to recentralize, the perception of partisanship by the protectors, and the transition from protectorate to full independence. First, during the protectorate each party finds it harder to signal its own commitment to observe the rules and to assess the commitments of others. Everyone knows that during this protectorate compliance by the previously warring parties is contingent on the threats and promises of the protector. Second, protectors may increase the natural instability of power sharing. Growing impatient with the politics of power sharing, the protectors may press for the recentralization of power. This in turn can fuel more intense resistance from the minorities empowered by the power-sharing arrangement. Third, the parties likely to intervene in conflicts are those with partisan attachment to one side or the other, and this increases the likelihood that the parties will see the arrangements themselves as biased. For example, in Lebanon the external protectors have privileged first the Maronites and then the Sunnis, causing dissatisfaction to grow in the other communities. Fourth, once the protectors withdraw, the aggrieved parties see new opportunities to undo the inequitable arrangements of the protectorate. In a sense the external powers serve as hegemons who enforce a set of rules and bring peace to the power-sharing system. Yet, as the theories of hegemonic stability and the power transition underscore (Organski 1968; Modelski and Thompson 1989), the decline or withdrawal of a hegemon and the rise of challengers who seek to impose a new hegemony can lead to extraordinary violence. The stability of power sharing becomes hostage to the changing interests of the outside powers. Zahar finds that Lebanon's 140-year experiment with power sharing brought peace when Ottoman, French, and Syrian protectors have been willing to maintain order, but destructive conflicts have accompanied transitions when one protector withdrew and another attempted to establish its predominance.

The recent experiments with international interventions in the conflicts of ethnically divided societies, and with international protectorates to make power-sharing arrangements work after these conflicts, are of such short duration that the authors in this volume have had to turn to most nearly comparable cases for insights into the longer-term consequences of power sharing in ethnically divided societies. Of course, this begs the question whether these findings are relevant to problems of ethnically divided societies after civil wars and whether they are relevant to international interventions and protectorates to induce regime change. Thus, as a plausibility probe, we use these lessons to see whether the consequences identified in previous chapters are beginning to manifest themselves in the recent power-sharing experiments after civil wars. At the moment the authors in this volume were completing their investigations, the international community maintained four ongoing power-sharing settlements under international trusteeship (Table 13.1). The longest-standing experiment with power sharing after a civil war is the General Framework Agreement for Peace in Bosnia and Herzegovina signed on November 21, 1995, in Dayton Ohio. This was followed in 2001 by three arrangements in Kosovo, Macedonia, and Afghanistan. The U.S. experiment with regime change in Iraq could be added to this list, but, since the broad outlines of its institutions were just emerging at the time this writing concluded, we have excluded this. Similarly, the implementation of experiments with power

Table 13.1. Power-sharing agreements after civil wars, 1995–2001

Conflict	Common name	Official title	Date
Bosnia	"Dayton Agreement"	General Framework Agreement for Peace in Bosnia and Herzegovina	November 21, 1995
Kosovo	"Constitutional Framework"	Constitutional Framework for Provisional Self-Government in Kosovo	May 15, 2001
Macedonia	"Ohrid Agreement"	Framework Agreement	August 13, 2001
Afghanistan	"Bonn Agreement"	Agreement on Provisional Arrangements in Afghanistan Pending the Re-Establishment of Permanent Government Institutions	December 22, 2001

sharing in a number of African countries such as Burundi and Sudan seemed too uncertain to be included at that time.

Seeking the immediate payoff of an end to the civil war in Bosnia, the international community seized on power sharing as a foundation for constructing a new state. The Dayton Agreement creates in Bosnia a classic power-sharing arrangement with inclusive and partitioned decisionmaking. According to the Agreement extensive territorial autonomy gives broad decisionmaking powers to the municipalities and the two Entities—the Federation of Bosnia and Herzegovina (for Bosniaks and Croats) and the Republika Srpska (for the Serbs). The central Bosnia-wide institutions—including the collective presidency, cabinet, and parliament—balance representation among the three major ethnic communities. Many contend that this was the only institutional arrangement that could have ended the civil war on terms that would keep Bosnia whole. Yet it has proved to be a fragile basis for state building (Ni Aolain 2001, 63).

In Kosovo the Constitutional Framework inaugurated on May 15, 2001, created a power-sharing arrangement. It promised elections to a 120-member Assembly that would guarantee inclusiveness through an electoral formula of proportional representation applied in a single 100-seat, Kosovo-wide constituency. An additional 10 seats were reserved for Serbs and another 10 seats were reserved for Kosovo's other minorities (Rom, Ashkali, Egyptian, Bosniak, Turk, and Gorani). A seven-member presidency of the Assembly balances the three largest (Albanian) political parties and also guarantees the Serbs one seat and the other minorities one seat (to rotate among these smaller groups). The government must include at least one Serb and one other minority in ministerial positions. None of the Kosovo participants agreed to these institutions in the negotiations; they were imposed by the Special Representative of the Secretary General, Hans Haekkerup, who headed the United Nations Interim Administration in Kosovo (UNMIK) (Allin 2002, 74–75; Chesterman 2001).

In Macedonia, the Ohrid Agreement signed on August 13, 2001, under intense pressure from the former French Minister of Defense François Léotard and U.S. Ambassador James Pardew, brought to an end the brief civil war. As a power-sharing arrangement, the agreement gives Macedonian and Albanian representatives mutual vetoes on all legislation of cultural or linguistic significance; such legislation requires a two-thirds majority in parliament plus a majority of the affected minority's representatives. It also guarantees proportionate appointments in administration and the police force (ICG 2001b). In addition, it promised future legislation that would grant territorial autonomy to the Albanian population within Macedonia.

In creating a postconflict government for Afghanistan, the Bonn Agreement, negotiated on December 22, 2001, left the creation of an Afghanistan Transitional Administration (ATA) until a Loya Jirga (Afghan Grand Assembly) could be assembled in six-months time—actually convened June 10–21, 2002. The Bonn Agreement planned that the Loya Jirga would lead to an interim arrangement until national elections could be called sometime before mid-2004. In fact, the implementation of the Bonn Agreement left most details to the secret negotiations within the ATA, with the Loya Jirga limited to formalistic ratification. Within the ATA, President Hamid Karzai developed a power-sharing arrangement: In Kabul his five vice presidents each represent one of the major ethnic groups, and outside Kabul regional warlords are left broad autonomy within their domains (Saikal 2002, 51).

Even in the initial months of these experiments, the problems associated with the dilemma of power sharing became evident—notably, the consolidation of political monopolies by the parties to the power-sharing arrangements, the exclusion of moderates and crosscutting interests from the political process, and the concentration of institutional weapons that permitted these local leaders to resist the central government. In Bosnia, leaders of the Serb, Croat, and Bosniak microstates were given the power to maintain separate armies, police forces, and judiciaries (Malik 2000). For example, by 1999 fully 93.7 percent of the police officers and 97.6 percent of the judges and prosecutors in the Republika Srpska were Serbs (ICG 2002a, 4; 2002b). They created separate administrations, including separate police forces, not only in the ethnically distinct regions but also in mixed areas (Okuizumi 2002, 731–732). In their respective cantons and even in such multiethnic districts as Brčko Bosnians, Croats, and Serbs maintained "three separate administrations, health care and education systems, pension systems, payment bureaus, and police forces" (Lyon 2000, 112; ICG 2002c, 6). Both police and judges routinely manifested bias in the enforcement of the law. Local ethnic elites discouraged moderation and opposition from within their communities: They intimidated voters so as to deter them from supporting opposition parties—particularly those making cross-ethnic appeals. As a consequence, in Bosnia's local elections in 1997, nationalist parties garnered 90 percent of the vote and fully 96 percent in the Republika Srpska (Pugh and Cobble 2001, 30, 34). International assistance funneled through the new power-sharing institutions enabled nationalist elites at Entity and local levels to tighten their grip on their communities. Roberto Belloni (2001, 173) noted that "by fostering community isolation, mobilization, and a general feeling of insecurity, ethnic elites legitimize each other and maintain a tight grip on their constituencies." And, as in other power-sharing systems, the empowered ethnic elites used their institutional weapons to weaken the common state (Malik 2000, 313). Andrea Kathryn Talentino (2002, 34) observed that at the all-Bosnia level "there is a structure of government but little interest in making it work, not least of all because those who control the entities prefer running them as fiefdoms rather than as subordinate units of a national whole."

During the short life of the Macedonian and Afghanistani accords, the problems associated with the dilemma of power sharing also began to emerge. In Macedonia, as the International Crisis Group ([IGG] 2002e, i, 3) warned, the Framework Agreement "invites outright collusion between ethnic leaders to heighten tensions and plays a substantial role in making the country ripe for conflict." "[I]nstead of attenuating ethnic differences through shared government, Macedonia's ruling parties have functioned as corrupt coalitions, dividing the turf among and within ministries and even on the ground for separate exploitation. The division of 'turf' functions as a rehearsal for division of territory as politicians cynically present themselves as defenders of the national interest while in fact conspiring with the other side for personal or party enrichment."

In Afghanistan the "light footprint" approach of Lakhdar Brahimi, the special representative of the Secretary General, created a personalistic form of power sharing that closely resembled hegemonic exchange (Rothchild 1997). In Kabul this emphasized relationships among personalities, such as Brahimi, Karzai, and the co-opted warlords, but made for a fragile regime and blocked the institutionalization of politics (Chesterman 2002, 40). Karzai's plan for creating a strong central government rallied support among Pashtuns, but this led to a confrontation with non-Pashtun delegates at the Loya Jirga and contributed to a divide within the government that continues to polarize politics along ethnic lines (ICG 2004b, 8).[2] Outside Kabul this personalistic power sharing left in place and strengthened the hand of regional warlords such as Amanullah Khan and Ismail Khan in the West, Gul Aqa in the South, Abdul Rashid Dostum in the North, Karim Khalili in the Center, and Muhammad Fahim in the Northeast. Their autonomy permitted the warlords to monopolize many of the rent-seeking opportunities

2. Amy Waldman, "Afghan Strife Exposes Deep and Wide Ethnic Tensions," *New York Times* September 6, 2004, A3.

within the Afghanistani state, such as customs posts, that funded their fiefdoms within the state at the expense of any imagined Afghan community. They stood in the way of institutions that would have been more supportive of sustainable peace and democracy. As Gordon Peake (2003, 190) observed about these warlords, "Few in the current crop of leaders appear to possess the basic skills of management required to help chaperone a shattered country. Well-versed in conflict and schooled in the politics of patronage and local networks, they have demonstrated little aptitude for the challenge of administration. With the ascendancy to leadership remaining tied to military deeds, other avenues that sometimes produce potential leaders, such as academia and business, remain essentially closed off." The warlords used their power to exercise leverage over decisions taken in Kabul. For example, they pressured the Loya Jirga Commission to pack the membership of the Loya Jirga itself with unelected delegates beholden to the warlords. The warlords' intimidation of delegates during the Loya Jirga sessions prevented the delegates from taking decisions that would limit warlord power (ICG 2002d, 1–3).

The identity and resource constraints on power sharing were also apparent in the recent experiments with internationally imposed power sharing—particularly in Bosnia. In the absence of a commitment to a common state, power sharing led to perverse political outcomes; this lack of commitment plus the limited resource base made Bosnia, Kosovo, and Afghanistan virtual dependencies of the international community. In Bosnia power sharing not only failed to paper over the absence of a shared sense of nationhood that could unite Bosniaks, Croats, and Serbs but also fostered the growth of separate extreme nationalisms. Ironically, the power-sharing arrangement seems to have paved the way for future partition by permitting consolidation of ethnically pure microstates under ethnic leaders (Malik 2000). The power-sharing institutions created a hothouse that kept alive and fostered Croat and Serb extremism within Bosnia at the very time radical nationalists were losing power in neighboring Serbia and Croatia (Chandler 2001, 114). Making this complex system work also proved to be expensive—well beyond the resources of the Bosnian peoples themselves—and only massive infusions of outside funds made it affordable. The duplication of parallel services was particularly expensive; indeed, maintaining three separate armed forces consumed about 40 percent of Bosnia's total public spending (Farkas 2001, 6). Estimates placed donor aid as high as one-third of Bosnia's gross domestic product and more than four times the per capita allotments of the Marshall Plan to Europe at the end of World War II (measured in constant prices) (Lyon 2000, 111; Belloni 2001, 164).

The recent experiments with internationally imposed power sharing also illustrate the ways in which international protectors may exacerbate the dilemmas of power sharing and introduce new dilemmas that thwart the consolidation of peace and democracy through power-sharing institutions. As a consequence, while the outside protectors have been indispensable in preserving the immediate peace, few expect that withdrawal anytime soon will leave behind an enduring peace. In Bosnia, for example, the survival of the shaky arrangement "depended upon a continuing level of international commitment that was . . . unlikely to be sustained" (Cousens 2002, 543).

International protectors have exacerbated the tendency toward recentralization and the resort to autocratic means as an antidote to the pressures for fragmentation, but this has in turn fueled stronger pressures for fragmentation. In Bosnia with each frustration over the deadlock in Bosnia's central, interethnic institutions and the immoderate policies of its Entities, the powers of the Office of the High Representative (OHR) grew. The Peace Implementation Council at its December 1997 Bonn meeting gave the OHR authority to impose laws where the local officials resisted reforms. In the next four years the OHR used its "Bonn powers" on over 100 occasions (Caplan 2002, 43). As a consequence, effective decisionmaking seldom took place within the institutions of the Bosnian, Entity, or local governments (Belloni 2001, 172; ICG 2003). For example, according to David Chandler (2001, 117), from the end of 1997 to early 2001 "not one law placed before the Bosnia Parliamentary Assembly has been drafted and ratified by Bosnia representatives themselves." Even the decisions to adopt a common license plate, flag, and currency had to be imposed on the collective Bosnian Presidency by the OHR (Farkas 2001, 12). Laws were often designed by experts from the Organization for Security and Cooperation in Europe (OSCE) and promulgated by the OHR. In hopes of consolidating the peace and making the Dayton Agreement work, the OHR intervened to remove immoderate nationalists from office. From March 1998 until early 2002, the OHR "dismissed, suspended, or banned from public office over 70 elected officials" at all levels (Caplan 2002, 44). On behalf of the stated objectives of "transparency, objectivity, and fairness" in the media (Talentino 2002, 37), the OHR with the aid of the Independent Media Commission silenced radical newspapers and broadcast outlets and sponsored journalists with a more moderate message.

These initiatives heightened the tension between international pressure for recentralization and minority pressures toward fragmentation. In Bosnia this tension was exemplified by the directing role of the OHR and the resistance at every step from the Entity governments regarding a July 2000 Constitutional Court decision. The Court ordered a change in the wording of the constitutions and legislation of the Entities so as to give all three "constituent peoples" co-equal status in both Entities. Yet, the narrow five-to-four decision of the Court resulted only because the three foreign justices from the international community sided with the two Bosniak justices against the two Croat and two Serb justices. The six-month delay as the Entity governments dragged their feet in implementing these decisions led the OHR to constitute new, interim constitutional commissions to draft amendments. When these Entity commissions could not draft so-called symmetrical amendments, the OHR brought the major parties' representatives to Sarajevo and, under explicit threat of sanctions from Western ambassadors, forced an agreement on the Entity representatives to make parallel changes in their laws. Yet, on returning to Banja Luka the Republika Srpska leaders at first refused to present the agreements to the Entity's National Assembly. After further international pressure, the Serbian Assembly brought the Constitutional Commission's proposals up for a vote, but rejected the agreements and adopted instead a new set of amendments prepared by 68 Serb delegates (ICG 2002a). In response the government of the Bosniak-Croat federation threatened to withdraw from the Sarajevo agreement because the Serbian amendments were not consistent with the agreement.

This recentralization made the international community a partisan in the inter- and intraethnic struggles associated with power sharing and this has undermined the legitimacy of these institutions. In Bosnia the OHR was clearly a partisan of the Bosniaks against Croats and Serbs and of moderate Croats and Serbs against extreme nationalists within those communities. International meddling, such as removing radical-nationalist incumbents and barring them from seeking office, ensured that moderates did better in the 2000 elections than previously (Chandler 2001, 117). Yet this moderation did not develop from within the communities, and international intervention on their behalf may have tainted the moderates as "collaborationists" who betrayed their peoples. Following the November 2000 elections, the OHR sponsored creation of the ten-party governing coalition known as the Democratic Alliance for Change to replace the radical nationalists in the Bosniak-Croat federation (ICG 2002c). Yet the intervention left behind festering resentment among segments of all communities that this moderation was engineered by outside manipulations that simply took sides in intra- and interethnic conflicts. It did not augur well for moderation once the protectorate was removed (Chandler 2000; 2001). Indeed, the October 2002 elections in Bosnia—touted as the first under indigenous administration—returned the nationalists to power at all levels, turning out many of the more moderate parties patronized by the international community.

Even in the much shorter history of the Kosovar, Macedonian, and Afghanistani power-sharing arrangements, the international community had to play a guiding role to make power sharing work, but in doing so it made the institutions and the international community's role appear to be partisan. In Kosovo just prior to the November 2001 elections a survey revealed that only 7.3 percent of Serb respondents thought that UNMIK treats Albanians and Serbs equally (ICG 2002f, II, 17). In Macedonia the power-sharing arrangements contained in the Framework Agreements signed at

Ohrid became highly partisan: Macedonians saw these as an imposition that favored Albanians (ICG 2002e). In Afghanistan, despite the commitment to a "light footprint" approach that was supposed to leave to the Afghans the leading role in rebuilding their country, the United States exercised a heavy hand in the partisan battles among the parties to the interim power-sharing arrangements. The U.S. decision to invite Karzai to speak at the Bonn meeting and the strong pressure from President George Bush's personal representative Zalmay Khalilzad that induced former king Mohammed Zahir Shah to withdraw in favor of Karzai influenced the choice of an interim president (Chesterman 2002; ICG 2002d, 3). Outside Kabul, according to Amin Saikal (2002, 50), "the dangers of fragmentation have been heightened by the US tactic of arming and otherwise supporting various strongmen for the purpose of hunting down Taliban and al-Qaeda remnants." The U.S. government foreclosed the option of appearing to be an honest broker and diminished the sense among Afghans that they had been empowered to select their own leaders through the institutions being crafted by the transitional or interim authority.

Mounting frustrations with these power-sharing arrangements have led many in governmental, intergovernmental, and nongovernmental communities to urge their governments to bypass power-sharing institutions and rule these regions more directly (ICG 2002a). In Kosovo foreign intervention plus power sharing have not moved the region closer to a multiethic society, and so increasingly Europeans talk of a long-term international protectorate for the region (e.g., Chesterman 2001; USIP 2001, 6–7). After the outbreak of ethnic cleansing on March 17, 2004, European representatives responsible for Kosovo increasingly acknowledged that four and a half years of attempting to establish power-sharing institutions had resulted in a "collapse in Kosovo" (ICG 2004a). Yet imposing solutions by fiat and restricting free speech undermined the legitimacy of these institutions and thwarted evolution toward self-governance and democracy (Caplan 2002, 54–60).

The Tactics of Stewardship

The nation-state stewardship strategy is a conclusion drawn from the investigations in previous chapters that seems to be borne out by these recent experiences in the Balkans and Afghanistan: When the international community chooses to intervene in the conflicts of ethnically divided societies or to induce regime change in these societies it should eschew power sharing and implement policies that emphasize a power-dividing approach to institution-building. The choice of specific tactics in this larger strategy will depend on the outcome of the civil war (that is, whether there is a victor and preponderant party), the objectives of the ethnic groups in fighting the civil war (that is, whether the issue of contention was secession and division of the existing state), and the willingness of outside parties to assume the long-term role of protector to oversee the establishment of viable institutions. The strategy is a complement and corrective to those studies of state building, nation building, and regime change that focus almost exclusively on the configuration of armed forces or the extent of economic assistance (compare Dobbins 2003–2004). The tasks of building states, nations, and democracies are first of all about politics and to an important extent about getting political institutions right. Nine policy implications follow from the analysis in previous chapters that we group under the three rubrics of objectives, form and timeline, and institutional legacies of stewardship.

Objectives of Stewardship

Our first two points concern the broader vision of what the international community seeks to achieve through the institutions it fosters after intense domestic conflicts in ethnically divided societies such as civil wars.

1. Constituting nation-states. After civil wars in ethnically divided societies, the international community should seek to create new states (such as Bosnia) or to hold together existing states (such as Macedonia) so that the parties in the state share a common sense of nationhood. That is, at a minimum the parties must agree to coexist within a common state. This shared sense of nationhood has been prominent in the success of democracy in ethnically divided societies such as India (Ahuja and Varshney, Chapter 10), South Africa (Sisk and Stefes, Chapter 12), and many unitary postcommunist states (Bunce and Watts, Chapter 6) (also see Roeder 1999). The international community must determine before it intervenes whether a viable nation exists that can sustain a state, and it should make its objective clear at the outset to keep or divide the existing state. In Kosovo, as Alexandros Yannis (2001) warns, the failure to address the issue of the future status of Kosovo is counterproductive because it leaves the Serbs and Albanians living within that state to work toward radically different objectives.

Thus the choice whether to foster existing states or to partition them is constrained by the basic objectives of parties in the previous conflict. Seeking to keep an existing state united after a civil war is a viable strategy when the ethnic groups share a commitment to a common state. In Angola and Mozambique, for example, the rebels did not seek secession, but sought greater power within the central government of the state. The same is also true in the Democratic Republic of the Congo during the conflict that sporadically ravaged that country after August 1998. Alternatively, maintenance of states is less likely to be a viable strategy for enduring peace and democracy after a civil war when one or the other ethnic group has raised the issue of secession. This is illustrated poignantly by the attempts to hold together Bosnia and to hold together Serbia-Kosovo-Montenegro. In the latter circumstances, partition of the parties into separate, independent, defensible states is often a better option. Each party can establish effective governance within its respective borders and forge its own ties to the international community of states. The raised costs involved in dividing existing states—in terms of population transfers, refugees, administrative and policing costs, and subsequent internationalized tensions—must, of course, be added to this calculation. Yet as the recent experience of the international community overseeing the separation of East Timor from Indonesia shows, partition can be managed so as to reduce levels of conflict and avoid extreme dislocations. Moreover, the costs of continuing association can be extremely high, and partition can be preferable to the uncertainty of living together in the same state.

2. *Limiting government.* The strategy of nation-state stewardship advises that in the establishment of central government organs, these must represent what is common to all parties and what constitutes the basis of nation-statehood, rather than simply a concatenation of the parts of the ethnically fragmented society. After a civil war, this means limiting the state and trusting to civil society and to private initiative in those areas that deeply divide the previously warring parties. The commonality among the individuals and groups that constitute the citizenry may be only a consensus that they should remain together in a single state that maintains domestic law and order and defends them against foreign enemies—a modern night-watchman state—but the central government should constitute both a symbolic and real representation of this consensus that citizens of all ethnic groups share in common. Sisk and Stefes' chapter on South Africa, Ahuja and Varshney's study of India, and Bunce and Watts' analysis of postcommunist states all link success in maintaining peace and democracy in ethnically divided societies to an effective central government that expresses and enforces at least this minimal basis for unity. In short, the strategy of nation-state stewardship advises that if the interethnic consensus that supports a common state is limited, then the reach of its government should be similarly limited.

Form and Timeline of Stewardship

Points three through six concern the form and timing of various interventions by the international community. Taken together these points underscore that foreign powers should be cautious and selective when deciding whether to intervene because both intervening too early and intervening with the expectation of withdrawing quickly can lead to longer-term problems.

3. Delaying intervention. If state builders are to be in a position to avoid power-sharing outcomes, it is often necessary to delay intervention until there is a clear sense who is likely to emerge victorious. The earlier the intervention, the less likely there is to be agreement among the parties about the likely winner. And the earlier the intervention, the more likely it is that the only agreement that will bring an end to the conflict will include formal power sharing that freezes the stalemate and the uncertainty about the outcome of a future contest of arms. Premature intervention plus power sharing may bring short-term relief from the violence, but it also increases the likelihood of more costly conflict—and even violence—in the long run. The evidence is strong that peace is more durable when one party is victorious, the parties do not need to resort to power sharing, and the parties can clearly foresee the outcome of a resumption of violence (Licklider 1995; Wagner 1993).

This advice, of course, emphasizes long-term benefits that sometimes may be gained only by accepting short-term costs. This stresses consolidating peace and democracy for the long term, yet the short-term loss of lives and property must be brought into the equation. This is not an easy calculation: On one hand, state builders must weigh the probability, expected intensity, and expected duration of continuing violence in the current conflict. These costs are immediate and easily imagined. On the other hand, state builders must weigh the probability, expected intensity, and expected duration of violence following power sharing, but these costs are more remote and much harder to estimate. Certainly there are circumstances in which the expected loss of life in the short term is so overwhelming that intervention without consideration for the longer-term consequences may be necessary. The nation-state stewardship strategy introduces an important caveat: Leaders and diplomats considering intervention in these unhappy circumstances must recognize that if immediate intervention necessitates power-sharing institutions, then compared to circumstances in which it would be possible to establish power-dividing institutions, the likelihood of recurrence of violence will be higher, the time until it recurs will probably be shorter, the violence is likely to be more intense, and the duration of the subsequent conflict is likely to be longer. These longer-term costs should not be ignored or wished away in a rush to intervene armed with the hope that power sharing will secure the peace.

4. Lengthening protectorates. Stewardship should be a long-term commitment because establishing durable democratic institutions in ethnically divided societies recently torn by conflicts is seldom completed quickly. As a review of America's experiments at nation building from 1945 to 2003 concluded, "the record suggests that, while staying for a long time does not guarantee success, leaving early ensures failure" (Dobbins 2003–2004, 103). For this reason, intervention should be avoided unless the external powers are willing to sustain a protectorate likely to last a decade or more. External protectors simplify the initiation of a transition from civil war, but, if they intend to stay only for the initial period, their presence may complicate the longer-term problems of consolidating peace and democracy. The incentives of parties to comply with the norms of the new institutions and the credibility of their commitments to abide by these norms in the early phases of implementation all remain contingent on the presence of the protector. The external party's withdrawal changes these incentives and anticipation of imminent withdrawal reduces the parties' incentives to compromise in the short run. In Bosnia, for example, President William Clinton's promise that U.S. soldiers would leave Bosnia after 12 months made voters more likely to cast their ballots for nationalists who would protect them and made Serbian politicians less inclined to compromise with the international authorities (Allin 2002, 40; Caplan 2002, 41). Conversely, intervening powers should be committed to remaining to oversee the transition to a locally negotiated form of democracy and into the period of consolidation. A longer-term commitment permits individual members of the separate communities to break ranks with the nationalist leaders without fearing retribution from either the nationalists or members of other communities in the near future. The lengthy commitment of the British and Irish governments in Northern Ireland to see the peace process through various institutional experiments, failures, and renewed efforts is both exemplary and cautionary. Yet this must also be a commitment to use the period of the protectorate to press the parties to move beyond the initial arrangements to a functioning democracy. The history of Lebanon is sad testimonial to the ways that 140 years of protectorates that simply replicated virtually the same power-sharing arrangement and failed to press Lebanese leaders closer to their stated goal of a nonconfessional democracy did not produce either durable peace or democracy.

5. *Building from the ground up.* Where the parties to a civil war cannot agree to a common integral state, but demand power sharing, then the institution-building strategy of the international stewards should delay creation of central governing institutions, should rule from the center, and should begin by building lower-level institutions of self-governance. Each lower-level institution should be limited both geographically and functionally—such as local school boards, water-district boards, and infrastructure development boards. Each local authority should be independent of the

others, have its own constituency of voters, possess only limited jurisdiction, and make decisions by simple majority votes. In the larger strategy of nation-state stewardship these become vested interests in creating a political order that represents these crosscutting interests and multiple majorities and therefore become the building blocks for a future divided-power state.

This is a heavy hand rather than a "light footprint." It recognizes the reality of international interventions so far and seeks to avoid jeopardizing the longer-term viability of the central institutions of governance by constant, short-term meddling in their operations. The proposed strategy of nation-state stewardship, unlike the light footprint approach practiced in Afghanistan, would delay creation of central organs for long-term governance and would seek to prevent the parties to the previous conflict from creating regionally dominant governing institutions on the periphery. The actions of Karzai as leader of the interim and then the transitional authority limited the possibilities of institutional development at each step. The "light footprint" left local warlords to create local monopolies that will be destructive to the long-term stability of society. That is, the Bonn Agreement sought to remedy one of the key problems of the Dayton Agreement by creating an ongoing process of negotiations among indigenous political actors rather than locking in national institutions. But by failing to empower new actors in many independent political centers, it simply handed over the task of establishing these institutions to many of the players who brought about the previous civil war. A similar dilemma would have materialized in Somalia had the UN's strategy of accommodating the country's 14 militia leaders become the basis for an elite pact in 1993 (Lyons and Samatar 1995, 44–47).

6. *Phasing withdrawal.* The strategy of nation-state stewardship advises that withdrawal of an international protectorate should be phased so as to coordinate with the tactics of institution-building from the ground up in individual functional areas. As local institutions of self-governance take hold, and then as central governing institutions begin to function, the protectorate can devolve step-by-step more responsibilities onto these and reduce its profile. In the end the protectorate may leave no troops or administrators but keep in place a commitment to protect the democracy against its enemies with future interventions.

Institutional Legacies of Stewardship

The final three tactics of the strategy of nation-state stewardship for ethnically divided societies after intense conflicts such as civil wars concern the institutions of governance.

7. *Dividing power.* The institutions created for the longer-term governance of these postconflict societies should not reproduce and reinforce the ethnic divisions that previously gave rise to the civil war—as power sharing typically does. For example, South Africa's stability since 1996 is a consequence of a regime that does not privilege racial or ethnic divisions within politics. It is a regime that extends broad civil rights of association, expression, and participation to all groups without giving precedence to the parties of the previous conflict. It multiplies the arenas in which decisions are taken, and differences are defined so that many minor cleavages—not one overarching divide—are manifest in politics. This outcome can be encouraged by careful institutional design in a strategy of power dividing rather than power sharing.

The power-dividing strategy lowers the ethnic stakes in politics by taking the most divisive cultural or identity issues out of the hands of government and entrusting these to civil society. As we discussed in the section on the objectives of stewardship, leaders in ethnically divided societies must rediscover the virtues of limited government. Only this will make politics less all-consuming and possibly less zero-sum in nature. So, for example, if the educational curriculum is so divisive in an ethnically divided society that it threatens to tear the political system apart, then the basic law may take the government out of the business of prescribing curriculum. In these circumstances vouchers that permit individual families to purchase education in the marketplace may prove a better solution.

Power dividing protects the rights of ethnic and other cultural minorities with civil rights that aggrieved individuals can enforce against one another and against government officials through legal action in the courts. The rights enjoyed by members of cultural minorities must be identical to those enjoyed by members of the cultural majority and must be enforceable through individual and class-action suits. In addition, the rights possessed by ethnic minorities must also be identical to the rights enjoyed by other types of majorities and minorities in civil society—such as the professions, labor, management, women's groups, students' associations, and so forth—so that ethnicity is not privileged as a basis for political participation. In the context of ethnically divided societies a major purpose of homogeneous individual civil rights is to encourage the proliferation of interests and, particularly, interests that cross ethnic groups in defense of civil rights. In these conditions, subgroups within the ethnic majority are more likely to jump to the defense of the rights of ethnic minorities to defend the rights they share in common.

Power dividing accepts democracy as rule by the majority but seeks to facilitate the emergence of multiple, alternative majorities. Insofar as political institutions can shape the types of political cleavages that emerge in society, power-dividing institutions seek to avoid privileging the ethnic cleavage above all others and to encourage the development of crosscutting social cleavages. Power dividing disperses political power among a variety of political institutions at the national and subnational levels and empowers different majorities within each. Thus, power dividing encourages fencing off the executive from the legislative branch and separating legislative chambers one from another. But this is not to engage in the sterile debate between advocates of presidentialism and parliamentarism; it is an argument for the actual dispersion of powers. From this perspective, where presidentialism leads to concentration of powers in a superpresidency, it is less desirable than the fused powers of parliamentarism; however, where, in ethnically divided societies, presidentialism leads to real separation of powers and significant checks and balances, it is preferable to parliamentarism. Rather than looking for one optimal set of rules for elections, advocates of power dividing argue that a stable regime should have distinct electoral rules for each representative organ that create institutions that represent alternative majorities. In the division of power between national and subnational governments, the power-dividing strategy advises against concentrating local powers in single jurisdictions; for this reason federalism can lead to destructive outcomes in ethnically divided societies. Instead, power-dividing advocates call for the creation of multiple overlapping jurisdictions at the subnational level with governing boards elected by distinctive majorities. Thus, school districts should not be coterminous with water basin districts or with transportation development districts or with port districts, and so forth.

8. Enlarging negotiations. In the negotiation of arrangements for the longer term, the strategy of nation-state stewardship advises international stewards to involve many participants other than the warring ethnic groups—and perhaps even to lengthen the negotiation process. This runs counter to the usual short-term interest in reaching a quick agreement on new governance structures by bringing the warring parties to the bargaining table and isolating them as much as possible from social pressures. The negotiations over enduring governance structures must involve diverse interests that work with and compete with ethnic interests; otherwise, the previously warring parties are likely to compromise on a power-sharing arrangement that privileges them against all challengers. So in the interest of longer-run political stability, negotiations over the constitution must include labor, management, professional organizations, women's groups, students' associations, and other important social interests that cut across and compete with ethnic groups when designing governance structures. In South Africa, a lengthier negotiation process permitted more interests to surface, and this expansion of the negotiation process beyond the circle of ethnic leaders in turn led to the design of more durable democratic institutions.

9. Limiting power sharing. If used at all, the best use of power sharing is as a short-term, pump-priming concession by the victor to initiate an end to civil war and to avoid the costs of fighting to an unconditional surrender. The offer of power sharing is a concession by a dominant party that signals a preparedness to act with moderation in the future. The preparedness of majority interests to send such signals of respect and concern for minority rights in the postconflict context can encourage the minorities' sense of inclusion. The political minority knows that the concessions are costly to the political majority and that they constitute a more credible commitment to respect the rights and interests of minorities in a postwar political arrangement. Meaningful concessions are possible where the dominant coalition does not feel threatened by allowing minority interests to take responsibility for their own ethnic and religious practices. The majority knows that such acts of empowerment can always be rescinded; hence this knowledge facilitates their decision to concede limited authorizations. If implemented in the initiation phase, the power-sharing arrangement should be crafted to allow for an emerging majoritarian democracy. Yet if power sharing is used as an interim device for initiating a transition from civil war, it should be institutionalized as little as possible. Not only is this an object lesson from the successful South African transition, it is seconded by Bunce and Watts' finding that postcommunist unitary states have used concessions of some rights associated with limited autonomy to reach accommodations with their minorities. Yet, as the rarity of such examples attests, it is uncommon for majorities to voluntarily concede such rights when they have an option not to concede. In these circumstances, power sharing cannot be imposed by the international community on an unwilling majority because this would signal to the minorities exactly the wrong message about majority intentions and therefore court disaster when the third party disengages.

If there is no victor in the domestic conflict and power sharing is the only governmental institution to which parties will agree, it is typically better for international stewards to rule directly (and possibly autocratically) for the interim. In these circumstances the best use of power sharing is in nonrecurring decisions limited to a single issue, such as the integration of the armed forces of the warring parties into a single chain of command. These measures use power sharing to facilitate the ending of a civil war but leave behind fewer obstacles to consolidation of peace and democracy in the future.

Interim power-sharing arrangements for the initiation phase can raise some troublesome trade-offs, and these all point to limiting the role of power-sharing institutions in the initiation phase. Weak power-sharing institutions that include a sunset provision (expiration date), like an extraordinary or one-time convocation of constituent assembly, may be less likely to jeopardize the development of viable institutions for the longer term but will increase the likelihood of instability in the initiation phase. Stronger interim power-sharing institutions provide immediate stability but create problems for the longer-term consolidation of democracy and peace. These strong power-sharing institutions established to initiate the transition, even if they are intended to be interim arrangements, empower political actors who shape the institutions for the consolidation phase in ways that are likely to preserve their privileged position. The failure of democracy in Lebanon, as Zahar underscores, can be attributed to strong institutions in which politicians have jealously guarded their prerogatives against attempts to open up the political process.

The chapters in this volume also underscore that the power-sharing institutions that are easiest to manipulate may be the least effective tools at the end of civil war. Diplomats and leaders should not expect that simple manipulation of electoral or fiscal formulas will remedy many problems left behind by the conflict. Reilly (Chapter 7) finds that the choice of electoral system may have less impact on the extent of executive inclusiveness or democratic stability in ethnically divided societies than the heated debates in political science would lead one to expect. Eduardo Alemán and Daniel Treisman in Chapter 8 explore the central government's use of fiscal decentralization and fiscal proportionality—two prominent elements of power sharing—to consolidate peace within federal states and avoid a resumption of secessionist violence from ethnic-minority regions. Examining the experiences of India, Pakistan, Nigeria, and the former Yugoslavia, they find no evidence that greater fiscal autonomy for ethnic minority regions in a federation has affected the intensity or frequency of secessionist violence. Nor is a specific pattern of fiscal allocation likely to be both effective and practical. Regarding the distribution of the central government's expenditures among regions, Alemán and Treisman find that proportionality may not be a sufficient policy measure to stave off secessionist violence. They find that to maintain a country's unity, minority regions must be appeased with disproportionate shares of the central government's resources, yet this type of fiscal appeasement is likely to be too costly for a central government to maintain. This is particularly true after civil wars when resources are scarce and most regions expect above-average allotments. Paradoxically, it is precisely because they are so easily manipulated by politicians that these forms of power-sharing institutions have attracted such attention in the debates over institutional choices for divided societies.

Conclusion

In sum, our study that began with the role of power sharing in peace making led to both a warning and an enlarged menu of choices available to diplomats and leaders seeking to sustain regime change in ethnically divided societies emerging from domestic conflicts such as civil wars. The usual debate that pits majoritarian democracy against power sharing and argues that we must choose between them sets up a false dichotomy. The offer of power sharing may be necessary to initiate a transition to peace, but only under specific and somewhat unique conditions will implementation of power sharing also be a prudent starting point for a successful transition to stable peace and democracy for the longer term. We need to consider longer-term consequences as well and to focus on the alternatives to power sharing that create new opportunities for nation- and state building. We have outlined one set of alternatives in our strategy of nation-state stewardship. In this we have argued that we should rediscover the values of the various forms of democracy, such as the separation of powers, that represent neither unalloyed majoritarianism nor power sharing. It is short-sighted and self-defeating, we believe, to view democracy without power sharing as automatically leading to tyrannical outcomes. Majorities vary in their behavior and often use their authority in a responsible manner. Regime change is too important a matter for leaders and diplomats to act on assumptions that have not been tested in systematic research and validated by empirical evidence. This is the unique contribution that can be made by social scientists, including the authors who have contributed to this volume.

References

Abbink, Jon. 1997. "Ethnicity and Constitutionalism in Contemporary Ethiopia." *Journal of African Law* 41:159–174.

Abdelal, Rawi. 2001. *National Purpose in the World Economy: Post-Soviet States in Comparative Perspective.* Ithaca: Cornell University Press.

Abraham, A. J. 1981. *Lebanon at Mid-Century: Maronite-Druze Relations in Lebanon, 1840–1860, A Prelude to Arab Nationalism.* New York: University Press of America.

Adebayo, Akanmu Gafari. 1993. *Embattled Federalism: History of Revenue Allocation in Nigeria 1946–1990.* New York: Peter Lang.

Adekanye, J. Bayo. 1998. "Power-Sharing in Multi-Ethnic Political Systems." *Security Dialogue* 29:25–26.

Africa Confidential. 2000. 41 (May 12):1–2.

Agbaegbu, Tobs. 1998. "I Want to Rule Again." *Newswatch* 28:20–22.

Ahmed, Samina. 1997. "Centralization, Authoritarianism, and the Mismanagement of Ethnic Relations in Pakistan." In *Government Policies and Ethnic Relations in Asia and the Pacific,* ed. Michael E. Brown and Sumit Ganguly, 83–127. Cambridge: MIT Press.

Alesina, Alberto, and Enrico Spolaore. 1997. "On the Number and Size of Nations." *Quarterly Journal of Economics* 112:1027–1056.

——. 2003. *The Size of Nations.* Cambridge: MIT Press.

Ali, Mehrunnisa. 1997. "Federalism and Regionalism in Pakistan." In *Political System in Pakistan.* 3rd ed., ed. Verinder Grover and Ranjana Arora, 111–131. New Delhi: Deep and Deep Publications.

Allin, Dana H. 2002. *NATO's Balkan Interventions.* International Institute for Strategic Studies, Adelphi Paper, no. 347. New York: Oxford University Press.

Altbach, Philip G., and Damtew Teferra. 1999. *Publishing in African Languages: Challenges and Prospects.* Boston: Bellagio Publishing Network.

Alter, Karen J. 1998. "'Who Are the Masters of the Treaty'? European Governments and the European Court of Justice." *International Organization* 52:121–147.

Anonymous. 1958. "The Lebanese Crisis in Perspective." *World Today* 14:369–380.

Anyanwu, John C. 1997. *Nigerian Public Finance.* Onitsha, Nigeria: Joanee Educational Publishers Ltd.

Aplon, Jason, and Victor Tanner. 2000. *Civil Society in Bosnia: Obstacles and Opportunities for Building Peace.* Washington, D.C.: Winston Foundation for World Peace.

Armstrong, John. 1982. *Nations before Nationalism.* Chapel Hill: University of North Carolina Press.

Aslund, Anders. 1999. "The Problem with Fiscal Federalism." *Journal of Democracy* 10:83–86.
Atlapedia Online. 2001. Available at http://www.atlapedia.com/online/country_index.htm.
Attanasio, John B. 1991. "The Rights of Ethnic Minorities: The Emerging Mosaic." *Notre Dame Law Review* 66:1195–1217.
Aulas, Marie-Christine. 1987. "The Socio-Ideological Development of the Maronite Community: The Emergence of the Phalanges and the Lebanese Forces." *Arab Studies Quarterly* 7:1–27.
Austin, Granville. 1999. *The Indian Constitution: Cornerstone of a Nation.* Delhi: Oxford University Press.
Azar, Edward. 1988. "Lebanon: The Role of External Forces in Confessional Pluralism." In *Ideology and Power in the Middle East: Studies in Honor of George Lenczowski*, ed. Peter Chelkowski and Robert Pranger, 325–336. Durham: Duke University Press.
Bahout, Joseph. 1993. "Liban: les élections législatives de l'été 1992." *Monde arabe Maghreb Machrek* 139:53–81.
Bajpai, Kanti. 1997. "Diversity, Democracy and Devolution in India." In *Government Policies and Ethnic Relations in Asia and the Pacific*, ed. Michael E. Brown and Sumit Ganguly, 33–81. Cambridge: MIT Press.
Barany, Zoltan D. 1998. "Ethnic Mobilization and the State: The Roma in Eastern Europe." *Ethnic and Racial Studies* 21:308–327.
——. 2002. *The Eastern European Gypsies: Regime Change, Marginality, and Ethnopolitics.* Cambridge: Cambridge University Press.
Barbarosie, Arcadie. 2001. "Understanding the Communist Electoral Victory in Moldova." *Transition: Newsletter about Reforming Economies* 12:9–10.
Bardhan, Prahab, and Dilip Mookherjee. 2000. "Capture and Governance at Local and National Levels." *American Economic Review* 90:135–139.
Barkan, Joel D. 1995. "Elections in Agrarian Societies." *Journal of Democracy* 6:106–116.
Barry, Brian. 1975. "The Consociational Model and Its Dangers." *European Journal of Political Research* 3:393–412.
Bean, Richard. 1973. "War and the Birth of the Nation State." *Journal of Economic History* 33:203–221.
Bebler, Anton. 1993. "Yugoslavia's Variety of Communist Federation and Her Demise." *Communist and Post-Communist Studies* 26:73–86.
Beck, Nathaniel, Jonathan N. Katz, and Richard Tucker. 1998. "Taking Time Seriously: Time-Series-Cross-Section Analysis with a Binary Dependent Variable." *American Journal of Political Science* 42:1260–1288.
Beck, Thorsten, George Clarke, Alberto Groff, Philip Keefer, and Patrick Walsh. n.d. *New Tools and New Tests in Comparative Political Economy: The Database of Political Institutions.* Washington, D.C.: World Bank.
Bednar, Jenna, William N. Eskridge, Jr., and John Ferejohn. 2001. "A Political Theory of Federalism." In *Constitutional Culture and Democratic Rule*, ed. John Ferejohn, Jack N. Rakove, and Jonathan Riley, 223–267. New York: Cambridge University Press.
Beissinger, Mark R. 2002. *Nationalist Mobilization and the Collapse of the Soviet State.* Cambridge: Cambridge University Press.
Belloni, Roberto. 2001. "Civil Society and Peacebuilding in Bosnia and Herzegovina." *Journal of Peace Research* 38:163–180.
Benson, Michelle, and Jacek Kugler. 1998. "Power Parity, Democracy, and the Severity of Internal Violence." *Journal of Conflict Resolution* 42:196–209.
Berdal, Mats R., and David M. Malone, eds. 2000. *Greed and Grievance: Economic Agendas in Civil Wars.* Boulder, Colo.: Lynne Rienner.

Bermeo, Nancy. 2002. "The Import of Institutions." *Journal of Democracy* 13:97–110.

Bhalla, Nita. 2001. "War 'devastated' Ethiopian economy." *BBC News*, August 7.

Bieber, Florian. 2001. "The Challenge of Democracy in Divided Societies: Lessons from Bosnia—Challenges for Kosovo." In *Reconstructing Multi-ethnic Societies: The Case of Bosnia-Herzegovina*, ed. Džemal Sakolović and Florian Bieber, 109–121. Burlington, Vt.: Ashgate.

Blais, André, and Stephanie Dion. 1990. "Electoral Systems and the Consolidation of New Democracies." In *Democratic Transition and Consolidation in Southern Europe, Latin America and Southeast Asia*, ed. Diane Ethier, 250–268. London: Macmillan Press.

Bloomfield, David. 1997. *Peacemaking Strategies in Northern Ireland: Building Complementarity in Conflict Management Theory*. London: Macmillan.

Bogdanor, Vernon. 1988. "Federalism in Switzerland." *Government and Opposition* 22:69–90.

Bohrer, Robert E., II. 1997. "Deviations from Proportionality and Survival in New Parliamentary Democracies." *Electoral Studies* 16:217–226.

Bolton, Patrick, Gérard Roland, and Enrico Spolaore. 1996. "Economic Theories of the Break-up and Integration of Nations." *European Economic Review* 40:697–705.

Bookman, Milica Zarkovic. 1992. "Economic Issues Underlying Secession: The Case of Slovenia and Slovakia." *Communist Economies and Economic Transformation* 4:111–134.

Bose, Sumantra. 2002. "Flawed Mediation, Chaotic Implementation: 1987 Indo-Sri Lankan Peace Agreement." In *Ending Civil Wars: The Implementation of Peace Agreements*, ed. Stephen John Stedman, Donald Rothchild, and Elizabeth M. Cousens, 631–659. Boulder, Colo.: Lynne Rienner.

Bossche, Geert Van den. 2004. "Political Renewal, Citizenship and Identity: The 'New Political Culture' in Belgium." *Acta Politica* 39:59–78.

Box-Steffensmeier, Janet M., and Bradford S. Jones. 1997. "Time Is of the Essence: Event History Models in Political Science." *American Journal of Political Science* 41:1414–1461.

Brass, Paul R. 1973. *Language, Religion, and Politics in North India*. London: Cambridge University Press.

——. 1991. *Ethnicity and Nationalism: Theory and Comparison*. New Delhi: Sage Publications.

Breton, Albert. 2000. "An Introduction to Decentralization Failure." Washington, D.C.: International Monetary Fund.

Breton, Roland. 1997. *Atlas of the Languages and Ethnic Communities in South Asia*. New Delhi: Sage Publications.

Breuilly, John. 1994. *Nationalism and the State*. 2nd ed. Chicago: University of Chicago Press.

Bromlei, Iu. V., ed. 1988. *Narody mira: istoriko-etnograficheskii spravochnik*. Moscow: Sovetskaia Entsiklopediia.

Brudny, Yitzhak. 1998. *Reinventing Russia: Russian Nationalism and the Soviet State, 1953–1991*. Cambridge: Harvard University Press.

——. 2001. "National Identity and Democracy in Postcommunist Russia." Unpublished manuscript. Jerusalem: Department of Political Science, The Hebrew University.

Bruk, S. I. 1986. *Naselenie mira: etnodemograficheskii spravochnik*. 2nd rev. ed. Moscow: Izdatel'stvo Nauka.

Bruk, S. I., and V. S. Apenchenko. 1964. *Atlas narodov mira*. Moscow: Glavnoe Upravlenie Geodezii i Kartografii Gosudarstvennogo Geologicheskogo Komiteta SSSR, Institut Etnografii im. Miklukho-Miklaia Akademii Nauk SSSR.

Brynen, Rex. 1990. *Sanctuary and Survival: The PLO in Lebanon*. Boulder, Colo.: Westview Press.

Bueno de Mesquita, Bruce, and David Lalman. 1992. *War and Reason: Domestic and International Imperatives.* New Haven: Yale University Press.

Bueno de Mesquita, Bruce, and Randolph M. Siverson. 1995. "War and the Survival of Political Leaders: A Comparative Study of Regime Types and Political Accountability." *American Political Science Review* 89:841–855.

Bulcha, Mekuria. 1997. "The Politics of Linguistic Homogenization in Ethiopia and the Conflict over the Status of Afaan Oromoo." *African Affairs* 96:325–352.

Bunce, Valerie. 1997. "Presidents and the Transition in Eastern Europe." In *Presidential Institutions and Democratic Politics,* ed. Kurt Von Mettenheim, 161–176. Baltimore: Johns Hopkins University Press.

——. 1999a. "The Political Economy of Postsocialism." *Slavic Review* 58:756–793.

——. 1999b. *Subversive Institutions: The Design and the Destruction of Socialism and the State.* Cambridge: Cambridge University Press.

——. 2001a. "Comparative Democratization: Lessons from Russia and the Postsocialist World." Unpublished manuscript. Ithaca: Department of Government, Cornell University.

——. 2001b. "What Postcommunist Regimes Have Taught Us about Democratization." Paper presented at the conference, "The Fall of Communism in Europe: Ten Years On," Majorie Mayrock Center for Russian, Eurasian, and East European Research, Hebrew University of Jerusalem, May 15–17.

——. 2003. "Rethinking Recent Democratization: Lessons from the Postcommunist Experience." *World Politics* 55:167–192.

——. 2004a. "Federalism, Nationalism, and Secession: The Communist and Postcommunist Experience." In *Federalism and Territorial Cleavages,* ed. Ugo M. Amoretti and Nancy Bermeo, 417–440. Baltimore: Johns Hopkins University Press.

——. 2004b. "Status Quo, Reformist, and Secessionist Politics: Explaining Variations in Center-Regional Bargaining in Postcommunist Ethnofederations." Paper presented at the Workshop in Eastern European Politics, Harvard University, Center for European Studies, Cambridge, Mass., May 14.

Burg, Steven L. 1993. "Why Yugoslavia Fell Apart." *Current History* 92:357–363.

Burki, Masood. 1996. *Blue Print for a Stable and Viable Pakistan.* Lahore: Ferozsons (Pvt.). Ltd.

Burki, Shahid Javed. 1980. *Pakistan Under Bhutto, 1971–1977.* London: Macmillan Press.

Butenschøn, Nils A. 1985. "Conflict Management in Plural Societies: The Consociational Formula." *Scandinavian Political Studies* 8:85–103.

Caplan, Richard. 2002. *A New Trusteeship: The International Administration of War-torn Territories.* International Institute for Strategic Studies, Adelphi Paper, no. 341. New York: Oxford University Press.

Carnegie Commission on Preventing Deadly Conflict. 1997a. *A House No Longer Divided: Progress and Prospects for Democratic Peace in South Africa.* Conference report. Washington, D.C.

——. 1997b. *Preventing Deadly Conflict: Final Report.* Washington, D.C.

Central Bank of Nigeria. 1981–1985. *Annual Report and Statement of Accounts.* Lagos.

Cerovic, Stojan. 2001. "Serbia, Montenegro: Reintegration, Divorce or Something Else?" U.S. Institute of Peace Special Report. Washington, D.C., April 2.

Chandler, David. 2000. *Bosnia: Faking Democracy after Dayton.* London: Pluto Press.

——. 2001. "Bosnia: The Democracy Paradox." *Current History* 100:114–119.

Chapman, David. 1991. *Can Civil Wars Be Avoided? Electoral and Constitutional Options for Ethnically Divided Countries.* London: Institute for Social Inventions.

Chesterman, Simon. 2001. "Kosovo in Limbo: State-Building and 'Substantial Autonomy.'" New York: International Peace Academy, August.

——. 2002. "Walking Softly in Afghanistan: The Future of UN State-Building." *Survival* 44:37–46.

Chipande, Graham H. R., and Asmamaw Enquobahrie. 1997. *Decentralization of Macro-economic Management in a Post-conflict State: The Ethiopian Experience.* Addis Ababa: United Nations Development Program Ethiopia, June.

Cicciomessere, Roberto, ed. 2001. "Political Resources on the Web." Available at http://www.politicalresources.net.

Cichock, Mark A. 1999. "Interdependence and Manipulation in the Russian-Baltic Relationship: 1993–97." *Journal of Baltic Studies* 30:89–116.

Coakley, John. 1994. "Approaches to the Resolution of Ethnic Conflict: The Strategy of Non-territorial Autonomy." *International Political Science Review* 15:297–314.

Cohen, Frank S. 1997. "Proportional versus Majoritarian Ethnic Conflict Management in Democracies." *Comparative Political Studies* 30:607–630.

Cohen, John M., and Stephen B. Peterson. 1999. *Administrative Decentralization: Strategies for Developing Countries.* West Hartford, Conn.: Kumarian Press.

Cohen, Lenard J. 1995. *Broken Bonds: Yugoslavia's Disintegration and Balkan Politics in Transition.* 2nd ed. Boulder, Colo.: Westview.

Colley, Linda. 1992. *Britons: Forging a Nation (1707–1837).* New Haven: Yale University Press.

Collier, Paul. 2000. *Economic Causes of Civil Conflicts and Their Implications for Policy.* Washington, D.C.: World Bank.

Collier, Paul, and Anke Hoeffler. 2002. "Greed and Grievance in Civil War." Washington, D.C.: World Bank.

Connor, Walker. 1994. *Ethno-nationalism: The Quest for Understanding.* Princeton: Princeton University Press.

Corbridge, Stuart. 1995. "Federalism, Hindu Nationalism and Mythologies of Governance in Modern India." In *Federalism: The Multiethnic Challenge,* ed. Graham Smith, 101–127. London: Longman.

Cousens, Elizabeth M. 2002. "From Missed Opportunities to Overcompensation: Implementing the Dayton Agreement on Bosnia." In *Ending Civil Wars: The Implementation of Peace Agreements,* ed. Stephen John Stedman, Donald Rothchild, and Elizabeth M. Cousens, 531–566. Boulder, Colo.: Lynne Rienner.

Crow, Ralph. 1962. "Religious Sectarianism in the Lebanese Political System." *The Journal of Politics* 24:489–520.

Crowther, William. 1997a. "Moldova: Caught between Nation and Empire." In *New States, New Politics: Building the Post-Soviet Nations,* ed. Ian Bremer and Ray Taras, 316–352. Cambridge: Cambridge University Press.

——. 1997b. "The Politics of Democratization in Postcommunist Moldova." In *Democratic Changes and Authoritarian Reactions in Russia, Ukraine, Belarus and Moldova,* ed. Karen Dawisha and Bruce Parrott, 282–329. Cambridge: Cambridge University Press.

Csergo, Zsuzsa. 2000. Language and Democracy: A Comparative Study of Contestations over Language Use in Romania and Slovakia. PhD diss. Washington, D.C.: George Washington University.

Daalder, Hans. 1974. "The Consociational Democracy Theme." *World Politics* 26:604–621.

Dahl, Robert A. 1971. *Polyarchy: Participation and Opposition.* New Haven: Yale University Press.

Danforth, John C. 2002. *Report to the President of the United States on the Outlook for Peace in Sudan.* Washington, D.C.: U.S. Department of State.

D'Anieri, Paul. 1997. "Nationalism and International Politics: Identity and Sovereignty in the Russian-Ukrainian Conflict." *Nationalism and Ethnic Politics* 3:1–28.

Darby, John, and Roger MacGinty, eds. 2000. *The Management of Peace Processes*. New York: St. Martin's Press.

Dasgupta, Jyotirinidra. 1995. "India: Democratic Becoming and Developmental Transition." In *Politics in Developing Countries: Comparing Experiences with Democracy*. 2nd ed., ed. Larry Diamond, Juan J. Linz, and Seymour Martin Lipset, 263–321. Boulder, Colo.: Lynne Rienner.

——. 2001. "India's Federal Design and Multicultural National Construction." In *The Success of India's Democracy*, ed. Atul Kohli, 49–77. Cambridge: Cambridge University Press.

Deeb, Mary-Jane, and Marius Deeb. 1995. "Internal Negotiations in a Centralist Conflict: Lebanon." In *Elusive Peace: Negotiating an End to Civil Wars*, ed. I. William Zartman, 125–146. Washington, D.C.: Brookings Institution.

De Jonge Oudraat, Chantal. 1996. "The United Nations and Internal Conflict." In *The International Dimensions of Ethnic Conflict*, ed. Michael E. Brown, 489–535. Cambridge: MIT Press.

Demichelis, Julia. 1998. *NGOs and Peacebuilding in Bosnia's Ethnically-divided Cities*. Washington, D.C.: United States Institute of Peace.

Deng, Francis M., and J. Stephen Morrison. 2001. *U.S. Policy to End Sudan's War: Report of the CSIS Task Force on U.S.-Sudan Policy*. Washington, D.C.: Center for Strategic and International Studies.

Dent, Martin. 1995. "Ethnicity and Territorial Politics in Nigeria." In *Federalism: The Multiethnic Challenge*, ed. Graham Smith, 128–154. London: Longman.

Denyer, Simon. 2000. "Analysis—Burundi Peace Talks Reach Moment of Truth." Reuters Ltd., July 21.

Derluguian, Georgi M. 1998. "The Tale of Two Resorts: Abkhazia and Ajaria Before and Since the Soviet Collapse." In *The Myth of 'Ethnic Conflict': Politics, Economics, and Cultural Violence*, ed. Beverly Crawford and Ronnie D. Lipschutz, 261–292. International and Area Studies, Research Series, no. 98. Berkeley: University of California.

——. 2001a. "The Forgotten Abkhazia." Program on New Approaches to Russian Security, Working Paper Series, no. 18. New York: Council on Foreign Relations, January.

——. 2001b. "How Adjaria Did Not Become Another Bosnia: Structure, Agency, and Congency in Chaotic Transitions." In *After the Fall: 1989 and the Future of Freedom*, ed. George Katsiaficas, 103–122. New York: Routledge.

Diamond, Larry. 1995. "Nigeria: The Uncivic Society and the Descent into Praetorianism." In *Politics in Developing Countries: Africa*. 2nd ed., ed. Larry Diamond, Juan J. Linz, and Seymour Martin Lipset, 33–91. Boulder, Colo.: Lynne Rienner.

——. 1997. *Prospects for Democratic Development in Africa*. Hoover Institution Essays in Public Policy, no. 74. Stanford University: Hoover Institution.

Dobbins, James F. 2003–2004. "America's Role in Nation-building: From Germany to Iraq." *Survival* 45:87–110.

Dubravcic, Dinko. 1993. "Economic Causes and Political Context of the Dissolution of a Multinational Federal State: The Case of Yugoslavia." *Communist Economies and Economic Transformation* 5:259–272.

Dudley, Ryan, and Ross A. Miller. 1998. "Group Rebellion in the 1980s." *Journal of Conflict Resolution* 42:77–96.

Du Toit, Pierre. 2001. *South Africa's Brittle Peace: The Problem of Post-Settlement Violence*. New York: Palgrave.

Easter, Gerald M. 1997. "Preference for Presidentialism: Postcommunist Regime Change in Russia and the NIS." *World Politics* 49:184–211.

Easterly, William. 2001. "Can Institutions Resolve Ethnic Conflict?" *Economic Development and Cultural Change* 49:687–706.

EBRD [European Bank for Reconstruction and Development]. 1999. *Transition Report 1999: Ten Years of Transition.* London.

Economist Intelligence Unit. 2001. *Country Reports and Country Profiles.* Available at http://www.eiu.com.

Egziabher, Tegegne Gebre. 1998. "The Influences of Decentralization on Some Aspects of Local and Regional Development Planning in Ethiopia." *Eastern Africa Social Science Research Review* 14:33–63.

Elazar, Daniel J., ed. 1982. *Governing Peoples and Territories.* Philadelphia: Institute for the Study of Human Issues.

——. 1985. "Federalism and Consociational Regimes." *Publius: The Journal of Federalism* 15:17–34.

——. 1994. *Federal Systems of the World: A Handbook of Federal, Confederal, and Autonomy Arrangements.* London: Longman.

——. 1998. *Constitutionalizing Globalization: The Postmodern Revival of Confederal Arrangements.* New York: Rowman and Littlefield.

Encarta. 2001. "Nagaland." Microsoft Encarta Online Encyclopedia. Available online at http://encarta.msn.com.

EPRDF [Ethiopian People's Revolutionary Democratic Front]. 2000. *EPRDF's Five-Year Program of Development, Peace, and Democracy.* Addis Ababa.

Ethiopia. 1994. *Constitution of the Democratic Republic of Ethiopia.* Addis Ababa. December 8.

Ethiopia. Central Statistical Authority. 1996. *1994 Population and Housing Census of Ethiopia.* Addis Ababa, June.

Ethiopia. Ministry of Education. 1999a. *Education Sector Development Program Action Plan.* Addis Ababa, June.

——. 1999b. *Indicators of the Ethiopian Education System.* Addis Ababa, December.

——. 2000. *Education Sector Development Program Report.* Addis Ababa, March.

——. 2001a. *Education Sector Development Programme (ESDP) Consolidated National Performance Report: 1999/00.* Addis Ababa, February.

——. 2001b. *Ethiopia Education Sector Development Programme (ESDP) Mid Term Review Mission,* 1 [Main Report]. Addis Ababa, March.

Ethiopia. Negarit Gazeta. 1992a. *Proclamation to Provide for the Establishment of National/Regional Self-Government*: Proclamation #7 of 1992. Addis Ababa.

——. 1992b. *1984 E.C. Budget Proclamation*: Proclamation #26 of 1992. Addis Ababa.

——. 1992c. *A Proclamation to Define the Sharing of Revenue Between the Central Government and the National/Regional Self-governments.* Proclamation #33 of 1992. Addis Ababa.

——. 1993. *Proclamation to Define the Powers and Duties of the Central and Regional Executive Organs of the Transitional Government of Ethiopia*: Proclamation #41 of 1993. Addis Ababa.

Ethiopia. Office of the Prime Minister of the Federal Democratic Republic of Ethiopia. 1994. *The System of Regional Administration in Ethiopia.* Addis Ababa.

Etienne, Gilbert. 1994. "Pakistan." In *Dictionnaire International du Federalism,* ed. Francois Saint-Ouen. Brussels: Etablissements Emile Bruylant.

Europa World Yearbook. 1987–1998. London: Europa Publications.

Facts on File. 1955–1999. New York: Facts on File News Services.

Farkas, Evelyn N. 2001. "US Policy Towards Secession in the Balkans and Effectiveness of *De Facto* Partition." Institute for National Security Studies Paper, no. 40, Regional Security Series. Colorado Springs, Colo.: U.S. Air Force Academy, June.

Faust, Jon. 1996. "Whom Can We Trust to Run the Fed? Theoretical Support for the Founders' Views." *Journal of Monetary Economics* 37:267–283.

Fearon, James. 1994. "Domestic Political Audiences and the Escalation of International Disputes." *American Political Science Review* 88:577–592.

——. 1998. "Commitment Problems and the Spread of Ethnic Conflict." In *The International Spread of Ethnic Conflict*, ed. David Lake and Donald Rothchild, 107–126. Princeton: Princeton University Press.

Filippov, Mikhail, Peter C. Ordeshook, and Olga Shvetsova. 2004. *Designing Federalism: A Theory of Self-Sustainable Federal Institutions.* New York: Cambridge University Press.

Fish, M. Steven. 1998. "The Determinants of Economic Reform in the Postcommunist World." *East European Politics and Societies* 12:31–78.

Fox, Jonathan. 1997. "The Salience of Religious Issues in Ethnic Conflict: A Large N Study." *Nationalism and Ethnic Politics* 3:1–19.

Freedom House. 1999. *Freedom in the World 1998–1999.* New York: Freedom House. Available online at www.freedomhouse.org.

——. 2000. *Freedom in the World 1999–2000.* New York: Freedom House. Available online at www.freedomhouse.org.

——. 2001. *Freedom in the World 2000–2001.* New York: Freedom House. Available online at www.freedomhouse.org.

Friedman, Steven. 1995. "South Africa." In *Encyclopedia of Democracy*, ed. Seymour Martin Lipset, 4:1161–1167. Washington, D.C.: Congressional Quarterly.

——. 1996. "No Easy Stroll to Dominance." *Towards Democracy* (Fourth Quarter), 4–13.

Friedrich, Carl J. 1968. *Trends of Federalism in Theory and Practice.* New York: Frederick A. Praeger.

Furnivall, J. S. 1944. *Netherlands India: A Study of Plural Economy.* New York: Macmillan.

Gagnon, Alain G., and Guy Laforest. 1994. "The Future of Federalism: Lessons from Canada and Quebec." In *Federalism and the New World Order*, ed. Stephen J. Randall and Roger Gibbins, 113–131. Calgary, Alberta: University of Calgary Press.

Gagnon, V. P., Jr. 1994/95. "Ethnic Nationalism and International Conflict: The Case of Serbia." *International Security* 19:130–166.

Gandhi, Mohandas K. 1938. *Hind Swaraj.* Ahmedabad: Navjivan Publishing House.

Gandhi, P. Jegadish, ed. 1999. *New Facets of Financial Federalism.* New Delhi: Deep and Deep Publications.

Garb, Paula. 1998. "Ethnicity, Alliance-Building, and the Limited Spread of Ethnic Conflict in the Caucasus." In *The International Spread of Ethnic Conflict*, ed. David Lake and Donald Rothchild, 185–200. Princeton: Princeton University Press.

Garrett, Geoffrey, R. Daniel Kelemen, and Heiner Schulz. 1998. "The European Court of Justice: National Governments, and Legal Integration in the European Union." *International Organization* 52:149–176.

Gasiorowski, Mark J. 1996. "An Overview of the Political Regime Change Dataset." *Comparative Political Studies* 29:469–483.

Gastrow, Peter. 1995. *Bargaining for Peace: South Africa and the National Peace Accord.* Washington, D.C.: United States Institute of Peace Press.

Gboyega, Alex. 1989. "The Public Service and Federal Character." In *Federal Character and Federalism in Nigeria*, ed. Peter P. Ekeh and Eghosa E. Osaghae, 164–187. Ibadan: Heinemann Educational Books.

Gellner, Ernest. 1983. *Nations and Nationalism.* Ithaca: Cornell University Press.

Ghai, Yash. 1998. "The Structure of the State: Federalism and Autonomy." In *Democracy and Deep-Rooted Conflict: Options for Negotiators*, ed. Peter Harris and Ben Reilly, 155–168. Stockholm: International Institute for Democracy and Electoral Assistance.

Giersch, Carsten. 2000. "Multilateral Conflict Regulation (MCR): The Case of Kosovo." Weatherhead Center for International Affairs, Working Paper Series, no. 00-04. Cambridge: Harvard University, August.

Gleditsch, Nils Petter, Peter Wallensteen, Mikael Eriksson, Margareta Sollenberg, and Håvard Strand. 2004. *Armed Conflict 1946–2002.* Oslo: International Peace Research Institute. Available online at www.prio.no/cwp/armedconflict/.

Goltz, Thomas. 2001. "Georgia on the Brink." *Perspectives* 11:1–8.

Gorenburg, Dmitry. 1999. "Regional Separatism in Russia: Ethnic Mobilization or Power Grab?" *Europe-Asia Studies* 51:245–274.

Gourevitch, Peter A. 1986. *Politics in Hard Times: Comparative Responses to International Economic Crises.* Ithaca: Cornell University Press.

——. 1999. "The Governance Problem in International Relations." In *Strategic Choice and International Relations,* ed. David A. Lake and Robert Powell, 137–164. Princeton: Princeton University Press.

Graf, William D. 1988. *The Nigerian State: Political Economy, State Class and Political System in the Post-Colonial Era.* London: James Currey.

Guibernau, Montserrat. 1995. "Spain: A Federation in the Making?" In *Federalism: The Multiethnic Challenge,* ed. Graham Smith, 239–254. London: Longman.

Gulati, I. S., and K. K. George. 1988. *Essays in Federal Financial Relations.* New Delhi: Oxford and IBH Publishing Co.

Gulick, Edward Vose. 1967. *Europe's Classical Balance of Power.* New York: W. W. Norton.

Gurr, Ted Robert. 1989. Polity II Codebook. Boulder: University of Colorado. Available at http://www.colorado.edu/IBS/GAD/spacetime/data/Polity.html.

——. 1990. "Ethnic Warfare and the Changing Priorities of Global Security." *Mediterranean Quarterly* 1:82–98.

——. 1999. "Minorities at Risk Project." College Park: University of Maryland. Available at http://www.bsos.umd.edu/cidcm/mar.

——. 2000. *Peoples Versus States: Minorities at Risk in the New Century.* Washington, D.C.: U.S. Institute of Peace.

Haas, Ernst B. 1986. "What Is Nationalism and Why Should We Study It?" *International Organization* 40:707–744.

Haile, Minasse. 1996. "The New Ethiopian Constitution: Its Impact Upon Unity, Human Rights, and Development." *Suffolk Transnational Law Review* 20:1–84.

Hale, Henry E. 2004. "Divided We Stand: Institutional Sources of Ethnofederal State Survival and Collapse." *World Politics* 56:165–193.

Hampson, Fen Osler. 1990. "Building a Stable Peace: Opportunities and Limits to Security Cooperation in Third World Regional Conflicts." *International Journal* 45:454–489.

Handley, Antoinette, and Jeffrey Herbst. 1997. "South Africa: The Perils of Normalcy." *Current History* 96:222–226.

Hanf, Theodor. 1991. "Reducing Conflict Through Cultural Autonomy: Karl Renner's Contribution." In *State and Nation in Multi-ethnic Societies: The Breakup of Multinational States,* ed. Uri Ra'anan, 33–52. New York: Manchester University Press.

Harik, Iliya. 1968. *Politics and Change in a Traditional Society: Lebanon, 1711–1845.* Princeton: Princeton University Press.

——. 1991. "The Maronites and the Future of Lebanon: A Case of Communal Conflict." In *Security Perspectives and Policies: Lebanon, Syria, Israel and the Palestinians,* ed. Steven Dorr and Neysa Slater, 45–56. Washington, D.C.: Defense Academic Research Support Program.

Harris, Peter, and Ben Reilly, eds. 1998. *Democracy and Deep-Rooted Conflict: Options for Negotiators.* Stockholm: International Institute for Democracy and Electoral Assistance.

Hartzell, Caroline A. 1999. "Explaining the Stability of Negotiated Settlements to Intrastate Wars." *Journal of Conflict Resolution* 43:3–22.

——. 2000. "Sticking With the Peace: Explanations for the Duration of Civil War Settlements." Paper presented at the annual meeting of the American Political Science Association, Washington, D.C., August 31–September 3.

Hartzell, Caroline, and Donald Rothchild. 1997. "Political Pacts as Negotiated Agreements: Comparing Ethnic and Non-Ethnic Cases." *International Negotiation* 2:147–171.

Hartzell, Caroline, and Matthew Hoddie. 2003. "Institutionalizing Peace: Power Sharing and Post-Civil War Conflict Management." *American Journal of Political Science* 47:318–332.

Hartzell, Caroline, Matthew Hoddie, and Donald Rothchild. 2001. "Stabilizing the Peace after Civil War: An Investigation of Some Key Variables." *International Organization* 55:183–208.

Hartzell, Caroline, Shaheen Mozaffar, and Donald Rothchild. 1999. "Negotiated Civil War Settlements and Post-conflict Governance: The Choice and Consequences of Institutional Design." Paper presented at the annual meeting of the American Political Science Association, Atlanta, September 2–5.

Hechter, Michael. 2000. *Containing Nationalism.* New York: Oxford University Press.

Herbst, Jeffrey. 2000. *States and Power in Africa: Lessons in Authority and Control.* Princeton: Princeton University Press.

Herring, Ronald. 2001. "Making Ethnic Conflict: The Civil War in Sri Lanka." In *Carrots, Sticks, and Ethnic Conflict: Rethinking Development Assistance,* ed. Milton J. Esman and Ronald J. Herring, 140–174. Ann Arbor: University of Michigan Press.

Hicks, Ursula. 1978. *Federalism: Failure and Success.* New York: Oxford University Press.

Hislope, Robert. 1997. "Intra-Ethnic Conflict in Croatia and Serbia: Flanking and the Consequences for Democracy." *East European Quarterly* 30:471–494.

Holmes, Stephen. 1995. *Passions and Constraint.* Chicago: University of Chicago Press.

Holsti, Kalevi J. 1996. *The State, War, and the State of War.* Cambridge: Cambridge University Press.

Horowitz, Donald L. 1985. *Ethnic Groups in Conflict.* Berkeley: University of California Press.

——. 1991. "Making Moderation Pay: The Comparative Politics of Ethnic Conflict Management." In *Conflict and Peacemaking in Multiethnic Societies,* ed. Joseph V. Montville, 451–475. New York: Lexington Books.

Hourani, Albert. 1946. *Syria and Lebanon: A Political Essay.* London: Oxford University Press.

——. 1966. "Lebanon: The Development of a Political Society." In *Politics in Lebanon,* ed. Leonard Binder, 13–29. New York: John Wiley and Sons.

——. 1988. "Visions of Lebanon." In *Toward a Viable Lebanon,* ed. Halim Barakat, 3–10. London and Sydney: Croom Helm; Washington, D.C.: Center for Contemporary Arab Studies, Georgetown University.

Hudson, Michael. 1978. "The Palestinian Factor in the Lebanese Civil War." *Middle East Journal* 32:262–267

——. 1988. "The Problem of Authoritative Power in Lebanese Politics: Why Consociationalism Failed." In *Lebanon: a History of Conflict and Consensus,* ed. Nadim Shehadi and Dana Haffar Mills, 226–234. London: Centre for Lebanese Studies, I.B. Tauris.

Huntington, Samuel P. 1968. *Political Order in Changing Societies.* New Haven: Yale University Press.

——. 1981. *American Politics: The Promise of Disharmony.* Cambridge: Harvard University Press.

——. 1991. *The Third Wave.* Norman: University of Oklahoma Press.

Hurlburt, Heather F. 2000. "Preventive Diplomacy: Success in the Baltics." In *Opportunities Missed, Opportunities Seized: Preventive Diplomacy in the Post-Cold War World,* ed. Bruce W. Jentleson, 91–107. Report of the Carnegie Commission on Preventing Deadly Conflict. Lanham, Maryland: Rowman and Littlefield Publishers.

Hutchinson, John. 1987. *The Dynamics of Cultural Nationalism.* London: Allen and Unwin.

Ibelema, Minabere. 2000. "Nigeria: The Politics of Marginalization." *Current History* 99:211–214.

ICG [International Crisis Group]. 2001a. "Macedonia: The Last Chance for Peace." ICG Balkans Report no. 113. Skopje/Brussels.

——. 2001b. "Macedonia: War on Hold." Skopje/Brussels, August 15.

——. 2001c. "Turning Strife to Advantage: A Blueprint to Integrate the Croats in Bosnia and Herzegovina." ICG Balkans Report no. 106. Skopje/Brussels, March 15.

——. 2002a. "Implementing Equality: The 'Constituent Peoples' Decision in Bosnia & Herzegovina." ICG Balkans Report no. 128. Sarajevo/Brussels, April 16.

——. 2002b. "Policing the Police in Bosnia: A Further Reform Agenda." ICG Balkans Report no. 130. Sarajevo/Brussels, May 10.

——. 2002c. "Bosnia's Alliance for (Smallish) Change." ICG Balkans Report no. 132. Sarajevo/Brussels, August 2.

——. 2002d. "The Afghan Transitional Administration: Prospects and Perils." Kabul/Brussels, July 30.

——. 2002e. "Macedonia's Public Secret: How Corruption Drags the Country Down." ICG Balkans Report no. 133. Skopje/Brussels, August 14.

——. 2002f. "A Kosovo Roadmap: Addressing Final Status," I-II. ICG Balkans Report no. 124–125. Pristina/Brussels, March 1.

——. 2003. "Bosnia's Nationalist Governments: Paddy Ashdown and the Paradoxes of State Building." ICG Balkans Report no. 146. Sarajevo/Brussels, July 22.

——. 2004a. "Collapse in Kosovo." ICG Europe Report no. 155. Pristina/Belgrade/Brussels, April 22.

——. 2004b. "Elections and Security in Afghanistan." Kabul/Brussels, March 30.

——. 2004c. "Elections in Burundi: The Peace Wager." Africa Briefing no. 20. Nairobi/Brussels, December 9.

Ikein, Augustine A., and Comfort Briggs-Anigboh. 1998. *Oil and Fiscal Federalism in Nigeria: The Political Economy of Resource Allocation in a Developing Country*. Aldershot, England: Ashgate.

India [Government of India]. 1965. Ministry of Finance. *Report of the Finance Commission 1965*. New Delhi.

——. 1981. Backward Classes Commission. *Report of the Backward Classes Commission 1980* [The Mandal Commission Report]. Delhi: Controller of Publications.

——. 1991. *Census of India, 1991*. New Delhi: Government Printing Office.

——. 2001. Ministry of Finance. *Report of the Eleventh Finance Commission*. New Delhi.

IPS [Institute of Policy Studies, Islamabad]. 1992. *Pakistan's Economic Challenges and the Government Response*. Islamabad.

Irwin, Zachary T. 1984. "Yugoslavia and Ethnonationalists." In *Ethnic Separatism and World Politics*, ed. Frederick L. Shields, 105–149. Lanham, Md.: University Press of America.

Jaggers, Keith, and Ted Robert Gurr. 1995. Polity III: Regime Change and Political Authority, 1800–1994 [Computer file]. 2nd ICPSR version. Boulder, Colo.: Keith Jaggers/College Park, Md.: Ted Robert Gurr [producers], 1995. Ann Arbor, Mich.: Inter-university Consortium for Political and Social Research [distributor], 1996.

Jarstad, Anna. 2001. *Changing the Game: Consociational Theory and Ethnic Quotas in Cyprus and New Zealand*. PhD diss. Uppsala, Sweden: Department of Peace and Conflict Research, Uppsala University.

Johnson, R.W., and Lawrence Schlemmer. 1996. *Launching Democracy in South Africa: The First Open Election, April 1994*. New Haven: Yale University Press.

Jones, Stephen. 1997. "Georgia: The Trauma of Statehood." In *New States, New Politics: Building the Post-Soviet Nations*, ed. Ian Bremer and Ray Taras, 505–546. Cambridge: Cambridge University Press.

Kahn, Herman. 1965. *On Escalation: Metaphors and Scenarios*. New York: Frederick A. Praeger, Publishers.

Kaplan, Cynthia. 1998. "Ethnicity and Sovereignty: Insights from Russian Negotiations with Estonia and Tatarstan." In *The International Spread of Ethnic Conflict*, ed. David Lake and Donald Rothchild, 251–274. Princeton: Princeton University Press.

Karatnycky, Adrian, Alexander Motyl, and Amanda Schnetzer, eds. 2001. *Nations in Transit, 2001: Civil Society, Democracy, and Markets in East Central Europe and the Newly Independent States*. New Brunswick, N.J.: Transaction Publishers.

Karklins, Rasma. 2000. "Ethnopluralism: Panacea for East Central Europe." *Nationalities Papers* 28:219–241.

Kaufman, Stuart. 2001. *Modern Hatreds: The Symbolic Politics of Ethnic Wars*. Ithaca: Cornell University Press.

Kaufmann, Chaim D. 1996. "Possible and Impossible Solutions to Ethnic Civil War." *International Security* 20:136–175.

——. 1999. "When All Else Fails: Evaluating Population Transfers and Partition as Solutions to Ethnic Conflict." In *Civil Wars, Insecurity, and Intervention*, ed. Barbara F. Walter and Jack Snyder, 221–260. New York: Columbia University Press.

Kaufmann, William W. 1956. "Limited Warfare." In *Military Policy and National Security*, ed. William W. Kaufmann, 102–136. Princeton: Princeton University Press.

Kedourie, Elie. 1960. *Nationalism*. London: Hutchinson.

Keesing's Contemporary Archives / Keesing's Record of World Events. 1955–1999. Bath: Longman Group.

Keller, Edmond J. 1988a. *Revolutionary Ethiopia: From Empire to Peoples' Republic*. Bloomington: Indiana University Press.

——. 1988b. "Remaking the Ethiopian State." In *Collapsed States: The Disintegration and Restoration of Legitimate Authority*, ed. I. William Zartman, 125–139. Boulder, Colo.: Lynne Rienner.

——. 1995. "Regime Change and Ethno-regionalism in Ethiopia: The Case of the Oromo." In *Oromo Nationalism and the Ethiopian Discourse*, edited by Asafa Jalata, 109–124. Lawrenceville, N.J.: Red Sea Press.

Kerr, Malcolm. 1959. *Lebanon in the Last Years of Feudalism, 1840–1868: A Contemporary Account by Antun Dahir al-ʿAqiqi and Other Documents*, translated with notes and commentaries. Publications of the Faculty of Arts and Sciences, Oriental Series no. 33. Beirut: American University of Beirut/Catholic Press.

Khalaf, Samir. 1997. "From a Geography of Fear to a Culture of Tolerance: Reflections on Protracted Strife and the Restoration of Civility in Lebanon." In *Conflict Resolution in the Arab World: Selected Essays*, ed. Paul Salem, 354–383. Beirut: American University of Beirut.

——. 2002. *Civil and Uncivil Violence in Lebanon: A History of the Internationalization of Communal Violence*. New York: Columbia University Press.

Khalidi, Walid. 1989. "Lebanon: Yesterday and Tomorrow." *Middle East Journal* 43: 375–387.

King, Charles. 2000. *The Moldovans: Romania, Russia and the Politics of Culture*. Stanford, Calif.: Hoover Institution Press.

——. 2001a. "Misreading or Misleading? Four Myths about Democratization in Post-Soviet Georgia." Unpublished manuscript. Washington, D.C.: Georgetown University.

——. 2001b. "The Benefits of Ethnic War: Understanding Eurasia's Unrecognized States." *World Politics* 53:524–552.

King, Gary, Michael Tomz, and Jason Wittenberg. 2000. "Making the Most of Statistical Analyses: Improving Interpretation and Presentation." *American Journal of Political Science* 44:347–361.

King, Robert D. 1997. *Nehru and the Language Politics of India*. Delhi: Oxford University Press.

Kionka, Riina, and Raivo Vetik. 1996. "Estonia and the Estonians." In *The Nationalities Question in the Post-Soviet States*, ed. Graham Smith, 129–146. London: Longman.

Kitschelt, Herbert, Dzenka Mansfeldova, Radoslaw Markowski, and Gabor Toka. 1999. *Postcommunist Party Systems: Competition, Representation, and Inter-Party Competition*. New York: Cambridge University Press.

Knox, Colin, and Pádraic Quirk. 2000. *Peace Building in Northern Ireland, Israel and South Africa: Transition, Transformation, and Reconciliation*. New York: St. Martin's Press.

Kohli, Atul. 1997. "Can Democracies Accommodate Ethnic Nationalism? The Rise and Decline of Self-Determination Movements in India." *Journal of Asian Studies* 56:325–344.

Kohn, Hans. 1945. *The Idea of Nationalism: A Study in Its Origins and Background*. New York: Macmillan.

Kolstø, Pål, and Tsilevich, Boris. 1997. "Patterns of Nation-Building and Political Integration in a Bifurcated Postcommunist State: Ethnic Aspects of Parliamentary Elections in Latvia." *East European Politics and Societies* 11:366–391.

Kopstein, Jeffrey, and David Reilly. 1999. "Explaining the Why of the Why: A Comment on Fish's Determinants of Economic Reform in the Postcommunist World." *East European Politics and Societies* 13:613–624.

Kraft, Evan. 1992. "Evaluating Regional Policy in Yugoslavia, 1966–1990." *Comparative Economic Studies* 34:11–33.

Kraft, Evan, and Milan Vodopivec. 1992. "How Soft Is the Budget Constraint for Yugoslav Firms?" *Journal of Comparative Economics* 16:432–455.

Krasner, Stephen D., and Daniel T. Froats. 1998. "Minority Rights and the Westphalian Model." In *The International Spread of Ethnic Conflict*, ed. David Lake and Donald Rothchild, 227–250. Princeton: Princeton University Press.

Krayem, Hassan. 1997. "The Lebanese Civil War and the Ta'if Agreement." In *Conflict Resolution in the Arab World: Selected Essays*, ed. Paul Salem, 411–435. Beirut: American University of Beirut.

Kugler, Jacek, and Douglas Lemke, eds. 1996. *Parity and War: Evaluations and Extensions of the War Ledger*. Ann Arbor: University of Michigan Press.

Kumar, Krishna. 1998. "Postconflict Elections and International Assistance." In *Postconflict Elections, Democratization and International Assistance*, ed. Krishna Kumar, 5–14. Boulder, Colo.: Lynne Rienner.

Kumar, Krishna, and Marina Ottaway. 1998. "General Conclusions and Priorities for Policy Research." In *Postconflict Elections, Democratization and International Assistance*, ed. Krishna Kumar, 229–237. Boulder, Colo.: Lynne Rienner.

Kuperman, Alan J. 1996. "The Other Lesson of Rwanda: Mediators Sometimes do More Harm Than Good." *SAIS Review* 15:221–240.

Kuran, Timur. 1991. "Now Out of Never: The Element of Surprise in the East European Revolution of 1989." *World Politics* 44:7–48.

——. 1998. "Ethnic Dissolution and Its International Diffusion." In *The International Spread of Ethnic Conflict*, ed. David Lake and Donald Rothchild, 35–60. Princeton: Princeton University Press.

Laitin, David D. 1987. "South Africa: Violence, Myths, and Democratic Reform." *World Politics* 39:258–279.

——. 1998. *Identity in Formation: The Russian-Speaking Populations in the Near Abroad*. Ithaca: Cornell University Press.

Lake, David A. 2003. "The New Sovereignty in International Relations." *International Studies Review* 5:303–323.

Lake, David A., and Matthew A. Baum. 2001. "The Invisible Hand of Democracy: Political Control and the Provision of Public Services." *Comparative Political Studies* 34:587–621.

Lake, David A., and Donald Rothchild. 1996. "Containing Fear: The Origins and Management of Ethnic Conflict." *International Security* 21:41–75.

——. eds. 1998. *The International Spread of Ethnic Conflict: Fear, Diffusion, and Escalation.* Princeton: Princeton University Press.

Lapidus, Gail. 1998. "Contested Sovereignty: The Tragedy of Chechnya." *International Security* 23:5–49.

Lapidus, Gail W., and Edward W. Walker. 1995. "Nationalism, Regionalism, and Federalism: Center-Periphery Relations in Post-Communist Russia." In *The New Russia: Troubled Transformation,* ed. Gail W. Lapidus, 79–113. Boulder, Colo.: Westview.

Leatherman, Janie, William DeMars, Patrick Gaffney, and Raimo Väyrynen. 1999. *Breaking Cycles of Violence: Conflict Prevention in Intrastate Crises.* West Hartford: Kumarian Press.

Lederach, John Paul. 1996. *Remember and Change.* Peace and Reconciliation Conference. Enniskillen, Northern Ireland: Fermanagh District Partnership.

——. 1997. *Building Peace: Sustainable Reconciliation in Divided Societies.* Washington, D.C.: U.S. Institute of Peace Press.

LeDuc, Lawrence, Richard G. Niemi, and Pipa Norris, eds. 1996. *Comparing Democracies: Elections and Voting in Global Perspective.* Thousand Oaks, Calif.: Sage.

Leites, Nathan, and Charles Wolf, Jr. 1970. *Rebellion and Authority: An Analytic Essay on Insurgent Conflicts.* Chicago: Markham.

Lembruch, Gerhard. 1975. "Consociational Democracy in the International System." *European Journal of Political Research* 3:377–391.

Lemco, Jonathan. 1991. *Political Stability in Federal Governments.* New York: Praeger.

Levinson, David, ed. 1991. *Encyclopedia of World Cultures,* 10 vols. Boston: G. K. Hall.

Lewis, W. Arthur. 1965. *Politics in West Africa.* London: George Allen and Unwin.

Licklider, Roy. 1995. "The Consequences of Negotiated Settlements in Civil Wars, 1945–1993." *American Political Science Review* 89:681–690.

Lieven, Anatol. 1998. *Chechnya: Tombstone of Russian Power.* New Haven: Yale University Press.

——. 2001. "Georgia: A Failing State?" *Eurasia Insight,* February 5. From Johnson's Russia List, no. 5077, February 7.

Lijphart, Arend. 1968. *The Politics of Accommodation: Pluralism and Democracy in the Netherlands.* Berkeley: University of California Press.

——. 1977. *Democracy in Plural Societies: A Comparative Exploration.* New Haven: Yale University Press.

——. 1984. *Democracies: Patterns of Majoritarian and Consensus Government in Twenty-One Countries.* New Haven: Yale University Press.

——. 1985. *Power Sharing in South Africa.* Policy Papers in International Affairs. Berkeley: University of California, Institute of International Studies.

——. 1990a. "Electoral Systems, Party Systems and Conflict Management in Segmented Societies." In *Critical Choices for South Africa: An Agenda for the 1990s,* ed. R. A. Schrire, 2–13. Capetown: Oxford University Press.

——. 1990b. "The Power-Sharing Approach." In *Conflict and Peacemaking in Multiethnic Societies,* ed. Joseph V. Montville, 491–510. Lexington, Mass.: DC Heath.

——. 1993. "Consociational Democracy." In *The Oxford Companion to Politics of the World,* ed. Joel Krieger, 188–189. New York: Oxford University Press.

——. 1994. "Prospects for Powersharing in the New South Africa." In *Election '94 South Africa: The Campaigns, Results, and Future Prospects,* ed. Andrew Reynolds, 221–231. Claremont: David Phillip Publishers.

——. 1995. "Multiethnic Democracy." In *The Encyclopedia of Democracy,* ed. Seymour Martin Lipset, 3:853–865. Washington, D.C.: Congressional Quarterly.

——. 1996. "The Puzzle of Indian Democracy: A Consociational Interpretation." *American Political Science Review* 90:258–268.

——. 1999. *Patterns of Democracy: Government Forms and Performance in Thirty-Six Countries*. New Haven: Yale University Press.

——. 2002. "The Wave of Power-Sharing Democracy." In *The Architecture of Democracy: Institutional Design, Conflict Management, and Democracy in the Late Twentieth Century*, ed. Andrew Reynolds, 37–54. Oxford: Oxford University Press.

Linder, Wolf. 1994. *Swiss Democracy: Possible Solutions to Conflict in Multicultural Societies*. New York: St. Martin's Press.

Linz, Juan J., and Alfred Stepan. 1996. *Problems of Democratic Transition and Consolidation: Southern Europe, South America, and Post-Communist Europe*. Baltimore: Johns Hopkins University Press.

Lipset, Seymour Martin. 1960. *Political Man*. Baltimore: Johns Hopkins University Press.

——. 1981. *Political Man: The Social Bases of Politics*. Expanded and updated edition. Baltimore: Johns Hopkins University Press.

Lodge, Tom. 1983. *Black Politics in South Africa since 1945*. London: Longman.

Lohmann, Susanne. 1994. "Dynamics of Informational Cascades: The Monday Demonstrations in Leipzig, East Germany, 1989–1991." *World Politics* 47:42–101.

López-Pintor, Rafael. 1997. "Reconciliation Elections: A Post-Cold War Experience." In *Rebuilding Societies After Civil War: Critical Roles for International Assistance*, ed. Krishna Kumar, 43–61. Boulder, Colo.: Lynne Rienner.

Lorwin, Val R. 1966. "Belgium: Religion, Class, and Language in National Politics." In *Political Oppositions in Western Democracies*, ed. Robert A. Dahl, 147–187. New Haven: Yale University Press.

Luttwak, Edward N. 1999. "Give War a Chance." *Foreign Affairs* 78:36–44.

Lyon, James M. B. 2000. "Will Bosnia Survive Dayton?" *Current History* 99:110–116.

Lyons, Terrence, and Ahmed I. Samatar. 1995. *Somalia: State Collapse, Multilateral Intervention, and Strategies for Political Reconstruction*. Washington, D.C.: Brookings Institution.

MacPherson, James C. 1994. "The Future of Federalism." In *Federalism and the New World Order*, ed. Stephen J. Randall and Roger Gibbins, 9–16. Calgary, Alberta: University of Calgary Press.

Madison, James. 1961 [1788]. *Federalist Papers no. 10 and 51*. Reprinted in *The Federalist Papers*, ed. Clinton Rossiter. New York: Penguin Books.

Maila, Joseph. 1994. "The Ta'if Accord: An Evaluation." In *Peace for Lebanon? From War to Reconstruction*, ed. Deirdre Collings, 31–44. Boulder, Colo.: Lynne Rienner.

Makdisi, Ussama. 2000. *The Culture of Sectarianism: Community, History, and Violence in Nineteenth-Century Ottoman Lebanon*. Berkeley: University California Press.

Malik, John. 2000. "The Dayton Agreement and Elections in Bosnia: Entrenching Ethnic Cleansing Through Democracy." *Stanford Journal of International Law* 36:303–355.

Manin, Bernard, Adam Przeworksi, and Susan C. Stokes. 1999. *Democracy, Accountability, and Representation*. Cambridge: Cambridge University Press.

Manor, James. 2001. "Centre-State Relations." In *The Success of India's Democracy*, ed. Atul Kohli, 78–102. Cambridge: Cambridge University Press.

Mansour, Albert. 1993. *Al-inqilab 'ala al-Ta'if* [The Coup Against Ta'if]. Beirut: Dar al-Jadid.

Marshall, Monty, and Keith Jaggers. 2000. "Polity IV: Political Regime Characteristics and Transitions, 1800–1999." Dataset User's Manual. Available at http://www.bsos.umd.edu/cidcm/polity/p4manual.pdf.

Martiniello, Marco. 1995. "The National Question and Political Construction of Ethnic Communities in Belgium." In *Racism, Ethnicity, and Politics in Contemporary Europe*, ed. Alec G. Hargreaves and Jeremy Leaman, 131–144. London: Edward Elgar.

——. 1998. "The Use of Images of Cultural Differences in Belgian Political Life." Paper presented at the conference, "Federalism, Nationalism and Secession," Cornell University, Ithaca, N.Y., May 1–2.

Mason, T. David, Joseph P. Weingarten, Jr., and Patrick J. Fett. 1999. "Win, Lose, Or Draw: Predicting the Outcome of Civil Wars." *Political Research Quarterly* 52:239–268.

Mastny, Vojtech. 2000. "The Historical Experience of Federalism in East Central Europe." *East European Politics and Societies* 14:64–96.

Mattli, Walter, and Anne-Marie Slaughter. 1998. "Revisiting the European Court of Justice." *International Organization* 52:177–209.

Mawhood, Philip. 1984. "The Politics of Survival: Federal States in the Third World." *International Political Science Review* 5:521–531.

McCarthy, John D., and Mayer N. Zald. 1987. "Resource Mobilization and Social Movements: A Partial Theory." In *Social Movements in an Organizational Society*, ed. Mayer N. Zald and John D. McCarthy, 15–42. New Brunswick, N.J.: Transaction Books.

McGarry, John, and Brendan O'Leary. 1993. "Introduction: The Macro-political Regulation of Ethnic Conflict." In *The Politics of Ethnic Conflict Regulation: Case Studies of Protracted Ethnic Conflicts*, ed. John McGarry and Brendan O'Leary, 1–40. London: Routledge.

McGarry, John, and S. J. R. Noel. 1989. "The Prospects for Consociational Democracy in South Africa." *Journal of Commonwealth and Comparative Politics* 27:3–22.

McKelvey, Richard. 1976. "Intransitivities in Multi-Dimensional Voting Models and Some Implications for Agenda Control." *Journal of Economic Theory* 12:472–482.

McLaurin, Ronald De. 1977. *Foreign-Policy Making in the Middle East: Domestic Influences on Policy in Egypt, Iraq, Israel and Syria.* New York: Praeger.

McNab, Christine. 1990. "Language Policy and Language Practice: Implementing Multilingual Literacy Education in Ethiopia." *African Studies Review* 33:65–82.

McRae, Kenneth D. 1975. "The Principle of Territoriality and the Principle of Personality in Multilingual States." *Linguistics* 158:33–54.

——. 1986. *Conflict and Compromise in Multilingual Societies: Belgium.* Waterloo, Ontario: Wilfrid Laurier University Press.

Mehta, Mandavi. 2001. "India's Turbulent Northeast." *South Asia Monitor*, no. 35 (July 5). Washington, D.C.: Center for Strategic and International Studies.

Melvin, Neil J. 2000. "Post-Imperial Ethnocracy and the Russophone Minorities of Estonia and Latvia." In *The Politics of National Minority Participation in Post-Communist Europe*, ed. Jonathan P. Stein, 129–166. East-West Institute. Armonk, N.Y.: M. E. Sharpe.

Menkhaus, Kenneth, and Louis Ortmayer. 2000. "Somalia: Misread Crises and Missed Opportunities." In *Opportunities Missed, Opportunities Seized: Preventive Diplomacy in the Post-Cold War World*, ed. Bruce W. Jentleson, 211–237. Report of the Carnegie Commission on Preventing Deadly Conflict. Lanham, Md.: Rowman and Littlefield.

Meo, Leila. 1976. *Lebanon, Improbable Nation: A Study in Political Development.* Westport, Conn.: Greenwood Press.

Mihaljek, Dubravko. 1993. "Intergovernmental Fiscal Relations in Yugoslavia, 1972–1990." In *Transition to Market: Studies in Fiscal Reform*, ed. Vito Tanzi, 177–201. Washington D.C.: International Monetary Fund.

Mill, John Stuart Mill. 1962 [1861]. *Considerations on Representative Government.* Chicago: Henry Regnery.

Minahan, James. 1996. *Nations Without States: A Historical Dictionary of Contemporary National Movements.* Westport, Conn.: Greenwood Press.

Minority Rights Group. 1997. *World Directory of Minorities.* London: Minority Rights Group International.

Mitchell, George J. 1996. *Northern Ireland: Report of the International Body on Decommissioning.* Typescript copy, January 22.

Modelski, George, and William R. Thompson. 1989. "Long Cycles and Global War." In *Handbook of War Studies,* ed. Manus I. Midlarsky, 23–54. Boston: Unwin Hyman.

Montesquieu. 1977 [1748]. *The Spirit of Laws.* Berkeley: University of California Press.

Moseley, Christopher, and R. E. Asher, eds. 1994. *Atlas of the World's Languages.* New York: Routledge.

Muller, Edward N. 1985. "Income Inequality, Regime Repressiveness, and Political Violence." *American Sociological Review* 50:47–61.

Muller, Edward N., and Erich Weede. 1994. "Theories of Rebellion: Relative Deprivation and Power Contention." *Rationality and Society* 6:40–57.

Muller, Siegfried H. 1964. *The World's Living Languages: Basic Facts of Their Structure, Kinship, Location and Number of Speakers.* New York: Ungar.

Murphy, Alexander. 1995. "Belgium's Regional Divergence: Along the Road to Federation." In *Federalism: The Multiethnic Challenge,* ed. Graham Smith, 73–100. London: Longman.

Musgrave, Thomas D. 1997. *Self-Determination and National Minorities.* Oxford: Clarendon Press.

Nagel, Joane. 1994. "Constructing Ethnicity: Creating and Recreating Ethnic Identity and Culture." *Social Problems* 41:152–176.

Nehru, Jawaharlal. 1990. *The Discovery of India.* Delhi: Oxford University Press.

Ni Aolain, Fionnuala. 2001. "A Fractured Soul of the Dayton Peace Agreement: A Legal Analysis." In *Reconstructing Multiethnic Societies: The Case of Bosnia-Herzegovina,* ed. Džemal Sokolović and Florian Bieber, 63–94. Burlington, Vt.: Ashgate.

Nnoli, Okwudiba. 1995. *Ethnicity and Development in Nigeria.* Aldershot, England: Avebury.

Noman, Omar. 1990. *Pakistan: Political and Economic History since 1947.* London: Kegan Paul International.

Nordlinger, Eric A. 1972. *Conflict Regulation in Divided Societies.* Cambridge: Center for International Affairs, Harvard University.

O'Leary, Brendan. 1989. "The Limits on Coercive Consociationalism in Northern Ireland." *Political Studies* 37:562–588.

Oates, Wallace E. 1972. *Fiscal Federalism.* New York: Harcourt Brace Jovanovich.

Offensend, David G. 1976. "Centralisation and Fiscal Arrangements in Nigeria." *Journal of Modern African Studies* 14:507–513.

Okuizumi, Kaoru. 2002. "Peacebuilding Mission: Lessons from the UN Mission in Bosnia and Herzegovina." *Human Rights Quarterly* 24:721–735.

Organski, A. F. K. 1958. *World Politics.* New York: Alfred Knopf.

——. 1968. *World Politics.* 2nd ed. New York: Alfred A. Knopf.

Osaghae, Eghosa E. 1986. "Do Ethnic Minorities Still Exist in Nigeria?" *The Journal of Commonwealth and Comparative Politics* 24:151–167.

Ottaway, Marina, and Anatol Lieven. 2002. *Rebuilding Afghanistan: Fantasy versus Reality.* Policy Brief. Washington, D.C.: Carnegie Endowment for International Peace, January 12.

Ould-Abdallah, Ahmedou. 2000. *Burundi on the Brink, 1993–1995.* Washington, D.C.: U.S. Institute of Peace Press.

Owen, John M., IV. 2002. "The Foreign Imposition of Domestic Institutions." *International Organization* 56:375–409.

Pakistan. Ministry of Finance. 1964–1971. *Pakistan Economic Survey.* Islamabad.

Pappalardo, Adriano. 1981. "The Conditions for Consociational Democracy: A Logical and Empirical Critique." *European Journal of Political Research* 9:365–390.

Paris, Roland. 2001. "Peacebuilding and the Limits of Liberal Internationalism." In *Nationalism and Ethnic Conflict.* Rev. ed., ed. Michael E. Brown, Owen R. Coté, Jr., Sean M. Lynn-Jones, and Steven E. Miller, 299–334. Cambridge: MIT Press.

Park, Andrus. 1994. "Ethnicity and Independence: The Case of Estonia in Comparative Perspective." *Europe-Asia Studies* 46:69–87.

Pasha, Hafiz A., and Mahnaz Fatima. 1999. "Fifty Years of Public Finance in Pakistan: A Trend Analysis." In *Fifty Years of Pakistan's Economy: Traditional Topics and Contemporary Concerns,* ed. Shahrukh Rafi Khan, 201–216. Oxford: Oxford University Press.

Pattanaik, Smruti S. 1998. "Ethnic Aspirations and Political Power: Defining Mohajirs' Grievances in Sindh." New Delhi, India: The Institute for Defence Studies and Analyses. Available at http://www.idsa-india.org.

Peake, Gordon. 2003. "From Warlords to Peacelords?" *Journal of International Affairs* 56:181–191.

Pevar, Stephen L. 1983. *The Rights of Indians and Tribes.* New York: Bantam Books.

Plestina, Dijana. 1992. *Regional Development in Communist Yugoslavia: Success, Failure, and Consequences.* Boulder, Colo.: Westview Press.

Pogge, Thomas W. 1997. "Groups Rights and Ethnicity." In *Ethnicity and Group Rights* (Nomos, no. 39), ed. Ian Shapiro and Will Kymlicka, 187–221. New York: New York University Press.

Posen, Barry R. 1993. "The Security Dilemma and Ethnic Conflict." *Survival* 35:27–47.

Powell, G. Bingham. 1982. *Contemporary Democracies: Participation, Stability, and Violence.* Cambridge: Harvard University Press.

Prakash, Siddhartha. 2000. "Political Economy of Kashmir since 1947." *Economic and Political Weekly,* June 10, 2051–2060.

Prendergast, John, and Emily Plumb. 2002. "Building Local Capacity: From Implementation to Peacebuilding." In *Ending Civil Wars: The Implementation of Peace Agreements,* ed. Stephen John Stedman, Donald Rothchild, and Elizabeth M. Cousens, 327–349. Boulder, Colo.: Lynne Rienner.

Price, Robert. 1990. *The Apartheid State in Crisis: Political Transformation in South Africa, 1975–1990.* Berkeley: University of California Press.

Przeworski, Adam. 1991. *Democracy and the Market: Political and Economic Reforms in Eastern Europe and Latin America.* Cambridge: Cambridge University Press.

Przeworski, Adam, Michael E. Alvarez, José Antonio Cheibub, and Fernando Limongi. 1995. *Sustainable Democracy.* Cambridge: Cambridge University Press.

——. 1996. "What Makes Democracies Endure?" *Journal of Democracy* 7:39–55.

Pugh, Michael, and Margaret Cobble. 2001. "Non-Nationalist Voting in Bosnia Municipal Elections: Implications for Democracy and Peacebuilding." *Journal of Peace Research* 39:27–47.

Pula, Besnik. 2001. *Contested Sovereignty and State Disintegration: The Rise of the Albanian Secessionist Movement in Kosova.* Master's thesis. Washington, D.C.: Georgetown University.

Putnam, Robert D. 1988. "Diplomacy and Domestic Politics: The Logic of Two-Level Games." *International Organization* 42:427–460.

Qian, Yingyi, and Barry R. Weingast. 1997. "Federalism as a Commitment to Market Preserving Incentives." *Journal of Economic Perspectives* 11:83–92.

Rabushka, Alvin, and Kenneth A. Shepsle. 1972. *Politics in Plural Societies: A Theory of Democratic Instability.* Columbus, Ohio: Charles E. Merrill.

Rakisits, C. G. P. 1988. "Center-Province Relations in Pakistan Under President Zia: The Government's and the Opposition's Approaches." *Pacific Affairs* 61:78–97.

Ramseyer, J. Mark, and Frances M. Rosenbluth. 1996. *The Politics of Oligarchy: Institutional Choice in Imperial Japan.* New York: Cambridge University Press.

Rao, M. Govinda. 1998. "India: Intergovernmental Fiscal Relations in a Planned Economy." In *Fiscal Decentralization in Developing Countries*, ed. Richard M. Bird and François Vaillancourt, 78–114. New York: Cambridge University Press.

Raun, Toivo U. 1997a. "Democratization and Political Development in Estonia, 1987–1996." In *The Consolidation of Democracy in East-Central Europe*, ed. Karen Dawisha and Bruce Parrott, 334–374. Cambridge: Cambridge University Press.

——. 1997b. "Estonia: Independence Redefined." In *New States, New Politics: Building the Post-Soviet Nations*, ed. Ian Bremmer and Ray Taras, 404–433. Cambridge: Cambridge University Press.

Rector, Chad. 2003. *Federations and International Relations.* PhD diss., University of California, San Diego, La Jolla.

Reilly, Ben. 2000/2001. "Democracy, Ethnic Fragmentation, and Internal Conflict: Confused Theories, Faulty Data, and the 'Crucial Case' of Papua New Guinea." *International Security* 25:162–185.

——. 2001. *Democracy in Divided Societies: Electoral Engineering for Conflict Management.* Cambridge: Cambridge University Press.

Reilly, Ben, and Andrew Reynolds. 1998. "Electoral Systems for Divided Societies." In *Democracy and Deep-Rooted Conflict: Options for Negotiators*, ed. Peter Harris and Ben Reilly, 191–204. Stockholm: International Institute for Democracy and Electoral Assistance.

——. 1999. *Electoral Systems and Conflict in Divided Societies.* Washington, D.C.: National Research Council.

Reno, William. 1998. *Warlord Politics and African States.* Boulder, Colo.: Lynne Rienner.

Reynolds, Andrew, and Timothy Sisk. 1998. "Elections and Electoral Systems: Implications for Conflict Management." In *Elections and Conflict Management in Africa*, ed. Timothy D. Sisk and Andrew Reynolds, 11–36. Washington, D.C.: U.S. Institute of Peace Press.

Riker, William H. 1964. *Federalism: Origin, Operation, Significance.* Boston: Little, Brown.

——. 1980. Implications from the Disequilibrium of Majority Rule for the Study of Institutions. *American Political Science Review* 74:432–446.

Roeder, Philip G. 1991. "Soviet Federalism and Ethnic Mobilization." *World Politics* 43:196–232.

——. 1993. *Red Sunset: The Failure of Soviet Politics.* Princeton: Princeton University Press.

——. 1999. "Peoples and States after 1989: The Political Costs of Incomplete National Revolutions." *Slavic Review* 58:854–882.

——. 2000. "The Robustness of Institutions in Ethnically Plural Societies." Paper presented at the annual meeting of the American Political Science Association, Washington, D.C., August 31–September 2.

——. 2001a. "The Rejection of Authoritarianism." In *Postcommunism and the Theory of Democracy*, by Richard D. Anderson, Jr., M. Steven Fish, Stephen E. Hanson, and Philip G. Roeder, 11–53. Princeton: Princeton University Press.

——. 2001b. "The Triumph of Nation-States: Lessons from the Collapse of the Soviet Union." Unpublished manuscript. San Diego: University of California, San Diego.

——. 2003. "Clash of Civilizations and Escalation of Domestic Ethnopolitical Conflict." *Comparative Political Studies* 36:509–540.

Rose, Richard. 2000. "The End of Consensus in Austria and Switzerland." *Journal of Democracy* 11:26–40.

Rossos, Andrew. 2000. "Great Britain and Macedonian Statehood and Unification, 1940–49." *East European Politics and Societies* 14:118–142.

Rothchild, Donald. 1970. "African Federations and the Diplomacy of Decolonization." *Journal of Developing Areas* 4:509–524.

——. 1986. "Hegemonial Exchange: An Alternative Model for Managing Conflict in Middle Africa." In *Ethnicity, Politics, and Development*, ed. Dennis L. Thompson and Dov Ronen, 65–104. Boulder, Colo.: Lynne Rienner.

——. 1997. *Managing Ethnic Conflict in Africa: Pressures and Incentives for Cooperation.* Washington, D.C.: Brookings Institution.

——. 1999. "Ethnic Insecurity, Peace Agreements, and State Building." In *State, Conflict, and Democracy in Africa*, ed. Richard Joseph, 319–337. Boulder, Colo.: Lynne Rienner.

——. 2001. "The Two-Phase Peace Implementation Process in Africa and Its Implications for Democratization." Paper presented at the annual meeting of the African Studies Association, Houston, November 15–18.

——. 2002. "The Effects of State Crisis on African Inter-State Relations—With Eurasian Parallels and Differences." In *Beyond State Crisis? Post-Colonial Africa and Post-Soviet Eurasia in Comparative Perspective*, ed. Mark R. Beissinger and Crawford Young, 189–214. Washington, D.C.: Woodrow Wilson Center Press.

Rothchild, Donald, and Robert L. Curry, Jr. 1978. *Scarcity, Choice, and Public Policy in Middle Africa.* Berkeley: University of California Press.

Rothstein, Paul, and Gary Hoover. 2000. "The Welfare Economics of Autarky, Federalism, and Federation Formation." Political Economy Working Paper, School of Business and Center in Political Economy, Washington University in St. Louis.

Roy, Naresh Chandra. 1962. *Federalism and Linguistic States.* Calcutta: Firma K. L. Mukhopadhyay.

Rubin, Barnett R. 1998. "Russian Hegemony and State Breakdown in the Periphery: Causes and Consequences of the Civil War in Tajikistan." In *Post-Soviet Political Order: Conflict and Statebuilding*, ed. Barnett R. Rubin and Jack Snyder, 128–161. London: Routledge.

Safran, William. 1994. "Non-separatist Policies Regarding Ethnic Minorities: Positive Approaches and Ambiguous Consequences." *International Political Science Review* 15:61–80.

Saideman, Stephen M. 1998. "Is Pandora's Box Half Empty or Half Full? The Limited Virulence of Secessions and the Domestic Sources of Dissent." In *The International Spread of Ethnic Conflict*, ed. David Lake and Donald Rothchild, 127–150. Princeton: Princeton University Press.

Saideman, Stephen M., David J. Lanoue, Michael Campenni, and Samuel Stanton. 2002. "Democratization, Political Institutions and Ethnic Conflict." *Comparative Political Studies* 35:103–129.

Saikal, Amin. 2002. "Afghanistan After the Loya Jirga." *Survival* 44:47–56.

Salem, Elie. 1967. "Cabinet Politics in Lebanon." *Middle East Journal* 21:488–502.

Salem, Paul. 1991a. "Documents: The Ta'if Agreement-Annotated Text." *Beirut Review* 1:110–172.

——. 1991b. "Two Years of Living Dangerously: General Awn and the Precarious Rise of Lebanon's Second Republic." *The Beirut Review* 1:62–87.

Salibi, Kamal. 1976. *Crossroads to Civil War: Lebanon 1958–1976.* Delmar, N.Y.: Caravan Books.

——. 1988. *A House of Many Mansions: The History of Lebanon Reconsidered.* Berkeley: University of California Press.

Sambanis, Nicholas. 2000. "Partition as a Solution to Ethnic War: An Empirical Critique of the Theoretical Literature." *World Politics* 52:437–483.

Santhanam, K. 1960. *Union-State Relations in India.* Bombay: Asia Publishing House.

Sato, Hiroshi. 1994. *Uneasy Federation: The Political Economy of Central Budgetary Transfers in South Asia.* Tokyo: Institute of Developing Economies.

Scarritt, James R., and Susan McMillan. 1995. "Protest and Rebellion in Africa: Explaining Conflicts Between Ethnic Minorities and the State in the 1980s." *Comparative Political Studies* 28:323–349.

Schoch, Bruno. 2000. *Switzerland—A Model for Solving Nationality Conflicts?* PRIF Reports no. 54. Frankfurt, Germany: Hessische Stiftung Friedens- und Konflikt-forschung, Peace Research Institute, February.

Schumpeter, Joseph. 1975 [1947]. *Capitalism, Socialism, and Democracy.* New York: Harper and Row.

Selznick, Philip. 1960. *The Organizational Weapon: A Study of Bolshevik Strategy and Tactics.* Glencoe, Ill.: The Free Press.

Sen, Amartya. 1999. "Democracy as a Universal Value." *Journal of Democracy* 10:3–17.

Sharma, P. K. 1969. *Political Aspects of States Reorganization in India.* New Delhi: Mohuni Publications.

Shepsle, Kenneth. 1979. "Institutional Arrangements and Equilibrium in Multi-Dimensional Voting Models." *American Journal of Political Science* 23:27–60.

Shin, Doh Chull. 1994. "On the Third Wave of Democratization: A Synthesis and Evaluation of Recent Theory and Research." *World Politics* 47:135–170.

Shugart, Matthew Soberg, and John M. Carey. 1992. *Presidents and Assemblies: Constitutional Designs and Electoral Mechanisms.* Cambridge: Cambridge University Press.

Simeon, Richard, and Daniel-Patrick Conway. 2001. "Federalism and the Management of Conflict in Multinational Societies." In *Multinational Democracy,* ed. Alain Gagnon and James Tully, 338–365. Cambridge: Cambridge University Press.

Singh, Atul Kumar. 1987. *Finance Commissions in India: an Analytical Study.* Allahabad, India: Chugh Publications.

Singh, Gurharpal. 2000. *Ethnic Conflict in India: A Case Study of Punjab.* London: Palgrave Macmillan.

SIPRI [Stockholm International Peace Research Institute]. 1987–1998. *SIPRI Yearbook: World Armaments and Disarmament,* annual editions. New York: Oxford University Press.

Sirriyeh, Hussein. 1976. "The Palestinian Armed Presence in Lebanon since 1967." In *Essays on the Crisis in Lebanon,* ed. Roger Owen, 73–89. London: Ithaca Press.

Sisk, Timothy D. 1995. *Democratization in South Africa: The Elusive Social Contract.* Princeton: Princeton University Press.

——. 1996. *Power Sharing and International Mediation in Ethnic Conflicts.* Washington, D.C.: U.S. Institute of Peace Press.

Sivard, Ruth Leger. 1996. *World Military and Social Expenditures, 1996.* 16th ed. Washington, D.C.: World Priorities.

Skvortsova, Alla. 1998. "The Russians in Moldova: Political Orientations." In *National Identities and Ethnic Minorities in Eastern Europe,* ed. Ray Taras, 159–178. London: Macmillan Press.

Slezkine, Yuri. 1994. "The USSR as a Communal Apartment, or How a Socialist State Promoted Ethnic Particularism." *Slavic Review* 53:414–452.

Small, Melvin, and J. David Singer. 1982. *Resort to Arms: International and Civil Wars, 1816–1980.* Beverly Hills: Sage.

Smith, Graham. 1995. "Mapping the Federal Condition: Ideology, Political Practice and Social Justice." In *Federalism: The Multiethnic Challenge,* ed. Graham Smith, 1–28. London: Longman.

Smith, Graham, Vivien Law, Andrew Wilson, Annette Bohr, and Edward Allworth. 1998. *Nation-Building in the Post-Soviet Borderlands: The Politics of National Identities.* Cambridge: Cambridge University Press.

Smith, Graham, and Andrew Wilson. 1997. "Rethinking Russia's Post-Soviet Diaspora: The Potential for Political Mobilisation in Eastern Ukraine and North-east Estonia." *Europe-Asia Studies* 49:845–864.

Smith, Michael G. 1969. "Institutional and Political Conditions of Pluralism." In *Pluralism in Africa*, ed. Leo Kuper and M. G. Smith, 27–65. Berkeley: University of California Press.

Smoke, Richard. 1977. *War: Controlling Escalation.* Cambridge: Harvard University Press.

Snyder, Jack, and Karen Ballentine. 1996. "Nationalism and the Marketplace of Ideas." *International Security* 21:5–40.

Solchanyk, Roman. 1994. "The Politics of State-building: Centre-Periphery Relations in Post-Soviet Ukraine." *Europe-Asia Studies* 46:47–68.

Southall, Roger. 1994. "The South African Elections of 1994: The Remaking of a Dominant-Party State." *Journal of Modern African Studies* 32:629–655.

Spence, Jack, David R. Dye, Mike Lanchin, and Geoff Thale with George Vickers. 1997. "Chapultepec: Five Years Later—El Salvador's Political Reality and Uncertain Future." Cambridge, Mass.: Hemisphere Initiatives.

Statesman's Yearbook. 1955–1999. New York: St Martin's Press.

Stedman, Stephen John, and Donald Rothchild. 1996. "Peace Operations: From Short-Term to Long-Term Commitment." *International Peacekeeping* 3:17–35.

Steen, Anton. 2000. "Ethnic Relations, Elites, and Democracy in the Baltic States." *Journal of Communist Studies and Transition Politics* 16:68–87.

Steiner, Jürg. 1969. "Nonviolent Conflict Resolution in Democratic Systems: Switzerland." *Journal of Conflict Resolution* 13:295–304.

——. 1974. *Amicable Agreement versus Majority Rule: Conflict Resolution in Switzerland.* Rev. ed. Chapel Hill: University of North Carolina Press.

——. 1987. "Consociational Democracy as a Policy Recommendation: The Case of South Africa." *Comparative Politics* 19:361–372.

——. 1998. "The Consociational Theory and Switzerland—Revisited Thirty Years Later." Paper presented at the conference "The Fate of Consociationalism," Center For European Studies, Harvard University, Cambridge, May 29–31.

Steiner, Jürg, and Robert H. Dorff. 1985. "Structure and Process in Consociationalism and Federalism." *Publius: The Journal of Federalism* 15:49–55.

Stepan, Alfred. 1999. "Federalism and Democracy: Beyond the U.S. Model." *Journal of Democracy* 10:19–34.

——. 2000. "Russian Federalism in Comparative Perspective." *Post-Soviet Affairs* 16:133–170.

Stern, Joseph J., and Walter P. Falcon. 1970. *Growth and Development in Pakistan, 1955–1969.* Cambridge: Center for International Affairs, Harvard University.

Stevens, Joe B. 1993. *The Economics of Collective Choice.* Boulder, Colo.: Westview Press.

Storey, David, and Dominique Woolridge. 2001. "Enhanced Participation in Local Governance: Lessons from South Africa." In *Democracy at the Local Level: The International IDEA Handbook on Participation, Representation, Conflict Management, and Governance*, ed. Timothy D. Sisk, 195–204. Stockholm: International Institute for Democracy and Electoral Assistance.

Suberu, Rotimi T. 1999. *Public Policies and National Unity in Nigeria.* Ibadan, Nigeria.

——. 2001. *Federalism and Ethnic Conflict in Nigeria.* Washington, D.C.: U.S. Institute of Peace Press.

Switzerland. 1993. Bundesamt für Statistik. *Eidgenössische Volkszählung 1990: Sprachen und Konfessionen.* vol. 16. Bern: Bundesamt für Statistik.

Szayna, Thomas S. 2000. *Identifying Potential Ethnic Conflict: Application of a Process Model.* Santa Monica, Calif.: Rand Corporation.

Talentino, Andrea Kathryn. 2002. "Intervention as Nation-Building: Illusion or Possibility?" *Security Dialogue* 33:27–43.

Tanzi, Vito. 1995. "Fiscal Federalism and Decentralization: A Review of Some Efficiency and Macroeconomic Aspects." In *Annual World Bank Conference on Development Economics 1995*, ed. Michael Bruno and Boris Pleskovic, 295–316. Washington D.C.: World Bank.

Tarrow, Sidney. 1989. *Struggle, Politics, and Reform: Collective Action, Social Movements, and Cycles of Protest.* Ithaca: Cornell University, Center for International Studies.

Taylor, Charles Lewis, and Michael C. Hudson 1972. *World Handbook of Political and Social Indicators.* 2nd ed. New Haven: Yale University Press.

Thimmaiah, G. 1985. *Burning Issues in Centre-State Financial Relations.* New Delhi: Ashish Publishing House.

Tiebout, Charles M. 1956. "A Pure Theory of Local Expenditures." *Journal of Political Economy* 64:416–424.

Touval, Saadia. 1982. *The Peace Brokers.* Princeton: Princeton University Press.

Treisman, Daniel. 1997. "Russia's 'Ethnic Revival': The Separatist Activism of Regional Leaders in a Postcommunist Order." *World Politics* 49:212–249.

——. 1999a. *After the Deluge: Regional Crises and Political Consolidation in Russia.* Ann Arbor: University of Michigan Press.

——. 1999b. "Political Decentralization and Economic Reform: A Game Theoretic Analysis." *American Journal of Political Science* 43:488–517.

——. 2002. "Rational Appeasement." Unpublished manuscript. Los Angeles: University of California at Los Angeles.

Tuéni, Ghassan. 1982. "Lebanon: A New Republic?" *Foreign Affairs* 61:84–99.

Tullberg, Jan, and Birgitta S. Tullberg. 1997. "Separation or Unity? A Model for Solving Ethnic Conflicts." *Politics and the Life Sciences* 16:237–248.

United Nations. 1980, 1985, 1986, 1990, 1995, 2001a. Department of Economic and Social Information and Policy Analysis. Statistical Division. *Statistical Yearbook*, annual editions. New York: United Nations.

——. 2001b. Department of Economic and Social Affairs. Population Division. *World Urbanization Prospects: 1999 Revision.* New York: United Nations.

United States. Bureau of the Census. 2001. *International Data Base.* Washington, D.C.: Bureau of the Census. Available at http://www.census.gov/ipc/www/idbprint.html.

United States. Central Intelligence Agency. 2000. *World Factbook 2000.* Washington, D.C. Available at http://www.odci.gov/cia/publications/factbook/indexgeo.html.

United States. Department of State. 2000. *1999 Country Reports on Human Rights Practices: Ethiopia.* Washington, D.C., Released February 25. Available at http://www.state.gov/www/global/humanrights/1999.

United States. Library of Congress. "Country Studies". Available at http://lcweb2.loc.gov/frd/cs/cshome.html.

USIP [United States Institute of Peace]. 2001. "Albanians in the Balkans." Special Report. Washington, D.C.: United States Institute of Peace, november 1.

Vanhanen, Tatu. 1997. *Prospects of Democracy: A Study of 172 Countries.* New York: Routledge.

Varshney, Ashutosh. 1993. "Contested Meanings: India's National Identity, Hindu Nationalism, and the Politics of Anxiety." *Daedalus* 122:227–261.

——. 2001. "Ethnic Conflict and Civil Society: India and Beyond." *World Politics* 53:362–398.

——. 2002. *Ethnic Conflict and Civic Life: Hindus and Muslims in India.* New Haven: Yale University Press.

Vejvoda, Ivan. 1996. "Yugoslavia 1945–1991—From Decentralisation Without Democracy to Dissolution." In *Yugoslavia and After: A Study in Fragmentation, Despair, and Rebirth,* ed. D. A. Dyker and I. Vejvoda, 9–27. London: Longman.

Venter, A. J. 1983. "Consociational Democracy." In *Political Alternatives for Southern Africa: Principles and Perspectives,* ed. D. J. van Vuuren and D. J. Kriek, 274–292. Durban/ Pretoria: Butterworth's.

Verney, Douglas V. 1995. "Federalism, Federative Systems, and Federations: The United States, Canada, and India." *Publius: The Journal of Federalism* 25:81–97.

Wagner, Robert Harrison. 1993. "The Causes of Peace." In *Stopping the Killing: How Civil Wars End,* ed. Roy Licklider, 235–268. New York: New York University Press.

Wallensteen, Peter, and Margareta Sollenberg. 1997. "Armed Conflicts, Conflict Termination and Peace Agreements, 1989–1996." *Journal of Peace Research* 34:339–358.

——. 1998. "Armed Conflict and Regional Conflict Complexes, 1989–1997." *Journal of Peace Research* 35:621–634.

Walter, Barbara F. 1997. "The Critical Barrier to Civil War Settlement." *International Organization* 51:335–364.

——. 1999a. "Designing Transitions from Civil War." In *Civil Wars, Insecurity, and Intervention,* ed. Barbara F. Walter and Jack Snyder, 38–69. New York: Columbia University Press.

——. 1999b. "Designing Transitions from Civil War: Demobilization, Democratization, and Commitments to Peace." *International Security* 24:127–155.

——. 2002. *Committing to Peace: The Successful Settlement of Civil Wars.* Princeton: Princeton University Press.

Walter, Barbara, and Jack Snyder, eds. 1999. *Civil Wars, Insecurity, and Intervention.* New York: Columbia University Press.

Wantchekon, Leonard, and Mario Simon. 1998. "Democracy as an Enforcement Mechanism for Elite Power-Sharing Contracts." Unpublished manuscript. New Haven: Yale University.

Waters, Mary C. 1990. *Ethnic Options: Choosing Identities in America.* Berkeley: University of California Press.

Weber, Eugen. 1976. *Peasants into Frenchmen: The Modernization of Rural France, 1870–1914.* Stanford: Stanford University Press.

Weingast, Barry. 1998. "Constructing Trust: The Political and Economic Roots of Ethnic and Regional Conflict." In *Institutions and Social Order,* ed. Karol Soltan, Eric M. Uslaner, and Virginia Haufler, 163–200. Ann Arbor: University of Michigan Press.

Weiss, Anita. 1999. "Pakistan: Some Progress, Sobering Challenges." In *India and Pakistan: The First Fifty Years,* ed. Selig S. Harrison and Paul H. Kreisberg, 132–152. New York: Cambridge University Press.

Werner, Suzanne. 1999. "The Precarious Nature of Peace: Resolving the Issues, Enforcing the Settlement, and Renegotiating the Terms." *American Journal of Political Science* 43:912–934.

Wheeler, Richard S. 1970. *The Politics of Pakistan: A Constitutional Quest.* Ithaca: Cornell University Press.

White, Osmar. 1972. *Parliament of a Thousand Tribes.* Melbourne: Wren.

Wilkinson, Steven. 2000. "Consociational Theory and Ethnic Violence." *Asian Survey* 40:767–791.

Williams, Colin H. 1995. "A Requiem for Canada?" In *Federalism: The Multiethnic Challenge,* ed. Graham Smith, 31–72. London: Longman.

Wittman, Donald. 2001. "War or Peace?" Unpublished manuscript. Santa Cruz: University of California, Santa Cruz, October 15.

Wolchik, Sharon. 1994. "The Politics of Ethnicity in Postcommunist Czechoslovakia." *East European Politics and Societies* 8:153–188.

Wood, Gordon. 1969. *The Creation of the American Republic, 1776–1787.* Chapel Hill: University of North Carolina Press.

Woodward, Susan L. 1995. *Balkan Tragedy: Chaos and Dissolution after the Cold War.* Washington, D.C.: Brookings Institution.

World Bank. 1975. *Yugoslavia: Development with Decentralization.* Baltimore: Johns Hopkins University Press.

——. 1998. *Ethiopia: Review of Public Finances.* 2 vols. Report no. 18369-ET. Washington, D.C., December 30.

——. 1999a. *Ethiopia: Regionalization Study.* Report no. 18898-ET. Washington, D.C., February 3.

——. 1999b. *World Development Indicators* [CD-Rom computer file]. Washington, D.C.

Wriggins, Howard. 1995. "Sri Lanka: Negotiations in a Secessionist Conflict." In *Elusive Peace: Negotiating an End to Civil Wars,* ed. I. William Zartman, 35–58. Washington, D.C.: Brookings Institution.

Yannis, Alexandros. 2001. "Kosovo Under International Administration." *Survival* 43:31–48.

Young, John. 1998. "Regionalism and Democracy in Ethiopia." *Third World Quarterly* 19:191–204.

——. 1999. "Along Ethiopia's Western Frontier: Gambella and Benishangul in Transition." *Journal of Modern African Studies* 37:321–346.

Yugoslavia. Federal Statistical Office. 1986. *Yugoslavia, 1945–1985: Statistical Review.* Belgrade.

——. 1988, 1990. *Statisticki Godisnjak Jugoslavije.* Belgrade.

Zacher, Mark W. 2001. "The Territorial Integrity Norm: International Boundaries and the Use of Force." *International Organization* 55:215–250.

Zahar, Marie Joelle. 2002. "Peace by Unconventional Means: Lebanon's Ta'if Agreement." In *Ending Civil Wars: The Implementation of Peace Agreements,* ed. Stephen John Stedman, Donald Rothchild, and Elizabeth M. Cousens, 567–597. Boulder, Colo.: Lynne Rienner.

Zamir, Meir. 1985. *The Formation of Modern Lebanon.* Ithaca: Cornell University Press.

——. 2000. *Lebanon's Quest: The Road to Statehood 1926–1939.* London: I. B. Tauris.

Zevelev, Igor. 2001. "The Redefinition of the Russian Nation: International Security and Stability." In *Russia in the New Century: Stability and Disorder,* ed. Victoria Bonnell and George W. Breslauer, 265–289. Boulder Colo.: Westview.

Contributors

Amit Ahuja is a PhD candidate in political science at the University of Michigan.

Eduardo Alemán is assistant professor of political science at the University of Houston.

Valerie Bunce is the Aaron Binenkorb Professor of International Studies and the Chair of the Government Department at Cornell University.

Caroline Hartzell is associate professor of Political Science at Gettysburg College.

Matthew Hoddie is assistant professor of political science at Texas A&M University.

Edmond J. Keller is professor of political science at the University of California, Los Angeles, and Director of UCLA's Globalization Research Center–Africa.

David A. Lake is professor of political science at the University of California, San Diego.

Benjamin Reilly is senior lecturer in the Asia Pacific School of Economics and Government at the Australian National University.

Philip G. Roeder is associate professor of political science at the University of California, San Diego.

Donald Rothchild is professor of political science at the University of California, Davis.

Timothy D. Sisk is associate professor in the Graduate School of International Studies, University of Denver.

Lahra Smith is a PhD candidate in the Department of Political Science at the University of California, Los Angeles.

Christoph Stefes is assistant professor for comparative European and post-Soviet studies at the Department of Political Science, University of Colorado, Denver.

Daniel Treisman is associate professor of political science at the University of California, Los Angeles.

Ashutosh Varshney is professor of political science at the University of Michigan, Ann Arbor.

Stephen Watts is a PhD candidate in the Department of Government at Cornell University.

Marie-Joëlle Zahar is assistant professor of political science at the Université de Montréal.

Index

Note: Page numbers with an *f* indicate figures; those with a *t* indicate tables; those with an *n* indicate footnotes.